GOOD TASTE, BAD TASTE, & CHRISTIAN TASTE

GOOD TASTE, BAD TASTE, & CHRISTIAN TASTE

Aesthetics in Religious Life

Frank Burch Brown

OXFORD
UNIVERSITY PRESS

2000

OXFORD
UNIVERSITY PRESS

Oxford New York
Athens Auckland Bangkok Bogota Bombay Buenos Aires
Calcutta Cape Town Dar es Salaam Delhi Florence Hong Kong
Istanbul Karachi Kuala Lumpur Madras Madrid Melbourne
Mexico City Nairobi Paris Singapore Taipei Tokyo Toronto

and associated companies in
Berlin Ibadan

Published by Oxford University Press, Inc.,
198 Madison Avenue, New York, New York 10016

Oxford is a registered trademark of Oxford University Press

Library of Congress Cataloging-in-Publication Data
Brown, Frank Burch, 1948–
Good taste, bad taste, and Christian taste : aesthetics in
religious life / Frank Burch Brown.
p. cm.
Includes bibliographical references and index.
ISBN 978-0-19-515872-4
1. Christianity and the arts. 2. Aesthetics—Religious aspects—Christianity. I. Title.
BR115.A8 B785 2000
246—dc21 99-086563

Printed in the United States of America
on acid-free paper

TO DAVID
AND TO CAMILLA

Contents

Figure 1. *Gustave Doré (1832–1883)*, The Empyrean (*Dante and Beatrice behold the Celestial Rose, Par. XXXI*). *From the Doré illustrations for Dante's* Divine Comedy, *1861.* (*Dover Pictorial Archive Series*)

Prologue

Religious Taste

Shared Taste: A Memoir

Taste may be subjective, but it is not merely private. Almost from the time of our earliest exchanges, my brother David and I have regularly attempted (with varying degrees of success) to share music we relish. Sometimes our efforts have been strenuous. Once we backpacked into the Uinta Mountains of Utah and at long last sat perspiring on a remote peak. There—using two pairs of headphones, an adapter plug, and a portable cassette player—we compared several different (but all remarkably elevated) performances of the "Sanctus" from Bach's Mass in B Minor.

That lofty concord and mutuality of tastes has plummeted at other times into abysmal discord and disagreement. My tastes in "classical" art and music have been eclectic and almost omnivorous, his more selective and discriminating. And I have always taken a greater interest than he in jazz and popular music, and in music worldwide. When serving as a composer-in-residence at various churches, I occasionally wrote music that he found too popular in its appeal, and therefore (to him) unappealing. But we have found that these conflicts in taste, a predictable feature of any shared passion for the arts, can also be fruitful. And our passion for the arts has persisted, having become integral to our lives more generally. David became a professional pianist, music teacher, and composer; I became a scholar-teacher in religion and the arts with opportunities to compose, direct a choir, and make music with the piano and sundry other instruments.

For both of us the arts (and not only music) have provided what one could fairly call "spiritual exercise." They have also served as a primary religious language. Sometime before David's eighteenth birthday, he confessed—professed, really—that were it not for Handel's *Messiah* he would probably not have had the capacity to remain a Christian up to that point. Odd as that may sound, he evidently meant something that I myself take seriously: it was through this music that the meaning of Christian faith came alive for him, transcending factors that are traditionally more decisive, such as doctrine and preaching. Since then, I have sometimes imagined I could chart the degree of my brother's variable proximity to the Christian tradition by the extent to which he could still care (or bear) to listen to yet another recording of *Messiah*. I have discovered that David's musical approach to faith has been shared by many Christians—including the Protestant theologian Friedrich Schleiermacher (1768–1834), who has a "theologically astute" character declare in a Christmas Eve dialogue: "Music such as Handel's *Messiah* is, for me, like a sweeping proclamation of Christianity as a whole."[1] And I have realized that for me, as well, the sense of Christian faith as something renewing and renewable has been conveyed and sustained to a significant degree through music and other art—classical, popular, and cross-cultural—and through the literary qualities of scripture itself.

By beginning on this personal note, I do not want to create a false impression. The book that follows is not primarily autobiographical. Even so, this project plainly has a basis in the aesthetic peak and pit experiences that began and still continue with my brother.

The Senses of "Taste"

Under the influence of such formative experiences, I have come to believe that matters of aesthetic taste—in a broad and nonelitist sense—are often intimately tied to various dimensions of morality (love, responsiveness, responsibility) and of religion (faith, worship, theology). While the notion of taste can seem somewhat alien to the context of religion, I believe it can be used to shed light on what animates and vexes Christian life and worship in a variety of ways that we can ill afford to ignore theologically or socially. Taste is involved in the delight Christians regularly take in singing songs, and in their frequent sense of perplexity or dismay at what certain other Christians choose to sing. Taste is essential to the enjoyment of those special works of art that help connect us with all we perceive to be holy; it is also involved in our disgust at things we regard as desecrating what is holy, or as somehow serving a purpose that is unholy—such as certain forms of violent or racist art.

Of course no capacity of the human mind, however sensitive or creative, can truly encompass the Holy as glimpsed in moments such as the Transfiguration; and nothing can fully capture the character of the profoundly Unholy, as witnessed in the unimaginable evil of the Holocaust. Even to mention aesthetics and taste in such contexts is to risk trivializing what is either unspeakably awe-inspiring or unspeakably awful. Yet it is in fact the unspeakable that often cries out for an artistic and symbolic medium to break through the limitations of ordinary thoughts and words. What has been meant, traditionally, by the very concept of the sublime is something that requires us to be able to feel, and even relish, genuine awe and terror. Eighteenth-century writers, who exhibited great interest in the sublime, often saw a connection between a taste for the sublime and the pursuit of religious experience at its most awe-inspiring and mysterious.[2] Recalling as well the scope of Dante's medieval pilgrimage from Hell through Purgatory to Paradise, I believe we can speak of two polar regions that religious taste avoids only at its peril: the exalted and sublime on the one hand, and the harrowing and abysmal on the other.

This is certainly not to say that, from my perspective, the transformative moments of artistic and religious experience—their respective epiphanies—have to do *simply* with taste, let alone with "good taste" in some conventional sense. For one thing, religious art that aspires to sublimity is for that very reason almost certain to violate the canons of "good taste" in some respect. Having overtly grand and lofty goals, the art of the sublime, when anything less than truly great, tends to cheapen its subject to some degree, which often results in at least traces of "kitsch." One thinks, for instance, of many of Gustave Doré's famous illustrations for Dante's *Divine Comedy*—even the undeniably striking depiction of the vast Rose formed by the saintly host in Paradise, as beheld by Dante and Beatrice (Figure 1). In any case, much of the best art defies prevalent norms of good taste. In the realm of "high art," one need only recall the "vulgar" passages in Dante's *Inferno* or the flagrantly nude figures of Michelangelo's Sistine Chapel, which church leaders with an acute sense of propriety soon made more discreet. In working and playing with the notion of good taste and bad, I mean, therefore, to be reshaping the ways we usually think about the norms of taste. And in linking various kinds of religious and artistic experience with taste, I am conscious of stretching the term—though not, I think, in an arbitrary fashion.

Many philosophers, beginning with Immanuel Kant (1724–1804), have thought of taste as essentially our capacity to judge whether something is beautiful, pleasing in itself. But that is just one of the senses of "taste" found in philosophy and criticism, not to mention everyday language. As I conceive of it here, taste primarily has to do with aesthetic response and responsiveness. Yet it has three elements or facets: perceiving, enjoying, and judging—which I like to term "apperception," "appreciation," and "appraisal." Taste, in short, has to do with the various elements of aesthetic discernment and response.[3]

But if taste is aesthetic, and if something aesthetic is to be enjoyed for its own sake, that creates a puzzle for a study such as this. Everyone would agree that an organist exercises taste (good or bad) in selecting and playing music for a church service. But if taste is aesthetic, how could it matter religiously? Why should it matter if the organist, during communion, feels moved to play a soft, slow version of "Take Me Out to the Ballgame"—something to which a student of mine once confessed? Isn't music simply music?[4] (Certain classical musicians and critics have been fond of saying exactly that.) And isn't aesthetic taste supposed to be something you can't really dispute in terms of religion or morality? (A great many philosophers since Kant have said that.)

Puzzling over these questions, we are forced to think about what we mean by "aesthetic." An unbridgeable gap between aesthetic taste and religious discernment does seem to be implied by one quite legitimate way in which we think about aesthetic values. When we think of something's aesthetic qualities, we do not think first of all about what makes it religious or moral. We think about what makes it rewarding just to look at or listen to, and so to savor in itself. Paraphrasing what medieval scholastics said of beauty as such, we can say that, at their simplest, aesthetic qualities please or displease in one's very perception of them. They are qualities we think of as formal, sensuous, expressive, or imaginative. All on its own, a snowflake on a pane of glass possesses a geometrical form we can appreciate, and a sensuous fragility expressive, perhaps, of a delicate serenity. In one's imagination the flake could be pictured almost as a microcosm—an orderly, harmonious world that is beautiful in itself, regardless of what one thinks the rest of the world is like. Such qualities are aesthetic, whether considered individually or in combination.

But while the aesthetic qualities of a snowflake might well be appreciated without thinking at all about what is morally good, really true, or required by God, the same cannot be said of Shakespeare's *Measure for Measure* or of the film *Dead Man Walking* (Tim Robbins, 1996). And it is not true of "Take Me Out to the Ballgame," once it becomes part of the artistry involved in worship. We call these works aesthetic, and they require taste; but they are not *merely* aesthetic in the narrow sense, and the taste they require needs to be informed morally and, in the one case, liturgically. It is therefore important to recognize—and many people do not—that aesthetic response comes in varying degrees of complexity. At one level taste has nothing to do with religion and everything to do with art or beauty that asks to be enjoyed simply in itself. At levels of increasing complexity, however, the artistry itself has a great deal to do with morality and religion. Taste must then assume a corresponding complexity, with a moral and religious dimension that is part of the aesthetic.

I have not forgotten that taste has also commonly been associated with such things as personal preferences (often trivial), with propriety and manners, with dress and class, and with what it takes to participate in what the eighteenth century termed the "polite world." Such matters, many of which smack of dilettantism or elitism, have some bearing on my concerns here; but there are other, more significant associations of the term "taste" on which I draw and to which readers need to be alerted at the outset.

On the religious side, it is pertinent, for instance, that Psalm 34:8 (often cited by Christian liturgists in discussion of Holy Communion) uses taste as a central metaphor in the invitation: "O taste and see that the Lord is good." Christian theology and spirituality since the early Middle Ages have in fact been concerned with the "spiritual senses," of which taste was one. The Puritans in England and America spoke of the "beauties" of salvation, for which the Christian was supposed to acquire a spiritual taste. And, as we will see, Schleiermacher represented a major stream within Romanticism when he referred to religion itself as "the sense and taste for the infinite." The extent to which religious taste might relate to taste for sensory beauty and imaginative art has been very much a question; but the connection has often been made, at least by analogy, and was acknowledged by Schleiermacher himself.

On the aesthetic side, as we will have occasion to note, the deeper significance of taste is not unrelated to the important Indian concept of *rasa*, which means, in part, an artwork's overall aesthetic savor or flavor, which depends for its effect on sensitivity and discernment. In India, the notion of *rasa*—that which one "tastes" and experiences aesthetically—has been extended and applied for many centuries to spiritual experience, especially to the mood or savor of religious devotion, or *bhakti*.

Even in the West, the idea of aesthetic taste did not emerge first as something neatly separable from other kinds of judgment and enjoyment. Indeed, in the late seventeenth and early eighteenth century, taste was something identified as a kind of common sense (*sensus communis*), meaning not only a sense that all human beings share in common but also a sense that can help create community.[5] That aesthetic sense, while responsive to artistic excellence and natural beauty, was seen as intimately tied to our moral sense, without which community cannot exist.

The present study recovers, as well, an assumption that once was common in both East and West, which is that taste pertains to the creative process itself. Thus I concur with those who claim that it is difficult, if not impossible, to create artistically without also becoming, as maker, a perceptive and receptive audience for what one is in the process of making.

Finally, as may be evident already, I am tapping into a way of thinking that understands taste to be integral to imagination, and vice versa—something already evident in the celebrated essays by Joseph Addison on the "Pleasures of the Imagination" (1712).[6] But whereas the notion of "imagination" typically conjures up a picture of an aspect of mind that is necessarily free and not necessarily disciplined, the idea of taste highlights the important function of discernment, discipline, and growth in aesthetic making and response. At the same time, "taste" brings to mind enjoyment, and possibly joy. Taste, then, unites delights with virtues. Good aesthetic taste values something intrinsically pleasing that, while valuable in its own right, is also good for human life.

Christian Taste

For there to be good taste, there must be such a thing as bad taste. But, again, taste has many dimensions. And no one's taste is entirely good or entirely bad. In any case, whether good or bad, what we call taste is common to all humans, being something exercised in perceiving, enjoying, and evaluating whatever is artistic or aesthetic. If aesthetic values had no religious importance, even good taste would be inconsequential for religion. But, as I have already been arguing, art and aesthetics enter into corporate religion and personal spirituality far more than is commonly realized. For this reason aesthetic taste has greater religious relevance than churches and theologians ordinarily suppose.

I am not suggesting that there is necessarily any one use or kind of taste that could be called Christian. While we are accustomed to the notion of Christian thought and Christian morality, the very notion of Christian taste is actually a bit surprising, even amusing. Christian tastes in art—everyone's tastes, in fact—can strike other people (and other Christians) as funny, sometimes even by design. But matters of religious taste are also acutely sensitive. And the fundamental issues are serious and, indeed, intimately related to Christian faith and practice. Much of what unites, and much that divides, communities and churches is connected with—though not, of course, reducible to—what various Christians perceive, enjoy, and value aesthetically.

I claim that, from a Christian point of view, aesthetic virtues should include—in the interests of love and community—the cultivation and appreciation of aesthetic diversity, rather than the exercise of rigidly exclusive likes and dislikes. Yet Christian tastes also need to learn to be discerning and discriminating. These opposing requirements, entailed in the critical pluralism I espouse, must be held in creative tension. If that is done, Christian taste can contribute to spiritual and moral virtues central to Christian life, including the capacity to love the neighbor, to "enjoy God" (as Calvinists have put it), and to love and worship imaginatively.

Many of the specific questions regarding Christian taste that I address in this study will be familiar to students of the arts and aesthetics, and perhaps even more to liturgists and church musicians. Some are practical, others theoretical. Although none of these questions have easy answers, a number can be phrased relatively simply. For instance: What, if anything, makes one style of art secular, another sacred? What are the values and limitations of popular styles as compared with classical or traditional, whether in church or in secular culture? What is wrong (or right?) with importing into a house of worship various kinds of music and media that are "worldly" in origin? By what criteria can one make a judgment? How can conflicting values—religious, moral, and aesthetic—be addressed by churches in a pluralistic context? When it comes to art and spirituality, how do differences in age, class, gender, race, and education factor into judgments of quality and appropriateness? Are certain kinds of spirituality, and of spiritual taste, more mature than others? Does the mature Christian need to have mature taste? Can the exercise of taste in the making of art be a viable spiritual discipline or religious vocation? What is the relation between religious vision and aesthetic imagination, and how do both relate to social action and ethical practice?

Some of these questions are doubtless more urgent than others. With respect to worship practices in particular, questions of taste (while often not identified as such) have become as vexed and potentially divisive as questions of doctrine. They may be raised when a community church in the American Midwest replaces its traditional music with contemporary Christian "soft rock," or when an Anglican Cathedral in England begins to explore the possibilities of liturgical dance after centuries of disinterest or disapproval. Taste (spiritual and aesthetic) can also become a question when an immense new Catholic basilica is erected in Africa's Ivory Coast, the architecture of which seems to disregard indigenous styles and the sheer cost of which, in a region of persistent poverty, threatens to obscure any religious aura attributable to its beauty.

Although my primary focus in this study is on Christianity, I refer selectively to matters of taste and religious practice beyond the bounds of Christian traditions. It is pertinent to this inquiry, for instance, that in India cassette recordings of religious music—sometimes using synthesizers and other "pop" sounds—now often accompany daily *puja* (the primary form of Hindu worship, public and domestic).[7] Whether this affects the character of the hospitality being shown to the relevant deity (such as Ganesha) is a question some would want to ponder. By keeping such non-Christian traditions at least within our peripheral vision, we can see the issues facing Christians in a different light, whether due to similarities or to differences. As I have already indicated, the very notion of taste itself, for example, is treated suggestively in India under the concept of *rasa*, which figures both in aesthetics and in various ideas of religious devotion.

A Brief Guide

What I am offering in this book is not primarily a historical study, either in terms of theology and theory or in terms of the arts and taste. Nevertheless, the historical aspects of the discussion are by no means incidental. People who are immediately engaged in disputes over art, taste, and religion tend to forget that today's arguments and their attendant confusions have a long genealogy. In point of fact, most Christians (even theologians) have only a very vague notion of how arts have figured in Christian theology and practice. The results are what one would expect: distorted impressions of what the arts must mean to Christianity itself, and ill-considered debates over style and taste that generate more heat than light.

Naturally, much of the history we need to understand has to do with the arts themselves: with how they have been practiced and perceived (or misperceived) by Christians and by others. Accordingly, having introduced in this Prologue some of the major assumptions and concepts of the book, I begin to flesh them out in the first full chapter. After that I provide something like a minicourse on different Christian ideas and uses of art. I go on to trace the modern development of the particular ideas of art that, for better or worse, have most decisively shaped present-day notions regarding art's relation to religion. Having reflected on these, I return to issues of taste per se.

The theological core of my treatment of taste is found in the fourth chapter, where I reflect at some length on crucial connections between the taste for art and the desire for God. That leads me back to matters that have direct relevance to the practice of Christianity: religious style, kitsch (high and low), aesthetic and religious pluralism, controversies in church music, the search for the sacred in architecture. I conclude by reflecting on the aesthetic formation of Christian practice and of faith itself through spiritual taste and art.

For my purposes, the art that invites closest attention is music. That is both because music has been of undeniable importance to Christian worship over the centuries and because no art form is presently more controversial. Of all the arts, whether in church or in society as a whole, music today is at once the most pervasive and the most stratified; it most clearly reflects and engenders values, identities, and divisions among social groups, frequently by "targeting" a specific age group, race, or class.

I refer to numerous artistic examples so that the intelligibility of my argument will not depend on a reader's familiarity with any one work or style. If a somewhat disproportionate number of these examples are North American, that is mainly because I am aware that I stand a better chance of interpreting the nuances of artistic tastes and styles with which I am most familiar. Because I pay considerable attention not only to formal, classical culture but also to informal and popular culture, a number of the sources I cite, and some of the artifacts I describe, are themselves popular and commercial rather than "elite" and academic. However timely, such examples are obviously far from timeless. By the time this book is published, will anyone still be dancing the Macarena? Will the Macarena have been adapted, eventually, for contemporary Christian worship? (Not surprisingly, the answers at this moment of final revision are "no" to the first question and "yes" to the second.) Fortunately, nothing depends on the currency of such examples.

This book is not intended only for specialists in theology and aesthetics or experts in some particular art such as church music. Yet, precisely because it ranges widely across the arts and media, and across the boundaries of religious and academic disciplines, readers can expect to make uneven progress. Every reader is bound to have more expertise in one area of the discussion than in another. Even where I have minimized jargon and have succeeded in creating a relatively level field of discussion, terrain that is less familiar is bound to be more difficult to negotiate. Besides, some parts of the book are consciously designed in such a way as to be more theoretical, technical, and specialized in character. As in mountain climbing, it is often possible to detour around the most difficult stretches and still get a good view of the whole. Chapter 1 is meant, in fact, to provide a kind of hilltop from which to view the main range of the discussion that lies ahead. From there, readers who are especially interested in practical issues and who find themselves impatient with delayed gratification may want to proceed to the fifth chapter ("Kitsch, Sacred and Profane") and read to the end before returning to chapters 2 through 4, which include a larger historical component, and a higher dose of theory.

I cannot claim to be equally competent, myself, in all the areas of study touched on here. I try to make the most of my interdisciplinary training in religion and the arts. I draw, as well, on my practical experience as a musician and as director of a master's program in church music for an ecumenical Protestant seminary in the American Midwest. While at work on this book, I have also participated in many different kinds of worship services in the United States and abroad; I have taught introductory courses in world religions to seminarians; and I have done research in Europe, North America, China, and India. It would be ludicrous, however, to think that any of this truly qualified me to elucidate the deeper mysteries of art and religion, of taste and imagination. I can only take comfort in the fact that my subject has in large part remained mysterious to minds more capacious and penetrating than my own. I am increasingly convinced that, like it or not, in matters of religion and the arts our species is basically one of amateurs.

Authors wanting to address a relatively broad range of readers frequently keep notes to a bare minimum and exclude debates with other scholars. Although I have exercised restraint in the matter of scholarly debate, I have quite intentionally provided rather ample notes. That is not because I have wanted to cater to specialists, but just the opposite. I have felt it important to guide even general readers to other sources and to alert them to alternative views. It is not as though the field I am covering were so well known that readers (even academic ones) could all easily fend for themselves if they wanted to pursue certain topics further. Specialists in any given area will at once recognize, even so, that my references are quite selective.

I must mention one bibliographical item in particular—my own book *Religious Aesthetics*.[8] Even before I had finished it, I knew that various topics I was addressing in the book were ones that would keep me occupied long after. Some of the most tenacious questions had surfaced in the chapters entitled "Sin and Bad Taste" and "Questioning the Classics." But I had no idea at the time that disputes over taste and quality, and over religious and secular styles, would soon demand attention from nearly everyone concerned about the arts, culture, and Christian life (particularly worship).

Reflecting such interests, and indeed worries, this new book has quite a different focus from the earlier one, and carries certain ideas much further. Overall, it places greater emphasis on practical aesthetics, looking more closely at issues confronted by churches in particular. In addition, the present treatment of taste includes many ingredients of a specifically Christian aesthetic, which is something I did not attempt previously.

Acknowledgments

The present book developed by stages, and only after much dialogue. Consequently, a number of acknowledgments are in order. Chapter 1 expands material first published in *The Papers of the Henry Luce III Fellows in Theology*, vol. 3.[9] Chapter 2 makes use of portions of an article entitled "Christian Theology's Dialogue with Culture," published in the *Companion Encyclopedia of Theology*, edited by Peter Byrne and Leslie Houlden.[10] An earlier version of chapter 7 was published in the journal *Encounter*.[11] Several chapters draw on an article published in *Theological Education*.[12] I am grateful to the editors and publishers for permission to reprint this material in modified form.

I am indebted to the Henry Luce Foundation for appointing me a Henry Luce III Fellow in Theology for 1996–97, for the express purpose of working on this project. I am likewise indebted to Christian Theological Seminary (Indianapolis) for helping to support that year's leave from my usual responsibilities of teaching and administration.

Much different versions of various parts of this study were delivered as invited multimedia presentations at: The second Seminary Musicians Conference of the American Guild of Organists in Dallas, Texas; Disciples Divinity House of the University of Chicago (Centennial Lecture); the 83rd Annual Conference of the Modern Churchpeople's Union in Hoddesdon, England; Wesleyan College in Macon, Georgia (Belk Lecture); Park Avenue Christian Church and Union Theological Seminary in New York City; Christian Theological Seminary; Valparaiso University (Institute of Liturgical Studies and Church Music Seminar); Northwestern University (Gerhardt C. Mars and John C. Shaffer Lecture);

United Theological Seminary of the Twin Cities and Andover Newton Theological School (inaugural Henry Luce Lectures in Theology and the Arts); and a keynote address at the Sixth International and Interdisciplinary Conference on Built Form and Culture Research (on "Making Sacred Places") at the University of Cincinnati. I am grateful to these institutions for their interest and generous support.

I am grateful as well to students in my classes at Christian Theological Seminary—particularly in the Church and the Arts, Theology and the Arts, Religion and Literature, and Spirituality and Artistic Creation. Their input has shaped my thinking in a number of ways. My ideas were likewise shaped at many points in the book by a series of symposia on the arts in theological education sponsored by the Yale Institute of Sacred Music, Worship and the Arts. They were stimulated more recently by my involvement on the Board of Advisors for the Theology Through the Arts project directed by Jeremy Begbie and sponsored by the Centre for Advanced Religious and Theological Studies at Cambridge University.

Colleagues and the readers for Oxford University Press who gave careful attention to earlier drafts of this study, in whole or in part, deserve my sincere thanks—and the thanks of readers, who have been spared a number of infelicities, inaccuracies, and confusions. I want to thank Charles Allen, Larry Bouchard, Graham Howes, and Richard Viladesau for their attention to the project as a whole. Joyce Krauser, my brother David Brown, and my parents Jane P. Brown and Ralph A. Brown, Jr. (shortly before his death) gave a most helpful perusal of much of the manuscript in its formative stages. The CTS faculty at a colloquium session commented helpfully on chapter 1. Members of the CTS Writers Group were kind enough to discuss chapter 2 with me. I thank Tex Sample for commenting especially on the chapters that deal with popular taste; E. Byron Anderson and Ted Gibboney for reviewing chapters on music and worship; Margaret Miles, Richard Kieckhefer, and J. Gerald Janzen for their reflections on chapter 6, particularly my discussion of Augustine's aesthetics; and Margaret Farley for helping me clarify issues there regarding the "ends" of both art and a moral life. Thomas Barrie, Judith Berling, Theodore Ludwig, Deborah Sommer, and co-members of a People-to-People delegation to China commented usefully on chapter 7. That chapter, in dealing with Chinese architecture, religion, and culture, required me to make a considerable stretch as a scholar. Paul Rozin alerted me to psychological and moral factors related to taste and disgust. My thanks to William Harmon, William Jackson, and Sunthar Visuvalingam for friendly advice in matters of cross-cultural aesthetics and religion, particularly Indian. Stephen Happel, Robin Jensen, David Morgan, Don Saliers, Janet Walton, and Wilson Yates gave encouragement and occasional guidance (or argument) at various stages along the way. Cynthia Read of Oxford

University Press deserves particular thanks for her support from the very beginning.

Needless to say, not all the views I express are ones my readers have endorsed. And most of the problems that remain are, of course, my own responsibility. It pleases me, however, to think that some of the remaining inadequacies may be the results of collective failure. That would fit with my belief that virtues and faults alike have a communal, corporate dimension.

I thank my daughter Joanna for touching up this Prologue, for discussing poetry and theology with me, and for keeping me apprised of artful aspects of youth culture. Finally, I am grateful to my wife Camilla for constant encouragement and timely dialogue without which I would never have been able to carry out this project.

Frank Burch Brown

GOOD TASTE, BAD TASTE, & CHRISTIAN TASTE

Good Taste, Bad Taste, and Christian Taste

The Religious Problem with Questions of Taste

Taste Perceived as Irrelevant to Religion

Compared with questions of morality and theology, issues of aesthetic taste generally strike Christians as relatively inconsequential. It is not that controversies involving taste never break out among Christians. On the contrary. Few things at present create more persistent conflict within Christian congregations than differences over worship style, music, and media (especially "contemporary" versus "traditional"). Outside the church, moreover, dedicated Christians throughout history have frequently found themselves at odds with prevailing styles of art and entertainment.

But whereas Christians are more or less accustomed to debating issues of morality and theology, and are often unapologetic about doing so, they usually find it embarrassing to be seriously worried—as many are—about such "trivial" things as taste and aesthetics. The Bible doesn't say much about these matters; and the people who care most about taste, and who therefore may be outspoken in their views, often strike others as aesthetes and elitists—as uncharitable in spirit and far removed from the poor and socially marginal folk beloved by Jesus.

In fact, Andrew Sullivan, a Roman Catholic and former editor of the *New Republic*, once went so far as to declare in an interview with the *Christian Century* that the very "tackiness" of the church is testimony to something greater working through it, and a sign of the power of the truth that survives the institution. "The Catholic Church is nothing if not tacky, in many respects," Sullivan said. He continued: "Religion is not interior design. It is not about the look of things."[1]

3

Even Christians devoted to the arts would quickly agree that Sullivan has a point—namely, that aesthetics per se is not the core of religion or spirituality. Indeed, to most Christians, aesthetic taste seems entirely peripheral to matters of faith. It is virtually inconceivable that the Jesus of the New Testament would ever have driven people out of the temple on account of their having decorated it in bad taste. And though the New Testament tells us that Jesus instructed his disciples in prayer, it never suggests that he tried to teach them to sing better.

At a practical level, of course, the church has employed a variety of arts; and the appreciation of art presumably requires taste, however minimally developed. But almost every Christian sect and denomination has used the arts selectively. And often churches look on their sacred rituals and artifacts as different from art per se. The "drama" of the liturgy and the "art" of the icon, for instance, are not understood chiefly as aesthetic objects, let alone as products of artistic genius. Thus, from an Eastern Orthodox point of view, supposing that the efficacy of icons depended in some way on artistic taste would be almost as heterodox as imagining that the efficacy of communion depended in some way on the communicant's physical sense of taste. From the viewpoint of Orthodox liturgy, nothing is gained spiritually by being a connoisseur of icons, any more than spiritual benefits would accrue from being (somehow) a communion gourmet.

Artistic Taste Seen as Theologically Suspect

The common Christian reluctance to consider artistic taste as having much religious significance is reinforced by the recurrent theological suspicion of, or disinterest in, things artistic and sensory. Whatever the practice of churches with respect to the arts, many theologians have said that the arts of sense, imagination, and material making are for the spiritually immature, the beginners. In their estimate, spiritual adults will prefer, rather, to contemplate intellectual or spiritual beauty, which is infinitely higher. With some notable exceptions, one finds variations on this theme reiterated from Augustine (354–430) and Pope Gregory the Great (c. 540–604) up to the present time.

To be sure, there is a venerable if subsidiary theological tradition that has reflected positively on the love of beauty. But the medieval Franciscan theologian Bonaventure (c. 1217–1274) was in no way atypical when he located material and sensuous beauty only at the lower levels of the pathway of the mind to God. (The Neo-Platonic tradition doubtless had much to do with that.) Like Bonaventure, a great many theologians have had a habit of hurrying over *artistic* beauty, due to its entanglements with the senses, materiality, and worldly imagination. Even Jonathan Edwards (1703–1758), well known for his love of spiritual taste and beauty, had relatively little to say about the arts.[2] There were, of course, Romantic thinkers and writers such as Friedrich Schlegel (1772–1829), William Blake (1757–1827), Samuel Taylor Coleridge (1772–1834)—and, in America, the Transcendentalist Ralph Waldo Emerson (1803–1882)—who celebrated the religious or quasi-religious powers of artistic imagination. They saw art as intimately connected with what we today might call "spirituality." But they occupied the outer margins of theology proper, both with respect to professional identity and with respect to orthodoxy. Friedrich Schleiermacher (1768–1834), the greatest theologian of Romanticism, likewise acknowledged profound parallels between aesthetic experience and religious experience, which he described as a sense and taste for the infinite. Yet he, too, held back from examining thoroughly the ways in which aesthetic pursuits and perceptions can contribute something distinctive to religious life itself, in the manner in which theological concepts can enrich prayerful reflection, for instance.

By the time that the Oxford Movement (1833–45) sought to recover a more aesthetically heightened liturgy for the Church of England, and certainly by the time Victorian critics such as John Ruskin (1819–1900) made their last efforts to renew a thoroughly moral approach to the arts, many of the more vigorous artists had retreated from the church itself. Indeed, ever since the Renaissance, patronage for the arts had become more and more secular, thereby encouraging the arts to enter more fully into the spirit of courtly, aristocratic, and bourgeois, middle-class life. It is not surprising that tastes in the arts, and ideas about the purposes of art, reflected such a shift in practice. Theorists recognized that art might at times emulate science, as one could see in the artistic fascination with optics, perspective, and observation of nature. They also saw that art could emulate or improve on social criticism, as in satire and comedies of manners, or in realist fiction. But even more, and above all, it became apparent that art could offer marvelously "useless" pleasure removed from other concerns.[3] Eventually, as the theories of taste and beauty earlier put forward by Immanuel Kant (1724–1804) were adapted—and often distorted—more broadly, the more progressive artists and critics alike were more and more tempted to think of all true art as essentially autonomous (something Kant had never quite said). By the end of the nineteenth century, and on into the twentieth, those "in the know" began to see true art as serving only itself and as appealing to a taste uncontaminated by moral, religious, or intellectual interests. Earlier theological suspicions of artistry and persistent ecclesiastical desires for control were now answered by artistic declarations of independence.

History seems, then, to have played a trick on anyone who might have hoped for a full-fledged theology of art and taste. Enlightenment thinkers had been the first clearly and systematically to distinguish aesthetic taste and fine art from a variety of other capacities and skills. In theory, that new conceptualization made possible a genuine theology of art or of taste. Yet the same line of reasoning that recognized aesthetic taste and art as distinctive also gave rise to the modernist impression (or conviction) that there is actually nothing about art and taste that could be intrinsically relevant to religion and theology, or indeed to morality. To value something for truly artistic and aesthetic reasons was now supposedly to accord it a value all its own. The taste for art was in principle divorced, therefore, from the spiritual taste that had been spoken of by scholastics, mystics, and Puritans alike, and to which this study will later return.[4]

That did not mean the end of art's spiritual aspirations. Even in the twentieth century, many artists—including pivotal avant-garde figures such as the painter Vassily Kandinsky (1866–1944), the poet T. S. Eliot (1888–1965), and the composer Arnold Schoenberg (1874–1951)—continued to produce works that in new ways expressed transcendental yearnings and that sometimes openly explored matters of moral, spiritual, and theological concern. Moreover, a certain number of religion scholars and theologically minded critics gave heed, despite the fact that in academic theory and criticism the spiritual aims of much modern art remained for a long time a well-kept secret, either unrecognized or suppressed.[5] By the middle of the century, numerous books, courses, and even graduate degree programs dealt explicitly with figures and topics in religion and the arts (especially literature and the visual arts). But it is telling that the late Catholic theologian Hans Urs von Balthasar (1905–1988), in his multivolume treatise on theological aesthetics, devoted but a small fraction of his discussion to the arts as such.[6] Among Protestants, Karl Barth (1886–1968) mostly confined himself to his beloved Mozart and to the *Isenheim Altarpiece* of Grünewald (1480?–1528).

Of the Protestant theologians and critics who began to take a keen interest in the arts, many looked to art mainly to expose signs of the depravity of the human condition and thus to ask and deepen existential questions that finally only theology could answer. Even when essentially affirmative of artistic beauty, as in the case of the Dutch Neo-Calvinist Abraham Kuyper (1837–1920), theologians still had a strong tendency to undercut art's more positive religious aspirations. As Kuyper's follower Herman Bavinck (1854–1921) argued: art glimpses Canaan from a distance; "it is not able even to dry our tears in the griefs of life."[7]

What therefore remained unclear was how any art—even religious art—could be spiritually empowering in a manner parallel to theology proper, or perhaps as a "sensuous" mode of theology in itself. An emphasis on the sheerly preparatory and critical function of art existed in tension with the older and often-repeated Protestant acclamation of J. S. Bach as the "Fifth Evangelist."[8] It contrasted, too, with the high praise that Luther (1483–1546) had for church music as a means of proclamation, second in value only to scripture or the verbal preaching of the gospel. In short, one whole line of modern Protestant theologizing on art (at least nonmusical art) tended to obscure how art might at times have a thoroughly Christian calling: to bear the good news with special grace, and not only to bear mere hints of hope or to bear the bad news (of sin and estrangement) with shattering power.

In this connection, it is revealing that the foremost Protestant theologian of art in the recent past, Paul Tillich (1886–1965), was most excited by the religious potential of expressionist art. What is revealing is that he favored such art in large part because he believed that a work that is "expressionistic" in style can shatter self-contained forms, exposing its truly ultimate concern by, in a sense, sacrificing its own coherence, sensuous appeal, and beauty,[9] becoming the kind of thing that literary critics would later call a self-consuming artifact.[10]

Postmodern critics have carried still further the fascination with artistic rupture, fragmentation, and fallibility even as they have broken down the notion that art and its appreciation are essentially walled off from other human interests. Critics in a deconstructive mode, led by Jacques Derrida, Paul de Man, J. Hillis Miller, and their Yale colleagues, have raised the suspicion of the arts to a new level by discovering in artistic "texts" unavoidable signs of formal and semantic instability. In their analysis, art never attains the perfection it allegedly aspires to, or produces meanings that are fully embodied, "present," and palpable. With most deconstructionists the motive for taking art apart is not theological, but it is in some sense antitheological: the removal of all vestiges of metaphysical authority, power, and ineffable truth—while sometimes hinting at a kind of negative theology.[11] In such postmodern eyes, wary of the illusions of both Enlightenment Reason and Pre-Enlightenment Religion, no uncontaminated space exists, even for art and taste—no perfect human or "spiritual" beauty.[12]

In keeping with that rejection of what we can call purist aesthetics, which was derived from the Enlightenment principle of artistic autonomy, most postmodern theorists see aesthetic judgments as deeply political. Sociologists such as Pierre Bourdieu thus interpret tastes and their expression in criticism as thoroughly ideological in nature: as prejudiced signs and tools of status, class, and entitlement.[13] Although such arguments as Bourdieu's quickly become reductive, they show how problematic it is simply to treat judgments of aesthetic taste as "disinterested," and free of all but purely aesthetic concerns. No longer can we trust the Kantian claim that judgments of taste are rooted strictly in individual judgment, uninfluenced by the opinions of others, and yet so representative of what humans share in common that they can claim to be universally applicable—warranting the assent of everyone.[14]

Taste Regarded as Prejudiced and Elitist

Of course, once such criticism exposes the connection between taste and the entrenched prejudices of class (or race), theologians and morally sensitive critics suddenly find yet another reason to avoid discussing taste, except in negative terms. For it seems more apparent than ever that the whole notion of taste is associated with a theologically and morally unacceptable elitism. In his book *Hard Living People and Mainstream Christians*, the Methodist theologian Tex Sample reports that the struggling, hard-living, working-class people he discusses relate to songs that other classes tend to scorn. Music, he says, is key in their worship.[15] But they don't respond favorably to imported organists and choir directors insistent on using Bach and Brahms to "lift" the musical tastes of the congregation. They don't much like musicians who feel compromised by the so-called musical debauchery of contemporary, gospel, and country music. Sample himself (with strong blue-collar connections) gets agitated just thinking about elitism in the context of the church. He writes:

> As a consultant to congregations around the country I have found any number of churches cowed by . . . musicians who continue to perform—and *perform* is the right word—for congregations where the overwhelming majority of people do not find their mono-type and elitist selections spiritually nourishing; indeed, they find them dull and boring. . . . If such musicians will not hear the concerned urgings of appropriate committees and officials, they should be lovingly fired.[16]

The point is by no means an incidental one for Sample. In fact, Sample extends and nuances his discussion of elitist taste and the politics of aesthetics in his later book, *White Soul: Country Music, the Church and Working Americans*.[17] Here his attack on elitist taste becomes part of a substantial theological defense not only of working-class resistance to the elitist values of the dominant culture but also of an alternative mode of being church that Sample calls, affectionately, the "trashy" church.[18]

Needless to say, such an attack on conventional cultivated tastes and elitist, "respectable" religiosity stands in stark contrast to many of the arguments now launched daily by defenders of traditional church arts, which are the very arts whose dominance Sample resists on behalf of "trash." Opposite Sample stands, for instance, the provocative book by Thomas Day entitled *Why Catholics Can't Sing: The Culture of Catholicism and the Triumph of Bad Taste*.[19] Significantly it is Day who, in questioning and indeed attacking recent trends in popular Catholic church music, is most comfortable retaining (rather than critiquing) the idea of taste. In his view, much music of that sort is definitely in bad taste; and bad taste is bad for religious life. By contrast, although Sample describes and defends what he regards as the better forms of country music by building on a nonelitist analysis of taste—my own, in fact—Sample is understandably leery of the idea of taste because of its association with elitism.[20]

"Taste" Irretrievable?

It appears, then, that there is little within either Christian habits, moral values, theological training, or secular theory to encourage a positive religious interest in aesthetic taste. Yet, as I want to argue, religious life and thought are nevertheless far more conditioned—both positively and negatively—by matters related to taste than has commonly been acknowledged, and in ways that deserve more careful attention. Even if one finds it prudent to circumvent or redefine the term "taste" per se in a variety of contexts, no other term or concept so effectively highlights the same complex of issues. For no other term so readily combines a concern for aesthetic delight with a concern for imaginative discernment and "formation" that, while often marking differences and creating conflicts, can be good for life, morally and spiritually, and communally as well as individually.

But clearly we cannot settle for existing assumptions about taste or suppose that we already know, intuitively, everything that a full-fledged theology of taste could teach us. Along with Tex Sample, we need to clear space for taking the existing religious and moral functions of popular arts and tastes seriously (and lightly, too); and, along with Thomas Day, we need to explore crucial dimensions of legitimate criticism and cultivation that go beyond enjoyments and judgments that are comfortable and popular. We are in search of a concept and theology of taste that is both spiritually challenging and nonelitist. It is my own judgment that, in an era in which imagination, sensory experience, and embodiment have become more theologically respectable, reconsiderations of taste might well contribute to new theological understandings of faith, community, and spiritual growth.

Preparing to Pursue Taste Theologically

Despite discouragements to pursuing taste as a religious and theological issue, I would suggest that there is something not only mischievous but also seriously misleading about either ignoring the aesthetics of religious practice or uncritically celebrating the spiritual assets of tackiness. If someone wants to take the first option, and so to dismiss taste as a subject worthy of argument and inquiry, that person is sure at some point to cite the Roman adage suggesting that there is no point in disputing matters of taste: *"De gustibus non disputandum est.*" But in the sphere of art, including religious art, there is good reason to believe that disputes over taste are not only inevitable (though sometimes regrettable) but also potentially productive. Perceptions, enjoyments, and judgments in the realm of taste are by no means beyond question or modification, and often they make a religious difference. The very fact that taste is almost never completely pure, and thus never completely disengaged from other values and commitments, suggests not that taste is irrelevant or private or indisputable but, rather, that religious and aesthetic judgments and enjoyments come together in a variety of significant ways that deserve recognition and discussion.

The most delicate aspect of such discussion concerns aesthetic judgments and delights that are near to the heart, personally and religiously. Among the most bonding of joys is the discovery that one's tastes are mutually shared. By the same token, among the most alienating of disappointments is the discovery that a beloved person or admired group rejects the very kinds of art and beauty that one cherishes or through which one worships. These are sensitive matters. If you attack my devotion to Arvo Pärt's contemporary musical style of spiritual minimalism, I may well feel that you don't understand something important about the inner meaning of my faith. If I criticize your unbridled enthusiasm for singing praise and worship choruses from texts projected onto a screen, that may strain our capacity to belong to the same local church. It may even strain the notion that we belong to the same church in a larger sense.

The association of patterns of Christian life with styles of art is not just an individual matter. We and our worshiping communities tend to identify with certain works and styles. The African American liberation theologian James Cone at one time argued, for instance, that white people had not earned the right to sing black spirituals. Spirituals, he said, belong to black experience and to the black church. To sing them the right way, people need to have come out of slavery and suffering. Although Cone eventually modified this interpretation of "singing rights," his earlier point cannot be dismissed lightly.[21]

The rule of love evidently requires sensitivity in matters of taste. It may require learning to attend in new ways to arts that are not historically a part of one's own tradition, and to let judgments of taste begin with the communities and individuals to whom a particular art is most indigenous. That does not mean, however, that a religion of love must happily tolerate, let alone promote, aesthetic carelessness or mediocrity.

We have already acknowledged that authentic religion can survive tackiness. But to say merely that tackiness is not fatal to religion is surely not to say enough, even from a religious perspective. We might ask, for example: Is it really a matter of religious indifference that Jesus was such a good storyteller? That his parables are not simply folksy anecdotes chock-full of greeting-card sentiments but are frequently artful and sometimes dense and difficult in the manner of poetry? Again, is the Roman Catholic Church in no way the beneficiary of the efforts of monks over the centuries to chant more or less in tune, and of choirs to harmonize? Was John Wesley completely off the mark when he praised a collection of hymns (many by his brother Charles) as not only free of "doggerel" and "patched rhymes" but also, in some measure, imbued with "the true spirit of poetry," which he thought could be confirmed by people "of taste"?[22] And does it matter hardly at all to Christian faith and practice that so many houses of worship are in some way beautiful? Or is it not rather the case that these efforts of artistry, requiring discipline and taste, generally enhance Christian life? And that diverse kinds of artistic excellence and beauty are part of the bounty of the religious life, not merely negligible products of human frailty that a gracious church must condescend to accept?

More pointedly: the evidence of scripture, tradition, and experience all suggest that art can sometimes mediate not only a sense of life but also a sense of grace and of the mystery that we call God. And since art cannot mediate without the aid of aesthetic imagination, response, and judgment—without taste, in short—we must consider the perhaps surprising possibility that taste at its most encompassing is no less crucial to religious life and faith than is intellectual understanding and moral commitment.

But what of religious art that many would regard as in some sense lesser in quality? Questions of aesthetic value obviously cannot be ignored from a theological perspective; but neither can they be answered apart from considerations of context. And even when the art in question seems aesthetically deficient, this hardly means that aesthetic factors are simply irrelevant to its religious function. It is surely worth contemplating that the very art that some trained critics and art lovers regard (with some reason) as sentimental kitsch is rarely regarded as cheap or inferior by the people for whom it serves devotional purposes. On the contrary, the religious admirers of such art (paintings by Warner Sallman, for instance) seem to find it either beautiful, heart-warming, or spiritually elevating.[23] Such heart-felt admiration, far from proving that the quality of that kind of art is a matter of religious indifference, shows rather that religious lovers of such art care in some fashion about its quality. They are attuned in particular ways to the art in question, and in particular aesthetic ways to faith and worship. Whatever we make of that, from the standpoint of theological aesthetics, it is not inconsequential. Whether highly cultivated or plainly unsophisticated, that sort of attunement, no less than particular notions of God and morality, doubtless affects the tone of Christian life and belief; it undeniably influences personal and communal theologies as well as styles of relating church to world. Evidently, then, there are religious reasons to examine the tastes manifest in the love of many sorts of religious art. Exploring those tastes could be a means of exploring religious sensibilities and identities. It might also uncover new ways of accepting, criticizing, or bridging differences.

In any case the current "worship wars," which so clearly reflect confusion and conflict in matters of Christian taste, indicate that we cannot afford the luxury of neglecting aesthetics. The kinds of Christians people imagine themselves to be, the kind of being they imagine God to be, and accordingly the kinds of Christian worship they regard as fitting and desirable, are often reflected or projected in aesthetic choices, whether recognized as such or not.[24] That questions of taste in religion are rarely amenable to conventional approaches to good art and bad, or to standard ways of demarcating sacred and secular styles, suggests not that questions of taste are irrelevant but that it is time to set aside certain habits of mind that tend to undermine fruitful discussion. Among them are elitism and dogmatism, on the one hand, and indiscriminate relativism on the other. Pursuing instead what we might term a critical pluralism, we can no longer assume that matters of taste should be left to take care of themselves or delegated to presumed authorities.

From a critical pluralist perspective, it appears that the most useful Christian exercise of taste today might be, in fact, to cultivate what I shall later discuss as "ecumenical taste." That would mean, among other things, developing forms of perception, enjoyment, and judgment that are able (1) to recognize and indeed relish certain aesthetic and religious differences without regarding them as inevitably and permanently alienating; (2) to learn to discern, as an act of love, what others find delightful and meaningful in art that has little appeal to oneself or one's group; and (3) to notice, both more precisely and more generally, points in life and worship where aesthetic aims and religious aspirations (or aversions) are wedded to one another, and thus to see how spiritual growth can have a properly artistic and aesthetic dimension subject to criticism, cultivation, and education. That sort of theological exploration of the aesthetic dimensions of faith and spirit can be profitable, however, only if our notions of art and taste are refined and deepened—though in a manner that at this early stage we must be content merely to adumbrate rather than expound.

Features of Taste for Theological Reflection

Three Elements of Taste

Joseph Haydn, in conversation with Leopold Mozart, once spoke highly of the latter's son Wolfgang, commending the younger Mozart for his wonderful taste and craft: "I tell you before God, as an honest man, your son is the greatest composer known to me in person and by name: he has taste, but above this he has the greatest knowledge of composition."[25] Indeed, despite his notoriously scatological taste in humor, Mozart is someone we can safely regard as having good taste in music. But if Mozart alone had had good taste, he would have had no appreciative audience, past or present, and no one qualified to praise him. There is the good taste exercised in the composer's making and judgment, and there is the audience's good taste in perceptively listening, appreciating, and appraising. There is also the relation of taste to other skills and capacities, as Haydn's remark makes plain. Taste is not one-dimensional.

Nor is taste evident only when it is astute and well cultivated. As noted before, the very possibility of good taste implies the possibility of bad. But good taste and bad taste both take many forms. And even bad taste can be put to good use. An art teacher who is quite indiscriminate in her tastes, who enthuses over practically everything that her students produce, may be showing poor judgment—poor taste—and in that respect she may not be helping her students to become more skilled as artists. But she may be helping them become more courageous and confident. There are doubtless worse kinds of charity than that, and much worse kinds of taste.

We all exercise taste in at least three ways: in aesthetic perceiving, enjoying, and judging (which, in more technical language, we can also term apperception, appreciation, and appraisal). Each of these aspects of taste has practical theological implications.

Taste as Aesthetic Perception

First, we exercise taste just in *perceiving* whatever is artistic or aesthetic—that is, in taking in the features of a particular work of art, or in noticing the aesthetic qualities of a natural object. This is not a question of physical perception alone. And our particular aesthetic perceptions are probably not shared by every perceptive creature. My dog Biscuit, for instance, has heard every note of Bach's Cantata 140, *Wachet Auf* (*Sleepers, Wake*), and in the process has probably heard a lot of high overtones that human beings cannot hear. Sometimes she even seems to like listening. But I would not say that Biscuit has ever listened to *Wachet Auf*. She has not heard the work that Bach composed. Certainly she has heard an array of sounds; beyond that she may have perceived qualities and patterns of sound that we could call in some sense aesthetic. The work as religious art, however, emerges from what we human beings hear *in* the sounds.

Not that humans all hear the same thing. None of us hears a Bach cantata in just the way that people in Bach's day did; performance practices have changed, sometimes in ways we cannot know; and so have listening practices. Much has happened culturally, musically, and liturgically since the eighteenth century. All of that affects what one apperceives in the very act of listening to the music

Bach wrote. It is also entirely possible that some who study Bach's church music today, and who work out of a long tradition related to that music, actually hear the music more rewardingly—and in ways Bach would have approved—than many people in his own congregations did. We should not assume that Bach's historical context establishes all the norms for what should count as hearing the music he wrote, which necessarily contains different possibilities for its realization in performance and hearing. What all this shows is that the taste required for making and hearing music is culturally shaped, and likewise evolves in relation to living traditions. But for that very reason, when it comes to taking in works of human art, my dog lacks taste.

There are human beings who are similarly inept. Certainly there are people in church who cannot tell when the organist is having an off day, any more than others can tell when the sermon is ill prepared. At such moments the organist can be grateful for tastes that, in this respect, are undeveloped.

A more serious ineptitude is one all human beings share. We are all to some extent culturally bounded, and limited in the number of styles to which we are attuned. That factor shows up, again, in our very perception of what is going on in a work of art, quite apart from whether we like the art or think it good. Let us go back to the Bach cantata. Even if we are of the opinion that some music is basically about itself, we tend to think of some actions and moods as compatible with a particular work of music, and of others as incompatible. I know from experience that a class of American undergraduate college students, when presented with this music, will usually say that they hear the opening chorus of *Wachet Auf* as peaceful, serene. (That is what they say about almost every kind of music they think of as classical.) Most classical listeners, by contrast, will declare that the music that opens this cantata sounds like an exalted wake-up call, orderly but transcendent: both a count-down and a celebrative procession moving in anticipation, the underlying pulses of three being grouped into larger units of twelve, tolling the hour of midnight. And that is not surprising, given that the text (which after all is asking sleepers to wake up) is based largely on the scripture in Matthew in which the sleeping bridesmaids are called to wake to meet the Bridegroom Christ. It is fitting, therefore, that listeners hear the music as at once expectant, full of anticipation, and yet by no means disorderly.

What explains the difference between the responses of the typical American college audience and those of the typical classical audience? The "peaceful" response of the college undergraduates is surely conditioned by the fact that they have mostly been listening to rock, rap, and heavy metal. They are *perceiving* the music of the cantata differently. They do not even notice certain features of the music by Bach—the sturdy beat, the intensity of certain rising musical lines played by the strings, the animated interweaving of the voices— because their frame of reference is different. The two audiences are simply not taking in the same work. We are safe in saying, in fact, that the typical college audience is not, at first listen, "apperceiving" the work that Bach wrote.

At a practical level, that kind of difference in taste has theological implications, even though (or perhaps because) it is a difference in basic perceptions that is often not recognized. In many churches today, for instance, one could not expect some of the most fitting perceptions of Bach's music to be widely shared. That is because a common range of aesthetic perception normally depends to a large extent on shared culture or tradition, and in that sense on a community of shared "taste." Where one has cultural diversity and widely differing aesthetic experience, aesthetic perceptions are predictably diverse as well. Very often, in fact, works of art indirectly favor particular groups over others, and establish insiders and outsiders, so that some people "get it" while others cannot, failing even to perceive what the insiders perceive. That kind of differentiation occurs despite the fact that music and art can also work in other ways to bridge cultural boundaries.

It follows that for a relatively diverse church to share anything but the most obvious and immediately accessible forms of expression, it must learn to transmit and share the "languages" of differing tastes, so that at least basic perceptions can begin to be shared. That process can occur only through cumulative and mutual learning and is perhaps never complete. But even when one cannot situate oneself fully within an alternative tradition of taste, one can be enriched by expanding one's capacities at least to the extent of making contact. In the case of the Bach cantata, the college audience at the end of merely ten to fifteen minutes of listening and discussion can often "tune in" to the music in such a way as to register much more fully what is going on in a choral work from the German Protestant Baroque. The process is not unlike learning the rules of a game as one begins to watch or participate. A cricket fan might not, after all, even "see" a bunting third strike in baseball unless informed as to what to look for, and in that case could not possibly get excited about such a strikeout. Bach's music may not be so inaccessible to listeners unfamiliar with its norms and strategies, its "rules." But a Bach cantata intended for church use today might best be introduced and discussed first in church school or at other times, just as one discusses (or hopes to discuss) theology and scripture.

Those trained in the "high arts" are well aware that experience and education are relevant to aesthetic perception. What those same people often fail to recognize is that different sorts of education and experience can be relevant to the experience of a variety of arts, even at a popular level. Many listeners familiar with jazz or European classical music, but uneducated in various forms of popular culture, perceive only boring, noisy, or confusing patterns when they first encounter a music video such as Joan Osborne's "One of Us," which in 1995 had remarkable staying power on MTV, besides serving as the driving force behind the platinum-selling, Grammy-nominated album *Relish*. In addition to bringing to the music and the images an inappropriate set of aesthetic expectations, such listeners often bring prejudices related to class and age.

"One of Us," written by Eric Bazilian,[26] is definitely targeted toward youth and others who may recognize but transgress sophisticated and middle-class standards. To "elite" tastes, therefore, such a song and its video version can seem at first nothing more than kitsch. Yet, upon repeated exposure to the video, initially skeptical viewers and listeners often come to detect layers of previously unsuspected meaning and to see a complex interplay of incarnational imagery in the mix of whimsical and off-beat musings. There is a plaintive, almost childishly inquisitive quality to the persistent, simply sung question: "What if God was one of us / Just a slob like one of us / Just a stranger on the bus / Trying to make his way home / No one calling on the phone / Except the Pope, maybe, in Rome?" Particularly in the music video version, an aura of slightly decadent—and thus faintly blasphemous—sanctity is generated as one views accompanying scenes and people from a carnival setting. One sees (among other things) an odd assortment of differently attired and oddly sized individuals, many from what could be considered underclasses. One by one they stick their heads into a cut-out opening in a two-dimensional replica of a figure from the Sistine Chapel. One soon realizes that those assorted human heads are appearing where God's head would have been seen in the Sistine representation of the creation of the sun and moon. At least, most viewers can guess the image is by Michelangelo.

At the same time, in a manner that is uniquely artistic and artfully theological, the music video produces an effect very different from anything found in Michelangelo's own art. At one point the voice asks: "If God had a face, what would it look like? / And would you want to see / If seeing meant you had to believe in things like heaven / And in Jesus and the saints and all the prophets?" This after already asking: "If God had a name, what would it be? / And would you call it to his face / If you were faced with him in all his glory? / And what would you ask / If you had just one question?" Piety and irony combine here unexpectedly to make something like a prayer that, in wondering out loud, simultaneously blesses and almost pities God—and ordinary human beings as well, as what God might ever and again choose to become.

To reiterate, experience and expectation condition what one actually hears or sees—what one perceives and thus "takes in." It is noteworthy that "One of Us" was heard by some Contemporary Christian Music (CCM) listeners as very much their own kind of song and was consequently given a certain amount of air play on CCM stations (even while reviled by others in CCM circles as sheer blasphemy). Rush Limbaugh plugged "One of Us" as signaling the return of American youth to fundamentalist religious values.

Perhaps because the song and its words could be so perceived (or misperceived), musicians at the other end of popular music spectrum soon found the song and video an irresistible object for parody. It certainly did not "catch on" with those who were taking their bearings from the alternative rock styles of albums such as *Mellon Collie and the Infinite Sadness*, from the Smashing Pumpkins (Virgin Records, 1995). Joan Osborne herself, knowing that a sweetly Christian image would be the kiss of death for her sort of musical ambitions, took to presenting the song in concert in ways that involved what *Spin* magazine characterized as "some biting revisionism." Reporting on a concert in Cologne, Germany, *Spin* observed: "She doesn't sound as sure about what to believe in anymore. 'Yeeeahh, yeeeahh,' she rasps, 'God is greeeat. . . .' The mike stand is now thrust way between her legs, and whether she realizes it or not, she's coming close to committing a most excellently lewd, even blasphemous, act."[27]

But other listeners (including Osborne herself) never perceived the song as one-dimensional. *Spin* reported how Osborne was thrilled to be invited by Nusrat Fateh Ali Khan, the immensely popular Pakistani Muslim qawaali singer, to join him in ritual singing—shortly before his death at age 48. She was by no means uninterested in "spiritual" ways of attuning to music, and was thus open to his hearing that potential in her own singing of "One of Us."

To be unable to hear either the unsettling implications of some of the questions in "One of Us" or the serious religious inquisitiveness behind its questions is surely to lack a perceptive faculty important to having a "taste" for it. Thus *perceiving* of that sort is, as we have noted, one aspect or function of what we call taste. But we also exercise taste in the act of appreciating: that is, in *enjoying* (or not) aesthetic perceptions; and then, last, in appraising or *judging* them as appropriate or inappropriate, as commendable or not.

Taste as Aesthetic Enjoyment

Of what theological relevance, then, is the second aspect of taste, the aspect of *enjoyment* or appreciation (or lack thereof)? For one thing, if I can be religious only in one mode or mood, there is probably little hope that I will appreciate the somewhat quirky religiosity of "One of Us." Similarly, if I am so jaded that I cannot take holy delight in fields of purple flowers—as Alice Walker proposed in her novel *The Color Purple*—my taste is apparently defective, and my religious sensibility as well. Again, if I no longer enjoy Isaac Watts hymns due to overfamiliarity, this dullness in taste diminishes my capacity to worship. In Book Ten of the *Confessions*, Augustine congratulates himself on having reached a point in life when he is no longer moved to tears by the music of the hymns he sings in church, and on having learned to value the songs mainly for the truth of the words. But in that respect, one could argue, Augustine's lurking dualism between flesh and spirit had corrupted his taste and his theology; for the truth as heard *through* the music, as heard delightfully and beautifully *in* the music, may be rather different from the truth abstractly conceived. Artistic embodiment may open up new levels of spiritual vision and create a satisfying sense of church and community that might otherwise remain inaccessible. But that can transpire only if one can appreciate, enjoy, or be moved by what one is perceiving in the art.

Aesthetic enjoyment (or disgust) may be spontaneous, but it is guided by cues provided by the work, its genre, and its context. A confusing mixture of cues can lead to a very mixed sort of pleasure. And when there is a dissonance between the perceived style of an artwork and the purpose it is meant to serve, a work that might otherwise please can actually disturb or disappoint. Recently a colleague and I listened to a Protestant Puerto Rican composer's arrangement of "A Mighty Fortress," which made use of bouncy, syncopated rhythms and slightly sassy singing. While we could easily enjoy the "beat" and the vocal styling, the stylistic cues themselves signaled a very light purpose for the music that seemed to conflict with the theological cues given by the chorale melody itself, and in turn by Luther's text (translated into Spanish). It was therefore by no means easy for us to *enjoy* this setting *as Christian music*, let alone as a musical setting of a text depicting God's capacity to defeat the greatest imaginable evils. The incongruity between form and purported content seemed too great.

We reminded ourselves that, according to the arranger, making "A Mighty Fortress" sound that way was an attempt to rejuvenate a traditional hymn and to make it more enjoyable, especially for young Puerto Ricans. It was clear to us that, in our much different cultural and ethnic setting, we were in no position to say exactly how this music would come across to its target audience, among whom it was at present selling very well. Yet if we were to take the text and chorale melody as providing legitimate cues to an appropriate musical arrangement, it seemed legitimate to ask whether the musical enjoyment in this case had any distinctly religious component; and, if so (if the religious meaning were one of celebrative conviviality, for instance), whether a great deal of the religious meaning of Luther's text might not have been distorted or lost in this musical translation. In short, for us the aesthetic question became theological: Is the character of God as capable of withstanding the onslaughts of utmost evil being compromised, and possibly trivialized, here? Is the way that the text and its theology is being treated, musically, tending to undermine what the words want to say? Is the kind of enjoyment called for by the medium actually undercutting the message?

The proper fit between style and content is seldom a simple question. Even so, one might say this in response to the light pop, syncopated setting of "A

Mighty Fortress": genuinely good after a fashion, but limited in the range and depth of what one is likely to enjoy. It would not be quite fair to consider such a setting to be the musical equivalent of fast-food communion, since it may very well fulfill its purpose in a manner that truly casual, quick communion would be hard pressed to do. But there is a sense in which no such rendition of "A Mighty Fortress" can adequately substitute for versions rooted more firmly in the tradition of the German chorale.

At the same time, it would be a mistake to think that the religious potential of the traditional chorale is itself unlimited. For one thing, the chorale style does not easily lend itself to self-effacing humor or infectious religious conviviality. Furthermore, one must be cautious about generalizing across cultural and generational boundaries. One can pose the question of appropriate style and fitting enjoyment, but, as already indicated, the setting in which the question is best answered is one to which the style in question is most indigenous. And the answer as to which enjoyments fit with various religious purposes may not come all at once, or from only one source, but over time and in a community involving worshipers, clergy, and artists alike.

Taste as Aesthetic Judgment

As the trajectory of this discussion has already indicated, questions of aesthetic *perception* (or "apperception") and of *enjoyment* (or "appreciation") are intimately related to questions pertinent to the third element of taste, aesthetic *judgment* (or "appraisal"). We commonly exercise taste in *judging* the quality of what we perceive and possibly enjoy, and that act of judging figures in much of our aesthetic (and religious) response to nature, art, and liturgy. The act of judging is rather different, however, in relation to works of nature than in relation to works of art. Whatever one may make of Oscar Wilde's inverting the relationship between art and nature, normally we do not judge a sunset or a storm to be superb, the way we might judge a Turner *painting* of a sunset or a storm to be. But we do choose whether to call a sunset to another person's attention, we decide whether to paint or perhaps photograph it, and we unconsciously decide whether to remember it for its unusually vivid colors. All of these acts involve aesthetic judgment, or appraisal (evaluation).

Whether concerned with nature or with art, judgment is different from enjoyment as such. Most students of twentieth-century art would judge many works by Picasso to be excellent; but for an increasing number of viewers it has become difficult (for reasons deriving mainly from the artist's biography) to enjoy a number of his paintings, particularly those that appear to dissect and exploit female subjects. Yet it is also true that we sometimes enjoy a work of art more highly than we would evaluate it in critical terms. This is typically true of art for which we say we have a soft spot—art we admit is sentimental or melodramatic, such as hymns learned in childhood, certain religious movies, or perhaps book illustrations, such as Gustav Doré's sometimes melodramatic illustrations for Dante and Milton.

Critics are not immune to such "guilty pleasures." For example, it is not uncommon for critics to exhibit a peculiar and inordinate fondness for certain third-rate works by a normally first-rate artist. One can also personally appreciate works that go against critical fashion without necessarily making a confident critical appraisal. Many classical musicians enjoyed compositions by Rachmaninoff at a time when his critical reputation was relatively low due to the regnant modernist canons. They considered this enjoyment more a matter of personal preference than of public judgment. Now that such musicians are again allowed to be eclectic and overtly emotional, many acclaim Rachmaninoff's works as major contributions to music of the twentieth century.

When it comes to religious art, I am prepared to argue that there is room both for sentiment and sentimentality, and thus for easy emotion and a kind of indulgence. That is true for many of the same reasons that Christians should be allowed or perhaps encouraged occasionally to revisit, nostalgically, feelings associated with a quite uncritical phase of love, with naive sympathy, or with a state of unabashed wonder. Sometimes indulging in easy emotion will open up a capacity to feel more deeply, when that is called for. (Adults whose hearts have been strangely warmed by the bedtime stories they have read to children know how this can happen, and how valuable it can be.) But when sentimentality dominates the religious space, it truncates religious development, at least in the aesthetic sphere. To acknowledge that sentimental and otherwise "defective" religious art has its place is not to forget the importance of evaluation but to recognize that various criteria enter into religious aesthetic judgment.

This brings us back to the question of how to judge, how to appraise, the suitability of a kind of enjoyment—especially the enjoyment that a certain style of art brings to a worship setting or even to Christian life in general. What if the enjoyment can fairly be characterized as a kind of entertainment? Again, this is a point at which issues of taste cannot well be avoided. But neither can they be treated in a one-dimensional fashion.

Today, with respect to *judging* the religious merits of certain kinds of enjoyment, the specific issue of entertainment in worship demands special attention. It arises repeatedly in connection with the easy-listening, lounge-style music featured at numerous alternative worship services—services frequently patterned on the well-known Seeker Services at Willow Creek Community Church in South Barrington, Illinois. In the ears of a good many listeners, a typical instrumental prelude to a Willow Creek service is virtually indistinguishable from the light fusion jazz one hears as background on the Weather Channel on American television. Yet that style of worship music is more and more commonly used in the United States (and elsewhere) not only for the seekers but also for finders. In other words, it is becoming mainstream, to the extent that any one worship stream can now be designated as "main." There is no question that many people in church today can enjoy such light, entertaining, undemanding music. The main question is one of judgment: judging whether that kind of enjoyment is one of the legitimate goals or means of worship, and, if so, whether it should be central.

In this context it must be emphasized again that the question of worshipful entertainment is more complicated than it appears. The most common criticism of so-called Contemporary Christian Music is that most of it settles for being entertaining, and that it does so by importing secular styles.[28] Yet anyone familiar with church music knows that secular styles have been imported into sacred contexts over and over again. And some of those styles have been highly entertaining. Much of the music already found in various of the older Christian hymnals makes use of secular tunes that provide relatively light entertainment, even as they "lift the heart toward the Lord." A similar thing can be said of much "art music" used in churches. Mozart masses, for instance, can be almost as entertaining in their florid melodies and animated accompaniment figurations as his operas are. Indeed, except for the *Requiem* and the more contrapuntal sections of the Mass in C Minor, Mozart masses tend to sound quite operatic. Simply to exclude entertainment from worship seems narrow and rigid.

Consequently we have to ask additional questions about the entertainment being provided: What is the tone and focus of the entertaining aspect of worship? Does it eclipse everything else? Or is it one moment within a larger worship context that, perhaps through the sermon, might at a later point confront one with dimensions of the divine and of faith itself that are radically awe-inspiring or that call for a seriously prophetic utterance? Like so many issues in aesthetics and ethics, this becomes partly a question of balance and proportion.

Beyond that, however, there is the question of the *kind* of entertainment provided by a given style of music. Most white musicians who visit African American churches where gospel music predominates notice this: that when gospel music is sung and played in church by people for whom it is a primary mode of spiritual expression, the entertaining side of the music is often charged with an extraordinary energy, concern, and passion that transforms what otherwise might be perceived as a kind of "show." All the vocal and instrumental animation is fused into a medium through which life cries out for God, cries out to God, listens to and for God, and encircles and embraces everyone gathered there. All in all, that is not much like the light musical entertainment that most middle-class white congregations engage in when they try out alternative styles in worship.

Evidently many middle-class white worshipers *feel* they need a church that provides escape and amusement, with only a gentle hint of something more serious and potentially demanding. Theologically, however, one can question that sense of need, especially as it is translated into an all-encompassing taste for easy listening and for "lite" worship. It is true that the lives of middle-class whites are stressed and strained; yet they are also privileged and protected, by world standards. One might argue that there are some stresses that are better relieved through worship in the form of demanding aesthetic exercise and spiritual discipline than in the form of relaxed amusement.

It may be that "lite" worship styles have a place not unlike that of the sentimental art styles I earlier defended in a qualified manner. They can be most valuable as interludes and religious diversions that work to free the spirit, somehow allowing "softer" feelings and less critical thoughts to emerge that tend to be squeezed or blocked out by more formal and demanding modes. But to treat either sentimental moments or light entertainment as normative for worship in comfortable middle-class settings may indicate questionable religious aesthetic judgment.

Of course this characterization of certain alternative worship experiences is itself not beyond question. One cannot simply assume that one knows fully what others must be hearing or seeking in a style that one perceives to be superficial. Nor can one assume that the deeper needs of the more traditional worshipers are in actuality already being addressed in most mainline church settings, especially when so much of the traditional music of such churches is perceived as relatively pale and unimaginative, and therefore received not as enjoyable or moving but as distinctly boring. What is required in forming such complex aesthetic judgments is dialogue and exploration rather than the uncritical application of artistic and liturgical principles—new or old—that are presumed to be fixed and universal.[29]

This is partly to acknowledge that, contrary to what has commonly been believed in the past, the grounds for evaluating art—including Christian art—can be quite varied, and appropriately so. There is no one set of criteria suitable for all works and in every circumstance. Recognizing that allows us to steer a middle course between the indiscriminate acceptance of every aesthetic choice and the rigid application of a particular set of aesthetic rules presumed to be universal. Standards can shift, depending on context, without this meaning that one must abandon standards altogether.

That is a point highly relevant to the arts of the church. For instance, professional artists and musicians in our time rarely encounter new forms of church art that they would consider first-rate in terms familiar to the art world. This fact should not be shrugged off by churches, since church artists may have much to learn from secular standards. But it is also true that, as the Christian philosopher Nicholas Wolterstorff has pointed out, the aims of secular art have for a long time been determined by norms of free self-expression or of daring formal innovation; and these norms are generally inappropriate to worship and to truly communal art.[30] It is hardly surprising, therefore, that avant-garde arts highly prized by secular professionals have had limited appeal to worshiping communities.

At the same time, it must be said that people of the church are ill served by the common notion that knowing what they already like should preclude questions as to its relative value. Perceiving, enjoying, and judging—all three aspects of taste have as much to do with stretching and with learning as they do with inherent disposition. If tastes were not to a large extent learned, it would be extremely odd that virtually all Asian Indians like some kind of Indian music whereas most people elsewhere find such music strange and perplexing on first exposure. And it would be hard to explain how someone to whom Indian musical styles are initially off-putting can eventually come to relish the *rasa* (or "flavor") of different morning or evening ragas. Taste is not just in the genes; it is also in communal conditioning, in learning, in expanding what one likes and also judges worthy of others' attention.

Excellence in Taste

What I have been leading up to is this: In all three of its aspects, taste plays a significant part in forming religious perceptions and identities, in creating and reinforcing religious differences, and in making possible a wide variety of religious and moral discernments and experiences. Matters of religion and morality cannot be reduced to aesthetics; neither can aesthetics be reduced to religion and morality. But these spheres overlap and interact in ways that we have barely begun to appreciate, even if we have never heard directly of Kant's fateful compartmentalization of the good, the true, and the beautiful.

At its highest, taste—as seen especially in the sense of beauty and in the sense of sublimity—enters into the sense of God and the sense of good. And though astute artistic taste and true religious maturity cannot simply be equated (otherwise all good Christians would have good taste), there are genuinely excellent artistic modes of spiritual exercise that are open to professional and amateur alike. That is easily forgotten by those who try to discipline their arts within the academy or in the circles of the more sophisticated. It is all too easy for them (and indeed for anyone) to suppose that excellence is to be found only in the sort of art that their own group happens to prize. Having cultivated a hard-earned taste for what is difficult and demanding, they can mistakenly assume that popular arts in particular are always arts of compromise, accommodation, and mediocrity. Such an attitude is particularly deadly in churches, where tastes generally need to include more than to exclude.

From a religious perspective, it may be salutary for dedicated artists and disciplined lovers of art to realize that common experience is itself filled with God-given excellence. The body constantly functions in miraculous ways, unconsciously, in every moment of its life. Through yoga one can become an expert at breathing, controlling the heart rate, or achieving sexual ecstasy. But the most ordinary breath, the most normal heartbeat, is done remarkably well. And the quite average physical embrace that harbors befuddled love is already wonderful, when seen in the right light. Something similar can be said regarding everyday artistic talents. To be among a group of perfectly average singers giving voice to perfectly average spiritual songs in a moderately reverberant space, to join them in a kind of "ordinary" singing that becomes genuine prayer and genuine praise—this is to experience how excellently graced our common life can be. Many a trained musician can quickly compose a tune that will make for a hymn that can inspire, or is able to improvise in a manner that lifts the spirit. The seeming ease of that should not be an embarrassment, as though ease were always a sign of weakness and disease. From a theological standpoint, we can say that it is a gift that God can make so much of so little. And in the end, that is surely what theology says God does with even the most that humans have to offer.

Nevertheless, certain dimensions of theological and spiritual maturity—of Christian formation—cannot be attained apart from cultivated aesthetic imagination and a mature taste that rejoices in crossing the boundaries of the predictable and of conventional delights. Such taste is open to the difficult, the awe-inspiring, and perhaps to the shocking or the grotesque as well as to the beautiful, pleasing, and amusing. Such a form of Christian taste learns to appreciate, too, the value of "alien" tastes it can never hope to enjoy personally, due to human limitations. To enjoy another's enjoyment is already an act of love.

Aftertaste—and Foretaste

Theologians would like to believe that good Christians have good religious ideas and good moral convictions. Yet neither theologians nor students of art and culture would normally assume that the majority of good Christians have good taste. Properly reconsidered, however, taste can and should be placed among the spiritual gifts and disciplines. For many people, indeed, the religious life requires artistic and aesthetic expression, as an exercise enriching and extending worship, prayer, and ethical practice. In negative terms, we can say that genuine impoverishment of taste can impoverish worship and the spiritual life as well. The person who cannot respond readily to poetry will miss part of the religious meaning of the Psalms; the person insensitive to paradox and irony will not have ears that are tuned to hear many of the nuances of the parables of Jesus. It seems fair to surmise that someone lacking in imagination and artistic sensitivity, like the person who is morally numb and imperceptive, presents a special challenge to the divine. How and what one responds to, aesthetically, can make a religious difference.

Although charity might seem to require that genuinely Christian taste (in which love is essential) manifest itself in an uncritical acceptance of everyone's aesthetic inclinations, such an attitude would actually be inconsistent with a more developed picture of the Christian life. Even ecumenical and inclusive Christian taste must also be in some ways discriminating. In the *Divine Comedy*, Dante's powers of perception as he rises higher through the spheres of reality must be trained and disciplined in ways experienced at first as extremely painful. By the grace of God, his increasingly discriminating yet expansive "taste" is led finally to a vision in which the potential redemption and beauty of the whole creation can be glimpsed. Yet the reader has seen at every stage of Dante's journey toward the beatific vision that in fallen reality not every beauty or pleasure is equal; and some tastes and desires are potentially deadly. Christian taste, though requiring grace at every stage, and though striving to be open to every source of excellence, is necessarily both charitable and critical. Such charitable yet discerning taste appears to be one virtue increasingly needed by churches as they consider various aesthetic forms and styles through which faith can live anew.

Our discussion up to now has introduced reasons for, and obstacles to, pursuing the issue of taste from a religious perspective, and has provided certain analytical tools for sorting out aspects of taste that have theological significance. We must next examine historical and theoretical evidence fundamental to a theology of taste. First we will look more carefully at Christian attitudes toward art. We will then scrutinize modern ideas of art in particular and trace the gradual (but by no means total) displacement of religious love by the love of art itself. Having done that, we can examine how and why the taste for art and the desire for God are related. This we will do by looking carefully at the possible conversion of artistic taste into a mode of loving God—and of loving art "in God," as Augustine will teach us to say. At that point we can return to more practical issues relating aesthetic taste to worship and to the Christian life.

TWO

Art in Christian Traditions

Religious Ambivalence toward Art

It is no secret that not everyone who follows a religious or spiritual path has a keen taste for the arts, or chooses to exercise that taste.[1] In fact, if a religious path happens to be monastic or ascetic, training will invariably entail weaning the aspiring disciple away from certain aesthetic pleasures. Buddhist monks, for example, typically vow to abstain from seeing or engaging in performances of song and dance and instrumental music.[2] But quite apart from the disciplines of monasticism per se, many of which have involved a purified artistry, the pursuit of true religion has often been taken to mean purging away artistic delights—something that has made an impression on popular imagination. One thinks, for example, of the infamous bonfires of cultural and artistic "vanities" built by zealots such as Savonarola and his followers in Renaissance Florence, or of the notorious Puritan banishment of artistic frivolity.

In truth, particular religious traditions almost invariably view some arts and styles as spiritually useful or edifying, and others as corrupting or polluting—just as they frequently treat certain acts, foods, places, or people as ritually clean or unclean, as permitted or forbidden. Islam (aside from Sufism) generally regards music as too profane for corporate worship and normally restricts representational (especially zoomorphic) art. Yet Islam makes use of artful, melismatic calls to prayer; it trains reciters in special styles of chanting the Qur'an, which are governed by the science of *tajwid*—literally "adornment" or "making beautiful"; it encourages the cultivation of exquisite, secluded gardens evocative of Paradise; and in its architecture, Islam often adorns the exterior and interior surfaces of mosques with calligraphy and intricate abstract visual designs of great beauty.[3]

Again, Eastern Orthodox Christianity avoids naturalistic paintings of religious subjects and rejects three-dimensional representations of saints and holy figures; yet it wants icons painted (or "written") correctly and faithfully, it honors a spiritually "lively" presence in images, and it treats images as means of prayer, as "windows on eternity," and even as sacramental objects mediating the grace and presence of God.[4] This same venerable tradition of Christianity omits the use of instruments in worship. But it glories in unaccompanied, monophonic chant and, over the past few centuries, has come to accept and promote harmonized singing by choirs.

Thus religions and their adherents are at once intensively involved in the arts and selective about them, even wary. In that sense religions are almost all ambivalent toward what we today call art. Even Hinduism, in many ways the religion least restrained in its overall use of the arts, has traditions that are severely ascetic; some of its most devoted *sadhus* (holy ones) and philosophers treat everything that is sensory as illusory or ensnaring.

But while we can speak of religious ambivalence toward art, the fact is that religions rarely think about "art" in the abstract—at least not in the sense of "fine art." There are at least three reasons for this. First, religions often have their roots and life in cultures in which the ideas of art, craft, and skill tend to be blended. Here there is no clear concept of art as something fundamentally aesthetic. Nor is there a concept of the "fine arts" (plural) as special skills and artifacts to be valued collectively for their beauty. Such ideas of art are Western and modern. As a matter of fact, in Western antiquity, and on through the Middle Ages, the term for art (*techne* in Greek, or *ars* in Latin) could apply to any activity or product of skillful, knowledgeable, and admirable making— everything from ordinary leather-work and masonry to painting and architecture. The stone cutter and the sculptor were both equally artists. Alternatively, "art" referred to intellectual accomplishment and teachable knowledge, as in the seven "liberal arts." If "art" could cover all this, it is no wonder that followers of Isis, Mithra, or Christ would give little thought to the relation between religion and art as a whole. While Christians had certain attitudes toward the things we today consider art, the question of Christians' being either for or against art as such is our way of posing an issue that simply did not occur to them in those terms.

There is a second reason why art in the abstract has traditionally been of only peripheral religious interest. Religious practice naturally leads one to focus not on art generally, but on the traits and purposes of individual arts such as choral singing, organ playing, fresco painting, or the making of stained glass. Because such varied kinds of artistry serve particular religious functions, their possible shared identity as art is unlikely to be perceived or thought important.

Third, as we have noted, many products of religious art that could otherwise be admired in a museum or enjoyed in a concert hall would not consciously be valued in the same way—purely as art—in churches or temples. Worshipers rarely prize such things only for their inventive or lovely forms, though such aesthetic features matter. Rather, worshipers focus on the fact that, in being beautifully made or properly performed, specific arts can become religiously inspiring, instructive, memorable, or meditative. The worth of such art is typically validated not by the critic but by a specific kind of community and tradition, and possibly by sacred texts.

When it comes to the classic theological writings of the Christian tradition, anyone expecting a full-fledged theology of art is bound to be disappointed. Not only is art as such generally ignored as a topic, but the particular arts (in our sense) are themselves given relatively little notice. In point of fact, beauty receives more attention than any art—and nonsensuous, spiritual, or intellectual beauty more attention (and praise) than anything sensory. Theologically, the chief aesthetic concern has been with elevating the mind and soul. From the start, neither Hellenistic Jewish wisdom nor Greek and Roman philosophy would have encouraged Christians to place much confidence in a spirituality based on the senses and human artifice. Believing God to be invisible and spiritual, theologians tended to assume they had good reason to place the invisible beauty of ideas and mental states above the sensory beauty of art.

Even so, the countervailing doctrine of the Incarnation, along with the whole idea of sacramentality, could and would be used to validate art in various forms. There is evidence, moreover, that the presumed hostility of early Christians to images, instrumental music, and the like has been overstated. In any case, practically speaking, Christians have always needed to find media suitable for particular religious purposes such as instructing the young, sanctifying worship places, making truths memorable, enlivening prayer and praise, and burying the dead. Like almost everyone else practicing a religion, therefore, Christians have employed various arts, and in various styles.[5]

In almost all religions the choice of which art and style to use for a given religious purpose is guided more or less rigorously by traditions, not by personal taste. This does not mean that taste is not involved, but only that taste has a communal dimension. Although Immanuel Kant would have us believe that authentic judgments of taste are strictly individual (albeit of universal validity), evidence suggests that every individual judgment of taste—a judgment regarding what is beautiful or pleasing or fitting from an aesthetic point of view—reflects social influences. Thus the religious music that one favors and judges to be excellent often attracts one's favor or attention because one has learned to savor it under the influence of those who have cultivated the appreciation of such music. To be sure, there are "archetypal" aesthetic patterns and religious symbols that evoke more-or-less immediate response and that have more-or-less universal appeal. But by the time they are made into art or shaped in ritual, they are invariably culturally inflected, and therefore are perceived rather differently by the "insiders" of a given religious group than by "outsiders." At the other opposite pole, there are patterns of making and perception that are highly innovative or personal, possibly being products of individual genius. Yet even these do not emerge from a social vacuum. While the modern artist or connoisseur frequently seeks to form radically independent creations or judgments—sometimes even in the sphere of liturgical art—it is nonetheless always the case that the very sense of what one is doing when creating a particular kind of art, or responding to it, is guided to some extent by conventions and prior expectations. In this sense aesthetic response and taste, while rooted deep in the psyche and soul, is seldom if ever simply self-generated.

Because the taste exercised in making and responding to art is neither private nor isolated, we cannot really understand how artistic taste functions religiously unless we pay attention to traditions. There are traditions of theologizing about the arts, and traditions of actually making and using the arts religiously. In this chapter we will consider both kinds of Christian tradition together: the religiously reflective (theological) and the practical (artistic). We will want to see important ways in which the arts, and ideas about them, shape the Christian tradition as a whole—not forgetting that Christianity, like every major religion, is in some sense both one tradition and many.

If the present study were strictly historical, we would attempt to trace Christian uses and ideas of art mainly along chronological lines. For our purposes, however, it will be more illuminating to examine basic patterns, paying attention to chronological development where that seems especially significant. Accordingly, we will proceed by examining two conflicting attitudes toward art found throughout Christian history and theology. These attitudes are exemplified at their extreme by the contrasting ideas of two representative thinkers, Søren Kierkegaard (1813–1855) and William Blake (1757–1827), whose fuller thoughts on these matters are admittedly more complex than our polarity would suggest. As we will see, various historical traditions of Christian thought and artistry manifest the tensions of that conflict even as they sometimes transcend—or bypass—them. In this chapter we will pay greater attention to the formative stages of these traditions, because of their privileged position in Christian history.

Art—Unchristian? Or Christian?

Kierkegaard's Criticisms

A theologian who wants to ascribe to art some sort of Christian vocation needs, sooner or later, to figure out a way to answer Søren Kierkegaard. With considerable irony, verging on outright sarcasm, Kierkegaard writes in his *Book on Adler* (1846): "They speak in lofty tones of the Apostle Paul's brilliance, profundity, about his beautiful metaphors etc.—sheer esthetics. . . . Only pastoral ignorance can hit upon the idea of praising him esthetically . . . as a stylist and an artist," because Paul "has no affinity, none whatever, with either Plato or Shakespeare."[6] From the provocative standpoint Kierkegaard adopts here, Paul's artistry and imagination are beside the point when it comes to his being an apostle.[7] Whereas the artistic genius is gifted, the apostle is called by divine authority, regardless of gifts or a lack thereof.

In *Practice in Christianity* (1850), Kierkegaard makes a related point.[8] Here he asserts that, quite apart from the question of artistic ability, he cannot imagine himself a painter or sculptor trying to depict Christ. And he pushes the point remarkably hard—in the very year in which a much-acclaimed sculptural group depicting Christ and the twelve apostles was permanently installed in the cathedral in Copenhagen, the Vor Frue Kirke.[9] Kierkegaard declares that, just as it is incomprehensible to him how a murderer can calmly sharpen the knife with which he will commit his crime, so is it incomprehensible to him how an artist can sit "year in and year out occupied in the work of painting Christ—without having it occur to him whether Christ would wish to be painted, would wish to have his portrait, however idealized it became, depicted by his master brush." Kierkegaard continues: "I do not comprehend how the artist would maintain his calm, that he would not notice Christ's displeasure, would not suddenly throw it all out, brushes and paints, far, far away, just as Judas did with the thirty pieces of silver."[10]

It seems to Kierkegaard that this should happen because the artist should surely realize that "Christ has required only imitators"—that is, people who would actually follow him and pattern their lives on his—and that Christ therefore "scarcely desired or desires that anyone after his death should waste his time, perhaps his eternal happiness, in painting him." Kierkegaard exclaims in exasperation, "I do not comprehend it; the brush would have fallen out of my hand the very second I was about to begin; very likely I would never have been the same again."[11]

Kierkegaard goes on to make it plain that what truly appalls him is indifference to true religious commitment. And that kind of indifference is something he sees as entailed in the artistic attitude, which Kierkegaard describes as "a callousness toward the religious impression of the religious."[12]

Given Kierkegaard's own manifest verbal artistry, why would he regard an artistic approach to the religious as necessarily callous? Because the religious as such is supposedly irrelevant to the aims of art, which are aesthetic. Religion calls for a change of life, he believes, whereas art calls for disinterested appreciation, or what later theorists would call aesthetic distance. Kierkegaard illustrates his point by imagining the situation of an artist who has painted a Crucifixion. Kierkegaard finds it entirely plausible that "the picture of the goddess of sensuality found in his studio occupied him just as much [as the Crucifixion scene] so that not until he finished it did he start to portray the crucified one." When the Crucifixion has at last been painted, what people admire illustrates Kierkegaard's thesis that in the making and enjoyment of art "the point of view of the religious is completely dislocated"; for "the beholder looks at the picture in the role of an art expert: whether it is a success, whether it is a masterpiece, whether the play of colors is right, and the shadows, whether blood looks like that, whether the suffering expression is artistically true." What was once the "actual suffering of the Holy One, the artist has somehow turned into money and admiration."[13]

Kierkegaard concludes that when Christianity looks to art for help—regardless of whether it is the art of the sculptor, orator, poet, or painter—both art and Christianity attract a flock of distant admirers rather than people engaged in the genuine imitation of Christ. Such an attitude is fatal to faith. That is why, in Kierkegaard's eyes, the religious artist can be said to exhibit something like the mindset of a murderer, prepared to sacrifice what is most life-giving and holy, as did Judas.

Blake's Affirmations

Faced with such a sharp theological indictment of art—one made most artfully, one might add—religious lovers of art are sure to scurry to find witnesses to testify on art's behalf. Such witnesses, as it happens, are not hard to find. At the opposite extreme from Kierkegaard, in fact, there is the great Romantic poet, artist, and visionary William Blake, who offers the following aphorisms: "A Poet, a Painter, a Musician, and Architect: the Man Or Woman who is not one of these is not a Christian." "Prayer is the Study of Art," Blake says. "Praise is the Practise of Art"; "Fasting and all relate to Art." "The Divine Body manifests itself in Works of Art." "Jesus, his Apostles & Disciples were all Artists."[14]

In his work *Jerusalem*, Blake expounds further on such thoughts. "I know of no other Christianity and no other Gospel than the liberty both of body & mind to exercise the Divine Arts of Imagination. . . . The Apostles knew of no other Gospel."[15] Elsewhere Blake declares that the great artistic accomplishments of the Egyptians and Hindus are no less sacred than those of the Jews. All originally had one language, and one religion, which was the same religion shared and proclaimed by Jesus. And their highest arts all qualify as unsurpassable gifts of the spirit.[16]

Blake, as he indicates in various letters, was consciously defending religious imagination or "spiritual sensation" against the aridity of Enlightenment empiricism, on the one hand, and an unimaginative religious dogmatism on the other.[17] He thought it crucial to recognize that the Bible, no less than Homer, Virgil, and Milton, is directly "addressed to the Imagination which is Spiritual Sensation & but mediately to the Understanding or Reason." For Blake, the Bible in its inspired artistry is "more Entertaining & Instructive than any other book."[18]

It must be admitted, however, that Blake's form of Christianity was most unusual and that what he meant by the Gospel and by spiritual gifts and senses was not just what other Christians have generally meant. It is doubtful that Hindus would entirely approve of his version of their religion, either. Blake was plainly eccentric. And Kierkegaard would have thought Blake crazy indeed to claim that all Christians need to be artists.

Although each represents an extreme, at least in our schematic interpretation, neither Kierkegaard nor Blake stands alone. Each has a host of Christian friends, sympathizing to a considerable extent with the spirit if not the letter of his respective statements on art and its status in true Christianity. What is of interest to us, however, is not merely the affirmative or negative stances of various Christian traditions of thought and practice with respect to art (or particular arts). It is also why such stances were taken, the reasons that may have been given, and the consequences for theology and worship. These matters, which we can only begin to consider here, will have a direct bearing on the issues of taste and Christian faith that will occupy us in later chapters.[19]

Christians for the Constraint of the Arts

Friends of Kierkegaard

In voicing reservations about art as a religious medium, Kierkegaard would obviously have many allies among Christians over the course of history. Christian theologians have insisted time and again that the association of the arts with the senses, with self-indulgence, with worldly entertainment, and with things purely fictitious can render the arts either trivial or dangerous. Christian anxieties about the arts have been known to reach the point of unwitting self-parody. The Puritan divine Richard Baxter (1615–1691) made a point of confessing in his published diary, for instance, that among his youthful failings were crimes of reading "romances, fables, and old tales."[20] That is simply a more extreme manifestation, however, of serious worries that find both ancient and modern expression.

Christian theologians have commonly acknowledged that the various arts, when properly supervised, prove themselves of religious use in several ways. They are useful in religious instruction, in aiding memory, in warming the hearts of the "sluggish" for prayer and praise—as Thomas Aquinas (c. 1225–1274) and Bonaventure (1217–1274) claimed with respect to images in particular[21]—and thus in moving the will to follow what the mind already knows to be true. But, according to a great many theologians, the arts have limited religious value compared with such things as catechesis, preaching, and interior or verbal prayer, and are therefore mainly a concession to the spiritually immature. Augustine, for one, exerted a large influence on later theologians (Protestant as well as Catholic) through an insistence that even the highest human and earthly beauty—exemplified by certain hymns of the church—provides but a dim shadow of invisible, intellectual beauty; art that appeals to the senses thus exists far beneath the beautifully divine truth probed in a superior way by theological reflection.[22]

Visual Art under Scrutiny

Condescension toward the arts is often evident even in theological statements made in their defense, as one sees in the classic justification for visual art provided in the sixth century by Pope Gregory the Great. Writing to Serenus, Bishop of Marseilles, who had destroyed some images in his church, the Pope states:

> We commend you for your zeal against anything made by hand being an object of adoration, but we declare that you should not have destroyed these images. Pictures are used in churches for this reason: that those who are ignorant of letters may at least read what they cannot read in books by looking at the walls. Therefore, my brother, you should have preserved the images and at the same time have prohibited the people from worshiping them.[23]

Accepting this genuine but circumscribed appreciation of the arts, theologians in the Roman Catholic tradition have widely agreed that works of visual art can become books of the illiterate (*libri idiotarum*) and that religious pictures can constitute a Bible for the poor (*biblia pauperum*). While seeing a need for visual arts, such an approach treats religious art as a convenient and sometimes necessary tool of instruction, rather than as a unique means of ongoing spiritual formation and of spiritually elevated piety and prayer—something more evident, to be sure, in the Baroque art of the Counter-Reformation. Defending images this way excuses those who are better educated and spiritually advanced from any need to look.

Now, any objective description of Roman Catholicism would be bound to conclude that one of its most remarkable features is the staggering amount of visual art that has been produced under Catholic patronage. Furthermore, as the art historian David Freedberg has amply demonstrated in his book *The Power of Images*, there is no question that images have exerted an enormous influence in the spiritual lives of the faithful.[24] There is an abundance of popular and informal testimony to that fact, not least in devotional manuals and in miracle legends, which from the thirteenth century on give careful attention to the power of the images of the Mother and Child and of the saints.[25]

It is all the more striking, therefore, that the formal theological justification of visual art has been so slender, relative to other matters of consequence, and that the defense has been framed to such an extent in terms of making concessions.[26] Even in Eastern Catholicism, the gap between developed practice and sparse theological or liturgical commentary is startling. Theological circumspection regarding images may partly be because the powers of art are evidently so difficult to contain or explain in the permissible theological categories. The typical theological approach obligates one, in principle, clearly to differentiate the spiritual object of worship from the material, visible object of veneration, when in practice a fusion or confusion of the two tends to occur, even among the most theologically circumspect. As Freedberg argues, the tension between theological rationale and actual practice may explain why "the theologians are always embarrassed by the phenomenon of cult and miraculous images"; it may also explain why, "despite the strong defences of images [in Eastern, or Byzantine, Christianity], there is so little about images as part of the apparatus of worship in the Byzantine liturgy but so many images, such a huge abundance of them, in every Byzantine church."[27] Whatever the explanation, Catholic theological justification and support of the visual arts has failed to match the intensity and complexity of the manner in which images have exerted their powers (or God's) in Christian lives.

One other example will illustrate the point. Responding to the Protestant Reformers, the Council of Trent (1545–63) recast a clear but essentially timid defense of art that was advanced long before by Thomas Aquinas and others, going back to the Second Council of Nicaea (787). That argument claims that the use of images in worship is justified because the honor or prayerful attitude shown toward the image is transferred to that which it represents (the saintly or divine "prototype"). If true, this defense answers the charge of idolatry. What it does not do is show how the specific artistic qualities of an image—the means by which it works artfully with the mind and soul through the senses and imagination—could be of special value for shaping prayer and contemplation or for mediating a sense of divine presence.

One reason no such argument was forthcoming, or at least not in detail, is that some of the requisite critical tools for the analysis of art itself would not be developed until much later, in the modern era. Another reason, however, is that theologians—even Catholic theologians—were simply inclined to give most of their attention to supposedly higher things. And those other things were regarded as higher because—despite doctrines of Incarnation and Sacrament—it has always been difficult for theologians to reconcile crucial claims regarding divine transcendence and ultimate ineffability with an equally crucial sense of divine immanence and earthly presence. If God is essentially transcendent and invisible, as classical theism has taught, what has this transcendent reality to do with what is material and visible? While theologians have naturally affirmed the ultimate miracle of the Incarnation of God in Christ and the importance of the sacraments as such, they have often served as guardians of God's transcendence. By contrast, worshipers, artists, and various clergy have tended to cherish divine immanence and signs of sacred presence.

It thus seems fair to say that, on the one hand, Roman Catholic theologians have been inclined to view visual art as a secondary *aid* to prayer rather than as a primary *site* or *process* of prayer and divine-human encounter. Eastern Catholicism, on the other hand, goes further in its religious affirmation of images. It describes the making and beholding of icons as prayerful in itself and indeed as sacramental in nature. Even so, as we have noted, the Eastern church is highly selective regarding which kind of image it affirms. Today's artist and theologian can doubtless find inspiration in the assertion of the contemporary Dominican priest Aidan Nichols that, in embracing icons, the Second Council of Nicaea "recognized that art has a virtually sacramental power to bring the intangible within our touching."[28] But the branch of the church that explicitly talks about images (icons) as sacramental does not consider icons to be art, in any of the usual senses, any more than it considers the scriptures to be literature in the usual sense. Nor does it necessarily understand icons to be a sign of what other arts might potentially become—although Nichols himself undertakes that task perceptively. Consequently, in Eastern Christianity, too, we have relatively little analysis of the specifically aesthetic dimension of images and of the kind of prayer or revelation made possible through human artistry as such, even when gifted and blessed.

We have been looking closely at the question of images, because intense controversy has surrounded their use in Christian traditions. In this connection, we would be remiss if we did not now face the fact that Christian attitudes toward visual arts have included not only condescension and circumspection but also condemnation.

A significant number of the Church Fathers, in the era following the birth of Christianity, subjected visual art to outright attack—among them Tertullian (c.160–c.225), who urged would-be Christians among the Carthaginian artisans to change their profession.[29] It is not hard to understand why apologists for the Christian cause would have found visual art in particular to be offensive. For them such art was closely associated with the cult of the Roman emperor and with attempts to coerce Christians into showing devotion to the emperor's image. Images were condemned by Christian defenders as pagan, as a mark of religious ignorance, and as a product and agency of idolatry. Such an outlook doubtless found its ultimate sanction in the prohibition against graven images in the Second of the Ten Commandments. And in view of Christianity's roots in Judaism, many Christians may have been operating almost instinctively out of a long-standing Jewish tradition of suspicion (or extreme restraint) when it came to religious images. Nevertheless, presumably for tactical reasons, Christian criticisms of images drew as much on Greek and Roman philosophy as they did on the Ten Commandments.[30]

In later centuries, debates over various kinds of visual art would become quite heated among Christians themselves. For a time during the fierce iconoclastic controversy of the eighth and ninth centuries, icons were banned by law in the Byzantine empire, despite being upheld by iconophiles as the epitome of piety.[31] During the Protestant Reformation of the sixteenth century, opponents of images (and often of other arts as well) represented true Christianity as promoting a spiritual life unconcerned with what is merely "external" and material. In a passage mirroring the views of the Renaissance humanist Erasmus, Ulrich Zwingli (1484–1531) declared:

> The common people think that God is placated by victims of cattle and by corporeal things. But even since God himself is spirit: mind: not body, it is obvious that like rejoices in like: doubtless he [God] is above all to be worshiped by purity of mind. And today the mass of Christians worship God through certain corporeal ceremonies: whereas the piety of the mind is the most pleasing worship.[32]

Naturally attitudes toward the visual arts have varied within Catholicism itself. Monks have been inclined to be more severe in their visual aesthetics than secular clergy have been. And even among monastic communities there is much difference. As is well known, the Cistercians of the High Middle Ages were associated with a much more austere visual aesthetic than the Cluniacs of the same period. And though monastic architecture has generally been known for restraint in ornamentation, the architecture and decoration of many great abbeys during the Baroque era (in southern Austria, for instance) displayed what has been called a truly "theatrical exuberance."[33]

A corresponding continuum can be found among Protestants in their taste for, and use of, visual art—with the difference that few if any Protestant theologians have ever embraced visual imagery with the enthusiasm of certain Catholics. Compared with other Protestants, Martin Luther (1483–1546) was exceptionally tolerant of images. Lutheran churches in his day made considerable use of altarpieces, for instance. Yet Luther vacillated regarding the use of visual arts, and even at his most positive he imposed restrictions, rejecting Marian images and most portrayals of the saints, and emphasizing the instructional over the devotional function of visual art. Although Luther saw visual religious images as external things that are permitted in Christian freedom, he was inclined, as Gregory the Great had been, to defend them mainly for the sake of children and the spiritually weak.[34]

Taking a more radical stance, Protestants in the Calvinist and Free Church traditions completely excluded paintings and sculptures from church. That was true even when—as in the case of John Calvin himself (1509–1564) and of Calvinists in the Netherlands—they accepted depictions of biblical subjects in civic and domestic settings, where the dangers of idolatry were presumably minimized. Taking at face value the Church Fathers' rhetoric of anti-idolatry, and citing the prohibition of graven images found in the Decalogue, Calvin argued that the Church in its relatively pristine apostolic and patristic periods avoided religious art:

> For about the first five hundred years, during which religion was still flourishing, and a purer doctrine thriving, Christian churches were commonly empty of images. Thus, it was when the purity of the ministry had somewhat degenerated that they were first introduced for the adornment of churches.[35]

In the mid-twentieth century Karl Barth simply mirrored and extended this Calvinist tradition when he declared: "Images and symbols have no place at all in a building designed for Protestant worship."[36] The tradition of constraint with regard to painting and sculpture still continues among such Protestant groups as Presbyterians, Baptists, and Pentecostals, and to a lesser extent among Protestants in general, becoming part of their identity.

Constraining Music

In matters of music, Christian practice has been more consistently affirmative. Music has certainly had powerful theological allies in most Christian traditions, not least of whom were Augustine, Luther, and the Wesleys. In practice, moreover, music has played a well-nigh ubiquitous role in Christian worship. Yet music, too, has been subject to Christian censure and constraint. Zwingli banned all music from his churches in Zurich, on the grounds that God has nowhere in scripture commanded anything but a purely spiritual worship. Zwingli was not unaware of the words from Colossians (traditionally attributed to Paul): "Let the word of Christ dwell in you richly in all wisdom; teaching and admonishing one another in psalms and hymns and spiritual songs, singing with grace [or gratitude] in your hearts to the Lord" (Col. 3:16). Zwingli had a response, and one with a lineage that can be traced back to the patristic era: Paul does not teach us "mumbling and murmuring in the churches, but shows us the true song that is pleasing to God, that we sing the praise and glory of God not with our voices, like the Jewish singers, but with our hearts."[37] Not long before, an equally radical Reformer, Karlstadt (c.1480–1541), had argued that, far from being prayerful, even "the chant which we call Gregorian puts a distance between the mind and God," because the mind must concentrate so intently on singing the music that prayer becomes a purely secondary concern.[38]

If music as self-effacing as unaccompanied chant has invited criticism, it should come as no surprise that elaborate, extroverted, or effusive music has aroused even greater theological objection. In the third and fourth centuries (though less frequently before), Christian writers began to rail against hand-clapping, instruments, and strong rhythm, along with dance. Continuing their earlier practice of singing psalms a cappella in church, Christians began to argue that the ancient use of instruments in Jewish temple worship had always been a divine concession to human weakness, to woo the Jews gradually away from the idolatry of their instrument-playing neighbors.[39]

During roughly the same period, Christian theologians developed symbolic interpretations of scriptural exhortations to praise God with lute, lyre, trumpet, flute, cymbals, and so forth. Greek-speaking Christians from Alexandria started reinterpreting in allegorical terms the references in the Psalms to instrumental music. Thus for Pseudo-Origen, the harp-like cithara mentioned in Psalm 32 (33 in other versions) means the body, and the plucked psaltery a soul; and the psaltery of ten strings is a symbol of the body with its five senses and five powers of the soul.[40] Apparently, in his view, it would be a mistake for Christians to take that sort of scripture literally and use it as a license for playing instruments in the worship of God. Augustine would later share that view.

Classically educated theologians in the Western part of the Roman Empire objected to the use of instrumental music outside the church as well. In part, that was because of the pagan cult of idols, which employed instruments. Even more, it was due to Christian convictions regarding the immorality of the people and practices associated with instrumental music. Like many of their educated pagan counterparts, Christians were aghast at the lewd behavior of theater musicians, the bawdiness of songs sung at marriage banquets, and the dubious profession of many female instrumentalists and singers.[41]

However ancient, such musical concerns by no means evaporated later from Christian tradition. Calvin, for instance, was adamant about singing only unison Psalms in church, and without instrumental accompaniment. Indeed, disputes still arise today over whether instruments are permissible in church and, if so, which are most suitable, and why. Some groups such as the Churches of Christ prohibit instruments altogether; others permit only organ (which was itself banned at one time); still others decry the use of guitars and synthesizers while accepting woodwinds (which for certain groups have been anathema).

In any case, whether instrumental or sung, the music that has received the highest approval of theologians from the first century to the present has not been ecstatic or even animated. It has tended to be simple and restrained. It is music that tempers the passions (as Plato would have wanted), or makes the heart malleable. It is prayerful, like chant—and memorable, such as the songs from Taizé. And in the past, at least, it has often been music that through its mathematical structure pleases the intellect even more than the senses.[42]

To certain modern Christians, of course, the idea that music for worship should be intellectually satisfying may seem odd. Yet such music long received special theological favor because, whereas the senses deal with passing things, the mind supposedly ascends to those eternal realities thought to be dearer and nearer to God. That outlook is evident in the words of a medieval discussion that borrows ideas directly from the Roman Christian philosopher Boethius (c.480–c.524), and indirectly from Pythagoras and the ancient Greeks:

> Music is entirely formed and fashioned after the image of numbers. And so it is number, by means of these fixed and established proportions of notes, that brings about whatever is pleasing to the ear in singing. . . . Notes pass away quickly; numbers, however, though stained by the corporeal touch of pitches and motions, remain.[43]

Such thinking helps explain why, for the many centuries when music was studied as a liberal art (basic for all university degrees, including theology), it was pondered mostly at a theoretical level—namely, in the analysis of harmony and in the study of speculative cosmology (contemplating the harmony of the spheres, for instance). Such *musica* was not so much an art (in our later sense of the word) as it was a close relative of geometry, mathematics, and astronomy, with which it was linked in the *quadrivium*. The actual making of music had no such place or prestige. But when Christian music achieved intellectual sophistication, it could be justified according to such principles. (Whether those or related principles might be applied more widely again in support of an intellectually elevated liturgical music remains to be seen.)

The truth is that, in almost every era of Christian music, and most notably at the Council of Trent (1545–63), musical complexity and flamboyance, while favored by the nobility, among others, has been censured.[44] So it is that complicated, polyphonic singing of sacred texts has repeatedly come under attack because of its tendency to obscure the words with overlapping musical phrases—the assumption being that verbal clarity is essential to religious expression. The modern Lutheran pastor and theologian Dietrich Bonhoeffer (1906–1945) emphasizes clarity and simplicity in a distinctly Protestant commentary on hymn singing that privileges the "Word" above all:

> Because it is bound wholly to the Word, the singing of the congregation, especially of the family congregation, is essentially singing in unison. Here words and music combine in a unique way. . . . The purity of unison singing, unaffected by alien motives of musical techniques, the clarity, unspoiled by the attempt to give musical art an autonomy of its own apart from the words, the simplicity and frugality, the humaneness and warmth of this way of singing is the essence of all congregational singing. . . . It becomes a question of a congregation's power of spiritual discernment whether it adopts unison singing along with discreet organ accompaniments to liturgical action.[45]

The emphasis on musical restraint appears even in Charles Wesley (1707–1788), whose Methodists have often been known for vociferous singing and for warmth in the spiritual life. After urging congregations to beware of singing as if they were half dead or half asleep, Wesley admonishes them in his fifth rule of singing hymns: "Sing modestly. Do not bawl."[46]

As for unconventional or popular "modern" music, Pope Pius X, in the major decree *Motu Proprio* (1903), articulated a view shared by many outside as well as inside Catholic circles when he wrote that such music can be employed when "good and serious and dignified enough to be worthy of liturgical use"; but great care must be taken that "nothing profane be allowed, nothing that is reminiscent of theatrical pieces, nothing based as to its form on the style of secular compositions."[47] The Pope went on to forbid the use of the piano in church, along with "noisy or frivolous instruments such as drums, cymbals, bells and the like." While not to be put squarely in the Pope's camp, the Protestant British musicologist Erik Routley invoked similar principles much later in the century when scolding popular church music for being immodest and calling too much attention to itself in church.[48]

No one would deny, however, that in fact music of an enthusiastic and ecstatic sort, along with music of great complexity and emotional range, has regularly found its way into churches. Churches have in various times and places welcomed everything from Monteverdi's spectacular *Vespers of the Blessed Virgin*, Bach's cantatas, and Mozart's often operatic Mass in C Minor to highly emotional revival songs and popular musicals such as *Godspell* and *Jesus Christ, Superstar*. More recently soft rock (and even heavy metal) has become a more common Christian idiom, employed in many nondenominational community churches and by some evangelicals in weekly worship and in broadcasts on Contemporary Christian radio. Moreover, since the Second Vatican Council (1962–65), Catholic music itself has undergone a veritable revolution that, for better or worse, has vastly broadened the scope of liturgically approved music.

Our examination of the deeply rooted traditions of musical constraint suggests why such departures from standards of order, restraint, and self-effacement have been significant. From the standpoint of much Christian tradition, such music can easily appear provocative and unchristian. Sooner or later controversy usually ensues regarding what, indeed, constitutes Christian music, what its legitimate purposes might be, and what criteria might possibly apply in different traditions. Clearly the very sense of what it means to worship as a Christian can be affected by such developments in style.

Distrusting Dance and Drama

We have been focusing on constraints imposed on visual arts and music; but even more severe controls have of course been imposed on a variety of other arts that never developed so fully in Christian use. These include dance and drama, which we can consider only briefly here. Because of the association of dance with paganism (ancient and modern) and with sensuous, bodily existence, it has aroused the greatest theological suspicion of all the arts and so has generally found itself very much on the margins of Christian life and worship. Where religious dance has played a significant part in Christian life, that has transpired mainly outside the ordinary venues of Christian worship. Although even the Puritans smiled on certain forms of social dance, the art of dancing has thrived as a Christian medium mainly in popular Christian festivals, and most especially in the religious festivals of Mediterranean and non-European countries. Only in the twentieth century has dance become employed relatively widely as a Christian liturgical art, due partly to pioneering efforts by Isadora Duncan, Ruth St Denis, and Ted Shawn, among others.[49] To this day, no other art in worship can so easily cause discomfort and consternation.

Drama likewise had pagan and immoral associations for early Christians, as a consequence of which it met with strong disapproval from Church Fathers such as Tertullian and Augustine. In the words of the former:

Clearly Liber and Venus are the patrons of the theatrical arts. That immodesty of gesture and bodily movement so peculiar and proper to the stage is dedicated to them, the one god dissolute in her sex, the other in his dress. While whatever transpires in voice, melody, instruments and writing is in the domain of Apollo, the Muses, Minerva and Mercury. O Christian, you will detest those things whose authors you cannot but detest![50]

Born in the religious and civic festivals of late archaic and classical Greece, European drama was reborn in and about the medieval church, taking the form of scripture interpretations—acted and sung tropes—and evolving soon into mystery and morality plays.[51] Drama remained a notable part of church services and of outdoor religious festivals until the Reformation—and in Spain long after, where it attracted the talents of Calderón (1600–1681). The liturgy itself took shape as a kind of drama and extended itself dramatically in such ways as the processions of the feast of Corpus Christi.[52] But the Reformation and Counter-Reformation brought about estrangement between church and drama, which persisted to a large extent in the modern era, despite occasional outstanding plays of a Christian or churchly character, such as those by T. S. Eliot, Christopher Fry, and Paul Claudel. After such general neglect, even the brief skits presented now as a regular part of certain casual styles of worship can seem fresh and novel. Constraints have always been abandoned, however, for special festivals, among them the medieval Feast of Fools. Today's Easter pageants with actors, singers, elaborate sets, sound effects, and staged ascensions have ample precedent. Christmas crèches with living animals go back to Francis of Assisi himself (1181–1226).

Our survey of Christian traditions of artistic constraint makes it plain that, when it comes to questioning and circumscribing the arts on religious and theological grounds, Kierkegaard does not stand alone. But, on the opposite and affirmative side, neither does Blake. In fact, as we will see, it is Blake who might find the greater sympathy among a good many practicing Christians, and certainly among many spiritually sensitive people for whom religious ideas without artistic embodiment seem barren or incomplete. Given that our study as a whole is weighted in favor of the encouragers of art, we can here confine our discussion to certain points most pertinent for later consideration.

Christians for the Encouragement of the Arts

Friends of Blake

The Christians who have turned most regularly to the arts and who have treasured them most as part of their religious heritage and life have seldom been the most prominent theologians. Rather, they have tended to be local clergy, laity, and monks, with bishops and "tall steeple" clergy taking the lead in supporting major and more costly projects such as cathedral building. Naturally motives have been mixed. Particularly in artistic enterprises such as building churches, installing pipe organs, and training multiple choirs, the desire for prestige and a favorable public image has rarely been completely absent. But mixed motives are not unique to artistic endeavors. And though Christian traditions have all been selective in the arts they have embraced, many Christian lay people of financial means have donated generously to the available religious arts (sometimes at the expense of the poor, as their theological critics tirelessly point out). Throughout history, moreover, the laity have often been eager and unreserved in donating their own artistry—that is, when clergy have been willing to accept it. (One recalls that for centuries the choirs of Catholic churches were restricted to clergy, and that all these clergy were male.)

Scripture as Mother of Literature

Looking at the history of Christian practice, we find no reason to suppose that the artistic impulse has always been external to, or imposed on, the religious. Quite the contrary. Literary artistry seems entirely integral to the Bible itself, for instance. Despite Kierkegaard's skepticism about the appropriateness of praising Paul for the artistry displayed in his letters, pious and studious readers of scripture from the patristic period to the present have often found the rhetorical art, and artful design, of Paul's Letter to the Romans, or of portions of First and Second Corinthians, to be highly germane to their theological depth and spiritual power. The same can be said of the narrative art of Genesis, the poetry of Psalms or Job, or the metaphoric power of the parables of Jesus. It was with good reason that Augustine insisted that scripture (including Pauline writing) has a kind of eloquence: "A preacher who cannot give pleasure with his words may give pleasure with his texts."[53] It is hardly news, moreover, that when biblical scholars and preachers have attended to the literary artistry (and artful rhetoric) of the Bible, they have usually done so not in order to bypass its religious import but in order to grasp—or be grasped by—that import and to penetrate it more deeply.[54] Hymn writing—one of the relatively few forms of literature to inhabit the church itself—has obviously had scripture as its primary basis, especially the Psalms. Beyond that, however, the frequent wedding of religion and art in Christian and Jewish literature throughout the centuries has a basis and justification in scripture. Not only has the Bible served as what Blake termed the "Great Code" of Western art, it has in some sense given birth to a great deal of Western literature itself.

It is true that the Bible could be used to deprecate other literature, whose mere fictions would compare unfavorably with its supreme reality. It is also true that for Christian interpreters such as Jerome, the language of the Bible was "harsh and barbaric" compared with classical literature—in which case, so much the worse for literary niceties![55] Even so, major Western writers have always employed and played off of biblical themes even as they have written for readers outside the church walls. One hears echoes of the Christ story in the Anglo-Saxon epic *Beowulf*. And the Christian and biblical imprint is unmistakable in later epics such as Dante's *Divine Comedy*, Edmund Spenser's *Faerie Queen* (which, however political, provided a poetic myth of Christian virtues), Milton's *Paradise Lost*, and indeed J. R. R. Tolkien's quasi-Christian prose epic of humble heroism, *Lord of the Rings*. Medieval Romances such as *Sir Gawain and the Green Knight* and the numerous retellings of the grail legend replayed Christian motifs. Allegory (of which John Bunyan's *Pilgrim's Progress* was a late flowering) and figurative language generally have drawn inspiration from patristic and medieval techniques of interpreting scripture at multiple levels. Modern novels, such as Ernest Hemingway's *The Old Man and the Sea* and Graham Greene's *The Power and the Glory*, are filled with "Christ figures." Christian themes and symbols likewise permeate the youth-oriented fiction of writers such as C. S. Lewis (*Chronicles of Narnia*) and Madeleine L'Engle (*A Wrinkle in Time*).

Celebrating Music

In addition to being artistic in themselves, the Christian scriptures point toward other arts, particularly music, as significant for Christian practice. Thus the New Testament shows that, from the very beginning, churches made use of psalms, canticles, and hymns—probably sung unaccompanied and often antiphonally. There is almost nothing in the Bible to support Zwingli's argument that, when the writer of Colossians and Ephesians urged singing with grateful hearts to the Lord, he meant that act to be confined strictly to the heart, and hence silent. Although we have seen that, long before Zwingli's time, some patristic writers had allegorized and spiritualized the notion of singing to God, ignoring or denying the physical act of singing, the New Testament itself refers unambiguously to hymn singing, such as at the Last Supper. In the Book of Revelation, moreover, the images of singing in the heavenly Jerusalem seem to suggest that vocal art can rightly claim a prominent place in Christian worship (although one must be cautious of reading too much into historical practice on the basis of apocalyptic literature). Christians have celebrated the musicianship of the harpist shepherd and king, David, whose psalms (in their traditional attribution) have formed the core of Christian song. It is surely significant, too, that in their early art Christians sometimes depicted Jesus with lyre in hand, as the new form of Orpheus—who in myth had tamed beasts with music before descending to the underworld and then ascending again to life.

A careful reexamination of Christian references to music from the first to the fifth centuries has prompted scholars to set aside the once prevalent notion that the earliest Christians, many of them poorly educated, were the most "puritanical" in matters of music-making, and therefore the most critical of pagan (Greco-Roman) music. In fact, the evidence suggests that Christian polemics against music—especially pagan instrumental music—became far more intense in the writings of classically educated Christians of the third and fourth centuries. Probably that is because these Christians were conscious of pagan philosophical criticism of the same sorts of music. The surviving references to music in the earliest Christian writings suggest an attitude that, by comparison, was relatively accommodating.[56]

Over the centuries, music came in many ways to epitomize Christian art.[57] One reason, no doubt, was that the Bible explicitly calls for the use of music in worship and contains, in the Psalms, a collection of songs. Another was that music, being intangible and invisible, often has seemed the most spiritual art. John Calvin spoke of music in a manner that in certain respects typified Christian views, both in his praise and in his caution. Singling music out from among things that give spiritual joy, he wrote:

> Now among the other things proper to recreate man and give him pleasure, music is either the first or one of the principal, and we must think that it is a gift of God deputed to that purpose. For which reason we must be the more careful not to abuse it. . . . For there is hardly anything in the world with more power to turn or bend, this way and that, the morals of men, as Plato has prudently considered.[58]

Martin Luther's enthusiasm for music could be quite unrestrained. In the music of the human voice, he wrote, the munificence and wisdom of the gracious Creator is abundantly present, though beyond comprehension. Indeed, he said, "Next to the Word of God, music deserves the highest praise." It can comfort the sad, terrify the happy, and encourage the despairing. "The Holy Ghost himself honors her as an instrument for his proper work," using music to move the listener's soul. When music is made artfully, then it is "possible to taste with wonder (yet not to comprehend) God's absolute and perfect wisdom in his wondrous work of music." Luther specifically commended the "divine dance" of polyphonic music, with its many voices, concluding: "But any who remain unaffected are clodhoppers indeed and are fit to hear only the words of dung-poets and the music of pigs."[59]

In more recent times, music has played a particularly vital role in most African American worship. It is not surprising that it is an African American musicologist who, in our own era, has called for a whole discipline of "theomusicology."[60] In thinking of the place of such a discipline in relation to African American religion in particular, Jon Michael Spencer acknowledges that some of what he terms "the sacred music of black religion" is by no means church music; in fact, it has sometimes been produced in protest against elements of hypocrisy and racism in the churches, both white and black. Yet even that music, he argues, has a moral force that reflects and projects Christian values. Much of the life that is given "raw religious reflection" in the blues, for instance, is a "reliving of the parable of the Prodigal Son."[61]

One of the best known Roman Catholic affirmations of music is likewise modern—less colorful than Luther's, and less wide-ranging than Spencer's, but nonetheless far-reaching in effect. The *Constitution on the Sacred Liturgy* (1963), which was a product of the Second Vatican Council, paved the way for extensive musical-liturgical reform with this assertion: "The musical tradition of the universal Church is a treasure of inestimable value, greater even than that of any other art. The main reason for this preeminence is that, as sacred song closely bound to the text, it forms a necessary or integral part of the solemn liturgy."[62] Still more recently, Catholic theologians of music such as Edward Foley have felt encouraged to affirm, in fact, that ritual music—especially in the form of the song of the assembled people—can attain a broadly sacramental function, becoming "an event of the presence of Christ."[63]

Recognizing Visual Arts

Such paeans to music are matched in other arts mainly in the praise of icons, of particular works of church architecture such as Chartres Cathedral, and of certain exceptional artists, such as the "divine" Michelangelo. Compared with the accolades heaped on music, Christian affirmations of visual art in particular have tended, as we have seen, to be more defensive or condescending. Yet the *Constitution on the Sacred Liturgy* resoundingly affirms the role of the visual arts, and of other fine arts as well, as "among the noblest activities of man's genius," especially when "directed toward expressing in some way the infinite beauty of God in works made by human hands."[64] The Dominican Fra Angelico (c.1400–1455) was beatified in our time largely in recognition of his frescoes of New Testament subjects for the Dominican convent of San Marco. There has also been a recent move to beatify the modern Spanish architect Antonio Gaudi. And beyond that, especially in Catholic traditions, visual arts have played a pervasive role in giving shape to faith and have not lacked for ecclesiastical supporters, including Michelangelo's irascible Pope Julius II.[65]

The importance of visual art and architecture in the formation of early Christianity has been recognized less clearly than that of music, with some of the evidence having come to light only recently. We have no concrete proof of any distinctively Christian visual art or architecture before the year 200. It has long been known that Christians of the first few centuries commonly met in private homes and that there they made little or no attempt to design special rooms for liturgy or to provide any Christian images for the interior spaces.

Yet modern archaeology indicates that visual art played a part in Christian worship surprisingly early on—surprising because the earliest Christians were Jews necessarily aware of biblical injunctions against images, or else they were converted pagans who would be eager to distance themselves from Roman idolatry. Modern scholars have concluded, partly on the basis of artwork found in a synagogue and a church excavated at a third-century site at Dura-Europos (in modern Syria), that age-old stereotypes of supposedly image-hating Jews and Christians are false. It now appears that in late antiquity, neither Jews nor Christians consistently interpreted the second commandment of the Decalogue as prohibiting images of all kinds or as entirely ruling out the use of imagery in spaces dedicated to worship.[66]

The Christian openness to images is undeniable at Dura. The church there is a relatively large house that has plainly been renovated for liturgical purposes. One of its six rooms was enlarged to make an assembly hall where at the focal East end stood a small platform for either a bishop's seat or a reader's stand. Another room was converted into a baptismal chamber in two levels. Housing a font and canopy, the baptistry was decorated with narrative frescoes on pertinent New Testament themes, including Peter walking on the water, the woman at the well (from John 4), and the healing of the lame (from John 5). The doorposts to both of these rooms bear symbols such as eyes, angels, and stars, which clearly designate them as sacred spaces.[67]

It is hard to know to what extent such a church at a fairly remote outpost of the Roman world is representative. But in relation to the whole question of early Christian attitudes toward visual art, it fits with something that scholars have lately noticed about early Christian rhetoric concerning visual art. As we have seen with Christian rhetoric concerning music, Christian polemics against visual art were rare and often mild in the beginning. They seem to escalate in the third and fourth centuries, at a time when educated Christians became aware of the criticisms of images on the part of pagan philosophers, and when certain Christians were without doubt actually producing or using art (in the burial chambers of the catacombs, for instance). Being defensive in character, these Christian attacks on art should not necessarily be taken at face value. They may not be entirely representative voices of their own time. Nor do they necessarily represent Christianity before that time. At least one prominent interpreter of early Christian art has concluded that the main reason we have so little early Christian art, and none before the third century, is not that Christians started out strongly opposing art or seeking pure, immaterial spirituality. The primary reason is more likely to have been that they lacked land and capital. In the beginning, Christians seldom came from classes that made use of art. Lacking wealth or a desire to create a sharply distinct cultural identity, they produced no distinctively material culture of their own.[68]

All that was soon to change. In the fourth century, following the Edict of the pro-Christian Constantine in 313, Christian art and architecture had begun to pervade the Roman world. In this connection art history helps bring to light what church historians themselves have generally left in the shadows—namely, that art was instrumental in bringing about the revolution wherein Christianity became a new spiritual force in the world, as well as a very public and popular movement with vast political influence and increasing social prestige.[69]

Architecture, for instance, became an especially important means by which Christians reinterpreted their identity in relation to the pagan world of classical antiquity. For their places of worship Christians widely adopted (and adapted) not the pagan temple but the Roman basilica. This rectangular civic building, when turned ninety degrees on its axis, would not only accommodate many worshipers in its nave but would orient them toward a focal point at the East end—the direction of sunrise and prayer, and the locus of the eucharistic altar table. Here Christians typically built an apse by inserting a triumphal arch at the termination of the interior hall and erecting immediately beyond it a semicircular structure that was roofed by a half dome. The latter they usually decorated with luminescent mosaics depicting Christ either enthroned or ascending into heaven. When transepts were added at right angles to the main hall, the cruciform shape further Christianized the whole design.

Whether such artistic Christian adaptations of classical culture were a sign of spiritual health remains debatable. The rise in monasticism that occurred during this period and afterward shows that many Christians became concerned about the compromises that accompanied Christianity's new worldliness, its political hegemony, and its popularity. Such compromises were reflected and projected in much art and architecture from that time onward. The greatest monuments of the new Christian era were all products of the temporal triumph of Christianity and not simply the triumph of spiritual vision and vigor. These include the first Saint Peter's Basilica in Rome, with its impressive size; the splendid art programs found in the churches of Ravenna, with their stunning mosaics;[70] and Justinian's magnificent multidomed Church of Hagia Sophia in Constantinople, with its multiple physical and symbolic levels (Figure 2). Upon viewing Hagia Sophia at its completion in 537, the Emperor Justinian was supposedly moved to exclaim: "Glory to God who has thought me worthy to finish this work. Solomon I have outdone you."[71] The glory Justinian here claims to be giving God is all too clearly linked with the glory he claims for himself in rivaling King Solomon the temple builder. The greater God's glory, the greater Justinian's.

Figure 2. *Hagia Sophia, Constantinople (Istanbul)—the Church of Holy Wisdom, long one of the greatest churches in the world, and later a great mosque. The Emperor Justinian, who built the church between 532 and 537, boasted that he had outdone Solomon. By contrast the historian Procopius, writing some twenty years after the dedication, declared that "whenever one enters the church to pray, one understands immediately that it has been fashioned not by any human power or skill but by the influence of God. And so the mind is lifted up to God and exalted, feeling that He cannot be far away but must love to dwell in this place which He has chosen." (Courtesy of Dumbarton Oaks)*

Art history also shows, however, that it would be wrong simply to assume that when Christians have invested power, energy, and money in art and architecture, this has always entailed religious and cultural compromise of the sort now often labeled and criticized as "Constantinian." One indication of certain distinctively Christian and often countercultural values in art is that, from the third to the sixth centuries, Christians developed a multifaceted visual christology whereby they interpreted Christ not only as Ruler of the universe (and hence as the one true Emperor) but also as an alternative to any earthly emperor. In early Christian art, Christ is sometimes seen as an anti-emperor who triumphs in humility, entering Jerusalem on a donkey; or as a worker of magic and miracles; as the Good Shepherd; as the new Orpheus who restores life; as the new Asclepius with boundless powers of healing; as the infinitely wise philosopher conversing with his inquiring disciples; as androgyne in whom opposite sexes are reconciled and united; or as the unique human whose halo and golden garments identify him as·nothing less than also truly God— possibly in refutation of Arianism. In all these instances, the art makes visible some significant feature of Christ that will at once dissociate him from merely pagan and worldly expectations while associating him with powers, functions, and realities that a pagan world could learn to recognize and worship. In this way the art functions to shape and vivify early Christian christology at its core.[72]

As we have already emphasized, moreover, the Eastern Church has affirmed a "glorified" visual art that is at once elevated in function and yet relatively humble in appearance. This is the art of icons, produced prayerfully, and under spiritual guidance. Rather than expressing the artist's personal vision, such art is confined to a rather strict set of conventions of representation that nevertheless give the image a sort of *dynamis*, or supernatural power, and allow it to serve as a virtually sacramental medium, opening a window on eternity and conveying a higher reality. Without reducing spirit to flesh and materiality, the icon reaches the human spirit and lifts it to the divine, through what is material. In the words of John of Damascus (c. 655–c.750):

It is clear that flesh is material. Therefore I adore, worship, and venerate the material by which my salvation was gained. I worship it not as God but as full of divine grace and efficacity. Is not the wood of the Cross most blessed and most happy? Is the sacred and venerable mount, the place of Calvary, not material? Is not the life-giving stone . . . ? Are not the ink and paper of the Gospels material? Are not the body and blood of our Lord material? Either remove all worship and adoration of these things, or allow, according to the tradition of the Church, the veneration of images dedicated to the name of God and his friends the saints, because they are in the shadow of the Holy Spirit.[73]

Some of the Eastern writers, such as the patriarch of Constantinople Nicephoros (758–828), argued that visible images are actually superior to words. His claim (however debatable) was that the words of sermons or holy texts require further thought (beyond perception) in order for them to make sense, whereas images of holy things, once their visible form is taken in, permit a virtually direct apprehension of holy reality. Images therefore can provide a convincing proof of faith.[74] Such a position stands at the opposite extreme, obviously, from that of the iconoclasts. It is in accord, however, with the belief that an icon such as St. Luke's Madonna in Venice is a faithful record, being such an "authentic" portrait that it could not be a product of merely human skill. In point of fact, the origins of such icons were long obscured by legend, so that they hardly seemed made by humans at all.[75]

The Diversity of Artistic Gifts

On the side of affirming the role of the arts in Christian traditions, it is important to point out that, over the centuries, arts of various kinds have not only illustrated both major and minor Christian tenets but have given them imaginative life, nurturing and challenging faith in a fashion unavailable to doctrine alone, and sometimes in tension with official dogma. Although we need not survey them all here, we should observe that these arts have not merely ornamented Christian doctrine; they have, as it were, given it flesh and blood.

Such diverse works of artistry as the sculptures of Chartres Cathedral, the epics of Dante and of John Milton, and the spiritual songs of African Americans have all in their own way reinterpreted the meaning of what theologians have sometimes called "salvation history." They have illuminated the despair and hope of human experience while enlivening a sense of God's involvement in shaping and transforming existence in time. The intellectually complex metaphysical poems of George Herbert's *The Temple* and the erotically tinged, fervent lyrics of the Spanish mystic St. John of the Cross probe the mysteries of sin, grace, and salvation. Rembrandt's peculiarly and powerfully Protestant art gives at times a palpable expression to the need for reliance on grace alone. At the level of devotional art, countless crucifixes and painted altarpieces and illustrated scriptures, whether or not conforming to the criteria of fine art, serve as objects before which, and because of which, prayer has continually been offered up. Within a monastic setting, Hildegard of Bingen's medieval poems and music together constitute prayer of exceptional intensity and beauty. In the sphere of secular culture, too, art animates religious perceptions and ideas. Mozart's treatment of the theme of human forgiveness in *The Marriage of Figaro* and other operas, for example, bestows on the act of forgiveness an ineffable graciousness that hints at divine grace as well. In our own day, films such as

The Mission and *Dead Man Walking* sharpen and deepen issues of conscience in relation to morally ambiguous and religiously divisive topics such as defensive violence and capital punishment, and of meaningful or meaningless suffering.

Artistic Genres and Christian Identities

Different kinds and uses of art have undeniably helped to define different religious groups within Christianity. Eastern Orthodox worship has of course been associated to a considerable degree with centrally planned, domed churches (whose interiors are free of pews or chairs) and with seemingly timeless rituals employing ancient arts. Preeminent among the latter are the icons, which in being venerated are kissed, are honored with lighted candles, are sometimes sung to, and are prominently displayed in processions and on the iconostasis separating the sanctuary from the nave of the church. The very sound of Orthodoxy is distinctive as well, as the singing is entirely unaccompanied.

Roman Catholicism can be distinguished aesthetically in small ways and large. Unlike the Orthodox, who use a cross with a flat likeness upon it, Roman Catholics have made prominent use of the crucifix—a cross bearing a three-dimensional "corpus" of Christ. Instead of producing icons as such, Roman Catholicism has found artistic expression in sculptures and in paintings that, depicting a wide array of subjects, often become overtly expressive. From the Renaissance and on through the Baroque in particular, Roman Catholic paintings have often taken on intensely dramatic qualities, not least through the use of dramatic lighting and contrasting darkness. Religious figures portrayed in such art become full-blown sacred "characters" whose psychological and spiritual states inspire devotion and identification. Roman Catholicism has often been visibly identified, too, with the distinctive forms of Romanesque and Gothic architecture and with later variations on the basilica style. At the audible level, Catholicism is distinguished from Orthodoxy by the use of instruments (now frequently vernacular, such as guitars). Moreover, Roman Catholics, unlike the Orthodox, have usually been free to employ musical counterpoint, polyphony, and harmony. Liturgically, both Roman and Eastern Orthodox Catholics differ from many Protestants in making much use of ceremony, formal gestures, processionals, vestments, and incense.

Protestantism typically sets itself apart from Catholic Christianity by visibly paring away and simplifying the objects within sight of worshipers. Few Protestant churches feature religious paintings, though many have stained glass. Only Lutherans consistently make use of the crucifix. Some Protestants avoid displaying even a cross. Instead of emphasizing the visual, Protestant worship and piety "foregrounds" the audible and verbal, cultivating the arts of preaching, Bible reading, and congregational singing, which in turn create a distinct sense of the centrality of the gathered people. Outside of worship settings, Protestant "material culture" since the nineteenth century bears a greater resemblance to Catholic practice in the use of images and devotional objects than the classic theological battles over the subject would ever lead one to expect. At the popular level—as seen in illustrated Sunday school literature, for example, and in the popularity of the biblical pictures hung in homes—evangelical Protestant piety in particular has by no means been only a piety of the word.[76] Yet, even within the home, the kinds of images employed by Catholics and Protestants are different, with Protestants keeping their distance from Marian images, rosaries, pictures honoring the Sacred Heart of Jesus, and the like.

Moreover, the aesthetic differences between different kinds of Christian piety have to do with more than the visual and auditory. Protestant worship services tend to be less formal and ceremonial. They typically differ from Catholic and Orthodox services even in their olfactory impression, since most Protestants have banished incense. And Protestants are less interested, in general, in marking the church space as sacred. Especially in "free church" traditions, their buildings are not so much houses of God as assembly houses and places for preaching. The modern use of neutral "worship centers" and auditoriums, absent even a steeple, fits with that tradition of de-sacralized space.

It should also be noted that, within both Catholic and Protestant traditions, there are strong regional and ethnic variations in artistic style that establish a strong sense of identity among particular groups. In African American worship, for instance, many churches encourage highly active congregational participation, with patterns of call and response, clapping and uplifted hands, spontaneous cries of "Amen!," and bodies in motion. To an extent that until recently has been unusual within Christian practice—especially outside Pentecostal and charismatic circles—such worship has often had an ecstatic quality. Ecstasy has been manifest both in the older ring-shouts and spirituals, and in modern gospel singing—the latter often accompanied by Hammond organ or piano, and by a band with percussion. Rather than fearing aesthetic freedom and the sense of release, African American worship has tended to foster those things as ways in which the Holy Spirit can move at will.[77]

Such differences in the aesthetics of worship not only help create bonds within communities, they also help create and reinforce differences that separate communities. As Hans Belting observes, for example, the schism between Eastern and Western churches that occurred in the eleventh century was not only doctrinal and political in motivation but also liturgical and (in our sense) "artistic." Thus there were great differences over the exact use of images—the manner of representing the crucified Christ, for instance. Later, in the fifteenth century, when Greek Christians came to a church council in Ferrara-Florence, they complained that they found themselves unable to pray before Western sacred images. Among the Greek visitors, Patriarch Gregory Melissenos argued against a proposal for church union by stating: "When I enter a Latin Church, I can pray to none of the saints depicted there because I recognize none of them. Although I do recognize Christ, I cannot even pray to him because I do not recognize the manner in which he is being depicted."[78] Perhaps needless to say, analogous differences over artistic styles and patterns of worship generate similar responses of mutual alienation among many worshipers today.

Certain styles and genres, such as hymnody, have been closely identified with Christianity and with church in general. But that identity has typically shifted over time. And certain kinds of artistic expression, when rejected for corporate worship by a major Christian group, are accepted in less sacred settings. In fact, when a dominant Christian tradition has minimized the arts, or a particular kind of art, within formal worship spaces, that has tended to encourage religious expression in the more secular sphere.

In European societies, the shifting venues of oratorio and cantata performance, for example, show how the very constraints imposed by churches encouraged religious art to develop in the world outside, making for a kind of secular religiosity. Oratorio began in a Catholic place of prayer (the Oratory of Philip Neri in late sixteenth-century Rome), and much later became a large-scale medium favored by Protestants in particular for special church occasions. Yet it was banished from Protestant churches in eighteenth-century England due to the puritanical opposition to religious theatrical works. Thus the oratorios of Handel (1685–1759), including *Messiah*, were rarely presented in the churches of his time, but rather on concert and theater stages. Oratorio was welcomed back in church during the era of Mendelssohn, exploring new heights in Liszt's unduly neglected masterpiece *Christus* (1866); and oratorio is heard in churches to this day. But it has prospered primarily on secular stages and in concert halls.

Cantatas and Passions were once the height of sacred church music. Church cantatas of Bach's time were part of an extended Service of the Word, being based primarily on the scriptures designated by the lectionary for a given Sunday. And Passions (going back to the Middle Ages) were designed for Holy Week, setting gospel texts concerning the suffering and death of Christ. But, following the peak of their artistic development, these forms waned as church art. Passion settings gave way to concert oratorios or were reduced to briefer works for Maundy Thursday or Good Friday, while cantatas were replaced in ordinary worship by shorter or less demanding forms that would no longer vie with sermons for the attention of the congregation. Today, while cantatas and even Passions make modest seasonal appearances in church, they live chiefly in concert or through recordings listened to at home, sanctifying the secular sphere.

Finally, while art has often had a religious, and indeed Christian, identity, the religious identity and purpose of art has differed with the character and context of the artwork, or with the particular Christian tradition to which it relates. Some art serves as prayer or praise; other art serves an overtly didactic purpose, informing the viewer about sacred history or church doctrine. Some art serves primarily to beautify the place and moment of worship; other art motivates religious or ethical action in the world. Some art endeavors to glorify God mainly by enhancing human life itself and by creating this-worldly beauty; other art, searching for God or for the depths of experience, agonizes and questions, sometimes undercutting in radical Protestant fashion every sense of its own worthiness. There is sacred art, which is made explicitly for church use; there is broadly religious art, which may be presented in a gallery or in the theater or on a concert stage; there is art that, by its very style or medium, establishes a special identity for a religious group; and there is art that, despite its ostensibly secular character, has religious or theological significance because of the depth of its human expression or because of the sense of transcendence that its beauty generates.

Arts and Theologies of Less and More

Two "Ways" of Sacred Art

Repeatedly throughout Christian history, theologians and church leaders have attempted to set forth more-or-less universal guidelines for sacred art, and even for religious art outside the church. As mentioned earlier, favorite *desiderata* for such art include: simplicity, dignity, order, restraint, beauty, harmony, sincerity, truthfulness. Nevertheless, much sacred art has been created with other aims in mind, especially when commissioned for special religious occasions. Particularly outside the more formal European traditions, and in various Christian communities around the world, Christian arts have shown considerable exuberance and playfulness, and a willingness to entertain in God's honor. In addition, donors, patrons, and artists themselves have frequently aimed at an art of splendor, glory, magnitude, and awe-inspiring complexity. The traditional theological predilection for artistic restraint is answered by artistic predilections for creative freedom and by lay predilections for emotional satisfaction.

In point of fact, sacred art tends everywhere to bifurcate into an art of "more" and an art of "less." Aesthetic abundance can have religious reasons often missed by theologians worried over worldly display. Likewise, aesthetic austerity can serve religious purposes that are misunderstood when viewed as merely bending to theological constraints. In pursuing religious goals creatively, a given art can use either abundance or poverty of means. One sees this clearly in the contrast between the aesthetically pleasing severity of Cistercian monastery churches of medieval France, and the grander, more elaborate architecture of Benedictine pilgrimage churches.

One contemporary instance of religious minimalism is the nonsectarian Rothko Chapel in Houston, with its low ceiling and abstract, meditative paintings whose color fields of muted tones quiet the mind ineffably while eluding any specific religious content. Such a space contrasts sharply with Antonio Gaudi's ornately extravagant (and unfinished) Church of the Holy Family (*Sagrada Familia*) in Barcelona, which is all restless exteriority and height. Again, there is the spiritually significant contrast between an "auditory church" in England designed in the seventeenth century by Christopher Wren, especially suitable for preaching, and a Rococo church built in Bavaria a half-century later. The former structure, enhancing lucid thought and discourse, features geometrical clarity, minimal reverberation, and unobstructed sight lines. The latter space locates the worshipper beneath a tall, dizzying dome with deceptive, *trompe-l'oeil* paintings. The worshiper is surrounded by curvilinear, lavishly decorated interior surfaces that overwhelm the eye and, by generating multiple echoes, possibly confuse the ear. Prayers here can surge and merge.

To reiterate, the way of "less" and the way of "more" can be equally artistic, and equally spiritual. Contrary to what theological statements often lead one to expect, the opposition between aesthetic spareness and abundance, or between emptiness and plenitude, does not always translate, religiously, into an opposition between pure spirituality and decadent worldliness. Most Christian listeners hear the sonic exuberance of the "Sanctus" from Bach's Baroque Mass in B Minor as anything but "worldly." Indeed, this music conveys a sense of holy convergence between heaven and earth, with everything filled with divine glory. Conversely, the often plaintive or rough-hewn quality of the Appalachian tunes published in *Southern Harmony* in 1835 creates an impression that their gospel message, far from being ethereal in its spirituality, is rooted firmly in the somewhat rocky soil of daily experience. It would thus seem that the art of privation and the art of superfluity both have religious legitimacy that is not fundamentally dependent on theological disapproval or approval.

Two Ways Defended; One Way Attacked

It is with regard to these two contrasting ways of art—"less" and "more"—that two of the most famous theological evaluations of visual art were formulated. Although the first theological statement more properly belongs to our discussion of Christian efforts to constrain art by attacking artistic "excesses," it can best be appreciated when paired here with its opposite. Both are medieval.

In a famous rebuke directed partly at the Benedictine monastery of Cluny and its dependencies, Bernard of Clairvaux in the year 1125 set a very high spiritual value on artistic austerity, and a low value on artistic extravagance. Using a rhetorical feint, he attacked the Cluny-style house of worship: "I say naught of the vast height of your churches, their immoderate length, their superfluous breadth, the costly polishings, the curious carvings and paintings which attract the worshipper's gaze and hinder his attention."[79] So he wrote, while acknowledging that where the church serves more worldly people its art may need to make a stronger appeal to the senses. Addressing the monastic setting, Bernard continued:

> But in the cloister, under the eyes of the Brethren who read there, what profit is there in those ridiculous monsters, in that marvellous and deformed comeliness, that comely deformity? To what purpose are those unclean apes, those fierce lions, those monstrous centaurs, those half-men, those striped tigers, those fighting knights, those hunters winding their horns? . . . So many and so marvellous are the varieties of divers shapes on every hand, that we are more tempted to read in the marble than in our books, and to spend the whole day in wondering at these things rather than in meditating [on] the law of God. For God's sake, if men are not ashamed of these follies, why at least do they not shrink from the expense?[80]

Bernard articulated some of the same concerns about art that we found in Kierkegaard. These arguments, furthermore, have no easy answers. But answers have been proposed, the best known of which is that of Bernard's contemporary Abbot Suger of St. Denis (c.1081–1151). Whereas Blake, in a later time, was most interested in defending artistic imagination, Suger defended the spiritual merits of aesthetic brilliance and splendor—a mark of the Gothic style inaugurated by renovations to Suger's abbey church, closely associated with the kings of France. Although Suger was not an author of theological treatises as such, his rationale for employing lavish beauty and artistry in the service of God was indeed theological. Just as Eastern iconophiles had defended their comparatively severe icons on the grounds that one's vision moves through and beyond the physical image to higher spiritual realities, so Suger in a Neo-Platonic vein argued that the luminous qualities of his church and its furnishings could, by appealing first to the senses, all the more effectively enlighten the mind and soul. Contemplating the bejeweled cross and golden altarpiece of the church, Suger wrote:

> Thus, when—out of my delight in the beauty of the house of God—the loveliness of the many-colored gems has called me away from external cares, and worthy meditation has induced me to reflect, transferring that which is material to that which is immaterial, on the diversity of the sacred virtues: then it

seems to me that I see myself dwelling, as it were, in some strange region of the universe which neither exists entirely in the slime of the earth nor entirely in the purity of Heaven; and that, by the grace of God, I can be transported from this inferior to that higher world in an anagogical manner.[81]

Suger affirms here the exceptional spiritual value of the lovely and precious objects that adorn his church, because they give sensory delight and because one does not get mired in the material level of enjoyment. The senses delighted in this way are transfigured by beauty, which transports the mind to a higher world. The religious value of the artistry is not dependent, therefore, on its having a particular—or any—religious subject. What counts is the beauty of the object and the "worthy meditation" that sees more in beauty than mere sensory stimulation. There is something about beauty, when it is appreciated rightly, that already begins to have a kind of sanctity and that points to a higher level of reality, beautiful in itself.

Suger among Theological Friends

In search of claims comparable to those advanced by Suger, one could certainly go back to the sixth century and the writings of Dionysius the Pseudo-Areopagite (c. 500). (His work was preserved and translated at the Abbey of St. Denis.) But one could also leap ahead to the modern Protestant theologian Paul Tillich. Describing his encounter with Botticelli's painting *Madonna and Child with Singing Angels*, Tillich declares:

Gazing up at it, I felt a state approaching ecstasy. In the beauty of the painting there was Beauty itself. It shone through the colors of the paint as the light of day shines through the stained-glass windows of a medieval church. As I stood there, bathed in the beauty its painter had envisioned so long ago, something of the divine source of all things came through to me. I turned away shaken.[82]

Insofar as art is beautiful, it has invited theological justification in such terms as these. In one's very perception of beauty, it delights and elevates the senses, and the mind. As an end in itself, beauty tends also to point by analogy to the divine, the first and final source of all beauty, and of truth and goodness and integrity, too. We find something like this argument in scholastic theology and likewise in neo-Thomists of the modern era, when they treat beauty as a "transcendental," present to some degree—along with goodness, truth, and oneness—in everything that exists, and united with these other transcendentals in the being of God, and serving with them as divine names.[83] Tillich and Suger put this more mystically, as a matter of experience rather than deduction.

That way of understanding art's religious efficacy has a perceptible affinity with another kind of theological defense of art. Christians most affirmative of the arts have frequently sought to legitimize the tangible and sensory realm of artistry by appealing to sacramental and incarnational theology.[84] If God could become flesh, they say, surely what is physical and sensory is not necessarily to be scorned. The sacramental elements—the water of baptism, and the bread and wine of communion—indicate as much. Perhaps art should not be thought of as a sacrament per se; but, according to this line of thought, it is sacramental.[85] Thus, borrowing Augustinian and Calvinist language regarding sacraments, theologians can say that art at times provides "an outward and visible sign of an inward and spiritual grace." As such, art meets our humanity through its sensuous, embodied forms of meaning. As John of Damascus wrote, defending icons against iconoclastic attackers: "Perhaps you [iconoclasts] are sublime and able to transcend what is material . . . but I, since I am a human being and bear a body, want to deal with holy things and behold them in a bodily manner."[86]

In the end, beauty—whether splendidly "more" or austerely "less," whether analogical or sacramental—has provided the most popular way for theologians to connect art and religion. Yet some theologians considering the arts insist on distinguishing not merely between degrees or genres of beauty but also between qualities within a specific kind of beauty. Karl Barth speaks of the beauty of Mozart's music as virtually unique in having the special capacity to take the utmost suffering and darkness into account and yet, through a sort of reversal, to transcend it gracefully, as light does darkness. On this basis, Barth testifies that he hears in Mozart's music parables of the kingdom of God.[87] Like Suger and Tillich, Barth recurs to the image of light when describing this beauty. Yet (in good Calvinist fashion) he emphasizes that the beauty of Mozart's music produces a light that is not wildly ecstatic but appropriately temperate: "The sun shines but does not blind."[88]

We have come a long way from the theological impulse to condescend toward art or to constrain it with the burdens of education or dour sobriety. We must remember, however, that, even in modern theologians like von Balthasar, the theological praise of beauty as such is rarely meant to apply fully to art. And even if beauty already has a kind of sanctity, at least by analogy with the good and the holy, it is nevertheless theologically unclear what makes some beauty spiritually luminous, and other beauty more carnal and worldly—whether it be a beauty of "less" or of "more." Finally, we should note that when theology comes to grips with modern arts in particular, it must ponder the possible religious value of art that disrupts and distorts, and in ways that are far from beautiful.

Toward an Integral Theology of Art—and of Taste

We end this stage of our inquiry with a measure of clarity accompanied by a degree of perplexity. One way or another, Christianity developed into one of the world's greatest patrons of the arts. We have seen, however, that if Christian art had relied strictly on formal theological endorsement, guidance, and interpretation, Christian traditions of artistry would have been far more circumscribed and modest than they have often turned out to be. The situation in monasteries, where many of the monks have been artists of some sort, is something of a special case; yet even there the specifically theological rationale for religious art—for chant, artful building, manuscript illumination, and so forth—has been less developed than the artistry itself.[89] And there, too, theology has imposed a high degree of constraint on the arts.

It would be wrong to conclude from this that theologians have all been, at heart, more akin to Kierkegaard than to Blake. For one thing, theologians have often been simply neutral about art or preoccupied with other topics, leaving artistic concerns to clergy, liturgists, and artists themselves. For another, theologians have periodically come up with strong defenses of some particular kind of art, even if they have generally lacked subtlety in describing what we would call aesthetic experience. They have also articulated theologies of beauty in general that from time to time have been applied suggestively to the arts, or at least to some of the arts.

Those theological strategies have worked less well in the modern era, however, as art has become less religious in any usual sense, more ironic and complex aesthetically, and intentionally less beautiful, often even grotesque.[90] Modern theologies also have faced the additional challenge that art in the present era has often been defined and prized in sheerly aesthetic terms that rule out any apparent connection with morality or religion.

Here we come upon the irony alluded to in chapter 1. In the time when art was most fully Christian, theologians themselves tended to be suspicious of artistic things. In any case, they had no unifying notion of art. That is to say, they did not conceive of poetry, music, painting, drama, architecture, dance, and the like as occupying one major sphere of culture, called art. Consequently, although there were Christian traditions of making this kind of art or that, there was no theology of art as such. When a unified concept of art finally came into existence in the modern era, that made it theoretically possible for there to be a theology of art, because for the first time there was an idea of art, in the aesthetic sense. Yet the very idea that made it possible to think of art as one kind of thing—as aesthetic—was conceived by many in such a way that religion was in principle left to the side. In spite of Romantic impulses to the contrary, it began to seem to many thinkers that if one valued something for its aesthetic qualities, for its beauty, and hence truly as art, one would not be valuing it for religious reasons, or for moral ones either. In a particular work of art, aesthetic and religious values (or "tastes") might coexist, but they would not consort. As we will see in the next chapter, that was the conclusion toward which much aesthetic theory moved in the modern era, eventually resulting in various kinds of purism, segregating art from everything else, and in ways that were to haunt much thinking about art in the twentieth century.

Yet it is precisely in the modern era (broadly speaking) that we actually begin to have sustained attempts to construct theologies of art. To repeat, that is the irony. Indeed, it seems something of a paradox. And it affects any attempt to reflect on the relation between religion and taste. For at the same time that the idea of the aesthetic took shape, taste came to be seen as crucial precisely in the making and experience of art.

But any extended treatment of taste as such must still be delayed. That is because, in the nineteenth century, emphasis on taste began to give way to an emphasis on artistic expression and aesthetic experience in a generic sense. For that reason, as we consider next the modern process by which the love of religion began to be replaced or transformed by the love of art, the notion of taste will appear more in the guise of aesthetic experience, imagination, or the love of art.

Even so, the ideas we will soon encounter can be combined, critically and selectively, with insights from the traditions of art and thought that we have already surveyed. That will allow us to reintroduce the idea of taste at a deeper level, and so to reexamine the powerful but puzzling conjunctions between art, taste, and religion. We will find that, while there are ways in which taste (and art) and religion must be differentiated, their relationship is in certain important respects more integral than most theologians or aestheticians have recognized. Blake may not be completely vindicated, nor Kierkegaard, but both will continue to have their say in the dialogue.

THREE

From the Love of Religion
to the Love of Art

Religion and the Love for Art

Ancient Attractions to Art

A great many Europeans over the past two millennia have professed a love for Christ and the Church. Yet, prior to the late seventeenth or early eighteenth century, there were no Europeans who considered themselves art lovers, none who professed to have a taste for art as such. That is because, as we have seen, no one in Europe (or apparently anywhere in the vicinity) had a general concept corresponding to what we usually think of as art, or of taste either.

Admitting many exceptions and variations, a work of art as we normally conceive of it today is a human artifact made with skill and know-how and a degree of inspiration or creativity; it is usually beautiful, imaginative, or expressive; it is shareable; and it can be appreciated to a large extent for aesthetic reasons, varying from pure delight in sensuous form to an enjoyment of richly imaginative insight. Up until the early 1800s, however, art in the aesthetic sense had not yet been clearly and systematically distinguished from the "liberal arts" such as grammar, mathematics, and astronomy on the one hand, and from the "mechanical arts" of manufacture and a whole array of knowledgeably applied skills on the other—carpentry, masonry, shipbuilding, and so forth. In short, the available concepts of art (Greek *techne*, Latin *ars*) had encompassed many things that we do not usually consider to be fine art and had excluded some things that we do.[1] Because there was not yet any general idea of art and taste in the aesthetic sense, neither was there any notion of being an art lover whose taste would be exercised in perceiving, appreciating, or evaluating art.

Even so, people since the beginning of time have undoubtedly loved various things they have regarded as beautiful. Medieval and Renaissance thinkers, for instance, characterized beautiful objects as pleasing, by virtue of being harmonious and integrated and well proportioned, with radiance, *claritas*, and splendor of form. Many such beautiful objects, and many throughout history that may have been more expressive or devout than beautiful, are ones that we today consider art, and ones that people evidently have loved. Certainly Christians have loved the artistry of hymns, stories of the saints, glittering mosaics, and lofty domes, which they have described as elevating, moving, beautiful, and good for the soul.

It seems very likely, moreover, that an ancient Greek's love of the *Odyssey*, King Saul's enjoyment of young David's harp music, and the medieval Abbot Suger's taste for richly ornamented devotional objects would all have something in common. These responses, which are various ways of loving art, would all be ones we would regard as in some measure aesthetic—an appreciation of the formal, expressive, or imaginative qualities of the artistry itself. They would all therefore involve what we would call taste—the capacity to perceive, enjoy, and judge aesthetic qualities. And because aesthetic taste would be involved, love of such art would necessarily go beyond interests of a strictly cognitive, moral, religious, or utilitarian nature.

The aesthetic reasons for valuing, or indeed loving, an artistic work may not always have been clearly recognized. But the lack of a general aesthetic concept of art did not stop earlier admirers and makers of a particular art such as sculpture or architecture from distinguishing traits we think of as aesthetic from traits we think of as more practical. For example, the Roman architect Pollio Vitruvius (first century B.C.E.) distinguished the beauty (*venustas*) of a building from its usefulness (*utilitas*) and its sturdiness (*firmitas*). And he made it plain that the work's beauty is what would be most likely to attract the beholder.

It is not that what we think of as arts—even fine arts—were traditionally loved or valued only for their beauty. Nor was beauty the only aesthetic value. For centuries it was commonly assumed that arts such as poetry, drama, oratory, music, or stoneworking could be appreciated for a variety of reasons. Poetry, for instance, could be treasured for being inspired by the gods as well as for being beautifully phrased and emotionally moving in its rhythms and sounds. From classical antiquity through the Middle Ages and the Renaissance people recognized, in fact, that various arts may be useful (or not), skillfully wrought, moving, pleasing, instructive, beautiful, and possibly inspired. Art could satisfy in any or all of these ways. Certain arts, as forms of *mimesis*, creatively "imitating" and perhaps improving on nature, were thought to be enjoyable mainly because *mimesis* is intrinsically pleasing for humans. Yet these, too, were believed to arouse or order the emotions, to enhance life, or possibly to honor the state or serve religion.

Modern Attractions to Art

As we have noted, thinkers during the eighteenth century began to use the terms "art" and "arts" in a new way. For the first time they classified as the "fine arts" those human artifacts and ways of making that seemed to exist primarily for the sake of their beauty. The lists of fine arts varied. Early on, gardening was often included as a fine art. Yet sometimes architecture was excluded, and literature. In time, however, "fine arts" generally meant music, painting, sculpture, drama, poetry, dance, and architecture.

To be able to perceive or judge art of this sort, one needed taste. As discussed by philosophers such as the Third Earl of Shaftesbury (1671–1713), David Hume (1711–1776), Immanuel Kant (1724–1804), and Edmund Burke (1729–1797), taste was fundamentally the power (or faculty) of discerning beauty. As such, taste involved perception and discrimination—along with imagination and a capacity for a certain kind of "disinterested" pleasure, since the beautiful pleases in one's very perception of it and not because it is useful or true or good.

Taste of that sort was regarded as aesthetic, being based on "perceptibles" (Greek, *aisthetika*) registering not just as sensation (like heat or cold) but as a kind of subjective feeling, produced (as Kant said) by the free play of the mental powers that make up imagination.[2] One cannot tell that a poem is beautiful by consulting the five senses alone, or by trying to assess its usefulness, nor yet by turning to science or religion. Taste is not based, finally, on sensation nor on pragmatic, cognitive, moral, or religious considerations. Taste attends to something else: the formal, expressive, and imaginative qualities of the aesthetic object, which please in the very process of being perceived (as the medieval scholastic philosophers had always said of beauty per se).

Although the feeling of pleasure that registers the perception of beauty is subjective, one still says that the object of taste—a rose, for instance—is what is beautiful, not the feelings themselves. And judgments of taste, while personal, are not private. Kant in particular insisted that judging something to be beautiful is different from expressing a purely personal liking (for caviar, for example) or from finding something merely agreeable (such as a certain fragrance). Judgments of taste call, instead, for the assent of anyone appropriately experienced and sensitive. In Kant's view, they claim to be universal, even though in actuality not everyone will happen to agree with any given aesthetic judgment.[3]

Following out ideas like these, a good many thinkers and artists began to see all art as existing mainly to afford aesthetic experience, and hence as free and autonomous. In time (from the mid-nineteenth century until the mid-twentieth) "absolute" music, along with lyric poetry, came to be regarded widely as the epitome of art—as the sort of thing toward which all art should aspire. And though a moral, even moralistic, notion of art was widespread in Victorian

England, a number of leading critics and artists moved toward some sort of aestheticism, which had already begun to take root in France. In its milder form, aestheticism claimed that art should be enjoyed sheerly for its own sake, for its sheer beauty or expressiveness, without any concern for morality or instruction, for religion or the outside world. In its bolder form, aestheticism made the experience of art the model for experiencing life itself.[4]

Yet any thoughtful person in the eighteenth and nineteenth centuries could also see that the arts are not identical and that even works of abstract music can in fact be valued for all sorts of reasons other than narrowly aesthetic ones. A symphony or a piano sonata was commonly understood to be more than purely formal design. It was not just aural wallpaper. Reaching "from the heart to the heart" (as Beethoven once said), a work of music could touch the soul and bring tears to the eyes. It was expressive, as people began to expect all art to be. For some thinkers—especially High Romantics, but including their many twentieth-century descendants—art's expressive and imaginative qualities united head and heart in such as way as to give it unique religious and cognitive powers. That was certainly true from the point of view of Blake and Coleridge, and of various German Romantics. Responding to Schleiermacher's *Speeches on Religion*, Friedrich Schlegel (1772–1829) described religion as poetry and philosophy combined, and yet saw artists, rather than religious prophets or preachers, as the apogee of humanity. From the poets' point of view, he said, the problem with religion is just that it is "a variety of poetry which, unsure of its own lovely playfulness, takes itself too seriously and too one-sidedly."[5] What is unclear in Schlegel's account is whether he assumed the poets (as the peak of humanity) were right about religion and, if so, whether this meant that, in the end, poetry and art are to replace religion and perhaps philosophy as well.

Shortly after Schlegel was musing in this vein, Hegel (1770–1831) saw a similar connection between art and religion of the past, but with the difference that, in Hegel's view, it would be art that must decrease while true philosophy—a Christianity somehow made fully rational—would increase. Art, Hegel said, is a medium in which "thought divests itself of itself" in such a way as to surrender its conceptual, rational character so as to become the sensuous embodiment of truth. But in modernity, according to Hegel, art finally yields to rational thought, which takes and transforms what art has to offer, moving its insights onto a higher plane. We "have passed beyond the point at which art is the highest mode under which the absolute is brought home to human consciousness," Hegel wrote. Indeed, although modern people will continue to make and enjoy art, "art is no longer able to discover that satisfaction of spirituals wants, which previous epochs and nations have sought for in it and exclusively found in it, a satisfaction which, at least on the religious side, was associated with art in the most intimate way."[6]

One could argue that Hegel himself had in actuality tried to go beyond not only art but also religion, since his ostensibly "rational Christianity" seemed to surrender the sense of mystery that is so vital to much religious sensibility and teaching. One could also argue—and many did—that Hegel had an insufficient appreciation of the powers of art. Many theorists and artists from the late eighteenth century to the present would retort that art can express the inner life, the life of feelings "too deep for words," which forever eludes purely rational thought and which may be related at least indirectly to religious experience. Be that as it may, fewer and fewer intellectuals and artists would agree with Hegel's notion that religion was more likely than art to thrive in an era of science and rationality. In point of fact, both art and religion would become embattled and defensive. But religion was more closely tied to dogmas and systems of authority that seemed especially vulnerable to rational critique, whereas art could at least be allowed to play in the realm of fantasy and feeling.

One way or another, then, art and religion would come apart. In the eyes of a few, religion would outlast art by becoming, in effect, philosophy or ethics. In the eyes of others, art would take the place of religion by becoming a refuge for feeling and imagination. In the eyes of still others, art's inner nature and true destiny had always been to take its leave of religion altogether and to satisfy itself with aesthetic form and expression for its own sake.

So this was the situation: When eighteenth-century philosophers and critics began to conceive of all the "arts of the beautiful" as comprising one sphere of culture—namely, art in the aesthetic sense—they were trying to allocate a special place for art. This autonomy seemed increasingly precious as time went by, because it meant that art would not be directly subject to rational attack on the one hand, or to moral and religious dictates on the other. Yet to give art a "room of its own," so to speak, theorists needed to specify in a consistent way precisely the nature of certain artistic purposes and pleasures. And that turned out to be hard to do. Old questions persisted for a time, but were rephrased and given new twists: Does art exist to please or to instruct? If art does both, does it please in order better to instruct, or just the reverse? If art has its own unique purposes, does art have any role in improving life and instilling moral virtue? Or is art actually amoral? Is artistry more a matter of representation (*mimesis*), or of free imagination? More a matter of beautiful making, or of creative expression? What differentiates the arts? Which arts, if any, are superior? Does the highest art exist simply for its own sake? And what is the nature of the artist, the creative genius?

Regarding the relation of art and religion in particular, the questions eventually took something like the following pattern: If the value of art has mainly to do with aesthetics—with matters of beauty and sublimity, of form and feeling, calling for taste—and if aesthetic values are somehow different from those of utility, knowledge, morality, and religion, what remains of the long-assumed connection between art and other things, including religion? If art is to have a realm of its own, with purposes unique to itself, how can it really serve morality, the public good, or religion? Even if art is enlisted in the service of religion or morality, isn't its heart always going to be elsewhere? Supposing art and religion are sometimes wedded in church, does not art's lingering urge to be self-directed or autonomous ultimately undermine the authority of religion itself? Wouldn't a taste for art then run contrary to any yearning for religious satisfaction, for God? How could the creative genius of the individual artist be fulfilled in the service of anything other than art itself?

With such issues unsettled, it is easy to see why Kierkegaard, writing in the mid-nineteenth century, could worry that an artist setting out to do a religious work such as a painting of the Crucifixion would inevitably end up betraying religion by appealing to a love of art rather than a love of Christ. Our next step is to place that kind of concern within the distinctly modern context and so to see how the issues of art and religion come to be framed as they often are today. That will help us to sort out the complex and often troubling issues that inevitably arise even now in any serious effort to understand or debate the religious dimensions of art and taste. For, every shift in understanding the nature of art marks a shift in how aesthetic values and taste are understood, and in how these are seen to relate to ultimate concerns or longings, and so to God.

To attempt a survey of modern aesthetic theory and artistic practice as a whole is of course out of the question. Instead, we will examine trends and figures that are especially relevant to our main aesthetic and religious concerns—concerns we identified first in terms of the contrasting views of art and religion posed by Kierkegaard and Blake. We will begin by tracing certain revolutionary (initially Romantic) developments in which arts of religious significance moved outside the bounds of institutional religion. We next note several nineteenth-century religious and artistic attempts to recover a humbler but genuinely religious role for the arts. Then we turn to modern and postmodern developments in art theory, which begin to be as influential as art itself. We will see how modern theories of art have tended to substitute the love of art for religious devotion and to isolate art from religious life and thought, even while acknowledging ties between aesthetic experience and religious feeling. Examining postmodern critiques of such purism, I make a plea on behalf of the integralist aesthetics that I myself have previously proposed and note ways in which it must be revised. In the end I expand the conversation to include an aspect of Jacques Derrida's deconstructionist thought that, when combined with the concerns of Kierkegaard and Blake, helps us prepare for the theological themes of the following chapter, which focuses on a theology of taste.

Art and the Love for Religion

Revolution in Religious Arts

When at the end of the Baroque era the energetic outpouring of religious art died down, European arts for the first time entered an era in which by far the greater percentage of artworks were produced for distinctly secular settings. These included places of business, civic buildings, private homes, salons, concert halls, and theaters. The works themselves involved genres such as landscapes, sporting art, portraits, history painting, comic and tragic drama, novels, lyric poetry, symphonies, songs, opera, and so forth.

Yet it must be said that many artists and thinkers of the late eighteenth and nineteenth centuries had no desire to sever art from everything religious or moral. On the contrary, even when their works were unorthodox, they sought in many cases a new religious and moral vision, freed from traditional religious dogmas and institutions but allied with a new sense of nature, history, and the human spirit (as exemplified by the genius of the artist).[7] The love of art became in some measure a religious love carried beyond the walls of institutional religion and into the aesthetic medium, in which assent to doctrines and ecclesiastical authority was of less concern.

The tendency within Romanticism in particular to seek the transformation of religion through artistic imagination is apparent in Blake's equating the true artist with the true Christian. One encounters a similarly expansive (and often ambiguous) reinterpretation of religion and religious experience in the poems and prose works of Hölderlin (1770–1843), Novalis (1772–1801), Coleridge (1772–1834), and Wordsworth (1770–1850), which frequently give voice to pantheistic or otherwise heterodox yearnings and intimations.[8]

The "natural supernaturalism" that begins to supplant the traditional supernaturalism of a God above and beyond nature is perhaps especially evident in Romantic visions of the Sublime.[9] In visual arts, one thinks of the paintings of the German artist Caspar David Friedrich (1774–1840). These evoke a quasi-religious sense of the awe-inspiring infinite by showing, for example, an isolated Alpine cross (with Christ's corpus), anchored in stone atop a lofty mountain that a woman, leading her male companion, has just ascended—with row upon row of distant, lower ranges in the background (Figure 11, p. 229). Alternatively, Friedrich depicts a monk standing alone by an expansive sea, or Gothic ruins in a snowy, evening landscape, silhouetted against a moonlit sky. A similar expansion and evocative naturalization of Christian visions of the world and the spirit occurs in American luminist landscapes and in the grander—sometimes grandiose—geological "cosmoramas" by Frederick Edwin Church (1826–1900) and Albert Bierstadt (1830–1902).[10]

In music a manifestation of related tendencies to transform the look and sound of religion can be heard in the myth-based *Ring* cycle of operas by Wagner (1813–83), and later in the Nietzchean symphonic poem by Richard Strauss (1864–1949) entitled *Also Sprach Zarathustra* (featured appropriately enough in the film *2001*), and still later in the Eighth Symphony of Gustav Mahler (1860–1911), the so-called *Symphony of a Thousand*. That work commences with a mammoth orchestral and choral setting of the medieval Pentecost hymn "*Veni Creator Spiritus*" and concludes with the paean to love and the Eternal Feminine that closes the second part of Goethe's *Faust*. Here mystical eroticism, or erotic mysticism, bursts forth into a new dimension. Compared with the ardor of Mahler's hymning of divine Eros, the guilt-laden sexuality of Wagner's immense revision of the grail legend in *Parsifal* can seem curiously repressed (while likewise using medieval sources).

Especially with the Romantic movement, then, art becomes a medium of religious evolution and revolution, often unauthorized from the religious side. Just such Romantic aspirations to unite art and religion at a higher level would surely have struck Kierkegaard as especially seductive and dangerous, given his insistence that art and religion are by no means to be put on the same plane.

The theological perplexity created by a "liberated" art did not escape the young liberal theologian Friedrich Schleiermacher writing in 1799 and thus in the heyday of Romanticism in Germany. A kind of Romantic himself, Schleiermacher was impressed with the place of feeling in religious experience, which, as we have noted, he described as a "sense and taste for the infinite."[11] Yet Schleiermacher felt that he had to remain content merely to acknowledge a largely hidden connection between aesthetic experience and religious. As he put it: religion and art, once allies in pagan antiquity, now "stand beside one another like two friendly souls whose inner affinity, whether or not they equally surmise it, is nevertheless still unknown to them."[12] That affinity Schleiermacher professed not to comprehend, though he would continue to find it fascinating. Certain artists were less reticent, taking on the mantle of religion yet without any clear religious commitment, thereby exposing themselves to Kierkegaard's kind of critique.

We have already observed how ironic it is that, once a relatively unified idea of art and aesthetic taste had finally become available to theology in the eighteenth century, it was far from obvious that a theology of art was called for. We should now be able to see that several things must have stood in the way of a full-scale theology of art (or of artistic taste). Not only was there the traditional Christian theological suspicion of, and condescension toward, the arts and artistic beauty. To that was added the new philosophical emphasis on the relative autonomy of art and aesthetic experience. As time went by there was also the increasingly undeniable fact that much of the new religious or quasi-religious creativity in the arts was leaving the church in both a physical and a spiritual sense. Protestant churches had already banished or repressed many arts, and the Catholic Church since the Counter-Reformation had in various ways been curtailing much of its patronage as well. Now art was making its own moves toward autonomy. It was not only separating itself from established religion but also widely refusing, even in its spiritual quests, to be subservient to theological norms or to the institutional church. Any full-scale theology of art (or taste) offered during the modern era would need therefore to take into account the religious significance of art that was conscious of its own powers and that flourished beyond the confines of orthodox creeds and religious institutions.

Attempting to Retrieve Art for the Church

Short of taking a daring plunge into the spiritual ferment of art outside the church and at the boundaries of traditional religion, various nineteenth-century theologians and clergy could and did attempt to renew the aesthetic life and spiritual depth of the church and its liturgy. They did so partly by encouraging church musicians, artisans, and architects to revive and update medieval Gothic styles—in the form of Gothic Revival architecture, for instance, along with a richer, more ceremonial liturgy and a refurbished patristic and medieval hymnody. It was in this way that members of the Oxford Movement and their high church descendants hoped to remedy the adverse spiritual effects of what many a Victorian complained of as the aesthetic drabness of British Christianity.

At about the same time, in a movement centered in Germany, Catholic clergy and church musicians were promoting the new Cecilian Society, dedicated to reviving Gregorian chant as well as polyphony in the sixteenth-century style of Palestrina. Their activities involved setting aside for good the legacy of the older ornate and operatic Viennese style of church music (Mozart, Haydn, and so forth) and suppressing the new growth of an effusive kind of musical Romanticism that Claude Debussy was later to call "hysterical mysticism."[13] (It must be said, however, that the musical moderation that they espoused led in most cases to an uninspiring blandness.) Later in the same century other Catholics, led by the Benedictines at Solesmes, France, made efforts to restore and promote the truer and more ancient forms of Gregorian chant. Meanwhile, in the visual arts, there were corresponding but less rigorous attempts on the part of certain groups to work in styles that would call to mind older, "purer" modes of Christian or quasi-Christian sensibility. Of these groups, the Nazarener in Vienna and the Pre-Raphaelite Brotherhood in England stood out. Even though such attempts by artists and musicians to revive the look and sound of an older religiosity made relatively minor ripples in art and music history, their effect within the Church was sometimes longlasting—as in the renewal of chant and Gothic style. During roughly the same period, popular hymnody flourished, though no one of the stature of Isaac Watts or Charles Wesley appeared. And in the middle of the nineteenth century, oratorio reached its greatest popularity, especially in England, and most notably with works such as Mendelssohn's *St. Paul* (1836) and *Elijah* (1846).

Without either reflecting or generating a fully developed theology of art, all of these movements revived an idea or assumption that had rather languished under Enlightenment rationalism—namely, that beauty and artistic expression are of considerable religious consequence. It is significant that after Cardinal Newman (1801–1890) had left behind what he perceived to be the current aesthetic shoddiness of Anglican liturgy, he proudly pictured the Roman Catholic Church as the font of art and beauty. Thus he declared: "Poetry is the refuge of those who have not the Catholic Church to fly to and repose upon; the church itself is the most sacred and venerable of poets."[14] The very source and mode of Christian revelation was something he saw as in a sense aesthetic: "Revealed Religion should be especially poetical—and it is so in fact. While its disclosures have an originality in them to engage the intellect, they have a beauty to satisfy the moral nature. It presents us with those ideal forms of excellence in which a poetical mind delights, and with which all grace and harmony are associated."[15] This is not to say that Newman was attracted to Catholicism only for aesthetic reasons. He disparaged those who would come to Catholicism and participate in church ceremonies "for their very beauty-sake, not asking themselves whether they are true, and having no real perception or mental hold of them."[16] Newman was clear that it is not enough to have "poetical feelings." He insisted that people must commit themselves.[17] It is fair to say, however, that Newman's form of religious faith was intensely aesthetic, without being exclusively so, and that his vision of the church was richly colored by his tastes in art and beauty, which, along with his faith, inclined toward Rome.

Taking Cognizance of Art outside the Church

But what of religious concerns for art and beauty outside the church itself? Certain Victorians sought, for one thing, to retrieve for art in general the humble but dignified role of much medieval art and artisanship, joining that ideal with the Romantic emphasis on feeling and imagination. Such sentiments were conducive to the arts and crafts movement. And various clergy called attention to the importance of the overall sense of beauty and of poetic imagination in culture at large, as either preparation for, or agent of, spiritual awakening. This theme recurred in the writings of John Keble (1792–1866) and in John Henry Newman.[18] It was Keble who wrote that "religion and poetry are akin because each is marked by a pure reserve, a kind of modesty or reverence."[19] And both Newman and Keble had imbibed from Wordsworth and Coleridge the sense of an affinity between poetry and religion, Newman declaring while still an Anglican that "the taste for poetry of a religious kind has in modern times in a certain sense taken the place of the deep contemplative spirit of the early Church. . . . Poetry then is our mysticism," penetrating beneath the surface of things—apparently even when not explicitly Christian—and drawing readers away from the material to the invisible world. To this extent, he said, the poetic and the religious characters of mind "answer to the same end."[20]

Not unlike Catholic thinkers of a later generation, such as Etienne Gilson (1884–1978) and Jacques Maritain (1882–1973), Newman wanted to honor art and would love it deeply, since beauty itself is already akin to religious value. Yet all these Christians exhibited a perceptible nostalgia for an era long past when the arts were (supposedly) humble enough to be genuine servants of the church and God.[21] This comes out when Cardinal Newman refers to the fine arts as "special attendants and handmaids of religion" that are "very apt to forget their place, and unless restrained with a firm hand, instead of being servants will aim at becoming principals."[22]

It could be argued, in fact, that none of the Christian thinkers we have named actually saw or stated any compelling reason for the theological enterprise to reexamine thoroughly and in fresh terms the relations between art, aesthetic response (or taste), and the religious life. Either the possible differences between the love of a duly humbled art and the love of religion were smoothed over (as with Newman, Keble, and the Gothic Revivalists), or (in the later case of Neo-Scholastics like Maritain) art and religion were made thoroughly amicable by being assigned to quite different but entirely compatible spheres.

Meanwhile many leading theorists and critics close to the arts themselves had begun to offer some heterodox views when it came to interpreting the relation between art and religion. In Britain, the cases of John Ruskin (1819–1900), Matthew Arnold (1822–88), Walter Pater (1839–94), and Clive Bell (1881–1964) are instructive in this regard, and warrant special though necessarily brief consideration.

The Love of Religion as the Love of Art

John Ruskin

Raised in a Calvinist form of evangelical Anglicanism, which he later left behind, John Ruskin exercised enormous influence through his prolific writings on painting and architecture, including the five volumes of *Modern Painters* (1846,

1853, 1856–60), *The Seven Lamps of Architecture* (1849), and *Stones of Venice* (1851). Although Ruskin's views underwent many changes over the course of his lifetime, it would be hard to find a theorist more eager in his prime to make both moral and religious claims for art and for the sense of Beauty. That was a sense he termed not "Aesthesis," which for Ruskin was nothing more than sensory response to pleasing stimuli, but rather "Theoria," which he defined as the "exulting, reverent, and grateful perception" of "the Beautiful as a gift of God."[23]

In the writings collected in *Modern Painters*, Ruskin provides what some have called a "natural theology of art."[24] One trait of Christian character, Ruskin says, is to love instinctively what he calls "Typical Beauty," such as appears in forms we term infinity, unity, symmetry, and moderation. Likewise, to love the "Vital Beauty" of nature requires "the entire perfection of the Christian character, for he who loves not God, nor his human brother, cannot love the grass beneath his feet and the creatures that fill those spaces in the universe which he needs not, and which live not for his uses."[25] In Ruskin's view, art is to be true to the beauty of nature and true also to thought and the artist's own vision and moral sense. Great works of architecture are thus the product of builders who exhibit moral quality. And all good art is moral in its origins and in its effects, being either truthful or admirably and beautifully useful. The highest arts, while occupied in the production of beautiful form or color, "relate to us the utmost ascertainable truth respecting visible things and moral feelings."[26]

All of this sounds exceptionally moral and highly Christian. But by the time Ruskin gave his inaugural lectures in 1870 as Slade Professor of Art at Oxford, his formerly orthodox faith had gone through a long period of erosion, leaving him a conventional Christian no longer. And though he retained a high view of art's morality, he now distanced art from religion in a number of ways.

Explicitly addressing in these lectures the relation of art to religion, to morals, and to practical use, Ruskin becomes equivocal when discussing the religious connection. Without completely severing art from religion or Christianity, he has almost nothing positive to say about the connection. He starts out by claiming that the great arts have had, and can have, but three principal purposes: enforcing religion, perfecting ethics, or doing material service (by which he turns out to mean, in short, "getting our country clean, and our people beautiful").[27] Then he criticizes ways in which religion and art have often been presumed to be related or have in fact, and unhappily, been mixed up together. Here he makes essentially three points.

First, Ruskin insists that art is not, as some suppose, a result of inspiration or religious vision but a product of wisely directed labor, drawing on the feelings common to humanity in general rather than the specially devout. The best art comes from people who are good, but not distinctively religious. Second—in a passage excised from the final version of the lecture—he asserts that art itself has not much benefited from religion. On the contrary: "Few of the greatest men," he declares, "ever painted religious subjects by choice, but only because they were either compelled by ecclesiastical authority, supported by its patronage, or invited by popular applause," with the consequence that their powers "were at once wasted and restrained."[28]

Last, Ruskin claims that religion, for its part, has not generally been helped by art, because religious art has encouraged people to believe in things that they would not normally and reasonably find credible, such as a heavenly, caring Madonna. Such art transgresses the bounds of harmless fiction or edifying symbolism; it constitutes outright deception that encourages false religion. Ruskin objects particularly to a kind of religious realism exemplified by certain grisly depictions of the sufferings of Christ such as those found often in Roman Catholic countries. That graphic realism is inappropriate, he says, because Christ in being crucified suffered no more physical pain than anyone else would. Art like that, Ruskin asserts, appeals not only to "the most vulgar desires for religious excitement but to the mere thirst for sensation of horror which characterises the uneducated orders of partially civilized countries." It especially occupies the sensibility of "tender and delicate women of Christendom," from whose hearts the image aims to wring out the last drops of pity.[29] The more truly Christlike thing would be to make people aware of, and attentive to, the massive everyday suffering in the world, and the horrors of war.

There is one more way that art can harm religion, according to Ruskin. It is harmful that art and architecture are used so often to make it seem that the divine presence belongs to one locality more than to another. Instead of consecrating one place through images and shrines, and thereby associating a manifestation of the divine with that particular area, we would do better to make most of the earth appear sacred and only a little of it profane.[30] Then human beings might be prevented from polluting and destroying the land and nature.

It is striking, to say the least, that someone who as art critic had championed Gothic Revival architecture, who had studied Catholic art in depth, and who was immersed in Christianity from the start, would now take such a dim view even of the historical relations between religion and the visual arts. We have seen that Kierkegaard, in his own way, might have concurred. But whereas Kierkegaard was normally willing to sacrifice art for the sake of Christianity, Ruskin in these lectures seems prepared to sacrifice Christianity—at least in its historical forms—in favor of art. It had not always been so. Earlier in life he had declared to a friend, "Religion must be, and always has been, the ground and moving spirit of all great art."[31] But at this juncture, his eyes having been opened (or some would say blinded) by modern experience and the industrial revolution, Christianity appears fraught with many untenable doctrines and irrational practices; it is guilty, moreover, of tolerating great ugliness, immense social suffering, and the human ravaging of nature. Art, by contrast, is something that Ruskin sees as by nature moral.

In private Ruskin had withdrawn further yet from Christianity, being something of an agnostic until 1875, when he apparently reclaimed a portion of his Christian heritage before falling seriously ill and eventually losing all mental coherence. What matters for our story is that when Ruskin retreated from Christianity, either publicly or privately, he tended to portray himself as moving into a position from which nature, art, morality—and possibly even God—could all be better served.[32] In this regard, the contrast with someone like John Henry Newman could hardly be greater, since for Newman art and beauty reach their apogee (however modest) within the Church.

Matthew Arnold and Walter Pater

Ruskin was in notable ways a conservative, an earnest moralist reluctant to criticize religion openly; but he did not support the status quo, socially, and in fact became an outspoken critic of capitalism. When one shifts to a cultural critic like his contemporary Matthew Arnold, who was socially much more conservative, one finds someone who was openly liberal in religious views: someone willing to assert plainly that, with the death of religious dogma, people would more and more need to turn to poetry. "At the present moment," wrote Arnold, "two things about the Christian religion must surely be clear to anybody with eyes in his head. One is, that men cannot do without it; the other, that they cannot do with it as it is."[33] From Arnold's perspective, the poetry capable of sustaining us would partly need to be the poetry of religion itself—religion (and the Bible) as literature. But in this form religion would no longer command the doctrinal assent that Newman thought essential for faith, nor the particular kind of commitment—a commitment transcending the ethical—that Kierkegaard considered crucial to Christianity.

"There is not a creed which is not shaken, not an accredited dogma which is not shown to be questionable," Arnold wrote. "More and more mankind will discover that we have to turn to poetry to interpret life for us, to console us, to sustain us. Without poetry, our science will appear incomplete; and most of what now passes with us for religion and philosophy will be replaced by poetry"—by which he meant (among other things) "the breath and finer spirit of knowledge."[34] Having made such a declaration, it is hardly surprising that Arnold went on to state: "The best poetry is what we want; the best poetry will be found to have a power of forming, sustaining, and delighting us, as nothing else can." That led Arnold to concentrate on the classic, the "truly excellent," as what deserves something we might term loving devotion.

Arnold, like Ruskin, quite consciously retained a use for religion. Yet Arnold's was even less a religion with specific dogmatic or metaphysical content. Unlike Ruskin, who in his last years still made reference to Christ's divinity (while remaining unclear about what he meant by that), Arnold paid homage to a Jesus who was no more than a supreme moral teacher. For the most part Arnold's God was reduced to a cipher, the great "not-ourselves" that he trusted somehow to underwrite the highest moral and cultural values.[35] While joining devotion to religion with devotion to poetry, Arnold was clearer about what it is that poetry has to offer—and much clearer about why poetry has a future.

In the waning years of the nineteenth century and the early decades of the twentieth, there would appear a more extreme way to shift affections from traditional Christianity to art. This would be to make art itself somehow suffice for the sanctification of life, and therefore in effect to substitute for religious devotion, without necessarily requiring art to reproduce even the moral teachings, stories, or images of traditional religion. Art could simply fulfill its own nature; that would be enough for the person properly attuned. Early signs of this development are evident even in the briefest inspection of the aestheticism (by no means frivolous) of the Oxford scholar and essayist Walter Pater, in many ways a successor to Ruskin.

In the famous conclusion of his best-known book, *The Renaissance: Studies in Art and Poetry*, the first edition of which appeared in 1873, Pater submitted a kind of creed:

> Well! we are all *condamnés*, as Victor Hugo says: we are all under sentence of death but with a sort of indefinite reprieve . . . : we have an interval, and then our place knows us no more. Some spend this interval in listlessness, some in high passions, the wisest, at least among "the children of this world," in art and song. For our one chance lies in expanding that interval, in getting as many pulsations as possible into the given time. Great passions may give us this quickened sense of life, ecstasy and sorrow of love, the various forms of enthusiastic activity, disinterested or otherwise, which come naturally to many of us. Only be sure it is passion—that it does yield you this fruit of a quickened, multiplied consciousness. Of such wisdom, the poetic passion, the desire of beauty, the love of art for its own sake, has most. For art comes to you proposing frankly to give nothing but the highest quality to your moments as they pass, and simply for those moments' sake.[36]

Now if art on its own can indeed give life's moments the "highest quality," it would not be surprising that some lovers of art might experience and describe such sheerly aesthetic moments as virtually mystical or transcendental. Pater himself, no longer able to give assent, intellectually, to Christian beliefs, came very close to transposing religious experience into something unmistakably aesthetic. In *Marius the Epicurean* (1885) he envisioned a fully aware and receptive life as in some sense "beatific."[37] He had already affirmed in a letter of 1883 that there is a "sort of religious phase possible for the modern mind,"[38] which he had it in mind soon to convey (in *Marius*). Before that, in his autobiographical essay "The Child in the House" (1878), he described how for the young child Florian (obviously doubling for Pater himself) "all the acts and accidents of daily life borrowed a sacred colour and significance; the very colours of things became themselves weighty with meanings like the sacred stuffs of Moses' tabernacle. . . . Sensibility—the desire of physical beauty—a strange biblical awe, which made any reference to the unseen act on him like solemn music—these qualities the child took away with him, when, at about the age of twelve years, he left the old house."[39] And now here, in *The Renaissance,* he wrote that the aesthetic heightening of consciousness could make it possible to "burn always with [a] hard, gem-like flame, to maintain this ecstasy."[40] Thus in Pater's writings—which scandalized many of his Oxford colleagues—the love of art became a poignant (because necessarily transitory) approximation of religious devotion.[41]

Clive Bell

Early in the next century, one member of London's Bloomsbury Group, the gifted art critic and influential theorist Clive Bell, saw aesthetic experience as still more exalted than Pater supposed, if that were possible. A formalist, Bell put forward his central theories in 1913 in a book simply entitled *Art.*

In *Art,* Bell proposes his best-known thesis, derived in part from Kant, but through many intermediaries: that aesthetic experience essentially depends on an artwork's "significant form," rather than on ideas or information or moral wisdom that the art may convey, or on representational veracity. Significant form has nothing to do with skillful representation, nor with any direct reference to life, nor yet with religious beliefs and institutions. In apprehending significant form in art, one's properly aesthetic response is pure, shut off from all other interests. Concentrating on "lines and colours, their relations and quantities and qualities," aesthetic attention is focused entirely on the work itself, and severed from any external sense of the significance of life.[42] Bell asserts that, even so, the aesthetic emotion which is thus induced, and which the artist means to express, is "one of the most valuable things in the world"—so valuable that one could be tempted to believe that "art might prove the world's salvation" (p. 32).

It will be recalled that Arnold likewise had spoken of turning to poetry to save us. But Bell is thinking in more private and (one might say) esoteric terms. He and his fellow art critic Roger Fry realized perfectly well that few people have the capacity to attend rightly to significant form. Pure aesthetic experience escapes them. Apparently if the world is to be saved through art, it will only be vicariously: through aesthetic virtuosi, as unacknowledged saints. In any case, Bell does not embrace Arnold's view that poetry and art provide a morally engaged criticism of life. In Bell's theory, art works as it does because it is *not* essentially concerned with life or morality or religion.

Bell takes us off guard, however, by going on to offer a second hypothesis, which treats aesthetic experience as having a metaphysical dimension. This hypothesis, ignored for the most part by modernist art theorists and critics otherwise indebted to Bell, leads shortly to claims that art is spiritual. Indeed, he says, art is a manifestation of the spirit of religion, though without being explicitly religious. Prior to that point, however, Bell frames the matter more philosophically. He asserts that when we respond to art as significant form, and therefore as an end in itself, we somehow obtain a sense of a deeper reality, of ultimate reality. That reality (evidently corresponding to Kant's unseen "noumenal" world behind the ordinary) is something we apprehend emotionally, in aesthetic experience. "The contemplation of pure form leads to a state of extraordinary exaltation," Bell writes; and it brings "complete detachment from the concerns of life" (p. 54). It is also revelatory. For it is in this experience that we become aware of the form's "essential reality, of the God in everything." Bell continues: "Call it by what name you will, the thing I am talking about is that which lies behind the appearance of all things—that which gives to all things their individual significance, the thing in itself, the ultimate reality" (p. 54).

That said, it is worth reiterating that, for Bell, art is not an expression of religion per se. Religion entails particular rituals and beliefs that are irrelevant to art as such. Yet Bell eventually declares that art and religion are twin manifestations of the same spirit (p. 63). There exists what he terms a "family alliance" between aesthetic and religious "rapture." In this extended sense, "all art is religious" (p. 68).

As we have noted, Bell acknowledges that not everyone will catch the essentially religious spirit of art, or what today would be termed its spirituality. Some will fail to do so because they confuse the external particulars of religious practice with the underlying spirit of religion. Others will miss out precisely because they have not learned to respond fully and deeply to art itself, to art as significant form; in short, they lack a certain capacity or acuity—what we might consider a kind of taste. But Bell believes that as long as one experiences the aesthetic emotion proper to art, nothing is lost by failing to see its religious roots.

When Bell discusses religion and art explicitly, he equates the source and the aim of art with the source and the aim of religion. The source of both is an imaginative sense of ultimate reality; the aim of both is ecstasy and a transformed sense of reality that removes one from worldly concerns. Religion is supposedly "an expression of the individual's sense of the emotional significance of the universe" (pp. 62–63), and Bell suggests that art is an expression of the same thing.

More or less subtly, therefore, Bell makes it possible to substitute art for religion. He expresses none of the nostalgia for religion that we find in Pater, and none of the poignant sense of the transitory nature of aesthetic moments. Bell seems unable to think of any reason for human beings to practice religion as such, as long as they have art. And he gives no reason why artists and art lovers need to think of the experience of art as religious, even if it is. He claims, rather, that the name for what is ultimately experienced in aesthetic emotion makes no difference: "Call it by what name you will." Even though Bell himself sees art and religion as twins, he prepares the way for artists and lovers of art to forget about religion entirely, by implying that religion offers nothing significant that they cannot have through art alone. From his perspective, it appears to be quite enough to love art well without confusing matters with religious doctrines and the "corrupt and stuttering expression" of "a thousand different creeds" (p. 69). The result is a virtual apotheosis of art.

Loving Art Purely

Two Trends

The approaches to art that we have just been examining tended to shift the love of religion to the love of art, partly by bequeathing to art the only assets of religion that were deemed worth saving: beautiful stories, poetic insights, patterns of symbolism, and exquisite feelings. These developments were harbingers of things to come in modern criticism and aesthetics. Indeed, they signaled two related and often concurrent trends. The first represents art (in the manner of Clive Bell) as a growth arising from the root system out of which religion sprung. The second represents art and religion as two different species of growth, with separate root systems and stems that earlier were intertwined because of having grown up together.

To understand more clearly where these notions fit in with modern ideas of art in general, we need to see their connection with two closely related lines of modernist theory of the arts—two forms of what I choose to call aesthetic purism. Even though these modern theories (and, lately, their postmodern rebuttals) quickly become technical and forbidding, many clues to their interpretation are provided already by the trends we have been discussing. We can therefore treat the pertinent theoretical developments succinctly. But treat them we must, because the thought patterns they represent have deeply influenced, and in some ways confused, even our ordinary efforts to understand what one loves when one loves art. (The need to sort out the pertinent issues surfaces every time a talented organist or former churchgoer says, "My religion is music," and really means it.)

Strict Purism

Students of aesthetics and literary theory will know that, until the last quarter of the twentieth century, nothing was more common than for theorists and critics to try to understand and appreciate art in its own terms, as itself and not another thing.[43] As already indicated, in aesthetics that has meant (until recently) the predominance of a purism that has appeared in two guises.[44] The stricter kind of purism—usually formalism of one sort or another—has treated art as a unique species of cultural activity. It has accepted something like Bell's hypothesis about significant form per se while rejecting his hypothesis about its metaphysical and religious import. When employed with subtlety and sophistication, as in the essays of the influential American art critic Clement Greenberg, purism of this sort takes into account the cultural and social matrix of art. But in evaluating art, it does not "confuse" social, historical, or moral issues with aesthetic ones. And it avoids the religious overtones heard in Ruskin, Pater, and Bell. Purism in this form could easily take as a motto Greenberg's words, used in describing modern sculpture in particular: "The arts are to achieve concreteness, 'purity,' by acting solely in terms of their separate and irreducible selves."[45] Or, as Archibald MacLeish said of literature, "A poem should not mean / But be."[46]

This means, of course, that to some extent strict purism has defied common sense. Poems do usually appear to be about something, to mean something. Paintings do often seem to represent something other than themselves. So strict purism has tried to convince us that this sort of meaning or manner of representation is finally done to create an aesthetic effect that is valuable or enjoyable in itself, apart from what the poem or painting appears to be "about." Ultimately the arts aspire to the condition of absolute music. Some just arrive there more directly than others. Art and taste (the "work of art" and the "aesthetic attitude") are essentially unrelated to other aspects of thought and experience, though the artwork may be constructed partly of historical, philosophical, or other materials. Even literature is basically self-referential and "auto-telic." As the linguist Roman Jakobson put it, the poetic function of language is to focus on the message not for referential purposes but for its own sake. Or, in the terms of formalist structuralism, a literary text is a closed system. Or again, to paraphrase some of the more "hard core" New Critics, literature is finally not about the world outside but about the fictive world it has constructed.[47] As the aesthetes of the turn of the previous century had already claimed, art exists for its own sake; and the pleasure one takes in art is *sui generis*.

Moderate Purism

The more moderate modes of purism have seen art as always somehow related to life, but in a unique fashion that sets it apart completely from any other form of cultural expression. Purists in this second mode often have drawn on ideas from their Romantic and German Idealist predecessors to speak of art as reaching beyond thoughts, or as expressing thoughts too deep (or too full of feeling) for words. Ernst Cassirer (1874–1945) and Susanne Langer (1895–1985) depicted art as a symbolic form altogether different from science or philosophy or religious thought. Thus, for Langer, art is a "nondiscursive" use of symbolic expression that gives form to the life of feeling—to tensions, movements, and rhythms of life. Without such artistic symbolism, she argued, there would be no vital religion, but what art provides is not yet fully religious. Similarly, philosophical idealists in the tradition of Benedetto Croce (1866–1952) and R. G. Collingwood (1889–1943) argued that art expresses particular perceptions or intuitions that constitute, as it were, the bottom of the mental food chain, making the other forms of mental life and expression possible. The more abstract forms of thought and the more complex forms of social organization feed continually on artistic expression. Art, however, does not use abstract concepts or serve social functions.

Seen in this way, art obviously does more than provide a unique sort of pleasure, though it may do that. Art also performs an indispensable and ongoing function in the life of the mind. So vital and highly evolved is this role of art that our food-chain analogy is in one way misleading. Although art may seem undeveloped and even primitive from a logical and scientific viewpoint, it is highly developed as an expressive means of opening up the subtleties of experience and making them "real" for us, for the first time. These are felt perceptions that tend to elude linear, abstract thinking. And that is why, according to such theorizing, art has no use for ideas as such, or for moral deliberation or religious commitment. It may respond to them, but it ceases to be art when it thinks abstractly or becomes engaged with life.

Martin Heidegger (1889–1976) and related phenomenologists (to employ the term loosely) took a different but not unrelated tack. Often using newly coined language, Heidegger pointed to the "originary" function of the work of art, indicating its capacity to disclose or unveil (in a uniquely veiled and inexplicable way) that which cannot be said plainly or thought unequivocally. For Heidegger, art opens up new possibilities of meaning and of being, calling attention to the radical particularity and irreducibility of what is, without grasping or controlling. Art thus makes available a world that transcends normal subject-object thinking and that therefore eludes logical, propositional language, and an instrumental, technological mentality.[48] Poetry gives us something vital in a time that (to speak poetically) exists between the era in which the gods fled and that in which they will return.

Such ways of imagining and valuing art have a venerable pedigree. Ever since Kant, one way of describing art has been to treat it as a kind of symbol language that, even in giving aesthetic pleasure, takes thought further than it could otherwise go, beyond the literally thinkable and sayable. Here is acknowledgment that, at some height or depth, art is immensely valuable to philosophy (or perhaps to genuine religion). Heidegger, for one, affirmed that truth is somehow "at work" in the work of art. And he was quite attached to the poet Hölderlin's assertion that "poetically, / Man dwells upon the earth." But dwelling is not philosophizing in the usual sense. And for Heidegger and his followers, art dwells at a distance from philosophical ideas and systems, and apparently from religious thought as well. Art's openness to the mystery of Being comes by way of means and ends that are purely its own.

In the past fifty years or more, those who have made a profession of studying literature have often adopted a moderate purism akin in spirit to what we have just described. New Critics such as Cleanth Brooks and Allen Tate, for instance, depicted literature as the use of special, "poetic" language. They described this language as organically unified and resonant with ambiguity and irony—a language of images, symbols, metaphors, fictions. What a poem (or any literary work) means is what it becomes as an integral whole, an art object like a well-wrought Grecian urn. For that reason, such critics insisted, the meaning of a work of literature emerges from close reading itself and cannot be paraphrased without leaving out its essence. A poem is not about ideas or even about "real life" emotions, but presents its own realities that are deeper or higher.[49] Literature thereby constitutes a special kind of cognition, an embodied and sensuous knowing.

Alternatively, the Neo-Aristotelians—sibling rivals of the New Critics—proposed to see literary art as a use of specific genres (tragedy, epic, lyric) to attain particular ends. But again the ends of art were seen as virtually unique. Art that is not sheerly didactic was supposed to constitute a special kind of *mimesis* giving a variety of pleasure that art alone can provide, which was usually described simply (if redundantly) as just the pleasure specific to creative "imitation." Although a poem might incidentally deal with things such as psychological themes or philosophical ideas, it allegedly puts them to strictly poetic use.[50]

Purist Principles Compared

It may be helpful to summarize: The stricter purists (nearly extinct) have pictured art in formalist terms, as essentially autonomous and with no inner or aesthetically significant relation to life or social reality (let alone to morality or religion). The more moderate purists (widely scattered but still abundant) have suggested that, insofar as art relates to life, it does so uniquely. As a special form of expression or as a special use of language, art offers something like a semblance of lived experience, or the world imagined freshly and uniquely by means of fictions and sensuously embodied ideas: organic wholes whose meanings are felt more than thought.

Whatever their particular strategies, both strict and moderate purists have tended to privilege and protect the realm of art. Religion, philosophy, morality, politics—these are all extrinsic to art. What exactly is intrinsic to art is harder to say, because nothing we can say can do justice to art; but whatever it is, art's inner purpose is not something that can be dictated by the theologian, moralist, or politician.

Purely Separating Art and Religion

Where does all this leave art in relation to religion, and the love of art in relation to religious devotion? Setting aside our botanical metaphors of root and stem, let us say that the stricter form of purist theory provides the final divorce papers for art and religion. If they ever again get together, it will be without license. And under any such temporary, ad hoc arrangement, they will retain their separate identities—as indeed they always have, albeit without the knowledge of the general public. Theirs was always a union in name only, perpetually unconsummated. Art might still do religion a favor now and again, or vice versa; but the aesthetic function of art, and the reason we love art as such, has nothing directly to do with its religious functions.

Like many of the stricter purists, moderate purists often have supposed that religion was formerly loved for reasons that can now be served better by art. But unlike the strict purists, moderates see that the connection between art and religion is real and persistent. Even so, they believe that art must be itself, which necessarily means being religious only indirectly or covertly. Religious symbols, stories, and themes have no special religious meaning when converted to the purposes of art. Their artistic purpose is to express, arouse, or focus aesthetic feeling. The connection with religion is mainly that the experience of art at its most profound is similar in kind to the feeling that gives rises to religious ideas, movements, and organizations. In this truncated sense artistic experience is religious—or spiritual, some would say. But one can just as easily call it aesthetic, and not mention religion or spirituality.

Some moderate purists—developing ideas hinted at in Arnold and beginning to flourish in Pater and Bell—have thought that religion might as well give up and become poetry, because religion at its heart is essentially a matter of feeling, and the only religious feeling worth preserving is expressed through the arts. What is most attractive about art, they have assumed, is akin to what is most attractive about religion; but religion in the cultural sense gets mired down in authoritarian structures, outworn creeds, and meaningless rituals.

Other moderate purists have allowed, intentionally or not, for the possibility that religion has legitimate tasks for which art in itself is unsuited. To an archetypal critic like Northrop Frye, for instance, art manifests concerns about life and society. But it does so as a kind of myth-language: hypothetically, and not directly. Unlike myth in its ideological and religious modes, however, art as such need not worry about engaging in actual moral deliberation, religious commitment, or theological interpretation. It deals rather in fictive possibilities and is therefore perfectly free to reshape as it wishes the limited number of primary story patterns that happen to relate to basic human concerns. Through its self-contained, secondary universe, literary art in particular explores those imaginative truths and patterns that indirectly inform our existence, enhancing the love of life. Thus literature does something that religion cannot do for itself. It invents and envisions at the level of sheer hypothesis. It pleases and plays with verbal design. And in doing so it refreshes the deeper spiritual springs through a renewal of the imagination.

What literature does not do, according to Frye's theories, is make moral choices, or really pray, or commit itself to what its words might mean outside the literary universe. Those things would alter the literary work's "centripetal" force that draws meanings into itself and creates a self-contained structure. Those other functions of language are for religion proper. When literary art is combined with religion, as in the Bible, it ceases to be literature, while remaining in some way literary. That being the case, however, religion is not necessarily rendered obsolete by literature itself, especially if it is religion that is undogmatic and nonauthoritarian, embracing its own crucial involvement in visionary mythmaking as Frye advocates.[51]

Taken as a whole, Frye's account of literary art is truly purist only at one point. What makes it purist is just his refusal to consider that it might be the function of some literature to assert in some manner, and to make claims on the reader. Because Frye is disinclined to recognize any properly literary function for certain kinds of "referential" language, this leads him to the purist conclusion that the Bible, whenever it stops being hypothetical, stops being literature. Were we to apply Frye's principle consistently, we would find it impossible to treat most of the Psalms as poetry. They all assert in some fashion, they exert pressures on the reader, and they reach beyond any self-contained poetic universe. To deny that they are poetry, on account of this, is indeed to cling to a purist principle.

Appraising Purism

The advantages of the various purist understandings of art are actually considerable. As perhaps the most sustained attempts in history to liberate art and to give art its due, they all preserve art's integrity, illuminate many of its special traits, and keep art from being reduced to politics or moralizing or preaching. Some purist theories also can be credited with acknowledging without embarrassment the ancient and ongoing alliances between art and religion, which seem too persistent and intense to be mere flings. There may be a natural connection, they say, because religion can always use its imagination refreshed and because art can always use its repertoire of symbols and subjects enriched.

A very real disadvantage of purist understandings of art, however, is the way in which even the moderate forms of purism divide up responsibilities between art and religion. Although a connection may be allowed at the level of preconceptual feeling, or at the level of sharing stories, there is little allowance for any thoroughgoing interaction between art and anything else, let alone actual belief and commitment. Such thinking cannot permit art *qua art* to make an overtly religious difference, or permit religious ideas and commitments to enter fully into the designs and aims of art. That is apparent from the sort of pronouncement one finds in the *New Catholic Encyclopedia* (1967), where, in the section on art and religion, we are told bluntly: "Art, even when it serves religion, is essentially concerned with beauty and with beauty only. . . . Art as such is autonomous."[52] The author of that statement evidently feared no contradiction. By then the view, which the author may have imagined to be medieval and scholastic in derivation, had become part of the modernist creed. But what was one to do with the horrific and grotesque painting of the Crucifixion in Grünewald's polyptych known as the *Isenheim Altarpiece*? Is this artwork, an acknowledged masterpiece, really "essentially concerned with beauty," and "with beauty only"? If it is expressive, is this a kind of expression that is essentially autonomous and therefore unrelated to religious belief and commitment?

The match, then, is far from perfect between purist art theory and the actual makeup and experience of art. Surely, whatever the intellectual suppositions of their makers, works such as the *Isenheim Altarpiece*, T. S. Eliot's *Four Quartets*, Benjamin Britten's *War Requiem,* and the AIDS memorial quilt all take into their very design as art the shaping and heightening of certain "real" responses to life and death. That is to say, in part, what T. S. Eliot himself said at one point (thereby contradicting some of his own purist pronouncements): "The author of a work of imagination is trying to affect us wholly, as human beings, whether he knows it or not; and we are affected by it, as human beings, whether we intend to be or not."[53]

Although it seems likely that Eliot's statement applies only to some art rather than to all, it gets to the heart of the problem with aesthetic purism of every sort. To be affected wholly is not to be affected only aesthetically, in the narrowest sense of "aesthetic" response: a delight in form or imaginative play for its own sake. Nor is it to be affected only at the level of feeling or purely intuitive knowledge, as though the feelings of profound artistic experience were ever utterly unaffected by, and had no effect on, convictions, commitments, and concepts. One is differently attuned and differently disposed after contact with certain works of art; one's ideas may begin to flow through new capillaries or even change direction. Any theory of art that leaves out the possibility for that kind of artistic engagement is too pure for its own good. And it is not good enough to account adequately for religiously significant art and taste.

Alternatives to the Pure Love of Art

Integrating the Love of Art with the Love of Religion

In view of its ever more apparent weaknesses, purism of every kind has in recent decades come under severe attack—along with much else that has come to us from the Enlightenment. One of the earlier lines of critical reaction stemmed from modern hermeneutics, particularly the work of Hans-Georg Gadamer (1900–).

In the course of reconsidering how understanding and interpretation transpire, Gadamer takes up the topic of taste, so often treated only implicity in modern theory. But Gadamer pictures taste not as a function of some highly distanced "cultured consciousness" concerned only for beautiful appearances, but as an outgrowth of the social life in which "what artists create and what the society values belong together in the unity of a style of life and an ideal of taste."[54] Gadamer thus rejects the "aesthetic differentiation" whereby the artwork loses all social and historical location.[55] And he calls into question the notion of an aesthetic consciousness removed from history and unconcerned with truth: "Since we meet the artwork in the world and encounter a world in the individual artwork, the work of art is not some alien universe into which we are magically transported for a time." Gadamer asks, rhetorically: "Is there to be no knowledge in art? Does not the experience of art contain a claim to truth which is certainly different from that of science, but just as certainly is not inferior to it? And is not the task of aesthetics precisely to ground the fact that the experience of art is a mode of knowledge of a unique kind?"[56] To these questions his own reply is unambiguous: "Art is knowledge and experiencing an artwork means sharing in that knowledge."[57]

Gadamer's approach, like that of certain moderate New Critics, is perhaps too quick to equate artistic experience with a special kind of knowledge—as though knowing were the primary element in one's response to a North Indian morning raga or even to the Taj Mahal. Moreover, Gadamer's treatment of artistic knowledge per se retains more than a hint of purism (albeit moderate), following Heidegger in making too sharp a distinction between the way truth "happens" in art and its other modes of appearing. Nevertheless, Gadamer provides one kind of theoretical leverage needed to move aesthetic experience back into relation to life.

How might we go further? One step further—and for now it is enough—is to realize that, as I have already suggested, there are gradations in the realm of the aesthetic. In art itself there are interactive and overlapping modes of thought and knowledge, and mixed forms of beauty (to borrow from Kant's allowance for "dependent" as well as "free" beauty). Some art, such as Bach's *Art of the Fugue*, may be prized for its own internal order above all; other art, such as the film *Babette's Feast* (Gabriel Axel, 1987), may be prized precisely because it engages "outside" interests such as those of religion and morality. One kind of art is not more aesthetic than the other. But their ways of being aesthetic are different.

I have argued along these lines, and in more detail, in previous books.[58] Needless to say, however, I have not been alone in proposing something like an integralist approach to aesthetics and art. One finds elements of this theory in John Dewey's *Art as Experience* (1934), for example.[59] Indeed, various aspects of such thinking about art are often assumed these days by those who pursue questions of religion, society, and the arts. But even today a truly integralist aesthetic is rarely articulated consistently, and hardly ever in terms of taste. And it now seems to me that an integralist approach is itself problematical if it overlooks genuine and profound tensions that emerge between art and religion. Certainly this oversight can occur if integralist approaches fail to take seriously enough Kierkegaard's sort of worry about art—as we are still endeavoring to do here.

Meanwhile, however, in the academy and in the world of art criticism, there is a related but more vehement line of attack on purism, which requires our attention. It is one that brings art back into contact with life. Yet in doing so, it gives little credence to aesthetic value as such and gives high visibility to the critical act itself. I am referring to the various contemporary approaches to culture and art now known collectively as postmodern (or poststructuralist).

Without pausing to decipher ideas that in some instances are notoriously difficult and nuanced with technical meaning, I nevertheless hope to map certain
strategies and claims that mark out paths that are significant here—paths taken
and paths not taken.

From the Love of Art to the Love of Criticism

To the extent that one can generalize, it seems fair to say that postmodern theories of culture do not see linguistic play, ambiguity, artifice, metaphor, and irony
as peculiar to art. Rather, they see these things as marks of contemporary, self-
critical consciousness and to some extent of all discourse. In contrast with the
high seriousness of much modernism, postmodern criticism and theory has
often been leery of depth, being more interested in playful and ironic surfaces, the interplay of texts, indeterminate meanings, and the force fields of
ideologies.

Postmodern theory tends to be iconoclastic, attacking the received images of
art, culture, religion, and rationality. In most of its forms, postmodern thought
tries to dispel the notion that there is any truly plain or "proper" sense firmly
established in language, any translucent referentiality, any reading apart from
misreading, or any perfectly reliable representation of reality, whether in art
or religion or philosophy. In denying any such "givens," postmodern theory
resists all totalizing systems—including theories that try to encompass all literary texts in a single system of interpretation—and all beguiling "supreme
fictions" (to borrow a term from the poet Wallace Stevens). Thus the most prominent representatives of postmodern thought—including Michel Foucault, Jean-
François Lyotard, Jacques Derrida, and the "Yale School" of deconstructionists
such as Paul de Man and J. Hillis Miller—have endeavored to undermine the
foundations of the fortress of Enlightenment reason and social theory, built on
assumptions of universally applicable, and universally acceptable, rational and
moral principles. Many postmodernists have largely replaced the question of truth
with questions of power and political persuasion. At the same time, they have
wanted to take apart what was left of the cathedral of religion, which they
have generally recognized at all only in its more authoritarian forms. For most
deconstructionists in particular, language about "God," as normally deployed in
religion and culture, epitomizes the futile "logocentric" and "onto-theological"
attempt to order the world metaphysically, to found a world centered on the
absolute and authoritative Word—typically as conceived in patriarchal terms.[60]

Postmodern criticism, instead of focusing on the organic harmony and integrity of the art object and its uniquely aesthetic mode of being, has paid more
attention to how art is perceived and used, to structural gaps often disguised
in the artwork, and to the impossibility of "pure presence" in artistic meaning

or being. Far from treating art and aesthetic theory as either disinterested or innocent, recent criticism has concerned itself with dismantling the ideologies of class, sex, and race that are embedded in art and in other cultural codes. Postmodern critics such as Paul de Man have attempted to expose an "aesthetic ideology" whereby the irrationalist mystique of the pure, organic work of art has been misapplied to the social and political sphere. In their view, that ideology has led to dehumanization, as individuals have been asked to sacrifice themselves for the sake of a "beautiful" ideal—and quite possibly for an idealized State seen as a beautifully organic entity, a veritable work of Art.[61] Postmodern theory has likewise called into question the supposedly universal claims of taste and the assumed status of the "classics" of the artistic canon. In point of fact, most ideological critics—particularly feminists and Marxists and various champions of multiculturalism—reject the whole notion of a pure, unprejudiced aesthetic taste, and likewise any sharp distinction between high art and low, or between art and other media. In that way they have joined with the more deconstructive theorists to remove art from its pedestal. Instead of privileging the work of art, in practice they have tended, if anything, to privilege the critical act, while in effect transposing the forbidding avant-garde styles of modern art into the idioms of cultural criticism and theory.[62]

Whereas modern theorists often pictured art as essentially about itself, as morally disengaged, and as uninterpretable in other terms—beyond paraphrase—postmodern thinkers such as Jean Baudrillard and Michel Foucault have been known to attribute much the same sort of self-enclosed character to culture and language in general. At times they have made it sound as though humanly perceived realities are, in their totality, linguistically and socially constructed, with language referring to nothing outside its own constructs. All reality is virtual, they have seemed to be saying. All is semblance and simulacrum. As various feminists, neo-Marxists, and other critics representing the latest in "ideology critique" have pointed out, the resulting relativism (ironically enough) can threaten to undermine any credible basis for protesting against injustice, oppression, sexism, or totalitarian propaganda.[63]

In the hypercritical atmosphere of postmodernity, the whole idea of loving art, not to mention loving art for the sake of God or the Church, seems more than a little naïve or passé. Yet, as we have seen, the stage had in some sense been set by modernism. By isolating and artificially elevating art, modernism itself over a period of time had already made art less approachable, and eventually less lovable. In a postmodern climate, at least the work of art has come to have a social location, and so to dwell among us. It is not entirely bad that art can no longer take such a superior stance vis-à-vis the rest of culture. There is reason to heed, as well, postmodern warnings about the prejudices of taste and aesthetic judgment. And there is much to commend the idea (which analytical philosophers had already derived from Ludwig Wittgenstein) that art has no one inviolable essence. Although, as various theorists have argued, the things we call "art" do bear important family resemblances, not the least of which are sensuous, formal, or imaginative qualities that are aesthetically "felt," the concept "art" is too elastic to denote any one and invariable set of defining characteristics.

But if what we call art has much internal variety in its nature and aims, and if aesthetic experience is not so uniform or airtight as modernist theories had supposed, there may be reason (*pace* de Man) to reconsider the love of various kinds of art in view of other longings and joys, including those of a religious sort. Our final move in the present chapter is to see this possibility through the eyes of the leading deconstructionist of our day.

Converting the Love of Art

To take the notion of loving art out of the realm of some purely disengaged aesthetic attitude, where it is often trapped, I want to call in another witness— a somewhat unlikely one in a work of Christian inquiry, since he is not only Jewish but also highly unorthodox. Even so, Jacques Derrida may assist us if we allow for a change in the manner of discourse, treating him as a kind of poetic philosopher, much as Kierkegaard was.

Derrida's book *Memoirs of the Blind* (1990/trans. 1993) contemplates images of blindness found in prints and drawings Derrida was invited to select for an exhibition at the Louvre Museum. These include, near the book's end, a sixteenth-century Flemish apocalyptic work called *Sacred Allegory*, by one Jan Provost (c.1470–1529). But Derrida's study is also concerned with artfully written texts, among them Augustine's autobiographical *Confessions*, which, as Derrida observes, is much occupied with sight and yet is filled with tears at every major turn. So Derrida looks deep down inside the eye that weeps and he meditates on the sort of semiblindness brought about by tears. He thinks about what the eye becomes when its sight is thus veiled. Pondering works of Christian artistry, Derrida views the eye within what he terms (somewhat opaquely) the "anthropo-theological space" of sacred allegory.[64] In this reading the eye and blindness function symbolically.

When he speaks of entering the space of sacred allegory, Derrida is evidently thinking not only of the allegorical (but to this day undecipherable) painting by Provost, but also of a whole system of Christian symbolism in which Augustine's thought likewise participates. Derrida is not, of course, prepared to accept this theological way of thinking at face value. He is interested in reading it differently, in deconstructing the allegedly tight structure of what it purports to be seeing and saying, so as to find what insinuates itself between the gaps.

Thus Derrida speculates, enigmatically as always: Perhaps as Augustine in the *Confessions* weeps for his deceased mother or for his son, or for many other things, the tears of grief and joy which well up and blind his eyes would constitute a welling up of nothing less than "the *truth* of the eyes, whose ultimate destination they would reveal." Derrida then describes this ultimate destination and truth of the eyes, of *human* eyes, at any rate. It is not to be able to gaze straight at the sun or at God or even at revealed Truth (as Christians have been prone to claim). It is "to have imploration rather than vision in sight, to address prayer, love, joy, or sadness rather than a look or a gaze. Even before it illuminates, revelation is the moment of the 'tears of joy.'" If so, human beings are destined to go beyond seeing and knowing by weeping (p. 126).

In other words—and here it is almost a shame to paraphrase Derrida, his phrasing is so much like poetry—there is sight on the one hand and blindness on the other: what structuralists call a binary opposition. What mediates is a third thing having to do with the eyes, but related both to sight and to blindness—namely tears, and the activity of weeping, which makes for a veiled kind of gazing (p. 127). What we have here is a revelatory or apocalyptic blindness, rather than blindness per se, and as such it is indifferent to blurred vision. The one blinded by weeping, as Augustine is, implores to know "from where and from whom this mourning or these tears of joy?" And this *act* of imploring already makes possible a kind of joy before the act ever becomes, *if indeed* it ever becomes, the longed-for vision of God. Such tearful imploring reveals the depths of human longing. It no longer has to do with ordinary sight, but with the conversion of sight (pp. 126–27).

Not accidentally, Derrida has led us into this phase of his discussion by considering Augustine's indictment of works of art, especially paintings, which Augustine in his *Confessions* refers to as "all these . . . additional temptations to the eye that men follow outwardly, inwardly forsaking the one by whom they [themselves] were made, ruining what he made of them." The delights of art are temptations not just for others but for Augustine himself, who says: "Finally I must confess how I am tempted through the eye. . . . The eyes delight in beautiful shapes of different sorts and bright and attractive colors." Derrida asks: "Would Saint Augustine thus condemn the temptations of *all* Christian painting?" And he answers: "Not at all, just so long as a conversion saves it" (p. 119).

The term "conversion" is not something thrown in only for effect. It is basic to the whole prolonged meditation that Derrida undertakes on eyes, blindness, tears, and sight.[65] Derrida reads Augustine in such a way as to say that conversion saves by a kind of blinding, thereby removing the sense of security and certainty given by sight, and by bringing forth imploring tears of insight. No longer does clear sight matter. But conversion does not lose sight of sight altogether, there being such a thing as memory of the visible world. Conversion is a way and process of seeing, perhaps of seeing art, or through art. "A Christian drawing should be a hymn, a work of praise, a prayer, an imploring eye" (p. 121), which amounts to "praying on the verge of tears" (p. 122). Art is no longer object but act. And conversion is not eradication but transformation having to do with what Derrida (on behalf of Augustine) terms making "the love of God grow within." This process appears to be at least one version of the same act that Derrida himself calls belief. He concludes his book with a quotation from Andrew Marvell, honoring the blind Milton, whom the poet has compared to the blind mythological seer Tiresias.

> Thus let your streams o'erflow your springs,
> Till eyes and tears be the same things:
> And each the other's difference bears;
> These weeping eyes, those seeing tears.

Derrida then has an unnamed interlocutor ask: "—Tears that see . . . Do you believe?" To which he replies, "—I don't know, one has to believe" (p. 129).

Which brings us back, for a moment, to Kierkegaard and Blake. What Kierkegaard sees in the love for art is desire that takes the form of unconverted vision. This is not unconverted vision in Derrida's sense, which among other things seeks certainty in revelation, and thus looks vainly for unmediated, direct knowledge of God. In Kierkegaard's discussion, the vision that is inadequate is attached, rather, to what is purely external, sensory, immediate in its pleasure, and finally superficial. Kierkegaard sees the limits of the purely aesthetic— in this case an immediate enjoyment of art for its own sake—and understands such an enjoyment of art to be sealed off from any direct commerce with the moral or the cognitive or the religious. Hence he judges that the very human taste for beautiful objects, and the enjoyment taken in freely exercising the imagination, is endless: the desire never ends. But it is not eternal: it leads back to itself. In pursuing art in such a way, artists and lovers of art do not give themselves to God. Nor, for that matter, do they feed the poor.

Blake, by contrast, sees art and imagination as already religious and moral. He discerns that some of the most important paths toward the love of God, of others, and of oneself as well, are disclosed through artistry and the imagination. What Blake does not see so clearly is that artistic vision is not inherently revealing. Without some sort of conversion, it can be religiously blind, however beautiful in other respects.

Derrida, for his part, shares the concern for finding a kind of vision (in several senses) that is transformed and transforming. This vision turns out to be a kind of blindness brought about by tears. Moreover, he sees—or I think he sees (one can never be sure)—that the tearful, apocalyptic, and hence converting sort of blindness can actually be brought about artistically, through autobiography such as the *Confessions* or through the paintings that Augustine thinks of as tempting. And those paintings really are tempting. Kierkegaard and Augustine are right about that. But the very powers that tempt are the powers that, when seen rightly, can penetrate the eye of mundane vision and virtually blind it; thus art can draw forth tears of grief and joy that express the greatest human yearning, the greatest human imploring possible, which seeks its source.

That source, from a Christian point of view, can only be God. "Our hearts are restless until they rest in Thee," to quote the familiar lines from the opening passage of the *Confessions*. Derrida is familiar—all too familiar—with this theological way of identifying the source and goal of our deepest yearning. But what counts for him is not seeing or reaching that Source, which is never present. What counts for him is the imploring, tearful, half-blind "making" that in joy and sorrow "grows the love of God." Such a revelation in the dark, as it were, takes place only when one loses the imagined possibility of direct vision and knows that one cannot know, but can only believe. Even so, as art is involved, this means that art can be a medium and agency that has ultimately to do with faith, and with what Augustine would call grace (hence the "joy" that Derrida mentions).

But is the taste for art, to begin with, always a deficient aesthetic desire that must first be converted, before art can reveal? Or does art itself act in any way to convert desire into a greater longing, a taste for the infinite? And if taste thirsts for God, why keep returning to art?

To pursue these questions may be taking things further than Derrida would want to go, though he plays poignantly with connections between tears, art, revealing blindness, and belief. In terms of our own project, the problem with stopping here is not only that Derrida obscures whatever commitments he has. It is also that he so little savors what is genuinely sensuous about art. Like many intellectuals, including a good many theologians, Derrida keeps his distance from the senses, even when commenting astutely on art, or on the supposed physicality of literature. What enters through his senses makes its impression and then is quickly drawn into the designs of intellection and verbal play. His is an imagination immersed in words.

Derrida makes no secret of it, really. In *Memoirs of the Blind* he touchingly confesses his anxieties about drawing—about either being able to draw or to look at drawing. He recalls that, growing up, he had felt jealous of an older, admired brother who produced graphite or India ink portraits and copies of pictures, all "religiously framed on the walls of every room." So the young Jacques renounced drawing, feeling himself called instead by the "graphics of invisible words." Even now, he says, "you can see very well that I still prefer them; I draw nets of language about drawing" (p. 37). And this in a book published in conjunction with a drawing exhibition that Derrida had been invited to organize, himself.

At the end of *Memoirs of the Blind* one has the sense that, despite hints to the contrary, the sensory and visibly aesthetic qualities of art are virtually surrendered in the celebrated moment of tears. The sensation of tears and weeping is converted into the idea of tears and of their meaning. Derrida gives sensory impressions and aesthetic perceptions a role mainly in memory, and without saying what that role is. To be sure, he is interpreting and deconstructing an allegory; and in this allegory, clinging to the sensory side of the aesthetic is supposed to be equivalent to giving in to the futile and finally superficial desire for sheer vision, presence, and clear (but in fact unobtainable) revelation of God's truth. It is unfaith, if I may put it that way. But what is the aesthetic sensorium outside the space of this allegory? What gives art its power?

What remains to be seen at present, then, is how the taste for art precisely as aesthetic feeds and is fed by the thirst for the invisible God. By attending to such things, while keeping in mind the considerable insights of ancient and modern theories and practices of art, we can hope to answer more fully Kierkegaard's objections to religious art and to qualify more carefully Blake's otherwise unqualified embrace of art as religious. Then we can hope to see why the art that one loves can bring tears of deep imploring and joy. These tears come not from the eye alone, but from the heart, testifying, finally, not just to a specific desire, but to an infinite longing and anticipation—a thirst for God.

FOUR

The Taste for Art and
the Thirst for God

Reorientation

The last chapter ended with a rather strenuous climb toward a vision of what we might call artistic conversion—religious conversion of and through artistic experience. The route was a bit tortuous, as we used Jacques Derrida as a kind of guide. Pausing to get our bearings, we recall that in the modern era it has been difficult to find a viable religious approach to art or taste, and largely because of the way that art has been pictured.

Not that there has been only one picture to work with. One option available since the late eighteenth century and the rise of Romanticism has been to picture art as something that by its very beauty, sublimity, or expressive power is at least quasi-religious. If such an image were altogether valid, a taste for art would always involve some sort of yearning for a higher joy, and possibly for the infinite. But that sort of Romantic theory fails to distinguish what, to be sure, cannot always be divided—aesthetic and religious yearning (or delight). Consequently it obscures something that we need to hold on to: religion is not just about aesthetics, nor is aesthetics always about religion.

In modern times it has been more common among academic theorists to picture art as something that is *not* religious at heart, but instead purely aesthetic (though a remarkably good substitute for religion). And if art does incidentally touch on something else such as religion, it supposedly does so only at the level of feeling, for the sake of aesthetic expression, without taking ideas or commitments seriously. But if that were completely true, a taste for art would have nothing to do with anything outside art. We would then have no reason to suppose, as almost everyone does nowadays, that art has anything to offer spirituality. And we should never have set out on this particular excursion.

Most recently, various postmodern alternatives have appeared that have displaced the aesthetic image of art in favor of one that is primarily political, social, and economic. Art has then become a matter chiefly for social analysis and cultural critique, with special attention to class, race, and gender. While bringing ideological factors into view that otherwise would remain disguised, postmodern approaches often miss what is distinctive about art. That happens when they overlook ways in which its aesthetic traits—the ones we first "taste"—transform and remake our other concerns, whether religious or social.

Hence the need for what I think of as a genuinely integralist approach to art and aesthetics, and to taste as well. Such an approach recognizes that when we love art, we focus on it attentively and aesthetically. That is to say, we attend closely to the look and sound and feel of things—the formal and expressive qualities of the medium—and to the imaginative weaving of stories that capture and enrapture selves and communities. The demands and intrinsic rewards of that attention are unique—if not exactly in kind, then in degree. Nothing else is quite like enjoying a Georgia O'Keeffe painting, a film by Akira Kurosawa, or a novel by Toni Morrison. (And these enjoyments are themselves rather different in kind.) Attending to art is not, therefore, just one more way of doing "business as usual," whether political or religious or recreational. But the satisfaction is not only intrinsic (which can be said of sports, too); it is peculiarly whole. An integralist approach to art recognizes that what we relish (or not) in attending to art is an outgrowth and transformation of all that makes us human, including our loves, fears, and fantasies.

As we now proceed further along our path, we will look for ways in which the distinctive and virtually unique traits of our enjoyment of art merge with—and diverge from—religious concerns and loves. We will be asking: What connection is possible between the taste for art and the thirst for God?[1] Between, one might say, a love for the visibly artistic and a love for the invisibly Holy?

The likelihood that there is such a connection, and perhaps more than one, is something we have envisioned all along. We last caught sight of a significant relation between the two tastes—artistic and religious—in pondering Jacques Derrida's difficult but tantalizing meditations on art, blinding tears, conversion, and Augustine's *Confessions*. In view of Derrida's discussion, although without his sanction, we can now perhaps venture to say that, at its highest, the taste for art can become an affair not of "tasting," merely, but also of somehow praying and praising. Literally or figuratively tearful, there is a kind of artistic vision that arises from the deepest imploring (and adoring) known to human being. In this mode, our engagement with art participates in a spiritual conversion whereby aesthetic taste is transformed into something more: into faithful longing and joyful anticipation of a kind that Christians call "eschatological" and perhaps "apocalyptic." The conversion of aesthetic perception and judgment, like Paul's blinding on the road to Damascus, can in the moment mark a profound if incomplete end (Greek *eschaton*) of one's everyday vision of things. And that sense of ending is also a new beginning, providing a brief foretaste and revelation (*apocalypsis*) of a new order within or beyond the old—yet without yielding a sheerly unmediated vision of God.

We have to admit that these answers are still preliminary. The view from here is still none too clear. But perhaps we could not expect more—nor, indeed, quite this much—from Derrida himself, who characteristically remains cryptic, and indefinite about his commitments.[2] Having come this far, we bid Derrida a grateful adieu, as Dante did to Virgil on a journey more arduous, but not unlike our own. We seek now to understand more fully, on the one hand, what it is about the love of art that can interfere with religious transformation and that therefore needs conversion; and, on the other hand, what it is about art that, nonetheless, can play a role both in converting taste and in converting religion itself to something less constricted and more richly imagined. Along the way, we will take the time to examine the recurrent but potentially confusing claim that all art is essentially religious or that, ultimately, all beauty is of God and therefore deserving of love.

With Dante, we accept that the ultimate goal is truly love divine, the love that moves the sun and the other stars and, indeed, everything that lives and moves and has being (*Paradiso* XXXIII; Acts 17:28). We want to see how the love of God feeds, and is fed by, the love of art. At this juncture we look for further guidance from scripture and theology—especially the theology of Augustine (354–430) as he argues with himself about the religious meaning of beauty and of love.

Loving Beauty Religiously

Religious yearning and artistic creation have a long history together. They converge memorably in the ancient Hebrew poem that we know as Psalm 42, which in English begins:

> As a deer longs for flowing streams,
>   so my soul longs for you, O God.
> My soul thirsts for God,
>   for the living God.
> When shall I come and behold
>   the face of God?
> My tears have been my food
>   day and night,
> while people say to me continually,
>   "Where is your God?" (NRSV)

The language of the Psalms can certainly be considered poetry (although it has not always been seen that way). Of this particular poem, which continues through to the end of Psalm 43, a recent commentator has written: "The pen of a master poet is exhibited here: in the intricate structure, the correspondence of imagery and mood, the play on words and sounds, and the momentum forward."[3] One can point to other literary traits: the progression of thought in pairs of parallel phrases (idea couplets, as it were), and the use of vividly figurative language that pictures longing as thirst, and tears as food. Even when the translated text (like the original Hebrew) is not set forth on the page in the manner we identify with poetry, it forms a rhythmic pattern for thought, letting the mind collect itself and return to its senses. Some modern literary theorists would call this use of language "expressive." It also has a kind of beauty. It has a savor, although for some readers it might be an acquired taste.

It would be hard to imagine that Kierkegaard could complain of this artistry that it disengages and distances one from religious commitment. The art of this psalm does not fit that description at all. It is no more disengaged than prayer is; indeed, it *is* a kind of prayer, a prayer of supplication. One wonders (*pace* Kierkegaard): could not a painting of the Crucifixion be equally a prayerful supplication—at least in the hands of some artists, and in the eyes of some viewers?

But if such things can be acts of faith or prayer, what is the point of their being artistic? Why should prayer ever want to take shape artfully, or art ever want to take shape prayerfully? What do we want from art, when we use it religiously? And what does art want from religion?

Such questions cannot be answered well without looking more closely at the traits of art, especially the matter of beauty. I have already pointed out that it is a mistake to suppose that art of every sort is concerned only with beauty. And no one believes that beauty has only to do with art. But there is no denying that the taste for art is often a taste for beauty of one kind or another. Furthermore, the religious use of art is in part an expression of the religious desire for its beauty, just as the religious fear of art is likewise in large part a fear of its beauty. No treatment of the religious taste for art can ignore beauty, therefore.

Understandably, Augustine is a theologian who often figures prominently in theological discussions of beauty and love. In a famous, climactic passage in the *Confessions* he addresses God with these words:

Late have I loved you, beauty so old and so new: late have I loved you. And see, you were within and I was in the external world and sought you there, and in my unlovely state I plunged into those lovely created things which you made. You were with me, and I was not with you. The lovely things kept me far from you, though if they did not have their existence in you, they had no existence at all. You called and cried out loud and shattered my deafness. You were radiant and resplendent, you put to flight my blindness. You were fragrant, and I drew in my breath and now pant after you. I tasted you, and I feel but hunger and thirst for you. You touched me, and I am set on fire to attain the peace which is yours.[4]

A master rhetorician, Augustine here crafts his prose almost in the manner of poetry. Augustine speaks metaphorically not only of seeing God's radiance (a perennial feature of spiritual literature), but also of breathing in God's fragrance, of tasting God, of hungering and thirsting for God (imagery clearly borrowed from the Psalms). He employs the language of yearning, a yearning all the more intense for having known moments in which the thirst was truly but briefly assuaged. The hint of divine fragrance, the taste of divine presence, the glimpse of divine beauty—these perceptions of the sacred all address the spiritual senses and awaken them to a greater longing, hunger, and thirst than before.

Augustine accepts such moments as a genuine foretaste of the ultimate fulfillment and joy in God—even if his discomfort with the very physical connotations of "taste" itself disposes him to favor hearing and, especially, sight as the exemplary spiritual senses. But what have any of these spiritual senses to do with the created and external loveliness that Augustine had earlier plunged into, and in which he had lost himself for so long? That loveliness derives from God, he acknowledges, but it did not, of itself, lead him to God. Why not? Could it have done so, if his aesthetic taste had not been so predisposed to savor only the outer layers, as it were, of those perceptible beauties? Could a taste for visible and audible art ever nurture the "spiritual senses," and indeed become spiritual itself?

Such questions arise pointedly when Augustine asks himself, "What is it, then, that I love when I love my God?" In loving God, he asserts, he is not loving "beauty of body nor transient grace, not this fair light which is now so friendly to my eyes, not melodious song in all its lovely harmonies, not the sweet fragrance of flowers or ointments or spices, not manna or honey, not limbs that draw me to carnal embrace: none of these do I love when I love my God."[5] And yet, he says, loving God does mean loving a kind of light, voice, fragrance, a food and an embrace—of the inmost self, where "something not snatched away by passing time sings for me."[6]

The object of Augustine's love is clearly higher than anything earthly, as he goes on to make plain. It is not the earth or sea or sun or stars. But these lower things, being made by God, tell of God by their beauty.[7] As Augustine will later affirm in the *City of God*, "The very order, disposition, beauty, change, and motion of the world and of all visible things silently proclaim that it could only have been made by God, the ineffably and invisibly great and the ineffably and invisibly beautiful."[8] This passage echoes one of Augustine's favorite scriptures, Romans 1:20, which declares that, ever since the creation of the world, God's "eternal power and divine nature, invisible though they are, have been understood and seen through the things he has made" (NRSV). But Augustine specifically names beauty as part of the goodness of the created order, which is not explicit in Romans. In highlighting beauty, Augustine reflects the influence of the Neo-Platonism of Plotinus (c. 205–270); but he may also have in mind another biblical passage, which he cites elsewhere—the thirteenth chapter of the Wisdom of Solomon (from the "Apocrypha"), which declares that "from the greatness and beauty of created things comes a corresponding perception of their Creator" (Wis. 13:5).[9] The idea of divinely created beauty is also at least implicit in Genesis, where God pronounces creation "good"—which the Greek translators who produced the Septuagint (Augustine's Greek Old Testament) rendered as *"kala,"* meaning "beautiful" or "good" in a very general sense.[10]

Now, if God made everything beautiful in its way, and if artists likewise make beautiful things—fictive worlds, designs, and representations—one might suppose that Augustine would conclude resoundingly that artists in their work are actualizing a God-given capacity latent within us all, and one that derives specifically from our having been made in the image of God. Augustine himself describes the world as a beautiful poem made by God. And as a matter of fact God is rather widely seen in the Middle Ages (and thereafter) as what we might think of as the Artist par excellence, the supremely knowledgeable and skillful maker of a world whose order is beautiful in the extreme.[11] That can be taken as a compliment and encouragement to artists, even if the emphasis in the Middle Ages is often placed on the rational knowledge and wonderful skill required for God's world-making, rather than on what we today would consider aesthetic imagination.

Alternatively, we might reasonably expect Augustine to conclude that loving all things bright and beautiful (works of art, for example) would be a reliable way of honoring or loving God, or at least of pointing oneself in God's direction, since God is the very fount of beauty. As our earlier discussion of Abbot Suger shows, that sort of claim likewise plays a part in Christian thought from the time of Augustine onward.

Acknowledging the reality of divine artistry and the divine call of beauty, Augustine is nonetheless too ambivalent about artistic and earthly beauty to embrace such straightforward affirmations without serious qualification. He would be the last person to forget that the very passage in the Wisdom of Solomon that speaks of the testimony of delightful beauty cautions against idolatry. Yet his ambivalence is itself instructive. For one thing, it may suggest to us that there was something a little misleading about our earlier division of Christians into opposing camps, the Friends of Kierkegaard and the Friends of Blake. If Augustine is any indication, Christians in either camp may well experience within themselves a certain amount of inner conflict. In this regard it is noteworthy that Kierkegaard himself wrote artistically and thought poetically, sometimes as he waxed eloquent in rejecting the religious pretensions of artistry. Indeed, in the first volume of *Either/Or,* Kierkegaard depicts quite convincingly the love that his fictitious author professes for opera, and particularly for Mozart's *Don Giovanni*—however sharply Kierkegaard himself would want to criticize the aesthetic life of sensuous immediacy that Don Juan and his music allegedly exemplify.[12] Augustine, for his part, writes with evident delight about artistic and sensuous beauties (especially those that please the eyes or that caress the ears), sometimes in the very passages in which he condemns them as seductive.

If such tensions are to be found within many Christians, it is all the more important to see how they play themselves out in the work of Augustine, whose influence on Christian thought has been almost as great as that of Plato on philosophy. Although Augustine's ambivalence toward earthly and artistic beauty is partly due to unresolved inconsistencies in his thought and life, it also comes from an authentic struggle (not unlike Kierkegaard's) to identify very real temptations that are specific to the realm of aesthetic taste. Those temptations are ones we cannot afford to gloss over in our eagerness to incorporate the love of art and beauty more fully into the life of Christian faith.

The Temptations of Art and Beauty

As early as the *Confessions*, but likewise in passages scattered throughout his voluminous works, Augustine gives us many reasons for exercising suspicion and caution in the realm of perceptible or imaginative beauty, the beauty that we perceive in nature and in much of art.

To begin with, beauty that we perceive through our senses—as contrasted with the highest intellectual or spiritual beauty—is necessarily mutable and transitory rather than changeless and eternal. As Augustine is aware, the Bible itself reminds us that the flower fades and the grass withers (Isaiah 40:7). Furthermore, the beauty seen by the eyes (or heard by the ears) has many forms and degrees rather than being one and absolute. Solomon arrayed in all his glory could not have matched the beauty of the lilies of the field (Luke 12:27). But their beauty in turn cannot be compared to that of the eternal Christ (or else the Church)—the Rose of Sharon and the Lily of the Valley, as patristic and medieval Christians deduced from an allegorical reading the Song of Solomon

(2:1). Augustine argues, therefore, that the beauty which appeals to our senses and human imaginations (as distinguished from our intellects) is deficient. It is deprived of full reality. As he says in Book 7 of the *Confessions*, "Contemplating other things below you [God], I saw that they do not in the fullest sense exist, nor yet are they completely non-beings: they are real because they are from you, but unreal inasmuch as they are not what you are."[13] The Christian cannot rest content, therefore, with loving physical and sensuous beauty. Even when untainted by falsity, earthly beauties are deficient because of their finitude and imperfection. The delight they provide is strictly limited and temporary. What is worse, such beauty is relatively superficial, more outer than inner.

To be sure, even beauty that appeals to our senses and imaginations can provide a rung for our ascent up the spiritual ladder, because, as we have noted, even that beauty can reflect or transmit something of the divine. In the *Confessions* Augustine states that "the beautiful objects designed by artists' souls and realized by skilled hands come from that beauty which is higher than souls; after that beauty my soul sighs day and night (Ps. 1: 2)." It is "from this higher beauty [that] the artists and connoisseurs of external beauty draw their criterion of judgement."[14] Unfortunately, as Augustine is then quick to point out, people "do not draw from there a principle for the right use of beautiful things." The principle he refers to is that they should not go to excess in their love of material beauties (*pulchra*) made by human beings but should, rather, save their strongest love for God. To cling to such lower forms of beauty, as people so often do, is to love them disproportionately. But the Christian life is nothing if not a commitment to order one's loves appropriately. As for why we find external beauty so alluring, Augustine attributes that to concupiscence—"the lust of the flesh which inheres in the delight given by all pleasures of the senses (those who are enslaved to it perish by putting themselves far from you [God])."[15]

If the right ordering of our loves is so important, we are bound to wonder just how much enjoyment of art and earthly beauty is permissible, and at what point it becomes excessive. Recalling that Augustine chose a celibate and semi-cloistered life after his conversion, on the assumption that such restraint would be required for fully Christian dedication, we can expect his ideals to be rigorous, with more than a touch of asceticism. And so they are. He complains in the *Confessions* that artists and artisans have entrapped our eyes by making clothing, vessels, pictures, and images of various kinds, many of which "go far beyond necessary and moderate requirements and pious symbols."[16]

Augustine admits that sometimes he errs on the side of "too much severity." He has sometimes gone so far, for instance, as to "wish to banish all the melodies and sweet chants commonly used for David's psalter from my ears and from the Church as well."[17] A better and more moderate course in worship, he proposes, would be to have the psalm chanted in a manner closer to reciting than to singing.

Yet, immediately after settling on this course of aesthetic moderation (which to us may still seem more severe than moderate), Augustine again vacillates, seemingly in the moment of writing. Almost relieved that in worship he is now more moved by the words that are sung than by the singing itself, he nevertheless recalls appreciatively the early days of his Christian life when tears poured out of his eyes while he rejoiced in the sung melodies. "Thus I fluctuate between the danger of pleasure and the experience of the beneficent effect, and I am more led to put forward the opinion (not as an irrevocable view) that the custom of singing in Church is to be approved, so that through the delights of the ear the weaker mind may rise up towards the devotion of worship." Even then, "If the music moves me more than the subject of the song, I confess myself to commit a sin."[18]

Augustine was not the only one in his day to have mixed feelings about the usefulness of music in worship. Henry Chadwick informs us that churches in Augustine's homeland of North Africa disagreed at that time on the whole question of whether music should be admitted to worship and, if so, of what kind.[19] Such controversy surely reflected larger questions regarding the relation of church to world, and of the spiritual to the physical.

Augustine, however, is not just concerned about church music, nor about music in general. He also disapproves of pagan myths and the "telling of idle tales."[20] And he censures theaters, where actors indulge false emotions, where the audiences relish the "repulsive" imitation of suffering in tragedy (which he himself so enjoyed in former years), and where people of loose morals imbibe the licentious atmosphere of comedy.[21] In much the same vein, Augustine denounces activities that strike us as rather far removed from the arts, such as sporting events and bloody gladiator shows.[22] And he does so without pausing to distinguish between that sort of pursuit and the pursuit of aesthetic beauty.

Clearly the theologically discriminating and ascetic side of Augustine fights with the side of him that not only appreciates the beauty he perceives but also rejoices in it personally and religiously. That leaves us with the task of trying to sort out which of his temptations to treat as peculiar to his personality and cultural situation, and which to treat as exemplifying persistent issues and dangers. We cannot identify the most persistent temptations, however—and they all have to do with misguided love—unless we understand more clearly how an Augustinian might suppose the love of art could ever be in accordance with the love of beauty that is beyond all human art. Adopting Augustine's ideas, and modifying them at crucial points, we will begin to see how to classify and evaluate tastes in artistic and earthly beauty, and what to make of the persistent but problematical idea that all beauty or art is religious.

The Love of God and the Lure of Beauty

Beauty's Goal, for God's Sake

Nothing is more common in modern theories of art than to assert in some fashion that we enjoy art for its own sake. It is a claim that seems to follow naturally from the related idea, found in Kant and indeed in antiquity, that we love what is beautiful simply because it is beautiful, and thus delightful in itself. The modern philosopher Alfred North Whitehead (1861–1947) even goes so far as to assert that beauty is "the one aim which by its very nature is self-justifying."[23] Whitehead is careful to add that beauty, in the absence of truth, occupies a lower level, just as truth in the absence of beauty sinks to triviality. Yet he maintains that "Truth matters because of Beauty,"[24] which in his view (though not in his words) is basically the intrinsically satisfying harmony of things as they exist and develop in right relation to each other and to the larger whole.[25]

Augustine in his Christian years never says that we should love human art for its own sake. That kind of love should, in his mind, be reserved for God. But Augustine will not be outdone in the praise of beauty; for he sees beauty— along with truth and goodness—as having its acme and source in the being of God. And the highest beauty, absolute beauty, is truly divine (albeit invisible), and therefore does deserve loving for its own sake. The heart's vision of God, of the beautiful but invisible Light, is our supreme reward, which is actually nothing other than an enjoyment of God and of each other in God.[26] And so it may be said that "our whole business in this life is to restore to health the eye of the heart whereby God may be seen."[27]

What the eye normally sees includes, however, some things that are anything but beautiful. There is both visible ugliness and moral ugliness. It is true that, having rejected Manichean dualism, Augustine insists that everything that exists is to some extent good.[28] After all, everything is made by God. Augustine also believes that everything that exists is to some degree beautiful, because God is beauty, and everything has its being in God; it participates at some level in God's reality. Augustine recognizes, however, that beauty exists in gradations. The lower we descend on the scale of reality, the lesser the quality of the beauty that we behold. Indeed, we on earth could be in danger of fixating so on the apparent ugliness and sinful corruption of some parts of the world that creation itself would appear flawed, which would in turn reflect badly on the Creator.

To prevent any such error on our part, Augustine argues that what counts fundamentally is the beauty of the overall design. Beauty derives from the balancing of contrasts and from the unity, order, rhythm, and harmony of the whole. As the Wisdom of Solomon proclaims, God has "arranged all things by measure and number and weight" (Wis. 11:20). There are indeed terrible monsters the mere sight of which "could kill by fright" (Wis. 11: 19b). Yet even these and other ugly monstrosities, when seen in their larger context, make a contribution to beauty.[29]

From there it is but a short step to Augustine's controversial "solution" to the problem of evil: That which appears evil and ugly when seen in isolation, and from our human perspective, is good when seen from the high vantage point of divine providence, which surveys the whole beautiful pattern of the "mosaic floor." Switching to a musical metaphor: that which sounds dissonant when heard in isolation contributes to the larger harmony.[30]

In these passages Augustine evidently contemplates something that can fairly be described as the aesthetic dimension of the redemption of creation. That the apparent ugliness of evil could and must be absorbed into the larger pattern of beauty, when viewed from a higher standpoint, accords with Augustine's insistence that evil has no independent reality, that it is finally a deprivation, a lack of goodness: "For you [God] evil has no being at all, and this is true not of yourself only but of everything you have created."[31] The attempt to weave apparent evil and ugliness into the beauty of the whole fabric of creation presents difficulties of its own, since it can seem to "aestheticize" and trivialize evil and suffering. Yet it does at least make it possible for Augustine and his theological progeny to avoid a strict dualism that, like that of the Manichees, would reject the material world as inherently evil and ugly.

If everything is in some sense good and beautiful from the very beginning and in the last analysis (eschatologically), then evil has no final claim even on what is material and finite. Indeed, the implication is that even hell, insofar as it exists, must contribute to a beautiful eternity for God and the saints. Augustine thus sets the tone for Anselm of Canterbury (c. 1033–1109), who, in explaining why God became human in Christ, takes it as a basic premise that God could not allow any evil to mar permanently the beauty of God's world and eternal plan.[32] Augustine and Anselm both ascribe to beauty an objective and eternal reality in God and see it as integral to salvation.

More to the present point, Augustine himself makes beauty pivotal in his whole concept of the final goal of the cosmos and human existence. Far from treating beauty at its highest as any sort of temptation, he treats it as essential to God's final design and to the ultimate satisfaction of the human soul. As such, beauty is integral to the being of God, the Alpha and Omega of history: "Late have I loved you, beauty so old and so new."[33]

Beauty, Body, and Spirit

But what, if anything, connects that ultimate beauty with the beauty of art or of nature? If only the highest beauty, God's beauty, is to be loved for its own sake, in what way are we to love beauty that is perceived by the bodily senses or created by the imagination?

With respect to the value of art and sensuous beauty, we have already seen that Augustine vacillates, in the manner of much neo-Platonic philosophy. On the one hand, even artistic beauty participates in the divine and can lift one toward the spiritual realm. On the other, such beauty is a kind of veil. It appeals more to the flesh than to the spirit, to the lower desires more than to the higher, to what is external more than to what is internal. In that way artistic and earthly beauty seduces one, deluding one into thinking it will be sufficient for happiness. In addition, human art can trap one with lies and false representations and can stir up inappropriate passions. Consequently, one easily forgets that one should not love such things for their own sake, but only for God's sake. They are for use (*uti*), not for enjoyment (*frui*) on their own account.

While indebted to Platonic philosophy, Augustine's line of thought, with its recourse to a series of polarities, draws equally on terms and concepts from the Bible, especially Paul: "Live by the Spirit, I say, and do not gratify the desires of the flesh" (Gal. 5:16). "Those who belong to Christ Jesus have crucified the flesh with its passions and desires" (Gal. 5:24). "Even though our outer nature is wasting away, our inner nature is being renewed day by day. . . . because we look not at what can be seen but at what cannot be seen" (2 Cor. 4:16, 18). "All of us, with unveiled faces, seeing the glory of the Lord as though reflected in a mirror, are being transformed into the same image from one degree of glory to another; for this comes from the Lord, the Spirit" (2 Cor. 3:18).

These and many other biblical descriptions of Christian temptation and aspiration could easily reinforce Augustine's disposition (Platonic and, earlier, Manichean) to deprecate what is sensory, outer, and material in favor of a more spiritual ascent from one degree of glory to another. It is true that early Christianity, like ancient Judaism, tended by and large to think of the soul as the unity of a human person, not as something separate from the body. It is also true that even in Paul's writing the "flesh" that is opposed to the "spirit" stands not just for physical desires but for sinful urges and vices that are nonphysical, such as hatred, envy, and pride. But the dualistic influence of the Hellenistic world is evident in the polarity Paul sets up between flesh and spirit, and in Paul's very choice of the term "flesh" to denote sinful urges of every kind.

Again, it is true that the Incarnation—which Christians naturally regard as the highest honor accorded to embodied human existence—is said to have had about it a visible glory, "full of grace and truth" (John 1:14). Augustine even speaks of the incarnate Christ as "beautiful on the Cross; beautiful in the Sepulchre."[34] Yet in Paul, especially, the Incarnation itself is also undeniably associated with the voluntary humiliation, and indeed self-emptying, of God on the Cross (Phil. 2: 5–8). This, too, Augustine recognizes, acknowledging that the beauty of Christ is an inner beauty that becomes profoundly hidden in the apparent ugliness and deformity of Christ crucified.[35] And though the physical body of the believer is to be raised in imperishable, spiritual glory, Paul says it was "sown in dishonor" (1 Cor. 15:42–43). However glorious and eternal the resurrected and glorified body of Christ, and of anyone raised in Christ (1 Cor. 15:42–50), it is still the body of the crucified or entombed Christ that most often epitomizes for Christians what human flesh per se comes to.

It is entirely understandable, then, that Augustine's first impulse as a Christian living in late antiquity is to say that the spiritual senses are *not* in any way physical. The fragrance, taste, touch, sound, and sight that is truly spiritual is without body. Stopping there would certainly minimize, however, the possibilities of blessing the beauties of artistry and of the natural creation. We might still have a theological "aesthetic." We could freely love intellectual or spiritual beauty insofar as it depended in no way on the senses and sensuous imagination. And we could look in a kindly way on the art and beauty around us to the extent that they can somehow be used to lift us completely beyond themselves, as pointers or analogies to be left behind on one's ascent. To treat such a spiritualized notion of beauty as aesthetic is to stretch the term, however, since aesthetics is by definition concerned in some way with "perceptibles."

In any case, art and nature appeal to us in a manner that is more palpably aesthetic. One cannot love art without in some way lingering with and attending to the senses and to sensuous imagination. Only as we employ and cultivate a taste that is receptive in this way can art manage to create an aesthetic feel by rendering the particulars of experience—the blade of grass, the look of dismay, the sense of a lost love—through a certain sonority, color, form, temporal flow, and the like. And only so can we enter the narrative and descriptive worlds of art, which are both like and unlike anything on earth. All this belongs to what Augustine thinks the truly spiritual realm is not. At least the ascetic and intellectual in him thinks that. Whereas, one might argue, it is all in fact pertinent to the very possibility of a rich and encompassing spiritual vision for creatures such as ourselves.

At least in principle, however, the step that is required now in order to return spirituality more fully to its aesthetic senses is not so very big. We can already agree with Augustine that the spiritual senses are not physical, if by that we mean merely that they are not *only* physical, or *merely* material, in some purely mundane sense. (It would be better actually to say that, however.) We can also agree that there must be some connection (symbolic or analogical at the very least) between beauty that is sensuous or imaginative and beauty that is spiritual.

That still does not necessarily recognize, however, a truly integral connection between our spiritual senses and anything sensuously aesthetic. From time to time, Augustine seems to glimpse something like that possibility as well. We could look, for instance, to his various comments on the dual veiling and revealing of sacraments and symbols, even though Augustine's treatment typically stresses verbal signification more than embodiment.[36] More significant for our purposes (though perhaps no less ambiguous) is the spiritual value Augustine sometimes places on physical sight, if faithfully converted.

As Margaret Miles has argued, Augustine can be found saying that the eye of the body and the eye of the mind can be unified in spiritual vision, at least for those with discipline and training.[37] Divine illumination comes from God, of course, and not simply from ourselves. But we are not sheerly passive recipients. Our wills, once energized by God, enable us to walk by faith. And though faith is more than sight, it makes of sight something special. In Augustine's words, you must have a willingness "to prepare the means of seeing what you love before you try to see it."[38] And what would a perfected spiritual use of physical vision be like? Augustine ventures to answer that question near the end of the *City of God*, which he completed at age seventy-two, in the waning days of the Roman Empire. There Augustine speculates that in heaven, as our wills move in perfect harmony with the will of God, our bodily eyes (restored and transformed at the resurrection) will behold things with a greatly enhanced power. We will surely not require these, the eyes of the spiritual body, in order to see God continuously and face to face. Yet our bodily vision may nevertheless attain such powers (which Augustine terms "intellectual") as are necessary to see directly what is invisible, including God. But even if they do not:

> Perhaps God will be known to us and visible to [the corporeal eyes of our spiritual bodies] in the sense that he will be spiritually perceived by each one of us in each one of us, perceived in one another, perceived by each in himself; he will be seen in the new heaven and the new earth, in the whole creation as it then will be; he will be seen in every body by means of bodies, wherever the eyes of the spiritual body are directed with their penetrating gaze.[39]

We can take this to provide a model of what, in Augustine's view, the highest spiritual use of our physical eyes could be. Although our bodies in the resurrection are changed and made spiritual, they are indeed flesh of a sort. Ideally, then, the flesh sees God in everyone, and in everything created by God.

Short of that heavenly ideal, we can conjecture that our own eyes can notice most easily the traces of God's reality in the more beautiful aspects of the created order. That this is the case is again suggested near the end of the *City of God*. In a poignant chapter that comes after he has recounted painfully the horrors of "this life of misery, a kind of hell on earth," Augustine contemplates what remains on earth of the original blessing from God. Augustine counts the arts of pottery and sculpture and painting among the many and varied remnants of those original blessings, although they are not enough to bring eternal felicity and are clearly subject to abuse.[40] He praises the rich diversity of poetry and "the delight given to the ears by the instruments of music and the melodies of all kinds that man has discovered."[41] These and many other things he praises, including the beauty of the human body, on account of which he looks forward to that heavenly day when "we shall enjoy one another's beauty for itself alone, without any lust." Then, finally, Augustine praises "the beauty and utility of the natural creation."

> How could any description do justice to all these blessings? The manifold diversity of beauty in sky and earth and sea; the abundance of light, and its miraculous loveliness, in sun and moon and stars; the dark shades of the woods, the colour and fragrance of flowers; the multitudinous varieties of birds, with their songs and their bright plumage; the countless different species of living creatures of all shapes and sizes, amongst whom it is the smallest in bulk that moves our greatest wonder—for we are more astonished at the activities of the tiny ants and bees than at the immense bulk of whales. Then there is the mighty spectacle of the sea itself, putting on its changing colours like different garments, now green, with all the many varied shades, now purple, now blue. Moreover, what a delightful sight it is when stormy, giving added pleasure to the spectator because of the agreeable thought that he is not a sailor tossed and heaved about on it. . . . Who could give a complete list of all these natural blessings?[42]

I have quoted at length because I cannot resist. Nowhere is it clearer that Augustine's eyes and heart take ineffable and almost endless joy in those things that will have an end, but which he longs to see restored and transfigured in the new heaven and the new earth.

The problem, which others have certainly noticed, is that Augustine's theories cannot do justice to his evident but intermittent appreciation of how spiritually rewarding earthly beauty can be.[43] What he does not see consistently or clearly is how much the vision of God and the enjoyment of the spiritual senses remain indebted to, and in dialogue with, the physical senses and their aesthetic transformation.

An Embodied Spirituality and Theology

Taking our cue from Augustine's picture of the mutuality between spirit and body in the New Jerusalem, we can go further than he was inclined to go. We can go so far as to affirm unabashedly that, with creatures such as ourselves, spirit and body are already mutually indwelling, even when uncooperative and uncoordinated. Our perceptions, thoughts, and imaginations lead us beyond our bodily boundaries to the far reaches of the mental and spiritual universe; we are not confined within our bodies. That is why we can think of the spirit as in some fashion transcending the body. From that perspective we can even say that the body inhabits the mind and spirit. But if so, it is not contained by the mind, as a moth might be contained by a jar. The body is *in* the mind, coloring its moods, giving weight and shape to its thoughts, lending the mind eyes and—in fact—body. That is evident from the easily forgotten fact that the bodily and sensuous language of metaphor structures even our intellectual constructs.[44]

At the same time, we can think of the spirit as inhabiting the body. We picture ourselves as exploring beyond our bodies; but we do not usually picture ourselves as *living* outside our bodies. Again, however, we are not "inside" our bodies merely as a prisoner is inside a cell—however trapped we may sometimes feel. We belong with and to our bodies. We recognize, for example, that what happens to our bodies happens in some way to ourselves. If you stab me or kiss me, either one, you have done it to *me*, not just to my body.

If we care to take the image of mutual indwelling to theological heights, we have only to think of Augustine's commentary on the Epistle of John, where he says of the self and God that "each mutually inhabits the other; He that holds and he that is held."[45] Just as my spirit and my body are mutually indwelling, so are God's spirit and my self.

What does all this have to say about the spiritual value of the beauty we can perceive bodily? We would be foolish to make some wild leap by arguing, for instance, that the only good Christian is a sensuous Christian, or that no good purposes can be served through curbing and denying the body and the senses. Augustine is only one of many witnesses to the spiritual value of trying, in some contexts, to minimize or eliminate some of the body's influence on the spirit. What we can affirm, minimally, is that denial or restraint of the senses (not to mention the imagination) is not inherently superior to training the physical eyes to see and enjoy spiritually. And now more boldly: Because we are embodied souls, and spirited bodies, the physical senses can themselves be spiritual senses, when rightly used and enjoyed. The fragrance, sweetness, and delightful taste that Augustine ascribes to the enjoyment of the spiritual senses ought to be enjoyed, also, in the enjoyment of art.

We can and ought to be fed spiritually from art, then, as long as it is art that is not designed to appeal to what is least spiritual about us. Simply put, art is able to address us "wholly, as persons" (as T. S. Eliot said).[46] If art is too "full of itself," that is an obstacle. There is always the chance that one will be tempted to rest in art. Every successful work of art turns us toward itself to some extent. But art can be both full of itself and full of the spirit. It can even become sacramental, in the broad sense to which Augustine subscribed: an outward sign of inward, spiritual grace (but with the inwardness of the grace being turned outward, and the outwardness of the sign being turned inward).

Art, however, does not generate its spiritual resources completely from within itself. It does not create all on its own the conditions for tasting the highest love, let alone for understanding and savoring the highest truth. Art (even religious art) is always shaped by other aspects of life, not the least of which is memory— as Augustine would emphasize—and the corporate form of memory that we know as tradition. In religion, art interacts not only with the church and its liturgical traditions but also with theology. Theology is part of what gives art its religious mind, so to speak, just as art is part of what gives theology its body and heart.[47] Each sphere forms and reforms the other. In balancing body and spirit, therefore, we have no reason to give absolute priority either to the relatively abstract theology favored by Augustine in his more intellectual moments or to the narrative and rhetorical art of the *Confessions*. Both have their limits, religiously, since God is beyond both (as negative theology and "apophatic" mysticism testify). Both have their value, religiously, since God allows Godself to be mediated and contemplated through both (as positive theology and "kataphatic" mysticism testify).

We have been working our way back to our guiding question of how to love both God and art, both holiness and beauty. We can continue by reflecting and building further on Augustine and his edifying struggles to honor God while living in the world. What we hope to discover in dialogue with Augustine (who again carries on a dialogue within himself) is a relatively simple but inclusive theological framework for validating and evaluating a spiritual taste for art. In Augustine's work, as we might expect, the path to that goal leads through love, and specifically through the idea of loving something or someone in God.

Loving "in God"

Loving the Neighbor in God

What, then, of love? Can love of God ever have a genuinely earthly focus, purpose, or attachment? Again and again Augustine returns to the Great Commandment as framed by Jesus: "You shall love the Lord your God with all your heart, and with all your soul, and with all your strength, and with all your mind; and your neighbor as yourself" (Luke 10:27). Augustine knows full well that one cannot abide by this commandment without loving neighbor and self as well as God. Even the highest love, therefore, includes not only God but the "other": "This reward is the supreme reward—that we may thoroughly enjoy [God] and that all of us who enjoy him may enjoy one another in him."[48]

Yet we are not God, any of us, even though we rightly seek God not only above ourselves but within. Accordingly, in Augustine's book *On Christian Teaching* (c. 392; expanded in c. 427), we find him saying that the best we can do in loving one another is to make "use" of each other on behalf of God. Distinguishing here between use (*uti*) and enjoyment (*frui*), Augustine says we use things when they serve some larger purpose. We can properly enjoy only that which we love for itself, and by which we are made happy. But only God can be loved that way, because only God, finally, can make us happy. We should not try to love or enjoy even our neighbor simply for the neighbor's sake.[49] "When you enjoy a human being in God, you are enjoying God rather than that human being. For you enjoy the one by whom you are made happy."[50] Again, this means that we can do no more than "use" each other lovingly. And since, for a classical theist like Augustine, God is completely self-sufficient and does not actually need us, it also means that "God does not enjoy us, but uses us," not to his advantage but for the sake of a goodness that is complete only in God.[51]

If we are to "use" other people, or to enjoy them (and ourselves) only on account of God, what becomes of the command to love one another? At this stage in Augustine's analysis, it is absorbed into the prior command to love God, because God requires the love of *all* one's heart, soul, mind, and strength. That all-absorbing love leaves "no part of our life free . . . to back out and enjoy some other thing; any other object of love that enters the mind should be swept towards the same destination as that to which the whole flood of our love is directed."[52] Loving self and neighbor entails relating that love "entirely to the love of God, which allows not the slightest trickle to flow away from it and thereby diminish it."[53]

We cannot but feel that the sentiment Augustine expresses here is in considerable tension with biblical and Christian values. At the very least his wording is infelicitous. The Great Commandment, after all, is hardly wanting to place on us the obligation of "using" one another, even for the sake of God. If I show love to a needy person only because I am thereby loving God, am I loving as Christ loved? Augustine himself seems to realize, in fact, that his ideas have troubling implications—although he persists, apparently engaged by the challenge of seeing whether he can make his unpromising formulation work out.

Hope comes when Augustine decides to explore further the idea of loving or enjoying something "in God," which he finds in Philemon 1:20.[54] There—in the translation used by Augustine—Paul tells Philemon: "So, brother, I shall enjoy you in the Lord." It is a usage found especially in Paul. In Romans 16:8, for instance, Paul speaks of Ampliatus as "my beloved in the Lord" (*en kurios*). Paul admonishes children to obey their parents in the Lord (Eph. 6:1). And he urges Philemon to take back the slave Onesimus as a beloved brother "both in the flesh and in the Lord" (Philem. 1:16).

So well does Augustine like the idea of loving someone in the Lord that he recycles and improves upon it in *The Trinity* (*De Trinitate*) (399–419). In *On Christian Teaching*, Augustine had found it necessary still to say that "when you enjoy a human being in God, you are enjoying God rather than that human being."[55] In the later work he states unequivocally that, at least in the case of a creature on a par with us, we can enjoy that creature in God. "Let us then enjoy both ourselves and our brothers in the Lord."[56] More than that, he acknowledges that sometimes scripture talks about love of neighbor without explicitly mentioning God. And that is because "if a man loves his neighbor, it follows that above all he loves love itself. *But God is love and whoever abides in love abides in God* (1 Jn. 4:16). So it follows that above all he loves God."[57]

What the phrase "in the Lord" or "in God" seems to do is set the context, indeed the ultimate context, for the love of self and others. If I receive someone as a beloved brother "in the Lord," I cannot very well treat that person in a manner that violates my relationship to the Lord. More than that, I am open to possibilities in that relationship that I may see in a new light precisely because I see it as somehow part of my relationship to the Lord. Moving beyond Augustine's discussion as such, we might recall that in the account of the Last Judgment given in Matthew 25, those who are blessed are surprised when the Lord tells them that they have given him food and drink, clothed him, and visited him in prison. The Lord then explains that, even as they have done it to the least of the members of his family, they have done it to him. That is to say, in effect, that they have performed these acts of love "in the Lord." One more relevant point is at least hinted at in Matthew. In the very moment when the blessed realize that their acts of neighborly love participate in nothing less than the love of Christ, they must understand more fully, now, the character and meaning of Christ for themselves and for the world. The deeper reason for the goodness of their loving acts is revealed to them. It is that those for whom they have sacrificed are already loved by a still greater love. The ones they have loved belong to a larger and higher order of things, which is itself nonetheless served by an earthly love that is attentive to what is present and immediate.

Loving Art and Beauty in God

With these Augustinian principles clarified and modified, can we say that artistic and earthly beauty warrants Christian love, and not just as a temporary springboard to something higher? We are not asking now simply for Augustine's own answers to the question, because we have seen that his mind vacillates with inner conflict. Instead, we are trying to reformulate Augustine's principles so as to come up with a more cogent Christian answer.

Some of those principles have to do with how *not* to love. And we have every reason to accept Augustine's judgment that, strictly speaking, love of anything has a religious or Christian sanction only when it somehow takes place "in God." If one loves something strictly for its own sake, completely apart from God, then one's love is in some respect deficient.

Not all deficiencies in love are the same, however. One kind of deficient love is a great love that is somehow misdirected. That could be an idolatrous love whereby one looks to something earthly as the sufficient source of one's overall happiness and clings to it inappropriately. A certain kind of aestheticism would surely fit that category.

A second sort of deficient love is one that is disproportionate or imbalanced. If I give all my goods to a child who asks for her inheritance in advance, leaving none for my other children, then the prodigality of my love will be a defect. After all, in the parable the generously prodigal father of the wastefully prodigal son does not give away the elder brother's inheritance, too. A relatively harmless example of disproportionate love in the realm of taste might be that of the graduate student in retreat from work who listens for hours every day to the Tchaikovsky Violin Concerto, and to nothing else.

Third, love can be too self-serving, too dominated by *eros*. There is in human life a place for a moderate degree of the desire that seeks self-gratification. But if one can only love out of a self-serving desire, which Augustine terms *cupiditas*, then one will not be able to give to the other person in a sacrificial way that denies the self. In terms of aesthetics, one might even make the mistake of demanding that the object of love always be beautiful in some immediately appealing way, instead of recognizing that love itself can call forth a deeper level of beauty. By contrast, in the Christian story, God loves sinful beings who have become unlovely, and does so with the intent that, in Christ, they will become a new creation (2 Cor. 5:16).

Love can thus be misdirected, disproportionate, and possibly inappropriate in kind. Augustine makes it plain that the love of art and earthly beauty is not excluded from any of these dangers. Such love is not always and necessarily "in God," therefore.

There is yet another form of deficiency in love, however. Love can simply be misidentified or imperfectly understood—a possibility that merits further exploration because of its special relevance to our later discussion of loving art. Suppose, for example, that I am a morally serious but agnostic person who decides to give financial aid to refugees from war. Not only do I not think of myself as obeying a divine command when I do so; I do not think of God at all. Yet I give expecting nothing in return, and I take a certain joy in the giving. It must be said that, from my perspective at the moment, I am not loving the refugees "in the Lord." But the act is good and loving, nonetheless. And if I were fully to understand why what I am doing is good—and if I were also fully to understand the true meaning of my incipient delight in giving aid sacrificially to other members of the human family—I would then see that such love and delight participates in, and anticipates, the reign of God. That fully religious realization could come as a kind of conversion in which I realize that I do not myself create the possibility or bear the core responsibility for the liberating and redemptive love at work in the world. I would then be loving willingly and gladly "in God."

But that still has to do with loving the neighbor, not with loving art. Isn't it time to admit that these are two very different sorts of love—one self-giving and the other essentially self-satisfying? And isn't there, consequently, an unbridgeable difference between loving a person "in God" and loving an object, no matter how artistic or beautiful? If so, about the only thing the concept of "loving in God" is good for, here, is to show that any love of art pretending to fit that category is defective, and downright sinful.

Certainly we cannot assume, without further discussion, that Augustine's essentially biblical idea of loving someone in God can be applied to the love of such nonhuman things as works of art (or, for that matter, nature). Augustine himself claims that we are to "use" created things that are lower than ourselves, rather than "enjoy" them.[58] And, as we have seen, his prime example of the act of loving "in God" is Paul's assertion that he will enjoy a person (Philemon) in the Lord.

At the same time, we have already emphasized that, according to Augustine, the beauty of the created order, having been made by the Author of creation, is such as to lead a perceptive and receptive mind to God (Wis. 13:4–5). Augustine never says we are really to quit loving the created beauty of what God has called good—even when we are in heaven. And Augustine states outright that the "beautiful objects designed by artists' souls and realized by skilled hands come from that beauty which is higher than souls," the same beauty for which Augustine's soul sighs day and night.[59] Both kinds of objects, therefore—natural and artistic—have the potential of continually leading the mind toward God, by virtue of their aesthetic qualities. What Augustine neglects to emphasize is that one cannot even perceive the beauty of these objects without focusing on them attentively and delighting in them, rather than focusing only on God and delighting only in sheer holiness (whatever that might mean). It is thus in God's interest, as it were, that we allow ourselves to enjoy and love created things as conditional "ends in themselves"—not as sufficient in themselves for our highest happiness but as ends whose enjoyment is good in itself while potentially leading to, or even adding to, the loving enjoyment of something greater.

Besides that, however, we need to consider something that Augustine appears to neglect altogether—the possibility that loving something artistic can be an integral part of loving human beings themselves. It is true that loving a work of art is not purely self-giving, let alone selfless. All the same, it can participate in giving—in self-giving and in reciprocity. Beautiful works of art are, as Augustine says, "designed by artists' souls," and not merely by artists' hands. For that reason they constitute extensions and expressions of who we are. Much of our shared delight as humans is artistic in nature. And much of our insight into what it means to be human comes from fiction, story, song, ritual enactment, and the like. These are gifts from the gifted. Although many art objects seem very far from existing as surrogate human beings—the most "thing-like" of abstract sculptures, for example—they nonetheless come to us as a kind of offering from their makers. Our act of attention and critical appreciation receives the artwork as a gift and incorporates it into the larger human world, no longer as mere object to be used but as something to be dwelled on and with.

All of which suggests, among other things, that Augustine's notion of "use" is misleading when applied to the love of art. (Augustine himself eventually dropped the whole distinction between *uti* and *frui*, apparently finding it awkward.) To say that one must use art instead of enjoying it is particularly confusing. A work of art has a kind of virtual life that makes it personal even in its ways of being object-like. If I intentionally destroy a beautiful Grecian urn you have given me, I have destroyed not only something that could have been a joy forever but also, for that reason, have possibly destroyed our relationship. Furthermore, because the love and enjoyment of other human beings is both enhanced and interpreted through art, it is partly by appreciating what others have made artistically that we can love one another. By the same token our disgust with the art loved by certain other people and groups can present a major obstacle to loving them—even recognizing that love does not consist merely (perhaps not even primarily) in feeling but also in willing and doing. This also means that Augustine is mistaken to think of the sensory beauty of art as inherently outward as opposed to inward in nature. What art can embody through its visible beauty and expressive qualities is not necessarily any more superficial than the expression on the face of a friend in love or in grief.

That still does not completely answer the question of what should count as loving something artistic "in God." We still do not know whether God has to be consciously in the picture before the enjoyment of a work of art or beautiful natural object can be considered a religiously significant act.

Here there could be much disagreement, reflecting very different Christian attitudes toward both nature and culture. Augustine himself, we might as well admit, was intent on relating everything as directly as possible to the love of God. He showed little interest in the natural sciences, for example. In his early years as a Christian, he even felt compunction about his own curiosity, reprimanding himself for becoming fascinated by the sight of a lizard catching flies.[60] We would not be likely to encounter this Bishop of Hippo at the local science museum, let alone at the Hippo Museum of Art. A little reflection should suggest, however, that there are many ways of relating an action or object to God, and of thus enjoying it "in God."

Let Me Count the Ways

To begin with, I could *dedicate* something to God, such as a song. In a sense, I am giving it to God. If it is a song I love, then all the better; because I am then better able to show my love to God. And if it is a song whose aesthetic excellence others can enjoy, that is better still. Our whole community is then united in the act. Perhaps the most famous example of the act of dedicating art to God is J. S. Bach's practice of inscribing *Soli Deo Gloria* (to God alone be the glory) on the scores of all his finished works, even humble musical exercises.

Similarly, I could *address* a poem to God, making it a prayer or a personal psalm. As poetry, it might well come from the heart, and my heart would therefore be in it. One recalls that Beethoven wrote on the first page of the score of the *Missa Solemnis* in D Major, "From the heart—may it go again to the heart." Whose heart is not specified. But the fervent pleas of "Dona nobis pacem" in the *Agnus Dei* seem to have both humanity and divinity in mind.

We can also *consecrate* something to God's service—a church building, for instance. It then becomes sacred, in the secondary sense that it is intimately associated with holy purposes. If poverty or urgent need prevents us from devoting special attention to matters of beauty or aesthetic quality, our consciences can be clear. In that case we are in fact "using" the building for God. But it is even better if we build the church lovingly (however simply), and in such a way as to be both practical and beautiful. Then it can glorify the Maker to whom it is consecrated and for whose sake it can be enjoyed.

We can also *receive* something artistic *on behalf of God* and of people who seek to love God. A song or melody that begins as in no obvious way religious can often be heard (received and perceived) by religious listeners in such a way that its joyful or elegant or haunting qualities turn into prayer or praise or lament.

In a variation on that process, we might imagine an act of aesthetic appreciation as something one is *sharing with God*. A biblical scholar—Gerald Janzen—was the person who first suggested the idea to me. He began by pointing out something I have noted here more than once: In Genesis God's creation of this or that aspect of the world is followed by God's appreciative "good"—as though, at that moment, God was simply "enjoying the objective beauty, rightness, fitness, 'thereness,' of what was there."[61] Augustine, as we know, could appreciate that point. Then my colleague segued to a scene from ordinary life: "I can look at a cardinal on my lawn and say, 'Oh God, what a beautiful sight! What a pert bird!' and I can go on to give thanks for a world fashioned so as to contain such a creature. And sometimes I wonder if God wants to say, 'Forget about me for a minute—just look at that bird—isn't that an amazingly beautiful creature in its own right, and for its own sake?'" My colleague concluded: "With all due respect to Augustine's distinction between loving something for its own sake, or as a substitute for God, and loving something for God's sake, or even loving it 'in God,' I would want to suggest another possibility as well: 'loving it with God.'" To those apt comments I would only add that, in my adaptation of Augustine, enjoying a work of art "with God" becomes a species of loving it "in God." Augustine's appreciative rhapsody on the original blessings of natural beauty shows that one side of him might welcome the sort of sanction that Gerald Janzen provides.

Here we must take a moment to reflect, however. It might seem odd to invite God to share an act of aesthetic appreciation (even metaphorically speaking), if the focus is not to be on God or if the art is not to be for God. How could that sharing be done "in God"? How could such appreciation be religious at all? Perhaps we can answer in this way: In the first place, to say that one is enjoying art in itself, but with God, says that such enjoyment is truly good—that, as Christian philosopher Nicholas Wolterstorff once wrote, it is a part of the peaceful flourishing or earthly *shalom* that God wants for us.[62] The religious sanction for enjoying art in itself, and sharing that with God, is not unlike the divine sanction for giving aid to refugees without thinking consciously of God at all, and later realizing that God shares in the giving (and in the receiving, too).

Second, however, we should not imagine that asking God to share in the enjoyment of the art makes no difference at all, just because one is paying more attention to art than to God. At the very least, it imposes a limit on the art one can choose to love "for its own sake." One could conceivably be the sort of person who would love only those artworks that tear the soul with their violence or that tend to plummet it into a state of profound melancholy or depression. At the opposite pole, one might love only art that is saccharine "fluff," virtually empty of substance. One might even love such works for their own sake, as enjoyable in themselves. Theologically, however, one would have difficulty asking God to share in the enjoyment of such art. Or if one could somehow ask God to do that once, one might hesitate to ask over and over. The question in that case would become one of proportion and balance. Some foods that are healthy or at least tolerable in moderation become sickening or poisonous when eaten in excess.

Be that as it may, we need to mention two more ways of loving something "in God." One of them is to *receive* or *perceive* something as somehow *from* God— like manna from heaven. That is true of the whole realm of nature, as normally conceived by Jews and Christians. In a somewhat complex fashion, that has also typically been the case with such scriptures as the poetry of the Psalms. Although Christians traditionally believe that the Psalms are part of "God's word," the psalms make no claim to speak for God, directly, as a prophetic text might. They speak of and to God (as in the earlier categories we discussed). And they do so under God's influence. In whatever sense we can speak of them as inspired by God, therefore, they are now words for *our* mouths that God originally called forth for the sake of God's people. In that sense the Psalms are *regarded as from* God, without being a manifestation or address of God.

The ways of loving art in God are beginning to add up. We can dedicate art to God, address art to God, consecrate it, receive it on God's behalf, invite God to share the enjoyment, and look at it as something from God. But finally, and most mysteriously, we need to say that a work of art can be loved in God when it has become, itself, a medium whereby God *becomes present* to us. The artwork or artistic medium is then transformed into something by which the transcendence of God is celebrated or genuinely mediated, not simply reported or honored. Then it is as though God adopted the medium as God's own.

Here idolatry is a great danger. But Christianity, like a great many other religions, worships a God whom it regards as both like and unlike, both above and within, things of this world. And for Christians art is a major part of the "cultural system" whereby a sense of God's reality is mediated—generally without supposing that the art is made by anything other than human hands. As we have seen, Suger looked in approximately that manner on the brightly beautiful objects in his Abbey church at St. Denis. Paul Tillich had a similar response to Botticelli's painting of the *Madonna and Child with Singing Angels* (Berlin–Dahlem Museum, Berlin). The aesthetic experience of transcendence is likewise a major premise of the film *Amadeus* (Milos Forman, 1984), based on Peter Shaffer's play. There the envious composer Antonio Salieri exclaims, after looking with a discerning eye at Mozart's musical scores, "I was staring through the cage of those meticulous ink strokes at—an Absolute Beauty!" It is a beauty that Salieri later refers to as the "voice of God."

Varieties of Aesthetic Transcendence

We are not quite done counting. One of the major themes of this study is that not all art is religious in the same way, when it is religious at all. It is important to see, therefore, that there are at least four modes in which a sense of the transcendent can be mediated aesthetically.[63]

Sometimes in the artistic mediation of the divine-human encounter, God appears only as the Absent One, as that which is signified only by the depth of the artfully expressed yearning. We can think of this perception as one of *negative transcendence*, which is more than hinted at in Derrida's meditations on blindness, tears, and Augustine's *Confessions*. One finds such a sense expressed in much Holocaust literature, if a sense of God is there at all. It also is evoked from the virtually infinite mourning, the endless *miserere*, that is given voice in almost all the works composed in the past decade by the Eastern European (Georgian) composer Giya Kancheli (1934–).

An art of *radical transcendence* conveys, instead, a sense of God as the Holy Other and infinitely distant one whom we cannot approach, though that Other can approach us and paradoxically can accommodate our incapacity. Here is Calvinist austerity, as seen in the beautifully bare and white interiors of Puritan meeting houses. Those were designed to purify the eye, to open the heart to God, and to direct the ear to the preached word, delivered literally from on high. Radical transcendence is also what one encounters (in quite another mode) in the blaze of fierce, awesome glory of the "Sanctus" of the *War Requiem* by Benjamin Britten (1913–76).

An art of *proximate transcendence*, by contrast, is sacramental, generating a sense of divine mystery and grace within and among and beyond things earthly and tangible. It is this that one beholds in the stained glass of medieval cathedrals as it colors—without changing—the light it transmits, just as (so medieval theologians said) flesh took on the reality of God in the Incarnation without changing the divine nature. An alternative genre of the art of proximate transcendence is informal and relatively earthy. One thinks of the many spirituals and gospel songs that convey a sense of God as the one who in Jesus knows intimately the conditions of bondage and pain, and in whose Spirit the believer can receive the promise of both earthly and heavenly liberation.

Finally, in an art of *immanent transcendence*, the sacred is altogether immersed in the ordinary. As such, it is never clearly distinguishable from the forms of the world and from the loves we know that are self-giving. We can perhaps see that sort of immanence in art of Diego Rivera, with its passionate love of the everyday Mexican people, or in the celebrative folk-style art of John August Swanson, where festive color and design depicts a this-worldly transformation of earth and society into the peaceable kingdom. Or one might find it in the photographs of Ansel Adams (1902–1984), which help awaken a new spiritual sense of the force and solemnity of nature, and indirectly call attention to our human responsibility for its preservation. Even immanence of this sort is a kind of transcendence, because it is pregnant with ineffable presence that is more than sheerly mundane.

We have been able to specify a great many ways in which art and natural beauty can be loved or enjoyed "in God." The mere fact that art can be enjoyed in God does not make it unique, of course. Almost anything that is permissible or good for life can receive some sort of religious blessing. Sports figures often dedicate their victories to God. Indeed, the Olympics originated in Greece as a kind of religious festival. And that is all well and good.

In the case of art, however, I have suggested that the religious connection is more intimate. Art not only allows itself to be blessed or dedicated or shared, religiously. As something that can engage us wholly, it can also enact faith and love, vivifying and in a real sense "converting" religious concerns sensuously and imaginatively, letting one taste and savor sacred delight. In such ways it gives a gracious foretaste of the reign of God that Christians believe will have no end.

That the work of art is transitory means that, in some sense, the greater the art's beauty, the greater the sense of yearning that it evokes. Even in those rare moments when the aesthetic experience becomes graciously transformed into a glimpse of genuine beatitude—and that is something no artist can guarantee—it soon fades, leaving behind something like a promise, an eschatological hope. And in the modern era in particular, the process of artistic questioning and imploring often takes place only distantly "in God."

It would be a mistake, however, to suppose that the note of longing sounded over and over in both Augustine and Derrida is the dominant tone of all art offered to God. Aside from the jubilation and even playfulness that marks much Christian art, there are works such as T. S. Eliot's *Four Quartets*, in which the longing itself is converted to quiet ecstasy, or can be. With that comes the possibility of a peace that passes understanding, not unlike—if we can speculate—the freedom from desire or craving that Buddhists have long contemplated and sought: the radiant enlightenment wherein even this one moment is enough, as though eternally blessed even in its passing. Of course none of this comes from art alone. But nothing at all exists alone. In the largest sense, it is all in God.

Art as Inherently Religious—Or Not

What, then, are we to make of the perennial idea that somehow all art is religious, and all beauty divine? One can find a version of the latter idea in Augustine himself. The idea reappears in Simone Weil, when she writes: "In everything which gives us the pure authentic feeling of beauty there really is the presence of God."[64] And it seems that at some point or other most spiritually inclined lovers of art are tempted to declare that all art is religious. We might recall Clive Bell's assertion that all art "is a manifestation of the religious sense" and that therefore "all artists are religious"[65] (a notion with which Blake would have concurred). That assertion is not unlike Paul Tillich's later claim that, because art indirectly expresses an ultimate concern through its style, "every artistic expression is religious in the larger sense of religion."[66] The idea is echoed in Bishop Richard Harries's insistence in his book *Art and the Beauty of God* that "all works of art, whatever their content, have a spiritual dimension."[67] Alejandro García–Rivera, in his recent study *The Community of the Beautiful: A Theological Aesthetics,* advances a similar claim, partly by quoting from Hans Urs von Balthasar: "All great art is religious, an act of homage before the glory of what exists."[68] And all these assertions bear some relation to a complex idea formulated by the Calvinist historian of religions Gerardus van der Leeuw: "Every true work of art is in a sense religious. Every true work of art bears within itself the germ of self-abolishment. The lines yearn to be erased, the colors to pale. Every true art is experienced as the incarnation of what is further distant from us, and different."[69]

Such assertions bear some resemblance to claims I have been making, myself. The claim that all art is religious is almost always accompanied, however, by an implicit disclaimer or qualification. Art is said to be religious "in some sense" or "in the larger sense." Or it is said that all "great art" or all "true art" is religious. And that is important.

But it may not be sufficient. Admitting that Puccini's *Tosca* is outstanding, musically, we may want to balk at calling it religious even "in some sense." And in what sense is the vocal art of Frank Sinatra or Celine Dion religious, however highly developed? Or Shakespeare's *Romeo and Juliet*? Or a morally intriguing novel (and film) such as *Wings of a Dove*, by Henry James? Are we to find "ultimate concern" in a Gainsborough portrait of an aristocratic lady poised prettily in the shade of a tree?

Of course, once the gauntlet is thrown down, the clever theorist can invariably think of *some* way in which the art in question can be thought of as religious. That still does not change the fact that, in general, the conviction that all art is religious is based, consciously or unconsciously, on a highly selective and often idealized notion of art or of aesthetic experience. And that can easily play into the hands of genuine aesthetes for whom art really is their religion, pure and simple.

With Augustine by our side, we can say that ultimately all of life exists in and for God; and that surely includes art. With the medieval scholastic tradition and its modern descendants, we can also observe that oneness, goodness, beauty, and truth are "transcendentals."[70] They pertain to everything that so much as exists, and have their ultimate grounding and fulfillment in God. Again, the beauty of art is included. But from this perspective everything is beautiful to some degree. That does not set art apart from anything else. It says nothing about art that does not even want to be beautiful. And it does not say what kinds of beauty are closest to holiness. Furthermore, none of the talk about beauty as a transcendental attribute of being addresses adequately what Augustine thought should be inescapably plain: the need for our experience and taste in beauty to undergo conversion. Not all art serves God directly. Nor does all art serve God indirectly, since some art tends to delude and distort, and so to be dissolute. Besides that, as Augustine forcefully reminds us, it is not just the art object that determines its spiritual power. It is also the spirituality and discernment—the faith, love, and "spiritual taste"—of the beholder that determines how edifying or illuminating the work will be.

So that's that—or could be. But simply to leave the matter there conveys almost nothing of the sense that so often surrounds encounters with art that we think of as highest. What persists is the feeling, evidently very deep, that such art is fulfilling what all art is meant to be. Not that all art needs to do that. It is enough that some does. And the art that does is indeed religious, often without going by that name. We could even go a bit further, crossing into terrain that Augustine would probably not care to enter. We could say that some of the art that fulfills the religious aspirations latent in the whole artistic endeavor— indeed in life—is religious partly by resisting what one already thought one understood by religion, or by God. It is by reflecting on such a work of art, and on one person's encounter with it, that I will bring to a close this stage of our inquiry into religious taste.

A Musical Coda

In a remarkable letter to a friend, the British composer Benjamin Britten (1913– 76) reflects on having listened late into the night to the long, final movement of Gustav Mahler's symphonic song-cycle of 1907–8, *Das Lied von der Erde* (*The Song of the Earth*), a setting of poems from the Chinese. The cycle ends with the "*Abschied*," or "Farewell," the last musical phrases of which keep returning at intervals to the word "*Ewig*" ("forever"), with which the music finally dies away.

557 Finchley Road [London]
29 June 1937 [postmark]

It is now well past mid-night & society dictates that I should stop playing the Abschied. Otherwise I might possibly have gone on repeating the last record indefinitely—for 'ewig' keit of course.

It is cruel, you know, that music should be so beautiful. It has the beauty of loneliness, & of pain: of strength & freedom. The beauty of disappointment & never-satisfied love. The cruel beauty of nature, and everlasting beauty of monotony.

And the essentially 'pretty' colours of the normal orchestral palette are used to paint this extraordinary picture of loveliness. And there is nothing morbid about it. The same harmonic progressions that Wagner used to colour his essentially morbid love-scenes (his 'Liebes' is naturally followed by 'Tod') are used here to paint a serenity literally supernatural. I cannot understand it—it passes over me like a tidal wave—and that matters not a jot either, because it goes on for ever, even if it is never performed again—that final chord is printed on the atmosphere.

Perhaps if I could understand some of the Indian philosophies I might approach it a little. At the moment I can do no more than bask in its Heavenly light—& and it is worth having lived to do that.[71]

Those words come from a young man of twenty-four who had already composed works of such Christian provenance as *A Hymn to the Virgin*, *A Boy was Born*, and a *Te Deum in C*, and who would later compose such works as the *Ceremony of Carols*, *Rejoice in the Lamb*, the *Missa Brevis in D*, the *Prodigal Son*, and the *War Requiem*, the last of which interweaves settings of war poems by Wilfred Owen with settings of the traditional Latin requiem liturgy. Britten is thus someone comparatively at home with Christian music and tradition.

Why, then, is Britten so transported by this piece of music composed by Mahler, a heterodox Catholic convert from unorthodox Judaism? What draws him to this music that turns toward the East, with its Chinese texts (freely translated into German by Hans Bethge and modified by Mahler himself), its pentatonic melodies and transparent textures—music that makes him think also of Indian philosophies? And why does Britten single out this particular music as at once unbearably beautiful and a source of such "Heavenly light" that it is worth having lived just to have experienced it?

In the case of *Das Lied von der Erde*, Britten and Mahler are both, in fact, crossing beyond the territory staked out by their native religio-cultural traditions and immersing themselves religiously in music that is in no explicit way religious. The more conventional versions of their respective religious traditions are ones with which neither Britten nor Mahler was ever completely at ease, it seems. And it appears that, with the music of *Das Lied*, both are going still farther from home, artistically and spiritually. They are doing so not as dabblers in exoticism but as artistic explorers looking toward the ultimate horizon of life, contemplating a final farewell to all human companionship and seeking transcendent communion with what the poetry set by the music describes as earth's ever-renewed, unending beauty.

It is not beyond the realm of possibility that for each musician the end of this artistic exploring could be, as T. S. Eliot would say in *Four Quartets*, to return home and know the place for the first time. But why leave, to begin with? It is not as though Christianity, or Judaism either, were without resources for contemplating death and earth in the ambient light of beauty. Nor is it as though these musicians were suddenly able, even if they had wanted, to see the world entirely through Asian eyes, as some forms of Orientalism might imagine.

One plausible reason for their mutual excursion beyond the familiar is that these particular people in their respective situations might not have arrived at the same place had they stayed within the confines of explicitly Christian traditions. Their musical undertaking is, for them, a spiritual exploration and discovery. For Britten, at least, this means reaching out to music of infinite yearning and sadness that is somehow also graced by a beauty that lights up in timeless fashion all that is temporal and fragile.

It seems superfluous to ask whether the making and partaking of this art can be religious. But if it can be, in what way? And can it be Christian? Britten's experience of listening to *Das Lied von der Erde* is undeniably aesthetic and religious. It is religious by being aesthetic in a certain manner. Without apprehending the particular and quite temporal beauty of the music, Britten would not have had this particular experience of aching longing (*Sehnsucht*) infused with a sense of eternity (*Ewigkeit*). And for him this beauty is itself evidently religious—or, as some would say, spiritual; for the beauty he apprehends in the music is not self-contained but overflows the realm of sound to bestow a sense of the very worth of existence.

Again, however, is this art also Christian? Is it even possibly Christian? The question cannot be answered simply. The experience afforded by *Das Lied von der Erde* obviously does not derive expressly from the Christian tradition or call for an explicitly Christian framework of response. That much is clear. But it seems equally likely that the quality of yearning and farewell pervading the last song emerges against a background not only of Asian concepts and images but also of Christian ones, especially regarding human longing and the goal of existence.

Mahler was the son of a free-thinking Jewish tavern keeper whose cruelty to his mother he found profoundly alienating. Obsessed with death at an early age, he had already envisioned some kind of immortality and eternity in his Second Symphony (1894), subtitled *Resurrection,* as well as in his Fourth Symphony

(1900) and in his Eighth Symphony (1907), which is a vast choral and instrumental setting of the Latin Pentecost hymn *"Veni Creator Spiritus,"* together with the last portion of Goethe's *Faust: Part II.* All of these works, without restricting themselves to a Christian frame of reference, obviously tie in with Christian concepts and impulses. Nothing in *Das Lied von der Erde* elicits a similarly Christian response. Mahler's struggles with the questions raised by mortality had taken a more negative turn late in life, following his forced resignation from the Vienna Opera, the death of his eldest daughter at age four, and medical confirmation of his own worsening heart condition. He is not, in this very late song cycle, embracing anything like a sanguine Christian faith in eternal life. Whatever affirmation he arrives at in this work might best be described as a qualified acceptance of personal finitude rather than as an affirmation of a personal immortality. But the terms of that acceptance are by no means sheerly stoic or strictly Buddhist. The undulations of the concluding music, and its gentle expansiveness, convey the sense that this finite human being, in the act of departure, participates in the earth's encompassing reality, ever renewed, and is thus enjoying something truly eternal in its beauty and significance. He is enjoying it in God, we might say.[72]

From a Christian perspective, such a limited but poignant affirmation can be seen in several possible ways, not all of which are mutually exclusive. And so we count once more, but more by way of wondering than asserting:

(1) The *"Abschied"* from *Das Lied von der Erde* could be interpreted by a Christian as expressive of an inappropriate, all-too-human mourning for sheerly temporal loss, coupled with an idolatrous or "pagan" glorification of the earth and a fatal lack of faith in God.

(2) A Christian could hear the music as revealing the genuine depths of human longing, and thus (however unintentionally) as showing the inner qualities of a desire that can, in the end, only be satisfied by the reality of a gracious God. A Christian could therefore regard the music as a preparation for hearing the Christian gospel.

(3) Christian listeners could hear the *"Abschied"* as expressing in musical language an almost resigned but genuine trust in that which is beyond the human, yet which meets and encompasses the human. While associated with the earth and its beauty, it is finally nothing other than God or Ultimate Reality.

(4) A Christian might hear the music of *Das Lied von der Erde* as representing an awakening awareness of the painful beauty of all things that must pass. And the fragility of life's beauty, its indescribable sweetness, along with the poignancy and emptiness of its passing—that could seem to be something that Christians might well learn to feel more keenly if they are to

love life and earthly things appropriately, even as lesser goods than the goodness of God who meets and encompasses all things transitory. At the same time, one might hear in the music a gesture toward surrendering life without any assurances beyond the fullness, and emptiness, of all that passes. And that gesture might seem somehow unchristian, or non-christian, but not insignificant.

Of these options, which are not meant to be exhaustive, only the first denies positive religious value to *Das Lied von der Erde*. The second grants it religious value, but as illuminating a stage of awareness preparatory to a fully Christian vision. The third option finds in the music a Christian vision expressed in veiled terms, more beautiful for being fresh and somewhat foreign.

The fourth is more complex, still, and needs more comment. It discovers something new in this art, which perhaps paradoxically conveys a transforming sense of eternal value in this truly transitory life and world. Our fourth approach regards that sense of things as something Christians would do well to ponder, even if the experience makes for subtle changes in the way their faith is lived and expressed. It could be that the tenderness and poignancy of this farewell to life would cause one to linger over the earth and friendship in a manner that Augustine, for example, would have thought inappropriate for truly Christian behavior. It might also suggest the possible goodness of letting go of life in a manner that has no sure goal in sight. That is not a usual part of training in Christianity. But there may be more than one legitimate Christian attitude toward the world, friendship, and death; and different attitudes may have their proper season in the life of any one Christian. Furthermore, it could somehow be a Christian act just to explore such an alternative sense of an ending, and be changed by it, at the very boundaries of Christian experience, and beyond. To taste of such art and in such a way might still be to enjoy it in God.

Kitsch, Sacred and Profane

The Question of Quality

Kitsch and the Question of Quality

What happens when the thirst for God is expressed, artistically, through kitsch? In asking that question, our fundamental concern here is with quality and with standards of evaluation. Kitsch forces us to raise the question of quality because no one thinks about kitsch, including religious kitsch, without thinking that it is in some sense bad art and somehow in bad taste. After translating Augustine's statement in *The Trinity* that "the physical face of the Lord is pictured with infinite variety by countless imaginations," Edmund Hill appends a note that says the face was "not yet stereotyped and sterilized by vile holy pictures and cheap commercialized religious art"—by which he clearly means kitsch.[1] The term itself first came into use in the mid-nineteenth century among painters and art dealers in Munich, Germany. Since that time, "kitsch" has always designated "cheap artistic stuff."[2] Yet kitsch is also art that some people think of as good—good for something, at any rate. To call something kitsch, therefore, is already to put into play certain ideas of what might make art bad or good.

Kitsch is by no means unappealing. Indeed, that seems to be part of the problem. It is art that appeals to many people, but for reasons that others find objectionable. And while various sophisticated people enjoy kitsch in some fashion even while recognizing it as kitsch, most people who think kitsch is good do not think of it as kitsch at all. To them it is ideal art: usually well crafted and generally heart-warming, filled with memories and dreams. It is art that is felt to be touching—sometimes as though, itself, "touched by an angel." A "kitschy" way of being touched can also cause the sorrows of life suddenly to well up and to dissolve into tears. Such sweet or sentimental effects, very different from the blinding and converting tears tasted by Derrida, may be disdained by the academic and certifiably serious art world. But they abound in the art that is beloved by bourgeois taste and by the masses of people who may not know or notice the difference between genuine art and its imitations.

Just then I was beginning to talk about kitsch in a dismissive manner that until recently was familiar in criticism—all too familiar. Nothing that I said was wrong, exactly. It could be defended in certain circles, at least, without much effort. But the idea that there is always a clear-cut difference between genuine art and imitation art is illusory. And to make general pronouncements about bourgeois taste and the tastes of the unsophisticated masses is quickly to dehumanize a very human subject. It is to risk stereotyping issues and people in a manner that is unwise and uncharitable—and basically unchristian.

One sees the danger when considering the criticisms of kitsch that Milan Kundera puts forward in his novel *The Unbearable Lightness of Being* (1984):

Kitsch causes two tears to flow in quick succession. The first tear says: how nice to see children running on the grass!

The second tear says: How nice to be moved, together with all mankind, by children running on the grass!

It is the second tear that makes kitsch kitsch.[3]

For Kundera, kitsch is a beautiful lie; it prettifies and falsifies the world, often by embracing, implicitly, a cause or an ideology that requires cheap emotion and an unqualified (but blinkered) acceptance of reality, a categorical "agreement with being" (p. 256). As Kundera puts it—consciously setting aside the norms of polite prose—kitsch tries to hide the existence of shit. Yet shit, too, is in fact real, and undeniable if one is to confront reality. Kundera insists that the denial of "shit" is essential to religion and totalitarian politics. In his view, both religion and politics need kitsch to cover up the fact that not everything conforms to their image of life as something that is finally completely agreeable, worked out in accordance with a higher purpose (to which they have special access), and leading ultimately toward a condition in which God or the State is all in all. Kitsch makes all that seem plausible. That is why kitsch is so amenable to political and religious uses. Or so Kundera claims.

And one can see why. Born in 1929 in Czechoslovakia, Kundera knows first-hand about the insidious effects of political kitsch—in this case Communist—and about religious kitsch, too. (What would he make of the Infant Jesus of Prague—a famous miracle-working wax figure displayed inside the Baroque church of St. Mary of the Victories, always wearing one or another of his thirty-nine costly robes?)[4] It is hard to deny that most of what people call kitsch (but which people?) is nothing if not comforting, or else fit for a "good cry": soft, not the least bit "edgy," devoid of genuine complexity or irony.

One thinks of the world of kitsch parodied in the film *The Truman Show* (Peter Weir, 1998), an artificial world by means of which Christof the "televisionary" producer creates and controls Truman Burbank's perfectly synthetic life so as to turn it into one unending TV show. Truman lives on a thoroughly nice, antiseptic island community called Seahaven, the streets of which are lined with what one film critic describes aptly as "architecturally tidy, strenuously pleasant dwellings." Truman himself lives "in a houseful of dimples with his too-perfect wife Meryl," who "coyly drops the brand names of cocoa and lawn mowers. She can exclaim 'I made macaroni!' in fiendishly ecstatic fashion."[5] As Kundera would have us expect, and as the film's director would surely want us to perceive, the kitsch of Truman's world is manipulative while appearing benign, sincere, and alluring.

From Truman's world—the fake world created for "True-man"—it is but a short step to the kitsch found in "real-life" advertising:

> Blue is the only color you can feel. You can see red. Look green. Have a tan. But blue is inside. Blue is a part of you. The deep blue of the sea stirs your soul. A bright blue sky lifts your spirits. The inky blue of midnight rouses passions deep within you.
>
> So it's no surprise that there is only one truly blue food. . . . One with a taste that's deep, ambrosial. A taste you experience. A taste you feel. The taste of blueberries.

That quasi-poetic reverie comes *gratis* by way of a box of Ralston Blueberry Pecan Muesli. It is harmless enough, since its designs on us are relatively transparent. One can have fun pretending that the poetry of life can be packaged, and the problems of life resolved, in a box of tasty cereal. It is a commonplace these days that some of the best art talents go into advertising. What saves artistry in advertising from being kitsch through and through is off-beat imagination and stylistic ingenuity. When churches try to replicate the techniques of advertising, the wit and imagination usually evaporate. What is left is a residue of nice sentiment. Again, that is just what Kundera would expect.

Yet there is something more than a little suspect about the extent of Kundera's suspicions of kitsch. For one thing, Kundera makes it sound as though religious art, like the political art of totalitarian regimes, must be kitsch by definition—a beautiful lie, a contrived sentiment, a false hope. But that would mean that even the epics of Milton and Dante should be regarded as kitsch (something that Kundera seems not actually to consider).

Another thing: Kundera's sword is two-edged and thus doubly cutting. To be sure, Kundera tries on occasion to be compassionate. He admits that all of us are seduced some of the time by kitsch. Take his character Sabina, for instance.

She could be touched by a "silly mawkish song about two shining windows and the happy family living behind them." And even so, she could be saved: "Though touched by the song, Sabina did not take her feeling seriously. She knew only too well that the song was a beautiful lie. As soon as kitsch is recognized for the lie it is, it moves into the context of non-kitsch, thus losing its authoritarian power and becoming as touching as any other human weakness" (p. 256).

Kundera thus allows that, if recognized for what it is, the sin of kitsch is forgivable. Yet mostly it goes unrecognized. And anything that smacks of traditional values or loyalties, Kundera labels as kitsch—such as a cold-war slogan decrying "the barbarity of Communism" (p. 262). Although it is hard to object to Kundera's targets in any given instance, he clearly spares nothing that would call for any genuine allegiance, any unchecked emotion, any faith.

Ironically, however, *The Unbearable Lightness of Being* is not, itself, immune to charges of propagating kitsch, although of a different sort. That is the other edge of the sword Kundera wields in his attack on kitsch, and one he fails to heed. Karsten Harries long ago pointed out that the modern artist or art lover who is proud of having unmasked the sweet and possibly erotic kitsch of the past too readily forgets that "modern art has produced its own clichés and its own brand of Kitsch."[6] Not all kitsch is sweet, says Harries (thereby concurring with the German novelist Hermann Broch). Some modern kitsch becomes downright sour, by taking itself too seriously in an effort to compensate for having lost religious weight.[7] These days, as Robert Solomon points out, it is often safer to be shocking or disgusting than sweet.[8] But the need to shock or disgust can become an affectation, itself, and a perverse sort of kitsch.

Kundera's novel could strike some readers as suffering from these very flaws. Its pervasive cynicism could easily seem mannered and pretentious—marred by pseudo-profundities, for all the talk of Nietzsche and Beethoven and Tolstoy's *Anna Karenina*. Kundera also invites criticism in that the women he portrays tend to appear peculiarly schematic, their worlds mostly orbiting around men, their habits sexually compliant in a manner one might have expected in fiction written for a more-or-less sophisticated men's magazine:

"The excitement she felt was all the greater because she was excited against her will. . . . For what made the soul so excited was that the body was acting against its will. . . ." (p. 155). Without indulging in soft feelings, Kundera nonetheless could be criticized for indulging in finely honed, male-oriented clichés about the resistant woman who secretly wants to be taken.

Nevertheless, Kundera's many fans would retort that to paint Kundera himself as somehow a purveyor of kitsch is to do him an injustice. And they would have a point, too. The accusation of kitsch rarely does the target of the accusation full justice. For many decades it was the habit of Marxist critics associated with the Frankfurt Institute to dismiss all popular art in capitalist societies as little more than kitsch, an art of "mass culture" corrupted by the economic conditions of its production and the commercial motivations of its aims. Such art they placed in direct opposition to the exalted realm of "high" or "autonomous" art. In his 1941 essay "Art and Mass Culture," for instance, Max Horkheimer claimed that "art, since it became autonomous, has preserved the utopia that evaporated from religion," whereas everything else (such as Disney-animated cartoons and Hollywood films) is to be rejected as "the contemptible trash of the day."[9] That kind of dichotomy hardly seems just, especially to the arts of the so-called masses.

Yet, as the example of Kundera's novel indicates, even art that is widely seen as "high" or at least traditional has not been exempt from being labeled kitsch. The charge of "kitsch" has sometimes been leveled at the eminently approachable but accomplished church music of John Rutter; at the ethereal "*In Paradiso*" section that concludes the ever popular Requiem of Gabriel Fauré (with which Rutter's Requiem has been compared unfavorably, however); and at the same section of the Benjamin Britten *War Requiem*.[10] It has likewise been leveled at Leonard Bernstein's eclectic *Mass*, at Gustav Mahler's music in general (as heard, for instance, by Ralph Vaughan Williams), at Ralph Vaughan Williams's music in general (as heard by more avant-garde composers), at the more orgiastic sections of Maurice Ravel's ballet music for *Daphnis and Chloe*, and at such certifiably avant-garde products as Krzysztof Penderecki's *Threnody to the Victims of Hiroshima*, the Golden Calf portion of Arnold Schoenberg's opera *Moses and Aaron*, and the entirety of Olivier Messiaen's *Turangalila* Symphony—all "high class kitsch," according to certain reputable sources.[11] The game is popular. It is a game of big kitsch eats little kitsch, the object being to see whose kitsch is the last to be eaten, and what (if anything) is left. Truly it is unjust simply to let all these works be swallowed up indiscriminately into the catch-all concept of "kitsch," just as it is true that Kundera's work is not done complete justice in that way.

Even truer is the fact that some of us have become increasingly leery these days about making any public judgments about quality in art, let alone about kitsch. In a chapter-length essay on "Christian Kitsch and the Rhetoric of Bad Taste," the historian of Christianity Colleen McDannell argues that factors of class, gender, status, and social identity all condition judgments as to what is kitsch. Yet, she says, the term is generally used in a such a way as to obscure that fact. "Kitsch" can be used, to be sure, in a cultural and relativist sense as "merely what one particular group does not appreciate in another group's culture."[12] That usage McDannell evidently approves. But it can also be used aesthetically, in the elitist manner of art critic Clement Greenberg (and to some extent Milan Kundera), to condemn popular art as a cheap imitation of the real thing. Or it can be used in an ethical sense, to point to a betrayal of the higher values summed up by James Lindsay when he asserts: "Art aims—as religion itself does—to teach and elevate, not merely to amuse, bewilder, and fascinate."[13] "Kitsch," in the context of that assertion, would be art that fails to teach or elevate. But who gets to decide? (Figures 3–5).

McDannell shows that in the modern era Catholics and Protestants alike have often worked with a simplistic and in fact untenable binary opposition between real art and kitsch, between good taste and bad. Along with art historian David Morgan, she argues that popular arts deserve better. They deserve the attention of serious historians, scholars, and students of religion.[14] And they do not deserve the rhetoric directed against them in the academy or in the church. Both scholars mount a persuasive attack on the elitist presuppositions behind the assumption that informal or vernacular art is by nature quite unlike "real art" and therefore unworthy of attention or appreciation.

McDannell and Morgan succeed admirably in complicating the question of kitsch and quality. What both understandably decline to do, as historians, is to develop, at a more complex level, nonelitist norms for appraising the aesthetic and religious quality of the work they persuade us to examine freshly. While they give us ample historical evidence indicating that there are religious aims that some sorts of "kitschy" religious art can apparently fulfill exceptionally well, they leave it to others to make a normative judgment as to the relative value of those aims. They also leave it to others to judge whether there are aims (aesthetic, moral, or theological) that such works really do tend to cheapen or to sell short—both for those who enjoy them and for those who do not. McDannell states bluntly: "It is not my intention to evaluate Christian material culture by a set of ethical and theological standards."[15]

Even scholars less constrained by the neutrally descriptive norms of historical interpretation are understandably reluctant these days to take up the task of aesthetic and theological evaluation. Sensitive to the multiple standards intrinsic to multiculturalism, and increasingly conscious of social and gender stereotypes, many in the academy are now painfully aware of the limitations inherent in their own "social location."[16] It is likewise increasingly apparent to theologians, liturgists, and church leaders that the standards applied in making judgments about liturgical art cannot simply be assumed to be universal.

In the sphere of religion, one result of such heightened and chastened sensitivity is a certain amount of nostalgia for the good old days when everyone (at least everyone in a given community) shared most of the same standards and tastes. Alternatively, many Christians seeking to avoid "worship wars" feel a powerful urge to set aside questions of artistic quality altogether. A good many Christians across the theological spectrum would just as soon treat arts as what theologians have termed "adiaphora"—things of religious indifference, being

Figures 3–5. Religious art that many people would call "kitsch" functions to witness, bless, and casually sanctify life in these mobile homes in Appalachian Virginia—even if occasionally in ways that can seem incongruous. (Photographs by Carol Burch)

Figure 4.

Figure 5.

permissible but of negligible importance. More accurately, they would wish to treat the *quality* of art and taste as a matter of indifference, religiously. They would happily sing Andrew Sullivan's theme song, introduced in chapter 1: The church is and always will be "tacky" in a number of ways; its survival in spite of all its "tackiness" is itself a testimony to something greater working through it.[17]

But for us to leave it at that is finally no more satisfactory here than it was when we first considered that option. In the preceding chapter, we examined at length a number of ways in which the taste for art can feed and be fed by the love of God. Art itself cannot, therefore, be treated as a matter of religious indifference. Nor can art be treated as automatically religious or perfectly innocent. Augustine made a convincing case that some kinds of art are inferior or indeed seductive from a religious perspective. If that is true, then the question of artistic quality and appropriateness must likewise be religiously relevant. We cannot have it both ways. We cannot say that the kind and quality of art makes no religious difference (à la Sullivan) and also say that some art is especially conducive to being enjoyed "in God."

In view of the increasing sensitivity and intensity of such controversies, it is probably time to find a new way of raising the question of aesthetic quality and appropriateness—a way that is pluralistic and nonelitist without being indiscriminate and irresponsible, either aesthetically or theologically. The first thing to notice (and we have indeed noticed it) is that the question of artistic quality matters, as does the corresponding question of aesthetic taste and judgment. The next thing to notice (and we have begun to do so) is that how that question matters and how it is answered depends to a large extent on who is asking the question. Even complicated in these ways, however, the question remains.

To see more clearly how the question of quality emerges naturally in relation to different perspectives on the same work of art, we will scrutinize more closely than usual several exceptionally strong candidates for classification as religious kitsch. Lest these examples seem either trivial or marginal, we would do well to remember that, as both McDannell and Morgan have shown, a taste for such art is a major component of specifically Christian taste and (arguably) a significant force in shaping and expressing contemporary Christian faith.

Sacred Kitsch: Appealing or Appalling?

It is surprising how few Christians outside the Eastern Orthodox tradition are acquainted with the most venerable story of how Christianity came to Russia. Just how much of the story is legend may never be known; what counts here is the point the narrative is making.

According to the *Russian Primary Chronicle,* Prince Vladimir of Kiev, in what was still pagan Russia, sent ambassadors to Constantinople in the year 987. Although they took the opportunity to observe Muslim worship, and the Roman liturgy, what most impressed them was the Byzantine liturgy and its aesthetic surroundings. This they witnessed at the great church of Hagia Sophia, where Basil II personally called their attention to the beauty of the architecture and of the chanting. Upon their return to Kiev they reported:

> We knew not whether we were in heaven or on earth. For on earth there is no such splendor or such beauty, and we are at a loss how to describe it. We know only that God dwells there among men, and their service is fairer than the ceremonies of other nations. For we cannot forget that beauty. Every man, after tasting something sweet, is afterward unwilling to accept that which is bitter, and therefore we cannot dwell longer here.[18]

Those who made the report did not, indeed, remain in their former condition but were baptized there in Russia into Orthodox Christianity, followed eventually by Vladimir and all his people.

It would be hard to think of a sharper contrast to the lofty, magnificent, and hierarchical style of Hagia Sophia than the relatively intimate, informal, and sweetly painted Precious Moments Chapel designed by Samuel Butcher (1939–). Set among the tree-covered hills outside Carthage, Missouri, and beside a peacefully flowing stream, the chapel has attracted almost a million visitors a year since its opening in 1989. That is due in part to its proximity to Branson, Missouri, which rivals Nashville as the country music "mecca." Loosely emulating on a smaller scale the design and "decor" of the Sistine Chapel in Rome, which Butcher had visited many years before, the Precious Moments Chapel displays fifty-three murals that Butcher painted on the more than five thousand square feet of its wall and ceiling surfaces. There are also thirty stained-glass windows made to his specifications, the largest of which comprises approximately thirteen hundred smaller pieces of glass. Much of this is described and selectively pictured on the virtual tour available at the Precious Moments Chapel web site, which should be consulted in conjunction with the following discussion.[19]

To reach the chapel, one passes through a multi-room gift shop and then walks down a paved path called the Avenue of Angels, entering the grounds through a large wrought-iron gate with elaborate, swirling vegetative patterns. The chapel is oriented toward the south and the nearby stream rather than toward the more traditional east; and those who describe it tend to use literal rather than liturgical directions. On the northeast wall of the chapel exterior is a nine-foot bronze plate with a scene representing God's law. In this scene the commandment tablets are held by a childlike angel who, backed by a second angel with a little sword, blocks the stairway to paradise—thereby symbolizing the futility of any attempt to reach God through good works alone. That bronze panel is paired with another on the northwest wall representing God's grace as shown in Christ (here depicted as a haloed child holding a cross) and continuing in the work of the Holy Spirit, symbolized by a waterfall. Two intricately carved wooden doors, weighing three hundred fifty pounds each, lead into the chapel.[20]

The interior side walls of the "sanctuary" have four main divisions, each: on the lowest level a series of elongated oval murals runs beneath a higher, parallel series of tall, rectangular panel paintings; these stand beneath a row of painted roundels, which in turn are beneath a top row of clerestory lancet windows. Stained-glass windows at ground level illuminate the side aisles, which are separated from the sanctuary itself by the walls with the murals.

On the left or east side of the main interior, the murals depict stories and heroes from the Old Testament. On the right or west side are scenes from the life of Christ and from the best known parables. Above, the ceiling is painted sky blue, with clouds at the edges and with pinkish white angels taking wing, resembling cupids but without a trace of Cupid's naughtiness. On the front of the balcony in the rear of the hall there are tributes to the artists of the Bible, while the back wall displays a series of murals showing the seven days of creation. In one mural, as God commands "Let there be light!," angel children shine their flashlights into the puffs of parting clouds.

At the front of the sanctuary the Hallelujah Square draws the most attention of any mural. It depicts an expansive scene in heaven, with two angelic children in the foreground holding up signs: "Welcome," followed by "To Your Heavenly Home," but with the welcome sign accidentally held upside down by the child in charge of it. Farther to the right, one child stands in front of a small golden doorway leading into the square itself. The door bears the words, "No More Tears." Friends on the other side greet one another. A mother and father evidently see their baby for the first time since he was taken away in death. (The artist and his wife had themselves lost a grown son.) All in all one sees some fifty-five figures in heaven, many of them representing specific children who have died. Half a dozen figures are people of color—which is more than one might have found in most American or European visions of heaven fifty years ago, although still hardly proportional. In the far distance of the scene, Jesus talks to clustered figures in white robes. Trees point skyward, beneath and behind an overarching rainbow.

In a half-hour video distributed commercially, Samuel ("Sam") Butcher narrates how he came to plan and design and paint the chapel.[21] He makes it plain there and elsewhere that the Hallelujah Square is heaven as seen through the eyes of a child. What he does not explain is why all the figures in the chapel—

whether they are supposed to be human adults or celestial beings or mere beginners in life—have the shape and look of preadolescent children.

But that will not surprise anyone familiar with the over fourteen hundred Precious Moments figurines that have been introduced to the public since the rights for their manufacture were purchased by the Enesco Corporation in 1979. As Enesco promotional material states, the teardrop-eyed children are a trademark and selling point of these "collectibles."[22] While the porcelain bisque figurines have been executed by a Japanese sculptor Yasuhei Fujioka and his workshop, Butcher supplies the drawings on which the figurines are based. Back in 1974, Butcher had already begun depicting the same sorts of teardrop-eyed children for Jonathan and David inspirational greeting cards; before that, he had worked as a staff artist for the International Child Evangelism Fellowship of Grand Rapids, Michigan. Clearly Butcher has always understood the experience of seeing the world through a child's eyes as something virtually inseparable from his faith and witness as a Christian artist. He seems to have taken as his motto Jesus' words that, unless we become as children, we cannot enter the Kingdom of Heaven (Matt. 18:3).

Samuel Butcher has spoken of the chapel as the culmination of his life's work.[23] Born in Jackson, Michigan, and raised in a family that was familiar with poverty, he later associated himself with Christian groups that took seriously their ministry to the young and relatively unsophisticated. Butcher studied art in high school, and in later years traveled abroad. In Italy, the Sistine Chapel made a lasting impression on him, as did other Italian Renaissance art. Butcher speaks of his use of "rich Renaissance colors" in the paintings and stained glass.[24] The large bronze plates outside the chapel appear to have taken their inspiration, although nothing of their style, from the famous bronze doors that Lorenzo Ghiberti provided in 1452 for the Baptistery in Florence. The whole program of the chapel is elaborately worked out, and the resources for the materials and labor were literally international. It could be argued that, in the Precious Moments Chapel, which as we have noted is modeled loosely on the Sistine, Butcher is trying to translate into an immediately accessible American vernacular something of the effect of the great religious art of the Renaissance.

The videotape and other verbal documentation associated with the chapel encourage us to believe that Butcher has succeeded. On the tape his high school art teacher speaks of feeling very fortunate when he discovered after six months that he had in his class a student who wanted to make real art, not just something to please family and friends, and who would surely become another Michelangelo. Butcher himself speaks on the tape of wanting to glorify God with his work and to communicate a sense of God's love. His manner is one of complete sincerity, and he seems touchingly grateful to be able to describe the chapel as a "spectacular" and "amazing" project. The promotional material, which

Butcher obviously endorses, is more eager to impress upon us the idea that the chapel is a "magnificent artwork," and indeed an unforgettable "Artistic Masterpiece."[25]

It is not hard to imagine what Milan Kundera would say about the Precious Moments Chapel. It exemplifies everything he condemns as sheer kitsch. Here all is sweetness and light. There is not the faintest hint of "shit." The words that recur repeatedly in descriptions of the chapel are "sweet," "precious," "tender," "inspirational," "touching." Visitors are frequently moved to tears.[26] And in Kundera's mind there would be no doubt that the first tear springs from thinking how nice it is to see the children in the role of angels or prophets or figures from the parables; a second tear would follow, tainted by the cloying awareness of how very nice it is to be here and to be moved—as everyone else is—by the sight of those dear children with teardrop eyes. The fact that the art is religious would only seal the case: the chapel is classic kitsch. The best Kundera could say, therefore, is that it indulges a forgivable weakness. At worst, he would conclude, it disguises a false ideology of God's universal love and perfectly wonderful world. In that respect it is a work that disseminates lies.

Karsten Harries, among others, might agree with Kundera about the effect. Kitsch, he says, is morally suspect. And though Harries does not write as a religious believer, he argues that religious kitsch "seeks to elicit religious emotion without an [authentic] encounter with God."[27]

But what might a Christian say—someone who in principle could be glad about the fact that the art aims to be religious? One can assume that, of the million or so visitors who come to the chapel each year, a high percentage are Christians. And a high percentage approve heartily of the art, if one can judge from the success of the gift shop that provides the only public access to the chapel and that is run by Precious Moments, Inc. (The chapel itself charges no admission.)

Although the visitors are predominantly middle or working class and American, they are not the only ones (Christian or non-Christian) that Butcher hopes to attract. Some even come from other lands. With that thought in mind, we might go so far as to ask ourselves: How might Prince Vladimir's emissaries from Russia a thousand years ago have reacted upon visiting such a Precious Moments Chapel? Would they have said, "We knew not whether we were in heaven or on earth. For on earth there is no such splendor or such beauty, and we are at a loss how to describe it"?

The question is obviously anachronistic, and any conceivable answer would be highly speculative. But it seems certain that the Russian ambassadors could not have had a good basis for judging the chapel to be kitsch, even had the concept been available. Not being familiar with any such style, they would have had little way of knowing the degree to which the chapel was either innovative or trite, either heart-felt or sentimental. In other words (in terms I introduced in the Prologue), while perceiving the lines, colors, and patterns of the chapel art, the Russian visitors, being unfamiliar with this artistic genre or its alternatives, might not have been able to "apperceive" with discerning eyes the features of the artwork as such, or the limited extent of the art's expressive range. In any case, I think we cannot completely rule out the possibility that the medieval Russians encountering such a chapel for the first time would have "appreciated" greatly what they saw, even to the point of responding with genuine wonder. And they might then have "appraised" the chapel highly, especially if their judgment was guided by the approving glance and word of a respected church leader (as at Hagia Sophia). One can just imagine, then, how different Russian Christianity would have looked following a thousand years of Precious Moments religious images.

It is safe to say, however, that to those who are now Russian or Eastern Orthodox, the idea of praying before an iconostasis of Precious Moments images—so different from the relative severity and dignity of traditional icons—would probably be extremely disconcerting. They might have great difficulty enjoying such art "in God." One has only to recall how the Greek Orthodox who attended the Council of Ferrara-Florence in 1438 found themselves unable to pray before Western sacred images, so unfamiliar was the style and subject matter.[28]

Yet, when it comes to distaste, Eastern Orthodox are not the only Christians who might have trouble with the Precious Moments style and subject matter. In fact, like Kundera, many Christians would consider the chapel and its art to be distinctly off-putting, precisely as kitsch. But, unlike Kundera, they might give reasons that, while based on aesthetic observation, are theological rather than anti-theological. It will be worth our while to examine some possible objections they might raise.

Christian critics put off by this art might be willing to grant that Butcher is motivated by something like a wish to translate certain of the values of the recognizably great religious art of the Renaissance into a devotional medium immediately appealing to the ordinary person today (and not only Americans). Indeed, if there ever was an art meant to be accessible to everyone, it is the art of the Precious Moments Chapel. Even the critical Christian might also concede that Butcher has a theological or scriptural basis for wanting to comfort mourners, both young and old, partly by looking at sacred stories and realities through the eyes of a child. Jesus asks us to become as little children in order to enter the kingdom of heaven.

Given that most of the dearly departed who are memorialized in the chapel's largest mural are children, any inclination to be critical of this "child's eye" view of the realities of faith might well be restrained. But Butcher was in his late forties when he began working on the chapel. And most of the visitors to the chapel are not in fact children, but adults. Nostalgia and idealization could easily enter the picture, therefore, coloring these efforts to see the world, faith, and death itself through the eyes of children. Indeed, many Christian educators would argue that the world actually experienced by most children bears little resemblance, overall, to the sweetly secure scenes envisioned throughout the chapel. Acquaintance with the religious literature that C. S. Lewis wrote for children would suggest, by contrast, that children's way of experiencing life and death is often full of conflicts, fears, and threats from without and within. Furthermore, as James Fowler's studies confirm, much about religion itself is confusing to many children, creating in their lives a mixture of fantasy, guilt, comfort, and exhilaration.[29]

Christian critics could bring scripture back into the discussion at this point. They could point out how Paul admonishes Christians to mature beyond the infant stage of needing milk as their spiritual food, and to learn how to find nourishment in something more solid (1 Cor. 3:2). Even in the passage in Matthew 18 in which Jesus encourages his followers to become as little children, Jesus is referring specifically to a need to adopt a humble attitude, not to any need to extend childhood in perpetuity. The Gospel of Luke takes pains to emphasize that Jesus himself grew up in every way, increasing in wisdom and stature and in divine and human favor—thereby, it seems, modeling a kind of adulthood toward which others might aspire (Luke 2:52).

In other ways as well, the vision of Christianity projected by the chapel and its murals might appear so partial and selective as to constitute a distortion of the gospel, not merely an accessible translation. The Crucifixion scene from the life of Christ sequence, for instance, occupies one rather small roundel in a series high above the main panels on the west wall. In the foreground of the scene we do not see the Crucifixion itself. Instead, we see children in the role of the women and disciples as they mourn amid happily flowering (or at least budding) shrubs. One little figure among the mourners already looks toward the next roundel, which shows the reassuring angel beside the empty tomb. In the background, the three stick-like crosses are barely visible on a distant hilltop.

Finally, at the front and center of the chapel, corresponding to the location where Michelangelo had painted the Last Judgment—with its dramatic images of redemption and damnation—Butcher gives us a kinder, gentler gospel: the mildest possible image of heavenly rewards, in a setting more placid than inspiring. That sin could possibly have dire consequences is never visualized at all, even if it is somehow presumed. While a great many modern Christians would welcome the displacement or moderation of punishment in the divine scheme, one might question such a global attempt to prettify the gospel.

To put the matter as delicately as possible, the Precious Moments Chapel could appear not merely childlike but somewhat childish in its spirituality and theology. The problem is not that the art is accessible. It is how it achieves that accessibility, and at what price. While ambitious (and perhaps overly so), it lacks the vigor, wit, and imaginative flair of an otherwise parallel enterprise of religious "translation"—the Dreamworks animated feature *Prince of Egypt*, based on the Moses story (Brenda Chapman, Steve Hickner, and Simon Wells, 1998). That production had the humility not to present itself as an Artistic Masterpiece on the order of Michelangelo's paintings for the Sistine. More than that, it displayed ethical subtlety in humanizing the Egyptians beyond anything usually encountered even in "high art" and formal preaching. Equally important, it built up a certain *gravitas* and sense of sublimity in such scenes as Moses' encounter with the Burning Bush and the parting of the Red Sea.

By contrast, the art of Butcher's chapel restricts itself to visual formulas more suitable to greeting cards—the endlessly repeated teardrop eyes being a perfect example. These are formulas that trigger a predictably tearful or heartwarming response but that offer no new insight, and in fact tend to trivialize genuine religious feeling, and so to profane what is sacred.

Thus to some Christians, especially those educated in theology and in the arts, Butcher's art would appear to work in a manner diametrically opposed to the goal of "reaching out without dumbing down," as Marva Dawn has recently urged in relation to Christian worship.[30] And yet this is art that makes high claims for itself. That the artistic rewards are not commensurate with the great cost and labor put into the work is all the more troubling in view of the fact that the art of the Precious Moments Chapel must, in one respect, shoulder an even greater burden than the art of the Sistine Chapel (to which winners of a Precious Moments raffle can travel for free). The Precious Moments Chapel is designed entirely for art rather than for liturgy or preaching. As a consequence, whatever religious experience is afforded by the chapel is guided completely by the art. And on that discouraging note the Christian critic might stop, having represented the sort of reaction one might expect from the more toughminded and academically trained student of art, or artistically trained student of theology.

That was not at all the reaction of one member of my extended family, however, when she visited the Precious Moments Chapel several years ago, not long after her husband had died. She was touched, along with many of her companions. It never occurred to her that this art was anything less than wonderful. After all, her tour had chosen the site specifically; they must have thought it was something exceptional. She had studied neither art nor theology. But she had been to Europe more than once and had attended church regularly since her youth. I suppose that Kundera would deny that her emotions, her tears, were genuine. That denial hardly seems necessary, however. Nor is it necessary to deny that her venture that day in Christian art and architecture could conceivably have carried her further in faith than the Sistine Chapel itself—which many a visitor has found overcrowded or simply overwhelming in scale and thus too much to take in. There have been people trained in theology and art who have been unmoved by the Sistine paintings (especially after their restoration, which many of us, to the contrary, do admire). Some other people, like a medievalist whom I count among my closest friends, enjoy Michelangelo's frescoes as paintings but are unable to see them as particularly religious in spirit or in effect, despite their overtly religious subject matter.

It may seem that I have come full circle, returning merely to affirm (with Andrew Sullivan) a precritical stage of appreciation or an uncritical kind of appraisal that Kundera had no wish to approve because of his own ideological commitments. But in fact I have not embraced entirely or uniformly any of the views of the chapel that I have tried to describe. Indeed, I have tried to show that some of the very things that make the Precious Moments Chapel appealing to some people could make it appalling to others. For those who are appalled, it may be that the only way to love the chapel "in God" would be to love the people who do just that, and to accept its art (in some measure) for their sake. That becomes easier when one recognizes that the chapel really does look very different to different people, depending on one's point of view—including one's theology, experience, and aesthetic taste. When it comes to appraising quality in the realm of religious art, therefore, we evidently need to take into account (among other things) the context of the individual viewer (or listener or reader), the context of the maker, and the context of the community—the various possible publics.

One implication of the discussion so far is that one cannot use the term "kitsch" as though it serves equally well in all contexts. If we care to call the Precious Moments Chapel a work of kitsch—and if anything is kitsch, this chapel would surely qualify—then it should be with a carefully qualified sense of what that means. Some artists and theorists cannot utter the term "kitsch" without also meaning to make the sweeping appraisal that the art is "rubbish" or worthless and quite probably insincere.[31] If that is inevitably what "kitsch" comes to, in one's mind, then one had better forget the term in religious circles; because, there, one will be surrounded by people whose hearts have truly been touched and whose spirits have genuinely been moved, at one time or another, by the supposed "kitsch" that one is dismissing as worthless. To explain that one means only that it is worthless as art rather than worthless as religion is not enough, since many Christians value such works as religious art.

I have been saving until now my own definition of kitsch, because it is normative and yet quite explicitly contextual, in the manner I have been attempting to justify. Kitsch can be regarded, broadly and simply, as that kind of successful work which most educated and disciplined artists in a given medium would be embarrassed to have produced, and which most established art institutions (as distinguished from entertainment venues) would be embarrassed to display or perform—because, to them, its success seems somehow cheap. Theologically speaking, it is art that educated, disciplined religious artists and their publics might be able enjoy "in God," but only with some sense of embarrassment, and with apologies to the Deity. To say this is not to deny that kitsch functions differently in different contexts, some of which minimize its weaknesses. Nor is it to deny that God is larger than any theology and subtler than any taste. It is only to affirm that, just as theologies can have characteristic inadequacies (and embarrassments), so can tastes.

In my account, not all commercial art is kitsch, nor is all popular art. And kitsch is not just bad art (and even bad art can be good in certain respects). Nor is kitsch always insincere. The aims of a work of kitsch, and the emotions it elicits, can be genuine, so far as they go. But, from the vantage point of most educated and disciplined artists, and of their institutions and clients, kitsch succeeds to an embarrassing extent. Its effects outrun its causes. At its worst, kitsch could be considered the aesthetic counterpart to what theologians (after Dietrich Bonhoeffer) have termed "cheap grace."[32]

Kitsch is designed and often calculated to tap into highly predictable responses in the viewer—responses not so deep as those tapped by artfully rendered archetypal symbols and the like, but more like emotional reflexes. Those reflexes are very real—rather like basic sexual responses. According to Ellen Laan, a psychologist at the University of Amsterdam, "for both men and women, when you show them a sexual cue, the body responds to it [whether or not they are aware of that]. It's an automatic response, it's probably hard-wired, and it's probably a good mechanism."[33] We have every reason to believe that similarly automatic responses are triggered by teardrop eyes and young children (whose typical looks are "designed" by nature to be adorable). Kitsch and erotic art are both primed to take advantage of such responses. Certain sophisticated viewers, being aware of this, are guarded against the slightest hint of kitsch. They learn to check what Kundera describes as the "second tear"—indulgent, unearned. But that protective mechanism is indeed learned, not natural.

Reflexive emotional responses are not all bad, however, nor is a guarded sensibility always good. Sometimes, as Robert Solomon has argued, the fear of sentiment and kitsch is altogether excessive and constricting, shutting down otherwise healthy and sensitive affections.[34] The veritable allergy that modern educated critics (predominantly male) have shown to any art they perceive as "soft" or "weak" or "sentimental" is often connected—as Colleen McDannell reminds us—with their sense of what should be dismissed as "effeminate."[35] There is reason to believe that the critical establishment at various levels is far too quick to label art as "kitsch" simply because it is touching and therefore supposedly feminine.

Kitsch itself (as defined above) can have a positive effect by releasing and exercising sentiments that otherwise might be so protected as to atrophy through disuse. There is a place for kitsch, therefore. Yet kitsch is forever immature— and often in a way that cries out to be counteracted and reformed at a more mature level. In and of itself, kitsch ordinarily conveys a distorted impression of the higher goals to which it typically alludes or aspires. And it cannot often carry one very far toward those goals.

One of the embarrassments of kitsch is that the religious experience afforded by religious kitsch tends to have something about it that is cheap or counterfeit—quick and easy, or illusory—yet impossible to criticize without seeming uncharitable. That is because, even in responding to kitsch, people do open their "hearts" and to some extent make themselves vulnerable, even if the overall impact and involvement is usually slight or superficial—as in a brief and abortive romance. To label the object of their affections as kitsch will be experienced and perceived as unkind, however true. Given that one goal of the Christian life is to care for the neighbor as for oneself, one dimension of that care is to be careful in criticism. It might also mean tempering one's internal criticism of the neighbor's kitsch with a degree of appreciation and enjoyment, recognizing that one's own negative judgment may be biased or uninformed, that the art in question may not deserve the label kitsch after all, that it is probably not worthless even if it is kitsch, and that, in any case, one might benefit on another occasion from a reciprocal act of charity.

A more annoying or indeed disturbing embarrassment is that the religious experience kitsch affords can at times be something entirely genuine and beyond reproach. It is disturbing to acknowledge that this is true because, if kitsch can sometimes work wonders religiously, that forces us to ask whether the aesthetic quality of art is of religious relevance. We have said all along that it is, or can be. But clearly we need to recognize that many factors go into perceiving, enjoying, and judging the religious worth of any work of art. Because of the several different elements of taste, good art can be abused, religiously; and bad art can be saved, religiously. It is time to see how, as we attempt further to develop flexible but genuine standards for evaluating art and taste theologically.

Taste Tests

A Taste of Appalachian Religion and Art

In her critically acclaimed novel *Saving Grace* (1995), Lee Smith narrates the youth, early adulthood, and middle years of Florida Grace Shepherd, who was born in Florida but raised in the Appalachians by a father who was a snake-handling preacher and by a mother who trusted the Lord to provide.[36] Though Grace had spiritual gifts, she came to know herself, in her family of believers, as ornery, full of fear and doubt, unable to love Jesus. She witnessed miraculous things, growing up. And she saw terrible things, too, including her mother's suicide by hanging. Grace was sexually exploited by a half-brother, who may have taken liberties with her mother as well. And she came to realize that her father, whose voice "made you feel good, like you were strong in the Lord" (p. 17), was faithless in love and marriage, and deceptive in many aspects of his piety.

After the death of Grace's mother, her father, Virgil, tried to leave behind his sordid reputation. So he took Grace from the relative safety of their little home beside Scrabble Creek, in a region of widespread poverty in North Carolina. Arriving in Tennessee, Virgil once again gave himself over to loose morals and charismatic ministry. He celebrated old-time religion, condemning the churches down the road that had wall-to-wall carpet, padded seats, "colored windows and Lawrence Welk music" (p. 139). As the Spirit moved in church and people started handling serpents, Grace stood over by the wall watching. But, as she says, "I could not keep my feet still, the music was so good" (p. 140). For the most part Virgil left her on her own, which was increasingly what she wanted.

Grace eventually married a truly kind preacher, Travis Word, who "got real scared every time he had any emotion that was not directly linked to God" (p. 170). His over-developed sense of sexual guilt and his squeamish attitude toward things of the flesh left her feeling undernourished. As several years went by, Grace found that even their two children were not enough to give her much sense of vitality, although she was not exactly bored. She concluded that "there are ways in which it is easier to live with a plaster saint like Daddy than with a real saint like Travis Word" (p. 197). It wasn't just the way Travis anguished over his sexual urges that bothered Grace. In her words: "Travis believed that everything in life happened for a purpose and fell into the great scheme of God, but I did not. I was still prone to question and agonize. I criticized God" (p. 202).

In time, at age thirty-three, Grace had a ravenous affair with a carefree house painter, which for a while made her feel rejuvenated and in some way "born again" (p. 225). That all ended in stupidity and meanness on both sides. "The fact is, I was not real good at modern life. I didn't even look good anymore after five years with Randy Newhouse" (p. 239).

It was winter and Christmas when things bottomed out. Grace was traveling, thinking of maybe getting back with Randy, when she pulled off the road at a little café which was "lighted up and friendly-looking. UNCLE SLIDELL'S DINER, the sign read, A CHRISTIAN RESTAURANT" (p. 248). Getting out of the car, although it was snowing outside, she heard something like the cry of a baby coming from a nearby putt-putt golf course marked by a sign, "UNCLE SLIDELL'S CHRISTIAN FUN GOLF." Approaching the course, she caught sight of a "love tour" starting, of course, with Hole Number One, which was the Garden of Eden—Adam and Eve, plastic fruit, and a red rubber snake. Hole Number Six was the Cross—the "old rugged cross," spelled "ruged." Grace noticed the Wedding at Cana, too, and of course the Ten Commandments. But for some reason, the First Christmas came after those, at Hole Number Ten. It featured ceramic barnyard animals and plywood cutouts of the Wise Men—with a whole host of angels hanging from a clothesline strung over the manger, where the baby lay crying (powered by some unseen source), dirty snow dripping in his face. The baby held out his chubby little arms to her. The sign said, TO: YOU FROM: GOD. And so it seemed to be, though what Grace says in narrating her story is that the glory of God shone all around. Later, a man from the diner helped her into her car. It turned out there was no Uncle Slidell. But that did not seem to matter. Grace started out on the interstate and ended up going back to North Carolina, to her abandoned former home up on Scrabble Creek. There she decided finally to return to church where, as she observes, she really would be coming to Jesus.

Once Grace returned home, the voice of the crying baby first heard at the Christian putt-putt golf course became, in her mind, also the voice of her mother, who appeared in a dream urging her, "*Come to me, Gracie,*" then, "*Oh come to Jesus honey.*" At this point in the story the reader is likely to ask what Grace does not: Is it Jesus who is calling? Or is it her mother? Or both? When Grace finally starts down the hill toward church the next morning, are we to interpret this act as a sign of her caving in to a need for confession and security? Or is it, rather, her discovery of the only way she can really heal—by surrendering to the gracious mystery of "joy in the Lord" and ecstasy in the Spirit (p. 271)?

Lee Smith seems to recognize that it might be hard for some readers to think of Grace's homecoming and impending conversion to life in Jesus as anything more than a retreat and final collapse into a childish faith. Smith goes out of her way, therefore, to depict Grace's change as a mature choice, although it means recovering a state of childlike openness and humility. Smith shows, for instance, that the people to whom Grace returns in repentance and gladness, Ruth and

Carlton Duty, have long since rejected the exploitive kind of Christianity prac-ticed by her father. And Smith has Grace distance herself from the hard-sell Christianity of Doyle Stacy, whose church on Zion Hill Road meets in a stone building that used to be a small-engine repair shop. Doyle is right about the main points of the gospel, but he is graceless in communicating them. Grace is finally shaping up, and in a profound way growing up, by being reborn (a term that Smith nevertheless avoids). Reflecting on how she has never yet been bap-tized, despite her Christian upbringing, Grace strips herself naked at home—as early Christians did for baptism itself—before carefully selecting her church-going clothes, in a manner approaching ritual. She knows she has not come home merely to retreat to a permanent womb: "When I leave here this time, it will be for good" (p. 270).

There is little doubt, then, where the "implied author" stands in regard to what we might as well call Grace's conversion into a life of faith. But just in case, Smith appends a note at the end of the book. She begins that note by say-ing: "In a way my writing is a lifelong search for belief. I have always been particularly interested in expressions of religious ecstasy, and in those moments when we are most truly 'out of ourselves' and experience the Spirit directly" (p. 274).

Saving Grace is very much concerned with what on earth to make of faith—its maturity or immaturity, its authenticity or inauthenticity, its powers to heal or wound. The novel captures well a particular narrator's voice and viewpoint, and her restless "spiritual journey" in and around a particular people and cul-ture. In so doing, it captures as well the tension between the wisdom of the world and the folly of faith, between experience and innocence, and shows something of what is at stake in finding a way for faith to be, in its own way, wise and experienced even while innocent and foolish. That would be what Paul Ricoeur has called a second naiveté, not uncritical and uninformed childishness.[37]

I would resist any attempt to label *Saving Grace* a work of kitsch, whatever its peculiar limitations and weaknesses. But in the novel, and from our own standpoint in this study, it is hardly insignificant that Grace's conversion is prompted by her encounter with "art" that we could easily call kitsch, if we think of it as art at all. The little religious vignettes at the Christian putt-putt golf course are decisive in bringing Grace to a realization of an alternative to her own wayward course. Jesus calls Grace, and extends saving grace to her, by assuming the form of a dirty-faced baby doll crying in an outdoor manger scene. The baby seems crying not so much for itself as for her. The possibility that such humble and tacky art could have such a profound effect is certainly meant to be ironic as well as "touching." And yet it seems perfectly consistent with Christian teaching, which rarely applauds the wisdom of the world or insists on the best sort of taste and art.

Again, however, the novel makes a crucial distinction between humble simplicity and contrived immaturity, both in art and in faith. The novel would not
have us conclude that Grace is being fooled by the golf course "art," or that
she is being manipulated. The art of the Christian putt-putt golf course is
incongruous, in view of the serious message it is intended to convey. In that
way it is kitsch. But it is anything but pretentious and slick, or in any way
coercive or seductive. It is miles from what Grace's father Virgil had criticized
as Lawrence Welk church music and padded pews. It is too crude, playful, and
genuinely simple for that.[38]

Such truly rudimentary and ingenuous (albeit ingenious) art has a narrow
range. Each of the scenes along the Christian Love Tour is little more than a
sign, a gesture. Such art hardly pretends to encompass, by itself, the height and
depth of the gospel. Like much religious art, only more so, it depends on a
broader and deeper religious context—a community of faith and a tradition of
worship—to say more fully what it means, and so to save it from utter triviality. But in the moment, and by its very manner and strategic placement, the
putt-putt art of biblical interpretation evidently could say what no Bible reading alone could say, and speak where no preacher could. And in its blessed
poverty of means, the putt-putt artistry had a very different flavor from what
visitors would normally detect at the Precious Moments Chapel.

Lee Smith knows, of course, that few readers of her book are likely to be so
much a part of the culture and mentality she is representing that they could
ever turn to Jesus on the basis of "artistic" scenes at a Christian miniature golf
course. More likely, her readers bear more resemblance to Smith herself, requiring
a more searching and subtle sort of art, and possibly even a more complex sort
of faith, though not necessarily anything more genuine. Certainly the art that
Smith herself practices is less didactic, less stuck to the literal surface of things.
Although the figure of the hypocritical preacher, for instance, is a stereotype,
Smith grants him a kind of spiritual power that, like that of the preacher E. R.
in the film *The Apostle* (Robert Duvall, 1997), is not to be gainsaid. And Smith
leaves room for the reader to establish some distance from Grace in her final
turning, just as Grace distances herself from Doyle.

If writing, for Lee Smith, is "in a way" a process of searching for belief, and
rejoicing in the signs that the search is not senseless, the process of reading her
writing might take on much the same quality. That means, however, that some
readers will be more adept and cooperative than others. Just how persuasive
the novel seems, in the end, will depend on whether the reader is willing to
take seriously the characters and their dilemmas, and the moral and religious
choices that shape their lives. One can easily imagine certain readers for whom
such a book would always appear sentimental and contrived, a rather sophisticated sort of kitsch—possibly one long and tiresome pun on the whole idea of

saving grace. The issue is not just aesthetic. It involves theology and spirituality and morality. But it is aesthetic in that the answer has everything to do with whether the novel will be felt to be compelling, and how. It all has to do, finally, with a discerning taste and with a breadth (or depth) of imaginative vision—with whether Christianity has either, and more particularly with whether this artistic interpretation of Christian conversion elicits and cultivates either. How is one to know? And who can say? It turns out that this is not just an individual judgment, or a matter of personal preference, but at least partly a function of whole communities of taste and faith. A few briefer examples will clarify, and show more clearly what is at stake.

A Sense of the Ending

Saving Grace ends quietly. Grace drinks from Scrabble Creek, thinks of her mother and her past, of the crying baby Jesus, and of snow angels she and her sister Billie Jean used to make when they were little. In the midst of such thoughts she starts her car. One supposes she is headed to church.

That conclusion—indeed the whole novel—is far too understated and open-ended to satisfy the purposes of most Contemporary Christian novelists. Certainly it would not appeal to writers such as Tim LaHaye and Jerry B. Jenkins, who team up for a series published by Tyndale House that deals with the last days of the earth—and that has sold over three million copies. The first of these novels, *Left Behind*, ends resolutely.[39] A pilot named Buck, who not long before has "received Christ," vows to join the "Tribulation Force." When his plane touches down, he joins three members of his family in Christ, who give thanks that God has protected him.

> They moved through the terminal toward the parking garage, striding four abreast, arms around each other's shoulders, knit with a common purpose. Rayford Steele, Chloe Steele, Buck Williams, and Bruce Barnes faced the gravest dangers anyone could face, and they knew their mission.
>
> The task of the Tribulation Force was clear and their goal nothing less than to stand and fight the enemies of God during the seven most chaotic years the planet would ever see. (LB, p. 468)

But we have gotten way ahead of ourselves. The novel begins by telling us what is on the mind of a different pilot—Rayford Steele, this time—as he routes his plane toward Heathrow airport. A family man, he is nonetheless thinking of Hattie Durham, a "drop-dead gorgeous" flight attendant. He is also thinking about how, lately, he has found himself repelled by his wife's obsession with religion, which seems all she can talk about.

God was OK with Rayford Steele. Rayford even enjoyed church occasionally. But since Irene had hooked up with a smaller congregation and was into weekly Bible studies and church every Sunday, Rayford had become uncomfortable. Hers was not a church where people gave you the benefit of the doubt, assumed the best about you, and let you be. People there had actually asked him, to his face, what God was doing in his life. (LB, pp. 1–2)

Rayford's reply, "Blessing my socks off," gets the church people off his back. But he still finds excuses to be busy on Sundays.

We quickly realize that *Left Behind* is going to expect us to take very seriously, and very literally, Mrs. Rayford Steele's preoccupation with "the end of the world, with the love of Jesus, with the salvation of souls," and finally with the "Rapture of the church" (p. 4). Before long, as it happens, the Rapture takes a number of Christian people right out of their seats on the plane, leaving others behind to hold up the clothes of the blissfully departed, and to gasp and shriek (pp. 16–23).

Now, the Rapture is not anything much discussed in the bulk of Christian literature and theology. It receives no entry in the hefty *Oxford Dictionary of the Christian Church*, third edition (1997). But the idea of being caught up in the air to meet Christ at his second coming is a major theme of some forms of millennialist and fundamentalist Christianity. By dramatizing the event and taking it seriously, *Left Behind* joins a rapidly growing body of Contemporary Christian literature that speaks vividly to people who are committed to such beliefs and the values associated with them. Such fiction, sold in great quantity through Christian bookstores, is valued all the more for being virtually the only literature (modern or otherwise) that gives respect and narrative life to the outlook of certain Christian believers often simply caricatured in fiction.

Not that this fiction is subtle. There is not a character or plot device in *Left Behind* that Charles Dickens or John Updike would find the least bit interesting; and no one would accuse Dickens or Updike of being unpopular or inaccessible. Nevertheless, just as science fiction written in a "pulp" style can raise very serious questions about the universe and our role in it, this Christian fiction boldly goes where no one has ever gone before. It is utterly contemporary, and yet utterly committed to a literal interpretation of Christian teachings as viewed through the lens of turn-of-the-millennium Christianity in its millenarian guise.

The *Celestine Prophecy* by James Redfield, together with its sequel *The Tenth Insight*, is likewise a kind of spiritual parable, though in some major respects less literal-minded.[40] It, too, is a bonafide bestseller, having sold more than five million copies and even occupied the number one position on the *New York Times* bestseller list. Endorsed by Elisabeth Kübler-Ross as a "fabulous book about experiencing life,"[41] it is the first of two stories (so far) that weave global history and New Age reflection (and speculation) into a saga of priests, mystics, politicians, technocrats, liberal secularists, and enamored lovers, with due representation of various ethnic and racial groups, especially Native American and African. The leading characters roam about in various Peruvian settings, and subsequently in the Appalachian hills, which seem to have some kind of magnetism for spiritual storytelling.

The Celestine Prophecy offers nine "key insights into life itself" that will lead toward "a completely spiritual culture on Earth," a new age of spiritual awareness. These ideas concern everything from the deeper meaning of seeming coincidences (the First Insight) to the causes of human conflict (the Fourth Insight), to truths about child rearing, such as the principle that children "need our energy, on a constant basis, unconditionally" (p. 193), which is an implication of the Eighth Insight.

The entire system of insights is built on a progressive, evolutionary view of history that includes virtually all beings in its eventual utopia. The very idea of such a spiritually inclusive evolution would horrify fans of Contemporary Christian literature, who see the end time of Jesus' Second Coming as establishing once and for all a great divide between the saved and the damned. Yet Jesus appears in Redfield's books, too. We are told that he is the one prophesized in an ancient and newly discovered Peruvian Manuscript from 600 B.C.[42] The Manuscript, which government and church had been trying to suppress, is being promoted by a kind of underground, including a few rebel Catholic priests. Evidently the ancient text predicts a future renaissance in consciousness, not "religious" but "spiritual" (CP, p. 13). It is a renaissance, or indeed revolution, whereby religions will be empowered to fulfill their promise of helping humankind find relationship to the higher source, the God within (CP, p. 248). The Manuscript prophecies the specific stages leading up to that development. There would be one person in particular who would come to set an example by grasping "the exact way of connecting with God's source of energy and direction," so as to actualize and interiorize divinity within himself (CP, p. 248; cf. TI, p. 120). The characters who hear the prophecy immediately identify that one as Jesus. But his achievement, they now realize, is the destiny of us all; for we can now consciously participate in a massive transformation of awareness and society—somewhat in the manner envisioned by the late Catholic theologian and paleontologist Teilhard de Chardin, cited in *The Tenth Insight*.

Like Christ, we are to become increasingly spiritual in our energy. But whereas *The Celestine Prophecy* sometimes makes that sound like a process of escaping completely from the weight of the material world, enabling us to walk lightly on water, for instance, *The Tenth Insight* speaks more of the transformation of the material and spiritual together. With increased "vibration and perception," we will have the capacity to see "incredible beauty and energy." The aim is thus aesthetic, as well as holistic in every conceivable way—environmental, social, psychological, scientific, religious. The ten insights are in some way analogous to the Ten Commandments, one could assume. But they do not give orders; they describe "key insights." And they do not focus on a particular Chosen People. Indeed, in their perspective on human life and thought, nothing of wisdom is left out, one might think. Everything is meant to be taken into account: Eastern philosophy, Western mysticism, Christian and Gnostic awareness, Franciscan ecological piety, Marxist social and economic reform, alternative medicine, organic nutrition, technological power (properly channeled) and human potential (properly understood). The stages of the ongoing utopian evolution—which cannot all be recounted here—are all summarized in *The Tenth Insight* (TI, pp. 105–34).

The Tenth Insight goes out of its way to acknowledge and reckon with the millenarian prophecies promoted relentlessly by those Christians who are addressed and enthralled by *Left Behind*. Redfield's writing even discusses the specific expectation of a "massive rapture" that "will begin among true believers, whoever they are," when they will be "snatched off the face of the Earth and lifted into Heaven" (TI, p. 50). It tries to take the story to another level, no longer literal. Lamenting the polarizing "culture war" between liberal permissiveness and fundamentalist authoritarianism, *The Tenth Insight* envisions a higher synthesis, moving beyond the literalism of the Christian Right and the cynical secularism of the Liberal Left (TI, pp. 45 ff., 129–33). Refusing to give in to fear, *The Tenth Insight* insists that all the opposing forces are just "souls attempting to wake up, like us" (TI 149). The higher way is to "stay centered in love" and to send others "love and energy" (TI 150). That is what *The Tenth Insight* is about: the need to project the Vision, and to hold it for the rest of humanity (TI, p. 217).

The target audience for *The Celestine Prophecy* and its sequel(s) is without doubt the large body of readers, worldwide, who are disaffected, or marginally connected, with what they perceive to be Western religion in its more dogmatic and controlling forms. Yet they are equally disaffected with a culture dominated by the ideals of a scientific and technological age that has appeared arid and soul-less. They find spiritual promise and fulfillment in the alternatives eclectically gathered under the New Age tent. Those alternatives are not just ideas; they have to do with "life style" and taste and tone, a sensibility that tries to blunt hard edges, that explores hidden and emerging possibilities, cultivates feeling and wonder, heightens contemplative awareness, blurs the rigid boundaries of rationality, and opens itself to the miraculous. The aesthetic of the New Age tends to be cross-cultural, esoteric, meditative, calming—or else celebrative without feeling driven or frantic or aggressive.

Redfield's efforts in this regard have found an immensely appreciative, international readership, despite his finding it necessary first to publish *The Celestine Prophecy* as a private venture. Yet it must be said that his writing could easily be classified as a kind of kitsch. Promoted by its New Age supporters as a masterpiece of fiction, a work of genius, and a distillation of the spiritual wisdom of the ages that accomplishes what the greatest storytellers across time and culture aspire to (see cover blurbs), *The Tenth Insight* will strike less sympathetic readers as amateurish. Most college English professors, if handed such a manuscript, would criticize it for stiff and unconvincing dialogue and for being unable to sustain a narrative without interrupting the story with dubious history and questionable philosophizing. The characters have little depth or interiority, despite all the emphasis on the inner life. They frequently mouth what critics sometimes unflatteringly refer to as psychobabble: "Maya reached over and touched me: 'Your comment was defensive. When you respond that way, the other person doesn't feel heard'" (TI, p. 176). Worse yet, readers are asked to find it somehow plausible that a manuscript from 600 B.C. could predict specifically that in the late twentieth century more and more human beings would develop a certain kind of consciousness—as though that method of dating time were actually available in 600 B.C. Indeed, everything depends on the fictional "possibility" that the same ancient manuscript could predict with great accuracy the reasons for the rise of modern science and foresee the problems of modern technology. The enormous success of this literature of the New Age can thus seem embarrassing to a more "literate" audience.

Evaluating Religious Kitsch

From the perspective of the theory of kitsch I have proposed, the work I have discussed here that would be least susceptible to being classified as kitsch is the novel *Saving Grace*. And to readers put off by a sympathetic treatment of public faith and private ecstasy, that could be classified as kitsch as well. The Precious Moments Chapel, the playful art of the Christian putt-putt golf course, the best-selling Contemporary Christian novel, and the two wildly popular New Age "adventure parables" all succeed, one might say, to an embarrassing extent—at least when judged by standards of many disciplined, educated artists, and by institutions and audiences most identified with the pursuit of artistic excellence. It is hard to imagine many teachers of studio art or creative writing or spiritual artistry who would regard works such as these as exemplary—as

things one would be altogether proud to have produced as an artist. The normative aspect of my definition of kitsch allows us to say not only that there is some
good reason to use the term "kitsch" in such cases, but also that people highly
trained and disciplined in the arts (popular as well as "elite") are among those
most likely to know the ways in which such kitsch takes short-cuts, exploiting
easy effects.

It is true that, in relation to every one of our test cases, the satisfied "target"
audience is in the best position to intuit or express the standards that such art
actually meets or exceeds. It is also true that economic values enter into the
picture in the appraisal and very survival of almost all forms of art, and not
only art that strikes people as cheap and commercial. Yet no one really thinks
that a good artwork is simply whatever various people happen to like, or like
to buy. Rather, we should say that a good work of art is one that, when it is
liked, is liked for good artistic reasons, perhaps the best of reasons. Although
those reasons arise in relation to a given tradition, however untraditional the
work's image, most judgments of taste implicitly reach out to a wider community, commending the art to everyone who could be positioned to give it a fair
hearing, viewing, or reading. That wider community will notice some things
that the "home" community will not. In the process, the ways in which the work
or style excels or falters (and almost every viable work or style has both strengths
and weaknesses) become part of the larger cultural dialogue, often cross-
cultural.

One can never state in so many words all the reasons why a work of art succeeds or fails, or in what respects. No set of criteria can adequately spell out
what makes for good art and what makes for bad. That is partly because the
words of criticism are not the words of art; if they were the same, there would
be no need for art. But even the art that is most elusive of verbal criticism is not
beyond critical response altogether. As George Steiner has emphasized, the best
and fullest criticism of works and kinds of art often comes indirectly, from other
works of art, whether or not they find a large audience.[43] The readers of *Left
Behind*, for example, could perceive in their fiction an implicit critique of Lee
Smith's approach as a novelist, which is designed to be ambiguous, at points,
even in treating a matter as serious as Christian conversion. Informed and conditioned by their favorite Christian fiction, they would hardly know what to
make of Smith's statement (reflected in her fiction) that in some way her writing is a lifelong search for belief. To them, that would indicate a sad confusion,
when it is clear to them that the answer lies in the Bible or in preaching (or literature) based squarely on the scriptures.

Lee Smith's fiction could, in turn, implicitly critique the art of *Left Behind*,
which starts with what it assumes is a biblical truth and then illustrates it. Smith
thinks she finds the truth as she uncovers and recovers it in the process of

writing. For her the act of writing, and therefore the act of reading, becomes new at every turn—stretching and criticizing and embodying what faith might mean. Her fiction is itself written that way, thereby criticizing the fiction that works mainly from prefabricated materials.

Then again, *The Celestine Prophecy* might suggest, for example, that the theological or spiritual vision of *Saving Grace* is rather too provincial, too private in its ecstasies. *Saving Grace* might suggest, in turn, that the abstractions tossed about in *The Celestine Prophecy* need more flesh and blood, and some sense of genuine intimacy with the Spirit. Attending to the mutual criticism of the arts develops our critical and appreciative powers, both. The result of being exposed critically and appreciatively to multiple styles is not, however, a capacity (or necessarily even the inclination) to declare an absolute winner, with all the opposition sent to shameful defeat.

Has my insistence on the importance of questions of quality and taste made my approach elitist, despite my disclaimers? Not as I understand the concept "elitist." It is not elitist to believe that some aesthetic choices are better than others. Every artist makes that assumption simply in choosing how to make a given work, or how to make it better. Nor is it elitist to believe that some artistic goals are more rewarding in kind and duration than others, however diverse those goals may be, and however conditioned by special communal interests and tastes. Every kind of art, even the most popular, has its relative "classics," and every community also singles out particular kinds of art as the most admirable and enduring. It is not even elitist to believe that some aesthetic styles are more promising than others for purposes of religious expression and exploration. We observed in an earlier chapter that virtually every religious tradition develops criteria as to which kinds of art are most appropriate for worship and devotion. Those standards may change, but they are anything but negligible. What is truly elitist (and cynical besides) is to believe that popular arts are not concerned with questions of quality, or that they are strictly for the "masses," or that they must always be mere kitsch. It is also truly elitist to think that "elite" and formal arts are always cheapened whenever they become popular and accessible.

One feature of my position that might indeed tend toward elitism is my belief that many important artistic values are discovered by artists who are both educated and highly disciplined (attributes I have intentionally left vaguely defined, however). That is actually not very different, however, from asserting in the sphere of religion that disciplined and trained theologians can say things that elude more casual and less educated interpretations of Christianity. Discipline and training does not guarantee superiority, but it does open up possibilities that are otherwise unavailable. It is true, of course, that the great religious figures such as Moses, Jesus, Mohammed, and the Buddha would not conform to today's ideals of education and discipline. The traditions surrounding them leave no doubt, however, that even their early followers viewed them as spiritually disciplined figures artfully offering wisdom that transcends anything one could imaginably consider "kitsch."

It remains to be seen how Christianity in the present era might best accommodate and encourage artistic excellence in a plurality of ways that are discerning and discriminating without being elitist and exclusive. The need, at least, seems real enough—even urgent. In a chapter that has considered several works of art concerned with the future and with the ends of faith, it seems fitting to close on a note of theological speculation related to this very point.

At the turn of the millennium the long-term viability of Christianity as a tradition of adventurous faith and profound aspiration appears to depend on (among other things) a new and renewed artistry. That means recovering and developing diverse modes of artistic creativity and discernment that are popular without being kitsch. It also means cultivating in a serious and sustained manner religiously significant art that is not afraid at certain points to be extraordinarily disciplined, theologically searching, and profoundly imaginative—even if that means being unpopular. Just how possible that may be is part of what we will consider in the chapters that follow, the next of which reflects on the medium of music, the context of worship, and the goal of an ecumenical taste and faith.

Ecumenical Taste

The Case of Music

Communities of Taste

A Diversity of Tastes

For reasons that are clear to almost everyone but theologians, musicians (even church musicians) do not generally make a habit of reading theology. If they have heard of a particular theologian, it is often because that theologian has had something to say about music—preferably something complimentary and quotable. Thus, recently, one Contemporary Christian Music distributor promoted the recordings of a Catholic singer by saying that, according to Augustine, "sung prayer has twice the impact of spoken prayer."[1] One can recognize in those words a creative translation of the well-known saying from Augustine that, in church, the person who sings prays twice—except that Augustine may not have said even that. He did say that he was tempted to give music more honor than is fitting, when he sensed that our souls are moved more by a Psalm when it is sung than when it is not.[2] And he remarked that the Alleluia one sings in church with the "mouth of the flesh" duplicates the continual praise sung silently in the "mouth of the heart."[3] But those cautious acknowledgments of music's power are not couched in the sort of catchy phrases that would either sell recordings or inspire congregational singing.

Musicians have not needed to be so creative in quoting from Karl Barth. Many know that, when this modern Protestant theologian thought of heaven, he immediately thought of music. Barth speculated that, in heaven, when the angels go about their task of praising God, they may play only Bach; but—Barth was quick to say—when playing for their own enjoyment, they surely play Mozart. On those occasions, too, according to Barth, God listens in with special pleasure.[4] A year before he made those remarks honoring his beloved Mozart, Barth had already spoken in a way that would warm many a musician's heart: "If I ever get to heaven, I would first of all seek out Mozart and only then inquire after Augustine, St. Thomas, Luther, Calvin, and Schleiermacher."[5]

Barth is not, of course, the only person to declare that certain kinds of earthly music are just the sort of thing one would want and expect to hear in heaven. But there are notable differences in the music nominated for heavenly status— something already implied by Barth's wish to accommodate, in different ways, both Bach and Mozart. Reviewers of the medieval music vocal quartet Anonymous 4 apparently regard the singing of that group as worthy of the Heavenly Paradise. The *American Record Guide* asserts: "Anonymous 4 produce some of the most exquisitely beautiful, expressive singing [to be heard]. . . . Surely this is the sound of heaven."[6] It is not only so-called classical music that evokes images of heaven. Writing in the *New York Post*, a reviewer opines: "If there is a heaven, and if there is music in it, the music probably sounds like the Chieftains"—no doubt still playing Irish jigs and reels. Bach, Mozart, Anonymous 4, the Chieftains—if such diverse music, and ever so much more, belongs in heaven, God would need to have immensely eclectic taste in order to enjoy it all. And so would the rest of the heavenly throng.

Conflicting Tastes, Family Tastes

At the other extreme from various kinds of heavenly music are the varieties of music associated with the nether regions. Many people still remember the 1986 Gary Larson *Far Side* cartoon that shows, in its upper half, an angel greeting each of the Blessed with the words: "Welcome to heaven . . . here's your harp." In the lower half of the frame, Larson shows a devil meeting the Damned, one by one, and saying, "Welcome to hell . . . here's your accordion."

I cannot think of that cartoon without recalling the fact that my mother used to banish my father to a large cedar closet in the basement whenever he wanted to play the accordion. The cartoon scene and that family memory have somehow merged in my mind. In my imaginary scene, my father is furnished with horns for his head and an accordion for his hands. He fumes just a little at being sent "below," but nonetheless plays energetically in his solitary confinement, welcoming the occasional visitor. From time to time he repeats the song of his I liked best: "Caravan," a tune from Duke Ellington (1899–1974) with pulsing rhythm and a modal touch, a hint of exoticism.[7]

A somewhat uncomfortable aspect of both the cartoon and the family memory—and of my imaginary conflation of the two—is the accompanying realization that much of the music that one group of people considers hellish is considered heavenly, or at least pleasurable, by the people actively playing and listening to it. When I ponder that fact, one more slightly discomfiting family memory rises to consciousness, rounding out this brief excursion into autobiography.

As a young boy, I spent a good many hours in the summer months talking with my great-grandfather, who died in 1972 at the age of 103.[8] Born soon after the end of the American Civil War, he had witnessed the advent of the first light bulb, the first telephone, the automobile, the airplane, the phonograph, and so forth. I learned from relatives that, while my great-grandfather was living and working on a farm in south Alabama (long before I came on the scene), he had purchased a fiddle from a Sears catalog. Married by then, and becoming a father in due course, he practiced the fiddle at home and soon played it with considerable skill—though, in the manner of many old-time country fiddlers, he supported it on his lap rather than placing it under his chin. In time he played for local country dances, and then in festivals in various parts of the American South. When his family moved to a house just outside the city of Birmingham, he became a butcher and then worked in a machine shop. He continued to play the fiddle, but less and less frequently. One day, while he was at work and his daughter (my grandmother) was at home, a nephew came by the house. The fiddle caught the nephew's eye and admiration, whereupon my grandmother, in her typical generosity, gave the fiddle away. Nothing was said when my great-grandfather came home. But one day he noticed that the fiddle was not where he had been keeping it. When he learned what had happened, he burst out in the closest thing to swearing that my grandmother was ever to hear from his lips. She hastened both to explain and defend what she had done: "Daddy, we don't live in the country any more. We're in the city. You know fiddling is for country people." He did not buy another fiddle, or play again.

Identity and Taste

If nothing of greater consequence ever came of differences in musical taste, we could say simply that musical tastes often are a sign or token of personal and social differences.[9] We might better say, however, that such differences and identities make themselves felt in music. That way it is clear that music can become an actual part of those differences and that the differences register on us quite palpably in musical form.[10]

Even then, we should be careful not to imply that music simply replicates in an audible medium the preexisting social and inner realities of our world. Rap music and the hip-hop culture of which it is an integral part are not just an expression of contemporary African American urban life as it already exists, or existed before. They constitute a new dimension of that life, and incarnate its pleasures and problems in ways never before heard or quite imagined. With rap, something innovative comes into being and hearing. On the one hand, gangsta rap gives voice to ferocious aggression, both in sounds and words. Known for heart-jarring rhythms, frequently misogynist lyrics, and "revenge fantasies," the gangsta rap of Snoop Doggy Dog, Tupac Shakur, and Ice-T has threatened to unleash actual violence—and sometimes has succeeded in doing just that. It has often met with considerable resistance from black communities and, more recently, with sometimes feeble imitation from whites. On the other hand, the rap idiom of groups like Public Enemy can act as a kind of exorcism, working through, and working out, what Michael Eric Dyson calls prophetic rage.[11] As another interpreter, Tricia Rose, observes in her book *Black Noise*: "In the postindustrial urban context of dwindling low-income housing, a trickle of meaningless jobs for young people, mounting police brutality, and increasingly draconian depictions of young inner city residents, hip hop style *is* urban renewal."[12]

If the differences between country people and city people, between urban ghetto blacks and suburban mall whites—or between Christians and Hindus— never showed up artistically, they would never be felt in the same way. And if the bonds between people were not both expressed and created in arts like music, neither would those bonds be experienced the same way. Music is not just a sign of the differences between different groups; it is one of the ways of establishing those differences and of showing that they matter. Neither is music just a sign of the blessed ties that bind; it is one of the ways of making those ties binding and blessed to begin with.[13]

An academic theorist of music might object that none of this has to do with the music proper, or with aesthetic taste in the pure and autonomous sense. Yet in churches, even more than elsewhere, various aesthetic, religious, and social perceptions are frequently bundled together. A whole host of messages can be transmitted simply by the choice to sing contemporary gospel music in a previously more traditional church, or by the decision to introduce newly composed but folk-based spiritual songs from the Iona Community in Scotland, or to revive Genevan Psalm tunes, or to open a service with twenty minutes of charismatic praise and worship choruses, or to blend any and all of the above styles. More than purely musical import is conveyed, as well, by the choice to use either a pipe organ or a Hammond B-3—or a piano or digital keyboard instead. Each of these musical choices not only opens up a whole realm of musical repertoire—as earlier opponents of the use of piano in worship knew and feared. Each choice is also a particular exercise of taste that suggests, rightly or wrongly, something about the ethos of a church, its theological mindset and spirituality, its social commitments, its predominant economic and racial mix, its "target" age groups. In the same manner—like it or not—the simple act of rephrasing a favorite hymn to make it more inclusive in language is often seen these days as an important cue as to a church's attitudes toward gender, society, or God.

In modern and postmodern societies, differences in taste assert themselves forcefully, and specifically as issues of identity. Doubtless the emphasis on difference is especially great when the pressures toward cultural assimilation and conformity grow, as is happening now as people are being brought into closer proximity through immigration, modern transportation, communication, and complex global economic networks. Given that ours is also largely a postcolonial era, with many newly independent nations struggling for political and economic stability, groups are highly motivated to claim their distinctive identities and values. At the same time they seek recognition, dialogue, and partnership. Hence the great attention now being given to "multiculturalism."[14]

Especially in the realm of music, as church historian Martin Marty has reported, modern culture is highly mixed up, and yet also divided up and stratified.[15] Marty cites, in particular, a 1994 General Social Survey that discerns a number of relatively discrete "music generations." When North Americans are asked to identify music on a range from "like it very much" to "dislike it very much," the generational differences are glaring. Over 35 percent of those born in or before the 1920s like "big band/swing," while that is true of only 6.7 percent of those born in the 1960s, and 3.7 percent of those born in the 1970s. And that is just the beginning of the differences in taste. Although 23.2 percent of those born in the 1960s, and 28 percent of those born in the 1970s, like "contemporary pop/rock," none of the pre-1920 cohort like it very much; nor do they like rap or heavy metal. And though 13 percent of those born in the 1970s like heavy metal, and 17 percent of them like rap, and another 5.5 percent like new age/space music, the figures drop to 7.1 percent, 2.9 percent, and 3.2 percent, respectively, for those born just a decade before. Classical fans are fairly constant across the generations, at between 14 and 20 percent. Country music and rock (including the "oldies") are especially popular in the youngest group. All of which prompts Marty to worry that churches may feel they have to create separate programs and worship forms for each age group. Any such attempt, he concludes, would be futile and self-defeating, presumably because the task could go on indefinitely, or at least to the point of fragmenting a church to death.

Liking a certain kind of music does not always entail liking to hear it in church. Only a small percentage of the oldest group cited, for instance, would regard their beloved big band music as particularly promising as a sacred style. My great-grandfather never brought his fiddle to church. Nor did my father have any urge to play his favorite accordion music in even the most informal of worship services. Yet in periods such as the 1960s and 1970s, and again at the present time, a large number of ethnic, racial, and generational groups have in fact made a point of trying to incorporate into worship the very kinds of music that they also favor for entertainment or leisure listening and that many other people, as it happens, usually hear as completely secular in tone. Never has there been more diversity in the kinds of music being offered for use in worship, or more difference as to preferences. In any part of heaven where Barth would be allowed to select the music, therefore, one can easily imagine a chorus of objections: "Where are the gospel songs and spirituals, the praise and worship choruses, the jazz masses and heavy metal rhapsodies, the songs from Taizé, the Gregorian chants?"

The Prospect of "Ecumenical" Taste

Surely people have every right to want to sing or hear music they like, whether in church or in heaven. Most Christians today would feel that there would be something wrong about asking anyone to attempt to glorify and enjoy God forever—which the Psalms, Augustine, and Calvinist confessions all describe as our purpose—while employing only music that seems alien to them, or inferior, or markedly inappropriate for worship. But how can people ever hope to discover music they could enjoy together in heaven, when it is increasingly difficult for them to find music they can enjoy together in a single church on earth?

Potential conflicts in taste are minimized, of course, when a religion or community succeeds in creating and maintaining a distinctive and relatively uniform culture of its own. A Christian veteran of the current "worship wars" cannot help marveling that, in a mosque in a typical city in the American Midwest, well over a thousand Muslims of every social class, age, and race—and from thirty or more countries around the world—worship gladly together every week. The ability to do so is in no small part due to the fact that the holy language of the Qur'an and of Islamic prayer remains Arabic, as it has always been; and the prescribed patterns of worship remain relatively invariable, despite certain regional and sectarian differences. Since music as such normally plays no part in public worship in Islam, and since in prayer halls visual artistry (apart from architecture) is generally kept to a minimum, the very simplicity and uniformity of the media employed in worship is conducive to making public prayer a point of convergence—a place where people of the most diverse backgrounds can find common holy ground. Not surprisingly, certain practices of the Sufi traditions, which tend to be more mystical and more artistic—often including dance and instrumental music, for example—are among the very ones that introduce the greatest differentiation among Muslims.[16]

At this point in history the challenges facing Christians are of another order altogether. The challenge of aggressively different Christian tastes in art and worship is especially pronounced now that even Roman Catholics—since the

Second Vatican Council of 1962–65—are free to adopt local and vernacular styles. And among Protestants, Evangelicals, and Pentecostals, matters of style in prayer, praise, and music increasingly assume the importance formerly reserved for doctrine, polity, and denominational identity.

At least in principle, however, the Church supposedly embraces people of every kind, having been made one in Christ. According to scripture, people of the Church, whatever their social differences, are to make "every effort to maintain the unity of the Spirit in the bond of peace," because they exist in "one body and one Spirit," with one faith, one baptism, and one God "who is above all and through all and in all" (Eph. 4:3–6). Christian groups committed to that principle have often repeated a saying that has sometimes been attributed (with insufficient reason) to Augustine: In essentials, unity; in nonessentials, liberty; in all things, charity.[17] That saying, which became popular among irenic souls of the Lutheran and German Reformed churches as early as the seventeenth century, makes a significant gesture toward harmony and cooperation. As such, it might tone down the exaggerated modern-day emphasis on individual preferences and taste, and likewise on identity politics.

I, too, want to urge charity in all things. But at this juncture in Christian history, resorting to the principle just cited will not be sufficient to address or solve conflicts over taste. On the one hand, the attempt to treat taste as a "nonessential" warranting complete liberty has too often meant ignoring the importance of aesthetic judgments and enjoyments in religious life. On the other hand, treating such things as musical taste as somehow essential has had liabilities of its own. It has too often resulted in attempts to regularize taste by decree, privileging the tastes of one group, silencing the voices of others, banning indigenous or local styles, or arbitrarily prohibiting instruments such as piano or guitar—and all without any attempt to engage in dialogue.

It would be unwise to suppose that, by thinking long and hard, we can now come up with some sort of global solution to matters of Christian aesthetic taste, whether musical or otherwise. No one theorist or set of experts, no matter how sagacious, can rightly presume to speak to all situations equally. What we can hope to articulate now is something more modest, but perhaps even more important: principles and guidelines.

In particular, what I hope to offer are aesthetic and theological principles, and a few representative practices, that might be conducive to a truly ecumenical taste. Any taste that I would want to describe and promote as "ecumenical" would in some way encompass, at least in theory, the sort of diversity of tastes at which we have already hinted. But it would do so in a discerning and discriminating way, rather than embracing uncritically every possible aesthetic preference or enjoyment.

By "ecumenical taste" I do not mean only something that is directly correlated with what is known among Christians as the ecumenical movement—an ambitious movement in the Church that has tried, with moderate success, to recover the sense and practice of unity among all believers in Christ. At its largest and most inclusive (perhaps irrationally so), ecumenical taste, as I picture it here, has to do with what the Greek *oikoumene* meant originally—namely, the "whole inhabited world." That large a scope is needed because, whatever the undeniable limitations imposed by our finitude and cultural conditioning, there is some sense in which aesthetic and religious taste want, in principle, to invite and include everyone.

At the microcosmic level, I am searching for a way in which members of a single church with diverse musical tastes can make music together for the enjoyment and edification of each other and for the greater glory of God. At the macrocosmic level, the ultimate religious goal I have in mind is for each spiritually sensing being to be free to share life and faith, praise and lamentation, with the whole community of creation. Expressed eschatologically, it is the hope for all beings to be liberated to join in the messianic banquet (Luke 14:15–24) at its widest and most abundant, savored momentarily here and now in the taste of a sacred meal and a spiritual song—yearning and ecstatic, beautiful and perhaps sublime.[18]

Nothing like that would be possible apart from a grace and bounty far beyond our power to produce in and of ourselves. The ultimate communion is not primarily our responsibility, though the vision and hope can guide our reflection even now. Having caught a glimpse of an encompassing ecumenical vision, we must next scrutinize the most basic obstacle to ecumenical taste.

Discrimination and Difference

A Nonmusical Musing

The viability of ecumenical taste depends on a capacity to discriminate in the positive sense of the term—that is, to differentiate and evaluate—without discriminating in the negative sense by disparaging whatever is different. Discrimination is crucial because discrimination recognizes difference.

In his recent book *The Community of the Beautiful: A Theological Aesthetics*, Alejandro García-Rivera describes a conflict of tastes that transpired between two groups within a single Christian denomination, both housed in a single church building. One was a Lutheran church of which García-Rivera was pastor—a church made up of mostly poor Hispanics who worshiped in a small, upstairs auditorium in a church building in a middle-sized city in Pennsylvania. The other was a church made up of English-speaking Lutherans who worshiped in the same building, but downstairs, in what was meant to be the church proper.

It was Christmas—the feast of the Incarnation—and the Christians downstairs put up a very large fir tree, which they decorated with simple white lights and white chrismon ornaments, using symbols that included the Greek "Chi-Rho" and the cross. Upstairs, in the small auditorium, the mostly Puerto-Rican community put up a small artificial tree that they covered with large quantities of tinsel and flashing colored lights and then topped with a rotating light that "swept the worship space in dizzying circles."[19] Around the tree the people of that congregation placed life-sized plywood cutouts representing a nativity scene, in the midst of which they hung a star that they borrowed from a Moravian community nearby. According to García-Rivera:

> When the community "downstairs" saw the Christmas decorations of the community "upstairs," they, recoiling in horror, would inevitably exclaim, "How gaudy!" When the community "upstairs" saw the Christmas decorations of the community "downstairs," they, also recoiling in horror, would inevitably exclaim, "How lifeless!" Such differences would be repeated over and over again in all the details that make up a parish's life. It was inevitable, then, that the host church decided that the Hispanic community might be happier somewhere else.[20]

Leaving us to surmise the irony of the phrase "it was inevitable," García-Rivera goes on to describe how he eventually left the Lutheran denomination altogether and returned to his roots as a Roman Catholic. More important, he tells how he heard the "call of Beauty"—first in an independent Hispanic Lutheran church that he had been permitted to establish upon being asked to leave the earlier site, and then within the Catholic context. Here at last was Beauty "at her most beautiful": Beauty that was both subversive and gracious; Beauty that crossed barriers and created community and that "loved difference." Such Beauty, he says, loved the Moravian star imported into the "Catholic" nativity scene in the little Hispanic Lutheran church.[21]

García-Rivera's story is both poignant and hopeful. In using it to launch his own study in theological aesthetics, García-Rivera sounds remarkably and admirably inclusive. One hardly notices on first reading that he never mentions Beauty as loving in any way the scene with the tall fir tree, its chrismons, and its austere white lights. What he actually says is that Beauty revels in the *contrast* between the very different kinds of decoration; and Beauty, he adds, loves the Moravian star imported into a Nativity scene constructed by the Hispanic community. He thus openly expresses gladness over an aspect of the Hispanic decorations upstairs while saying nothing appreciative about the downstairs decorations as such. The reason García-Rivera apparently struggles in his response to the downstairs decorations must be this: For understandable reasons, García-Rivera seems to regard that style of decoration, and everything it symbolizes, as inherently exclusive in its discriminating taste. That formal, homogeneous approach may be beautiful in a way, but it leaves out too many alternatives; it cannot be Beauty "at her most beautiful."

But one might wonder. At least one might, if one is an "Anglo" ecumenical Protestant whose own church has sometimes put up a tree decorated in much the manner García-Rivera has trouble enjoying. Could not even the more pristine aesthetic be Beautiful, and fully enjoyable "in God" (to borrow Augustine's language), if it were not taken by its advocates to reflect a standard by which all Christmas decoration should be judged, and often rejected as cheap? What if that homogeneous and restrained manner of decorating were upheld simply as the most "native" style of a welcoming and hospitable church community? What if that community had made it clear in some fashion that it could honor, likewise, the eclectic beauty of the Hispanic community—with their Christmas decorations that at first sight (one conjectures) might have seemed just so much kitsch? Is García-Rivera really wanting to insist that all liturgical art be radically eclectic—indeed, radically popular and informal? Just how inclusive would that kind of aesthetic be, really? Is eclecticism the only way to honor difference? Or is it not the case that eclecticism sometimes compromises or erases what is distinctive about the different gifts it collects?

Yet perhaps inclusiveness is not García-Rivera's primary concern, and perhaps it should not be. It is one thing to represent difference and another to include diversity. The main responsibility for including greater diversity lies, surely, with those who are a part of currently dominant classes and traditions and who thus occupy positions of greater privilege and power. The priorities are bound to be different for those who are in minority or marginalized or subordinated groups. They would want, first of all, to establish a sense of their own identity and the integrity of their "difference," and hence to confirm the worth of their own cultural values—including their aesthetic tastes, whether in church or outside. Such confirmation cannot, to be sure, optimally take place without a degree of *recognition* from others, including the dominant culture.[22] But for that very reason the dominant culture, especially when it is religious or churchly, is morally obligated to make room for alternative styles and points of view.

Discrimination in Disguise

Much of the history of cultural interaction has been one of alternating imitation (both admiring and envious) and rejection. It has been a history, still often glossed over, of disguised discrimination and at times undisguised disgust.[23]

Yet those who attempt to subordinate and deprecate different and rival tastes are rarely conscious of discrimination, in the negative sense. Often, on the contrary, they have every intention of making their judgments on the basis of the best in education, science, or philosophy, not to mention religion. Thomas Jefferson (1743–1826) was in the midst of trying to give a conscientious and scientific analysis of human nature and culture when he deprecated the artistry of blacks. He had just praised American Indians for their artistic skills, elevated imagination, and "sublime oratory," in what was already a conventional gesture invoking the notion of the Noble Savage.[24] Then Jefferson proceeded to write:

> Never yet could I find that a black had uttered a thought above the level of plain narration; never see even an elementary trait of painting or sculpture. In music they are more generally gifted than the whites with accurate ears for tune and time. . . . Whether they will be equal to the composition of a more extensive run of melody, or of complicated harmony, is yet to be proved. Misery is often the parent of the most affecting touches in poetry.—Among the blacks is misery enough, God knows, but no poetry.[25]

Jefferson went on to assert that, in terms of their natural endowments, blacks are inferior to whites and are therefore always much "improved" in both body and mind when mixed with the latter race—an interesting assertion, given his own probable relationship with, and illegitimate fatherhood through, his slave Sally Hemings.[26]

Not quite a quarter century before Jefferson was penning those thoughts, Immanuel Kant (1724–1804) was writing his early *Observations on the Feeling of the Beautiful and Sublime* (1764). There Kant said very little about art itself, and more about manners, feelings, natural phenomena, and gender differences.[27] In the section in which he takes a "fleeting glance at other parts of the world," Kant characterizes the noble, wild, and adventurous Arabs as, so to speak, the "Spaniards of the Orient," and the sophisticated, poetic Persians as the "French of Asia."[28] He asserts that the Asian Indians, by contrast, "have a dominating taste of the grotesque. . . . Their religion consists of grotesqueries," featuring "idols of monstrous form."[29] Chinese paintings are likewise strange, unnatural, and grotesque. Meanwhile, "the Negroes of Africa have by nature no feeling that rises above the trifling." In support of this judgment, Kant cites the views of David Hume (1711–1776), when the latter argues that, among the thousands of blacks who have been captured and transported into slavery, "not a single one was ever found who presented anything great in art or science or any other praiseworthy quality."[30]

It would be superfluous, I hope, to trace all the ways in which ostensibly informed and discriminating European and North American taste continued, from the nineteenth century up to the present, to make judgments that unconsciously reflected discrimination in a negative sense. Kant's comments about the monstrous Indian gods and sculptures, for example, have since been echoed by countless (though by no means all) European visitors to the Indian subcontinent.[31] As Edward Said has shown in his study *Orientalism*, even the fact that an alien culture has been in some respects profoundly attractive has not served to protect that Other from being construed in largely prefabricated or fantasized ideas and self-serving discourse.[32]

Regrettably, every way of attending aesthetically includes a certain amount of distortion. At present, what people hear (and dislike) in listening to the religious music of others seems often to bear little resemblance to what the "other people" hear (and like) who belong to the music's home community or church. And the sound of the music itself is often drowned out by the noise of negative discrimination and misperceptions.

It would seem that our time is one that calls for Christians and others to pay special attention to the art of appreciative discernment even while learning to be more positively discriminating, and in ways that are both hospitable and informed. On this side of utopia, any attempt to cross the barriers to a truly ecumenical taste must be approximate and imperfect. Perhaps there is some hope, however, if we understand better the nature of taste itself and how ideas and ideals of taste can be reformed so as to become more ecumenical.

Taste, Judgment, and Generosity

Beginning with Kant

To see how ecumenical Christian taste could be conceivable at all, we need to attain a more adequate conception of how taste could ever be both inclusive and discriminating, both generous and exacting. To that end, I want to spell out philosophically what is involved in the reformed understanding of taste being proposed here. I say "reformed" because it reshapes in significant ways the prevalent modern ideas of taste, which were formed above all by Immanuel Kant (1724–1804) and, secondarily, by philosophers such as David Hume (1711–1776).

The problem is not, of course, that too many people have been reading Kant, or Hume either. The problem is that Kant in particular expresses in a sophisticated way many of the kinds of convictions and habits of mind that do, in fact, underlie our everyday ways of thinking about taste, some of which are misconceived. And he puts his philosophical weight behind some ideas that tend to take modern theory and criticism far away from any conception of aesthetic taste that could be considered either ecumenical or religious.

Although the term "taste" itself eventually dropped out of favor in modern philosophies of art and beauty, no philosopher had more influence on the development of modern Western aesthetics than Kant. And for Kant, aesthetics was largely a philosophy of taste. Using the term "taste" more rigorously than many of his predecessors, Kant restricted taste mainly to one function. Especially in his later writing, Kant described taste as essentially our capacity to judge whether something is beautiful.[33] Accordingly, he saw taste as responsive only to beauty, not to sublimity (or to any other aesthetic quality, such as the grotesque). In his later work Kant showed little interest in the possible varieties of beauty itself, or in varieties of aesthetic taste. Furthermore, in his view, what is sublime has to do with feeling, not taste, and finally with a feeling of one's own rational and moral superiority as a human being when confronting the formless and unimaginably vast realms of nature.[34] While Kant's attempt to limit the scope and function of taste may seem innocuous, he carried it out in such a way as to create problems for any approach to taste that would aim to be pluralistic, let alone religious or in any way Christian.

Kant's main emphasis was on giving aesthetic taste its own validity and value. That meant demonstrating that taste and beauty are not subject to the dictates of intellectual understanding, morality, or religion. With respect to intellectual criteria, Kant's maintains that there are no rules one can simply conceive and apply either to make something beautiful or to judge that it has been beautifully made. What we perceive as beautiful has a pleasing form. But the fact that a particular form is beautiful and pleasing is not something known through cognition or susceptible of proof; beauty is not an objective property. Otherwise, we could have a science of the beautiful, which is impossible.

As we have noted, establishing the autonomy of taste also meant, for Kant, removing the possibility that taste as such could genuinely be religious and aesthetic at once, or aesthetic and moral. Although Kant saw an indirect connection between taste and morality,[35] Kant assigned taste to a realm of its own, thereby keeping religion and morality from interfering with judgments of taste, and vice versa. Unlike many of his modern followers, Kant acknowledged that, as art participates in culture, it is not so free or autonomous.[36] Yet taste, for Kant, has primarily to do with our response to "free" beauty.

It is especially pertinent to our project that, according to Kant in his maturity— most notably in the *Critique of Judgment* (1790)—taste is not a matter of degree or difference; a person is either exercising it or not. Something is either recognized as beautiful or it is not. And taste can no more be bad than intelligence can be bad. Since anyone, in principle, can exercise taste, that might seem admirably egalitarian. But because Kant thinks true taste is everywhere the same, at least when it is being exercised, he also thinks that everyone's taste ought to agree. And if whole communities disagree about what is beautiful, then so much the worse for the ones who evidently lack taste. (The tone is mine; the implications are Kant's.)

In fact, however, Kant was not much concerned about communities of taste, for all his early interest in national traits. He described judgments of taste as strictly individual and thus as essentially free of communal influence. And he did so while portraying the claims of taste as ones with which everyone ought, nonetheless, to agree, given our common nature as human beings.

Much that Kant says about taste makes a great deal of sense. We have every reason to agree with Kant that taste and art have a kind of integrity in themselves. Aesthetic excellence is never governed entirely by rules or rational concepts or ulterior purposes. That is part of what medieval scholastics meant when they said that something beautiful gives delight in one's very perception of it. Kant is persuasive, too, in asserting that taste goes well beyond having personal preferences (for the color purple, for instance) or finding something agreeable (such as the flavor of asparagus, as opposed to spinach). Preferences are a personal matter; taste is not only that. To call something beautiful is to say more than just, "I like it." It tries to make the claim public in some way. Finally, Kant makes a significant point when he argues that one cannot make a judgment of taste without in some sense making it for oneself. If I simply mimic the aesthetic opinions of others whom I respect, that hardly shows that my own taste is at work. It only proves that I am too insecure to exercise my own judgment in any way.

There are crucial areas, however, in which we would do well to differ with Kant. It is in relation to these that I can best set forth my own "reformed" and more ecumenical views of taste.

Taste as Potentially Religious

Kant did not discuss, because he did not recognize, just how complex the functions of taste would need to be in order to respond adequately to art, especially when it is religious. In proposing alternatives to Kant's views of taste, therefore, it must first of all be said—as I have emphasized from the beginning—that our more complex sorts of aesthetic taste are never exercised apart from other concerns, which may indeed be religious or theological. I might love the hymn "Amazing Grace" for a variety of reasons that have a bearing on how the song sounds to me. I might like it because the words come from the pen of a repentant former slave trader whose talk of sin and grace conveys therefore a certain moral gravity. Or I might like it because the music makes the very idea of grace sound more gracious, or because it was the last song my father ever sang, or because the melody has an interesting contour, or because of the way a particular singer projects and inflects it. (Judy Collins, for instance, did much to take the song out of the church context and into the broader secular world.)

Not all these factors are equally important, aesthetically. But if I judge the expressive quality and beauty of "Amazing Grace" without considering the genuinely religious shaping of the sound of its music as heard by people of faith, my taste in this respect is defective, no matter how refined in other ways. And that kind of defect would certainly make my taste less than useful in church. Similarly, it would be a serious category mistake to judge the merits of "Amazing Grace" when sung in church in exactly the same terms used to evaluate a free and autonomous art, though believer and nonbeliever alike may be drawn spiritually to the song's sheerly musical qualities, its "primordial pentatony, ebbing and flowing in triple meter, with the height and depth of a full octave compass."[37] One sometimes hears that "music is just music." But the statement is patently false—as Kant himself recognized, obliquely, with his category of "dependent beauty."

Because the requirements of taste in a religious setting are complex, it is not likely that any one person would combine equally well the different capacities needed to exercise taste well in a religious context. Many a musician who exhibits wonderful powers of perception and discrimination in matters that are purely musical is relatively inept at judging what sorts of music function well religiously and liturgically. By the same token, many a minister who is theologically informed and liturgically literate is musically rather insensitive, or relatively undiscriminating in aesthetics. Yet all these abilities are needed in order to exercise taste effectively in the context of religious practice. Kant's theory of taste, being profoundly impractical, gives little guidance about such things. According to our reformed understanding of taste, however, we could reach quite practical conclusions. We could say, for instance, that it makes little sense, aesthetically and liturgically, to leave all the judgments in church music either to professional musicians or to professional clergy. It makes better sense to train both musicians and clergy to appreciate each other's arts and to complement each other's tastes.

Taste as Potentially Inclusive

Our second major area of divergence from Kant has to do with the crucial matter of the alleged universality of the claims of taste. It will be recalled that, according to Kant, if I assert that something is beautiful—perhaps the symphonic poem *And God Created Great Whales* (1970), by Alan Hovhaness (b. 1911), or

Kirk Franklin's contemporary gospel song "Melodies of Heaven, Rain Down on Me"—I am rightly and necessarily claiming that all people of taste ought to concur when positioned to judge for themselves. Kant's thesis may sound a little odd, because we all know in advance that not everyone will agree with our judgments. But Kant challenges us to explain how, apart from claiming that everyone ought to concur, we could justify our conviction that the objects we admire as beautiful really deserve the attention of discerning people.

In point of fact, Kant's interest in universality does reflect a crucial impulse found within the claims that people make about the art they regard as exceptionally commendable. For example, the same internet site that uses the "quotation" from Augustine to promote the music of a contemporary Catholic singer, Donna Cori Gibson, makes a point of claiming that "she sings Catholic music with a universal appeal."[38] Again, the Most Reverend Franzo W. King, of the African Orthodox Church of Saint John Coltrane, in San Francisco, praises Coltrane's gifts in jazz composition and saxophone performance by saying, "We are fully aware of the universality of John Coltrane's music . . . and that his spirit and legacy does reach and touch the lives of people of many different faiths, creeds, and religions."[39] Similarly, lovers of classical music, who know that some of what they admire is normally an acquired taste even for themselves, nevertheless tend to claim that the appeal of the genuine classics is universal. That conviction is apparent in a nonelitist form when Hans Kollwitz, the son of the famous German Expressionist artist Käthe Kollwitz, writes: "In general mother was not a musical person; she did not 'know anything about music.' But the great works of music which strike responsive chords deep within all people, aside from any musical background, meant a great deal to her—the Bach passions, Beethoven's symphonies, Brahms's *Requiem*."[40] A corresponding assumption lies behind the claims of proponents of various kinds of church music. The editors of the 1906 and 1938 editions of the *English Hymnal* are bold to say that the great hymns of all ages, which are free from the sentimentalism, weakness, and "unreality" of much popular hymnody, "are for all sorts and conditions of men."[41] We cannot blithely ignore the extent to which groups want to claim their greatest arts as universal, and therefore as classics of a kind, without our misunderstanding the purpose of making certain kinds of "taste claims" to begin with.

Yet, even if it were the case that all the music cited above could be appreciated universally, is that a necessary precondition for calling it beautiful? Could there not be art and music of a less universal sort, which is also to be treasured? All of the sources quoted above clearly assume so, and wisely. Besides, not to put too fine a point on it, we have no evidence to suggest that everyone whose taste is astute would or should agree even on the aesthetic merits of the works that are referred to above as truly universal in their appeal.

What makes universal claims in matters of taste inherently implausible is not that people share nothing in common as human beings, or no common values in the realm of taste. It is that everything we share in common is to some extent culturally and socially conditioned. We can never hope, therefore, to be positioned all in the same way with respect to works of art. And in the sphere of art, unlike mathematics or logic, the particular positioning and attunement of even the most astute audience, reader, or viewer has everything to do with the range of possible responses. If a large number of the most musically alert listeners in the world are unable to hear anything of merit in Philip Glass's opera *Satyagraha* (1980), parts of which I regard as quite moving, that rightly gives me pause. I agree with one commentator that this "is a work written entirely on a moral, even religious, plane—more ritual than entertainment, more mystery than opera."[42] That may help explain why I can be moved by it, even while many listeners find themselves painfully bored. In any case, however, it ill behooves me to be making the claim that people of taste should universally agree with my judgment.

It is one thing to invite, to commend, to attempt to include; it is another to declare that those who demur necessarily lack taste. The trajectory of a judgment of taste normally leads beyond any specific community; it seeks to be inclusive. But there is nothing to prevent its doing so in a generous spirit, rather than insisting that everyone with any taste at all ought to pledge allegiance to the particular beauty being commended. Samuel Taylor Coleridge once stated: "We *declare* an object beautiful, and feel an inward right to *expect* that others should coincide with us. But we feel no right to *demand* it."[43] It now seems we should go even further and temper even the *expectation* that the tastes of responsive people everywhere should coincide with our own.

Taste as Critical yet Plural

Clearly I am embracing a kind of pluralism in matters of taste. As I have indicated, I would accept Kant's point that taste has the urge to make a claim that is universally valid. But I think we must be more modest in interpreting the scope and character of that claim, if it is to be legitimate. It helps if we acknowledge that even good taste comes in many forms.

This essential but sometimes elusive point warrants an extended illustration. Suppose, setting aside musical examples for a moment, we think about the more easily envisioned art of architecture. Let us say that I admire the National Cathedral in Washington, D.C., a belated contribution (recently completed) to Gothic Revival style. I may commend its aesthetic excellence to the attention of everyone, including people trained in architecture around the world. In that sense I am making a wide open appeal. In doing so, I invite and urge people to concur in my judgment, and in my enjoyment as well. If some do not, I can rightly feel disappointed, as one is naturally disappointed in not being able to share something one loves. I can even go on to provide evidence or hints that might eventually persuade those who at first disagreed with me. Then, if some remain unpersuaded, they might provide a convincing counterargument, showing how my judgment was based on a sentimental attachment to Gothic style, for instance, or to a merely romantic predilection for its revival.

In any case, however, I should realize from the start that not all varieties of beauty have universal appeal. Maybe none do, in actual fact. And that allows me to respect a great many judgments that differ from mine. I might well recall that when perceptive Renaissance writers on architecture used the word "Gothic" for a style of medieval building, they were not paying such architecture a compliment. They meant that it was barbaric—the sort of thing one would expect from the Goths. Not every discriminating lover of architecture, therefore, should be expected to concur with the aesthetic judgments of every other. Good tastes can conflict, and without necessarily negating each other. None of this is possible according to Kant's theory of taste. All of it is consistent with the critical pluralism I embrace.

Taste as Intersubjective and Transcendental

Does my critical sort of pluralism entail sheer subjectivism or complete relativism, both of which Kant was eager to avoid? It does not. For one thing, I have been presuming that judgments of taste can have intersubjective validity, even while not qualifying as universal. And the kind of pluralism I am advocating is meant to be discriminating as well as inclusive. It is a critical pluralism, not a total relativism. Judgments of taste are rooted first of all in the context of the communities most at home with a given style or kind of work. But that does not make such judgments purely local, let alone merely private. Nor does it entail the literally untenable belief that all aesthetic judgments are equal.

Furthermore, we need not hold that human beings simply impose their impressions of beauty on the external world. As a Christian aesthetician, I am committed to the belief—the faith, even—that in God, and for God, the world itself is somehow transcendentally beautiful and sublime, and that this is part of its goodness. We do not invent the world's beauty, though we have unique and different perspectives on it. What we respond to subjectively is not merely and thoroughly subjective.[44] And on that metaphysical point, I might add, there is some affinity with Kant, because he eventually comes to the point of indicating (however inconsistently) that taste is mysteriously related to the noumenal, "supersensible" reality behind the phenomenal world of ordinary experience.[45]

Moreover, unlike Kant, I believe that when we respond specifically to the sublime in nature as something awe-inspiring in its unimaginable immensity or infinite grandeur, that response should not (and usually does not) result in our thinking of ourselves as utterly distinct from nature, due to our mental powers and moral superiority as humans. Nor should it result in our finally relocating sublimity per se within our own mental and moral capacity, as Kant does. To do so denies the very element of radical "otherness" that is essential to the whole experience of sublimity, which after all entails an awareness (without comprehension) of something that in its magnitude or apparent infinity eludes our grasp. The experience of the sublime should, and does, more often move us toward a radically expanded sense of the Whole in which we are permitted to participate as creatures. It is altogether fitting that many of us find ourselves taking sublime works of literature, art, or nature as symbols or metaphors—or indeed as mysterious manifestations—of the Holy reality that encompasses us.[46]

That sort of connection between the experience of sublimity and the sense of the Holy is acknowledged less well by Kant than by Hegel, who asserts that "the art of sublimity is *the* sacred art as such which can be called exclusively sacred because it gives honour to God alone."[47] Unfortunately, Hegel restricts the art of the sublime to the literary and treats nothing in nature as truly sublime but rather as, at most, a "glorifying accessory for the praise of God."[48]

Be that as it may, Kant was surely right to think that there is no one-to-one correspondence between my perception of something's aesthetic qualities, however sublime, and ultimate reality. We have no reason to believe that human valuations of sublimity, or of beauty either, are anchored directly in divine aesthetic judgment, which is neither available to us nor possible for us as creatures.

Taste as Multifaceted

There is yet another point at which we need to separate ourselves from Kant, however. Taste need not be restricted to judgment, let alone to judgment that is narrowly aesthetic. As I have been saying from the start, taste actually has to do with three basic elements of aesthetic response, each of which is a function and element of taste. First, there is one's "apperception" (more or less adequate) of something's aesthetic features, which in relation to an artwork is simply the act of discerning or taking in the work itself. Second, there is one's personal "appreciation" (or possibly dislike) of the aesthetic object. And, third, there one's "appraisal" (positive or negative) of whether the aesthetic object is actually commendable in a public way. Consisting of those three elements, taste involves more than what Kant called the "free play" of all the cognitive faculties. In requiring thought and imagination, sense and sensibility, it is an integral part of our humanness, our loves, our existence as embodied and living souls.[49]

One thing that this division within the functions of taste allows us to see quite clearly is that tastes can be both good and bad, and in varying ways and degrees. Thus, a perception or judgment of taste is not often simply right or wrong, valid or invalid. A Christian worship leader in middle age may find some type of nominally secular music to be enjoyable but incongruous in the context of worship. And from one perspective that perception may be warranted. Yet a young person may perceive different features of the style in question, or enjoy them differently, and therefore judge that the style of music could be spiritually enlivening and potentially worshipful. That both perspectives could have areas of discernment and deficiency is not something Kant discusses or allows. But it fits with the theory proposed here and helps explain why, contrary to what Kant supposed, we have a number of different bases for differing and disputing in matters of taste, even if Kant was right to think that there is no strictly objective basis for judgment.

Taste as Communal

That taste has multiple facets also helps explain why taste and its judgments are naturally communal, which is something excluded by Kant's curiously individualistic universalism. Judgments of taste, as I have been insisting, belong to the social world, not merely to private experience. At the very least, the degree of our aesthetic pleasure is enhanced or depressed by the judgments of others. I think we can understand why, if we bring into the discussion the views of Kant's older conversation partner, the British philosopher David Hume. More than Kant, Hume recognizes many of the factors involved in taste, even if he is unabashedly elitist in what he makes of them. And Hume does not leave us on our own to judge what is beautiful.

Hume, as is well known, places great confidence in the exemplary judgments of certain arbiters of taste. In his classic essay "Of the Standard of Taste" (1757), Hume writes that, "though the principles of taste be universal, and, nearly, if not entirely the same in all men; yet few are qualified to give judgment on any work of art, or establish their own sentiment as the standard of beauty."[50] The reason why only a few people are qualified to judge in matters of taste is that inexperience, cultural prejudice, insensitivity, and lack of good sense all commonly cloud aesthetic judgment.

Who, then, is qualified to be "a true judge in the finer arts"? Hume answers in this way: "Strong sense, united to delicate sentiment, improved by practice, perfected by comparison, and cleared of all prejudice, can alone entitle critics to this valuable character; and the joint verdict of such, wherever they are to be found, is the true standard of taste and beauty."[51]

Hume is often accused of circularity in his argument. He admits that the standards of taste are not objective rules that everyone can point to. Rather, they are aesthetic values recognized in the judgments of people with impeccable taste. But how could we ever establish which judges are truly reliable without having impeccable taste, ourselves? And how would we know we had impeccable taste, without having it confirmed by reliable judges?

Hume admits that such questions are potentially embarrassing. He defends himself by arguing that, whereas the question of exactly which judges are reliable in taste might always in fact be discussed and disputed, everyone nevertheless recognizes, in principle, that some people are indeed much better judges than others, and actually exemplary. "They are easily to be distinguished in society, by the soundness of their understanding and the superiority of their faculties."[52] We can confirm for ourselves that their guidance in matters of taste helps us to understand our own aesthetic perceptions even better. That is to say, the more one attends to their judgments, the more persuasive they seem. One doesn't have to be an exemplary judge of taste overall in order to recognize elements of superiority in the taste of a teacher who is at work alerting one to artistic traits one might otherwise miss or misjudge.

When Hume expounds on how the arbiters of taste are "easily distinguished in society," one has no doubt that the society he has in mind, himself, is very polite, literate, civilized, and financially at ease, since in his view it would otherwise be "prejudiced." Hume is truly an elitist. But Hume recognizes that even the views of the aesthetic elite must be corroborated by a whole group of their peers; their verdicts must be "joint," he says. He thus admits that there must be some sort of community of taste. And he suggests that, finally, other human beings trust the verdicts of the few only because, as they try them out, they find their own perceptions sharpened and illumined.

That is a quite perceptive description of how critical judgments take hold. Most of us do, in fact, tend to give special heed to those who have the most experience with the art in question, who have shown good judgment in the relevant ways in the past, and who seem attentive and not unduly prejudiced. That is particularly true in relation to arts with high cultural status, where recognized critics play an especially important role.[53] What Hume fails to notice is that there is not just one circle of exemplars. There are many such circles, and in many strata of society, and in relation to many different arts. The elite among high society and academia are bound to have a certain amount of prejudice against those outside their own circles—and vice versa. Hume also makes too little of the fact that, once works of art earn a degree of recognition, they themselves set standards for other art. Artists themselves do not look foremost to critics for guidance and inspiration, but to other artworks. And that is probably true for the rest of us.

Once one ponders Hume's impressive list specifying all the necessary qualifications for a reliable judge in matters of taste, one realizes that no one person or group could possibly qualify. It begins to be no mystery at all why taste is and must be a communal enterprise, with different groups of trusted and experienced guides. Although Hume would never say so, an essential component of good taste should therefore be generosity, or its close relation charity—or, if you will, compassion. For all tastes have limitations and need mutual tolerance and encouragement as well as mutual correction.

Some of the limitations inherent in the exercise of taste have to do not so much with the fallibility and variety internal to human personality and society as with the variety and difference internal to art itself. At this point in history it should be obvious to almost everyone that aesthetic excellence itself is of many kinds, requiring differently cultivated tastes. Hume notes, for instance, that the works we love in our youth may not be the ones we favor in old age. He also states that every culture and era has favored styles, reflecting different customs and morals that the person of taste must take into account.

Going beyond Hume, we can say that, in all likelihood, one community of taste is more prepared to appreciate and judge Hindu temples while another group is more prepared to appreciate and judge Gothic churches, and still another to enjoy or judge the styles that we call Classical or Neo-classical, with their emphasis on dynamic balance and serenely harmonious beauty. When it comes to music, rather different audiences and tastes are ideally suited to judge a Flemish Renaissance setting of the Mass, a Celtic Mass by John Cameron (1998) or Philip Green (1971), a Flamenco Mass by Paco Peña (1988), the African *Missa Luba* (c. 1970s) based on traditional melodies, the Hispano-American *Misa Criolla* of Ariel Ramirez (1964), and the "New Age" *Missa Gaia* (*Earth Mass*) by the Paul Winter Consort (1982). Perhaps people with a truly eclectic taste are those best prepared to relish a wideranging, "ecumenical" work such as Hannibal Lokumbe's *One Heart Beating* (1999). Such works vary considerably in the qualities they present for appreciation and in the communities to which they primarily appeal.

Even within one community, however, sharp differences can arise. That is certainly true in the case of music as a liturgical art, where one is considering not only how it functions all on its own but, more important, how it functions in relation to a liturgy that, while not a work of art in the usual aesthetic sense, needs nonetheless to be artful.[54] The question of liturgical appropriateness is one factor we must attend to more closely as we now examine a cluster of issues pertinent to music and the church.

Musical "Ecumenical" Taste

Beauty So Old and So New

We have recognized from the beginning of this study that there is no overall consensus among Christians as to which music is best suited to the purposes of worship. Indeed, there is no consensus among Christians overall about the nature and style of worship itself. That is partly because the charter document of the Church—the Bible—has little to say on the topic of musical style; and it is relatively vague in what it says about the specific character and structure of worship.

As we saw in chapter 2, however, Christian musical practices were in fact prescribed and circumscribed by custom from the very beginning—continuing the synagogue pattern of making little or no use of instruments, for example. And among particular Christian denominations very definite, and very different, traditions of music-making developed over the next two millennia. From a standpoint outside any one of those traditions, some of the norms seem arbitrary. It appears an accident of history that the Catholic church at various times has restricted the use of all wind instruments—not just the loudest—while celebrating the spirituality of pipe organs, most of which include woodwind stops (flute, oboe, and the like).[55] Other musical practices seem much less contingent on circumstantial factors. While the Roman Catholic Church has backed away from an earlier privileging of Gregorian chant as the church's universal musical language, chant of various kinds is in fact one of the most widely employed religious practices worldwide. It evidently lends itself especially well to such purposes as prayer.

In church circles, judgments of musical taste are almost always tied closely to questions of tradition—and for good reason; for it is tradition that determines, in part, what sorts of music will seem appropriate. It is tradition that helps train a given community to hear certain kinds of religious meaning in particular kinds of music—the chorale, the spiritual, the very sound of the organ.

This is not to suggest that music has nothing to say on its own, without specific words and specific worship contexts. The sound of music, heard in itself, not only has well-attested powers but invites a certain range of meaningful response. Few people, no matter how musically inexperienced, would mistake the jubilant choral finale of Beethoven's Ninth Symphony as mournful, for instance, though neither would they necessarily picture to themselves an embrace of millions and a heavenly joy on earth, as specified in the text by Schiller. Again, even without the words, the melody and harmony of "We Shall Overcome" would never be associated with passive resignation. But neither do those sounds necessarily connote a determination to seek freedom and to find solidarity. And when that very music is sung now in its "original" form as a hymn, and in a predominantly African American service, it sounds different still: more spiritually and theologically grounded in its aim of social transformation.

We can say, then, that music's meaning is in some respects remarkably indeterminate; music lacks the conceptual precision of verbal language. Yet music is both more refined and more powerful than mere words when it comes to giving voice to the inner and "felt" meaning of thoughts, especially once those thoughts are uttered within the orbit of musical expression.[56] One thing that traditions of music-making in church accomplish over time, therefore, is to cultivate the connections between particular sorts of music and particular goals of worship—those goals being not only feelings of some sort but also commitments and beliefs, and the liturgical actions conducive to them.

Once any musical tradition is in place in church, subsequent decisions about how to worship and make Christian music cannot depart markedly from the pattern without altering a community's sense of identity and, perhaps, its sense of Christian faith itself. It may be that, as George Lindbeck has argued, doctrine is what generally provides the "rules" for which practices should count as Christian, or as Christian of a certain sort.[57] But a great many religions are guided less by doctrine than by social and ritual practices, including the arts.

Even those Christian groups most emphatic about creeds, confessions, or scriptural authority take their bearings, more than one might suppose, from their worship practices and musical traditions. Music gives voice to the heart of prayer and interprets the very meaning of doctrine. It was in no way atypical when, at a 1959 Sacred Harp singing convention in Northern Alabama, a woman named Joyce Smith stood up to testify: "You know this is somethin' we can all enjoy. Lot of times preachers get up and preach and it don't seem like it has any effect on anybody, but you let a band of God's children get together and get to singin'—people's gonna feel it" [a voice shouts "Amen!"].[58] For a great many people, singing is a primary Christian practice.[59]

The critical correlation between the "rule" or pattern of public worship (*lex orandi*) and the pattern of belief (*lex credendi*) has been long attested. What has not been recognized so clearly is the role of the arts in shaping prayer and interpreting belief, and indeed in inspiring and guiding a community's moral intentions and actions, its *lex agendi*.[60]

Even so, the integrity and vitality of Christian faith depends less on some uniform pattern of orthopraxis or on some unchanging theological orthodoxy than it depends on the integrity and reality of a God whose Beauty is always, in Augustine's words, both "old and new." Christianity does not need to have some monolithic and unchanging character in order to be faithful to such a God. That judgment is itself a theological one, however, and one that certain Christians would want to dispute.

"Ecumenical" Practices in Matters of Music

I have already indicated at various points in this study that, within the framework of Christian theology overall, the arts of worship need to be able somehow to encompass, or at least acknowledge and represent symbolically, the full range of religious and moral experience—from the relatively mundane to the sublimely elevated or horribly abysmal. They need to do so in such a way that the reality and hope of transformation and liberation (which together comprise salvation in the largest sense) becomes new and efficacious within the lives of the gathered people.

What I have been less emphatic in stating is that this requires that the arts actually make contact with lives. If such contact always occurs in relation to specific traditions, and if the lives of the gathered people are as personally and culturally diverse as the church would both expect and want, the question naturally arises as to how to make the breadth and fullness of the gospel truly accessible. What would that mean, artistically and musically?

No worship service can literally present the fullness of God in all its glory or the range of human experience in all its variety. Yet certain ways of gathering, singing, and celebrating are more theological encompassing and culturally inclusive than others.[61]

Catholic Guidance

In terms of music, the problem has been addressed in the Roman Catholic tradition by a series of documents.[62] For our purposes, two are especially pertinent and suggestive, although both are North American and neither is a formal and official statement of the Roman Catholic Church itself. The first, a 1992 report from the Milwaukee Symposia for Church Composers,[63] which included Protestant voices as well, could hardly be said to have been prepared in haste. A product of ten years of discussion, it builds on and responds to previous documents, particularly "Music in Catholic Worship"[64] and "Liturgical Music Today."[65]

Several points are of particular significance here. The "Milwaukee Symposia Report" moves decisively away from the earlier Roman Catholic conception of the holiness of music as something inherent in any one style and it emphasizes the whole ritual function of music-making in the liturgy. It thus regards church musicianship as integrally related to the work of architects, liturgists, poets, and so forth; and it makes clear the invariable intention of worship music to serve the word (a somewhat ambiguous though common observation to which we will return in chapter 9).

The "Milwaukee Report" stresses the need to select and compose music that is "within the assembly's grasp," that stands up to the repetition inevitable in liturgy—music that is simple enough to be sung relatively well on first hearing and that is nevertheless substantial enough to continue to inspire the sung prayer. Such music needs to meet musical, liturgical, and pastoral criteria, which the document treats as intimately connected. A work cannot be appropriate, truly, unless it is also of good quality. But quality concerns the actual presentation of the music, some of which may not exist in the form of a score. And finally, in view of the importance of artistic and cultural traditions, quality must be judged within the context of a given style and genre, not in the abstract.

Accordingly, the document has a whole section on cross-cultural music making (Paragraphs 56–63). It particularly recommends that different cultures learn to sing each other's music, preferably led by pastoral musicians representing the cultures involved. The document concludes:

> Of all the contexts influencing this musical-liturgical-pastoral judgment, the cultural one is the most decisive. Different cultures, language groups, and ethnic communities provide different contexts and raise particular questions when rendering the musical-liturgical-pastoral judgment about worship music. It is important to respect each culture. . . . This entails consciously avoiding the ethnocentrism that judges the music of one particular culture and era as superior and the model of all other Christian ritual music. To avoid this hazard, it is indispensable that appropriate representatives of those cultures providing the context for worship be central to the decision-making process. In particular, it is important to engage competent musicians, versed in the music of the cultures providing the context for worship. They will be key in helping their colleagues especially in the musical facet of the musical-liturgical-pastoral judgment. (Paragraph no. 86)

The claims made in the "Milwaukee Report" parallel in many respects the ideas proposed in the present study, which were formed largely independently. The main point of possible divergence concerns the apparent willingness of the "Milwaukee Report" to leave all criteria regarding quality per se in the hands of a given style's home culture or community.

That concern is one that our second document notices and attempts to address. It was composed after a series of consultations and discussions among various Catholic liturgists and musicians in the English-speaking world between 1992 and 1995. Because the first of these consultations took place in Snowbird, Utah, the document is called the "Snowbird Statement on Catholic Liturgical Music."[66]

Compared with the "Milwaukee Report," the "Snowbird Statement" places much more emphasis on aesthetic criteria, especially beauty, which it regards as not only liturgically effective but "even sacramental," being a sign of God's presence and action in the world. It affirms the concept of ritual music as clarifying how intimately music is tied to ritual forms. But it seeks a renewal of choirs and of academically trained musical leadership. Overall, the statement is concerned more directly with artistic quality as something essential to making rituals "more powerful and more engaging." It seeks to counteract any willingness to settle for the merely utilitarian.

Unlike the "Milwaukee Report," the "Snowbird Statement" affirms that, while musical standards are not absolute and unchanging, the elements entailed in musical judgment are "objective and are something more than mere assertions of personal preference or of social or historical convention" (Paragraph 6). It thus argues that "a discussion of musical quality across stylistic boundaries is valid and necessary," even if it is difficult to state the objective elements of musical quality.

The statement goes on to affirm a distinctive Catholic ethos, one that it regards as evident in music "that elaborates the sacramental mysteries in a manner attentive to the public, cosmic, and transcendent character of religion, rather than in styles of music that are overly personalized, introverted, or privatized" (Paragraph 8). The statement urges that such music, which has been employed by countless generations of Catholic Christians, be used as a starting point and guide for new developments. It discourages the use of recorded music (as did the "Milwaukee Report," for that matter) and insists that the "experimentation with guitars, pianos and other instruments over the past three decades has only proved the greater effectiveness of the organ." It also urges a more critical attitude toward electronic instruments.

Both of the above documents, which include more much that is of considerable interest, are valuable attempts to address the question of how to attain musical integrity and quality in a situation of great change and diversity. They deserve the attention of Protestants and Catholics alike. But, as we have seen, they have different emphases and do not always see eye to eye. The "Snowbird Statement" expresses far greater confidence in "objective" norms (however difficult to verbalize), and it ventures the claim that there is a spirit or ethos of Catholicism—as a cultural tradition, one might say—that must be respected regardless of the specific style of music employed in worship. In both of these ways it argues that aesthetic judgments regarding quality cannot be left strictly to those who are most at home with a given musical style.

Both statements affirm that praise and prayer can be offered in different ways. That is not at issue between them. But the "Milwaukee Report" stresses the necessity for churches to seek input from a wide range of expertise representing different cultural styles. This would apply especially to churches serving diverse language groups and ethnic communities. The "Snowbird Statement" stops short of saying that; in effect, it counters with the following question: At what point does difference obscure or violate the integrity of a tradition? At what point does stylistic difference become a difference in substance or meaning? Stepping out of the Roman Catholic sphere, one might ask: Could a Greek Orthodox church import drum sets, electronic keyboards, and rock music and still have anything like the same identity—anything like the same sense of what it means to come before God in reverence, and to conform oneself to the transforming image of Christ?

If the "Snowbird Statement" seems a little too nostalgic and too attached to one sort of ethos, the "Milwaukee Report" seems a little too quick to surrender questions of quality entirely into the hands of those associated with the community to which a given style is indigenous. While the "Milwaukee Report" insists on the importance of cross-cultural dialogue, it seems, at least by implication, to restrict that dialogue to an exchange in which each group informs the other of how its musical and cultural materials are best used. Nothing in the report sets forth unambiguously a goal or possibility of mutual criticism, even criticism that gives special status to every cultural community's own self-understanding.

Cross-Cultural Taste

Presumably, the reason why designers of the "Milwaukee Report" give scant attention to cross-cultural and cross-stylistic judgment (as distinct from exchange) is precisely in order to enhance diversity and to promote inclusiveness. They would not be puzzled by Tex Sample's claim that only working-class people can hear country music in certain ways because they are the only people well positioned to appreciate the particular kinds of social resistance and defiance expressed in country music.[67]

Ironically, however, if one presses too hard on the premise that one cannot make judgments of quality outside one's own community, one effectively cuts off the possibility of any sense of ecumenicity or unity-in-diversity. At any given time, or for any given worship service, the effect can of course be liberating for a group whose voice has in other respects been silenced or marginalized. But as a general procedure and principle, leaving critical judgments all to the "insiders" (even if they have otherwise been "outsiders") is no less univocal and monocultural than if one advocated the validity of only one set of objective standards. In order for people to share music together, in church or elsewhere, they must be able somehow to perceive, enjoy, and value each other's music. But if people can learn to do that, to some extent, they are then already beginning to be in a position to make certain judgments about the music—perhaps even to notice something about its possibilities and liabilities that its "home" users would never notice, given their complete familiarity with it.[68]

In any case, a strictly communal or local approach to questions of quality appears to be based on what is now widely regarded as an inadequate and perhaps idealized notion of the unity and coherence of communities and cultures.[69] We are all members of multiple communities, often overlapping. Indeed, if various psychologists are right, each of us constitutes in our own psyches something like a whole community of voices, all of which must learn to interact in cooperative rather than destructive ways. Our identities as persons and as communities are all to some extent constructed rather than being unchangeable and inherent in ourselves or our situations. Furthermore, every tradition in the world of culture is made up of multiple sub-traditions. Within the sphere of so-called classical music alone, there is enormous variety—greater, perhaps, than in any other body of music on earth. It ranges from medieval chant to Renaissance polyphony; from the sweet and melodious English madrigal and the splendidly contrapuntal Baroque cantata to the highly dissonant twelve-tone operas of Schoenberg and Berg. If there are a number of listeners who can meaningfully and enjoyably tune in to those different styles, many of which are only distantly related, there is little reason to suppose that musical values cannot be shared in some real measure across temporal and cultural boundaries.

To share both critical and appreciative cross-cultural perceptions and queries is not necessarily to presume one's taste is omni-competent. Western classical reviewers who attempt to review North Indian classical music will usually recognize that the art of Ali Akbar Khan on the sarod, or of Ravi Shankar or the late Nikhil Banerjee on the sitar, is something special; they will register due amazement at the artistry of Zakir Hussain on the tabla. They will almost always admit, however, that they are less than perfectly familiar with the ragas being performed and with all the fine points of interpretation and improvisation. That does not render their judgment superfluous or force them merely to parrot the opinions of their Asian counterparts; it suggests, rather, that their views will be based on a selective perception of the elements of the music-making.

Such cross-cultural interchange always entails distortions. Yet, for the same reasons, it affords new insight and expanded awareness, and on all sides. One can think of parallels in the acquisition of foreign languages. Rarely does a nonnative speaker ever learn to speak a foreign language without an accent. It is something that generally only children can do. Nor can the outsider expect to hear the full range of connotation and overtone in a language acquired in later life. That is why most poetry is written by natives to a given tongue. Yet the foreign speaker brings perspectives that native speakers lack. A native speaker, for instance, can never hear just the sound of the native language as distinct from its meaning. The very moment the native speaker begins really to listen to a linguistic phrase, the meaning floods over the sound, and the sense disguises the sheer sensation. The foreigner is slower to perceive the meaning, but for that very reason hears more of the sheer sound. But it is even more complicated and interesting than that. The native speaker actually detects in the sounds of the language tiny nuances of intonation and enunciation that would otherwise be undetectable and that color the meanings being expressed. Yet the only reason those tiny inflections are noticed is that they are perceived to be meaningful. And the minute they become meaningful, they cannot be heard as sheer sound! In any case, the outsider to the language can often notice many fascinating idioms and structural patterns that the insider will never have thought about at all, so intent is the insider on using the language in ways that seem entirely natural and indeed unremarkable.

What one must recognize is that any such cross-boundary listening requires special discipline and special humility. One must learn to listen with others and to "listen through" cultural dialects and musical accents, as it were, which only comes with practice. One must learn to perceive attentively before judging, and to judge provisionally even when enjoying (or not). One must also learn to listen differently to different styles. Anyone who approaches classical Indian ragas expecting rich harmonies and contrapuntal melodies will be disappointed. Such a listener may then be too incapacitated to appreciate a level of melodic invention and rhythmic complexity rarely approached in Western music of any sort. In any case, however, if a situation is such that dialogue is not invited—if the greater need of a given minority church, for instance, is to establish and maintain an independent and indigenous style—it is imperative that such a situation be honored rather than any sort of interaction be coerced.

Bad Habits and Bad Taste

If the phrasing of parts of the "Milwaukee Report" seems to incline toward an unsatisfactory yet open-minded cultural relativism, the "Snowbird Statement" could be said to err in the opposite direction, aspiring to a kind of "objective" taste that we have reason to believe is illusory. One recalls that, not infrequently, aesthetic judgments have been meted out by church musicians or church authorities in a manner and tone that has assumed that matters of taste are every bit as universal as Kant imagined, and even more objective—perhaps, in the case of the Church, imitating the voice of God. Even in its milder and more circumspect forms, a misplaced confidence in the objectivity and universality of taste, when combined with a sense of the moral and religious importance of its judgments, has often had the effect of silencing opposition and of squelching dialogue.

In his role as musical editor of the *English Hymnal* (1906 and 1933), Ralph Vaughan Williams pointed out the difficulty of providing congregations with good familiar tunes to sing. Many of the popular tunes, he explained, are not only unsuitable; "they are positively harmful to those who sing and hear them." He went on to state that the usual defense of "bad music" is that the people want and like something simple. Vaughan Williams retorted: "As for simplicity, what could be simpler than 'St. Anne' or 'The Old Hundredth,' and what could be finer?" Besides—warming up to his topic—"It is indeed a moral rather than a musical issue." It may take a certain effort to tune oneself to the "moral atmosphere implied by a fine melody." It may be far easier to "dwell in the miasma of the languishing and sentimental hymn tunes which so often disfigure our services. Such poverty of heart may not be uncommon. . . ." Nevertheless, "It ought no longer to be true anywhere that the most exalted moments of a church-goer's week are associated with music that would not be tolerated in any place of secular entertainment."[70]

Vaughan Williams, who contributed some notable music of his own to this remarkable hymnal, is making an argument that deserves to be taken very seriously. The pity is that it is phrased in such a way as to assume that any clergyman or organist with good training and decent taste would agree on which hymns are good and which are bad. Furthermore, the wording leaves no room for the possibility that some of the people out in the pews may have some legitimate notions of high quality music that Vaughan Williams and his committee would never have considered—more of the music from the former colonies, for instance.

It is impossible to say for certain how many of the editors of the *English Hymnal* would have subscribed to the aesthetic views of that exemplary member of the Oxford Movement John Keble (1792–1866). Perhaps they would not have embraced without qualification Keble's Victorian assertion that "religion and poetry are akin because each is marked by a pure reserve, a kind of modesty or reverence. . . . You are led upwards from beauty to beauty, quietly and serenely, step by step, with no sudden leap from depths to height."[71] Vaughan Williams himself disavows any bias toward "colourless music" as opposed to that which is "vigorous and bright." But, considering the full range of possibilities, it is apparent that neither Keble in his time, nor Vaughan Williams and his hymnal committee in theirs, comprehended just how many legitimate kinds of Christian expression could be excluded by an aesthetic of either earnest dignity or quiet reverence, however leavened. The committee members do admit in their part of the hymnal preface that "literary, musical, and religious standards vary."[72] Yet their aesthetic as actually practiced, and as verbalized by Vaughan Williams as music editor, appears entirely too tame to accommodate much from the *Sacred Harp* or *Southern Harmony*, let alone anything wildly ecstatic from the Caribbean or Africa, given that such effects might demand something like a "leap from depths to height."

For an English hymnal of that time, to be sure, the selections make much musical and liturgical sense. What is mainly problematical is the rationale and the rhetoric. That particular problem is a recurrent one. I recently received a letter that included the following judgment, which I quote here anonymously, with permission: "My work in the music business has had me laboring predominantly in the field of so-called Contemporary Christian Music, which I like to point out is seldom contemporary, only nominally Christian, and scandalously unmusical." (One recalls how Vaughan Williams condemned certain popular forms of hymnody as both musically and morally reprehensible—a plausible enough idea, but not when applied without proper qualification.) My correspondent has agreed that, in its sheer generality and exaggeration, his statement is bound to play on stereotypes of all sorts. It belongs to the language of crusades and culture wars. However useful such rhetoric may be for purposes of energizing resistance, where needed, it is by no means ecumenical in spirit—and perhaps, in that respect, it is not in good taste (nor meant to be).

Ecumenism with Teeth (but No Fangs)

In promoting ecumenical taste, I may seem to have fallen into that well-meaning but toothless sort of tolerance and aesthetic civility that John Murray Cuddihy describes and sometimes chides in his book *No Offense: Civil Religion and Protestant Taste*.[73] Cuddihy argues that, in order to cultivate a genuinely pluralistic, democratic society and to mute sectarian and ethnic rivalries, modern Americans with education and sophistication have learned to discourage any grand religious or aesthetic claims and pretensions. They have come to think it embarrassing and ill-mannered for one group to claim to be either God's chosen people or the one true church; similarly, they have come to regard it as in bad taste for any art to exhibit a polished "high" style or to strive to be truly lofty and sublime. Both impulses seem to them undemocratic and "vulgar." In terms of aesthetics, this means that upper-middle-class Americans with good taste prefer a certain honest roughness, "skilled carelessness," or artful imperfection. Their modernist aesthetic—while in its own way studied, and not merely casual or careless—shuns a sharp hierarchy of styles, craftily blurring distinctions between popular and elite. Attracted to the commonplace, this aesthetic of modesty, according to Cuddihy, constitutes a secular but essentially Puritan variation on Christian humility—a "decorum of imperfection" that is traceable, utimately, back to Augustine and the Bible.

Cuddihy observes that a hidden price is paid for this religious civility and self-effacing religious aesthetic, which places an interim taboo on "glory" until the Parousia, the Second Coming. A religion can be compromised, and its sense of its own communal identity weakened, when it promotes tolerance over religious commitment, and charity over truth. And taste that is of the "homely Protestant" variety, while apparently rooted in Christian values of a Calvinist sort, can result in art that is undistinguished and undramatic. It is a chastened art, and thus very different from the "high art" associated with certain alternative tastes—traditionally Catholic, for instance (and Spanish or Mexican especially).

It could be argued that the values of civility and tolerance become ever more important globally as societies grow more diverse and interconnected and as religious groups themselves become more multicultural. But Cuddihy is right that aesthetic modesty and religious tolerance can displace or compromise "high" or exuberant approaches to beauty and truth, and can efface a core sense of identity. While he seems willing, finally, to accept that compromise as the most Christian way, it is not—in my book—the only fully Christian way.

I want to emphasize, therefore, that, although the ecumenical taste I have described and promoted invites cross-traditional dialogue and mutual charity, it is not a matter of mere tolerance and civility. Nor does it embrace aesthetic modesty as the only truly Christian style or taste, shunning everything flamboyant, exotic, or ambitious. Nor, finally, does my pursuit of ecumenical taste assume that all arts and taste are to be regarded as entirely equal and therefore as already perfected, or at least good enough. Ecumenical taste as I understand it is not uncritical. It has teeth (although no fangs).

Even disgust is not entirely ruled out of the sphere of ecumenical taste. Various forms of disgust are valuable in causing one to withdraw from foods, objects, and behaviors that are potentially harmful. But disgust, while not something simply to be repressed, is certainly not beyond criticism, itself. The psychologist Paul Rozin points out that North Americans find it virtually impossible to drink a glass of their favorite juice in which a dead cockroach has been dipped, even when they are shown that the roach has been completely sterilized. The cultural repugnance (not shared by everyone in the world) is simply too strong.[74] As Rozin argues, one's disgust often has moral overtones that carry over to the people associated with the food preferences one finds disgusting and that likewise transfer from certain people one finds disgusting to their tastes in food. The good news is that, through education and experience, someone thoroughly and permanently disgusted by the idea of eating insects can learn, nevertheless, to overcome a corresponding disgust for those who find insects delectable. A similar recognition and critique of disgust is surely warranted in the area of aesthetic taste.

Even so—keeping in mind the distinctions between perceiving, enjoying, and judging—we can say that the goal of ecumenical musical taste is not necessarily to enjoy, personally, the arts and worship styles favored by various other people and groups. As André Maurois once said, "In literature as in love, we are astonished at what is chosen by others."[75] The greater and more useful goal is to try to perceive for oneself what others are perceiving in forms of art and worship that one finds alien; to go on to enjoy their enjoyment (without necessarily liking what they enjoy); and eventually to appraise provisionally those more "alien" tastes in relation to the arts and worship styles one finds more congenial. That approach, when applied to liturgy, can make it possible for people with different tastes to worship more fully together, setting aside the music (for instance) that is most questionable on all sides, and discerning together what is most promising.

The process I have just described seldom takes place spontaneously, "naturally." In the effort to establish some communion between diverse communities of taste, even within a given church, people must often clarify for themselves and others what exactly they are claiming, or should be claiming, when they say that they regard a certain kind of art or music as good, and as good for worship. Is the person who is making the claim trying to persuade everyone on earth, or just some? Is the person commending the art or manner of worship as good for every group and cultural situation, or as especially good in a particular kind of context?

With respect to the claims of taste, I believe we can distinguish at least four concentric circles of judgment, each broader in scope than the one before. The first circle is small. It is the circle inscribed by a judgment made purely for oneself. For years I could not stand to listen to the Ballades of Chopin because, when I was young, my brother practiced them each day (it seemed) while my mother cooked in the kitchen. Years later, I could not abide that music because I could not hear it at any time without smelling cheap hamburger and other food odors in my mental nose. I would not expect anyone else in the world to share that idiosyncratic response to Chopin. To this day, despite my eventual fondness for the music, I have no reliable "gut-level" intuition as to whether a Chopin Ballade could find a suitable place in church. Such purely personal judgments, which are not the sole basis of taste anyway, obviously should not be used as a basis for decisions regarding public worship and its music.

A second kind of judgment, broader in scope, has one affirming something for a particular community and time. The local church choir may sing exceptionally well, perhaps well enough to warrant producing a recording for the enjoyment of people in the area. But the choir's singing may sound best to those who know them and who can, for that very reason, hear special things in the singing. The music-making of children's choirs often has a similarly wonderful but community-based appeal. What matters here is not just the sound but who is producing it and whatever is involved in the whole activity of their participating in church with sometimes wavering, untuned voices.

Judgments inscribing the third circle, still broader in scope, make claims that are unrestricted and "open to the public," but without expecting more than a limited number of "takers." The contemporary Swiss composer Frank Martin (1890–1974) is someone whose religious music I regard as, in its own way, among the greatest in the twentieth century. But Martin's vocal setting of monologues from *Everyman*, for instance, is definitely an acquired taste, blending distant influences from French Impressionism with hints of German serial techniques and considerable dissonance. Some highly trained listeners find nothing attractive in the music, but listeners responsive to this music often regard it as a spiritual and musical revelation. In relation to a more vernacular mode of music, something of the sort could be said of certain songs sung by the contemporary African American group Sweet Honey in the Rock—some of their African adaptations, for instance, which have sonorities and rhythms that listeners elsewhere can find strange. This group's unaccompanied, intense singing, though certainly more popular in appeal than Frank Martin's, can make stringent demands on the relatively select, devoted audience.

Finally, there is the judgment regarding a work that one considers "universal" in its greatness and potential appeal—what we might call a "classic" of its kind. That sort of judgment is based least of all on merely personal experience; it takes into account the testimonies of others. Even then there will inevitably be many people whom the work will miss. Nevertheless, people of various ages and classes who manage to gain access to a classic work almost all come away intensely rewarded, and on repeated occasions, and possibly in different eras and areas. The Taj Mahal and Chartres Cathedral would fall into this category. In music so would Bach's *Magnificat in D*, and Duke Ellington's *Black, Brown, and Beige: Tone Parallel to the American Negro* (1943), and (on a lesser scale) the hymn "A Mighty Fortress." Sometimes it is not a work but a particular performance that becomes just such a classic—Marian Anderson singing spirituals, for instance, or Miles Davis on the trumpet on the album *Kind of Blue* (1959). It can happen that a whole style becomes something of a religious classic. Gothic comes readily to mind (almost as a cliché, in fact), along with the Dravidian style of temple building in South India.

Church musicians are aware that much of their music must make its mark within a particular community or tradition, or not at all. Yet within that tradition, a musician will want to distinguish between work that is good for very special purposes and for a limited time and other work that promises to be far more enduring and of more than local appeal. That judgment must be ratified, of course, by some significant portion of a church community. A church cannot reach any such judgments, however, without experiencing various possibilities for itself. Certainly it cannot explore the appropriateness and quality of specific works and styles without attending carefully to what different groups within the community may actually be hearing *in* the music they find worship-ful. For that purpose, as the Milwaukee report makes plain, a simple conversa-tion is rarely sufficient. Dialogue must be accompanied by musical encounters.

Exercising Musical Taste

Since the experience of music can never fully be conveyed in words, the ways of communicating what music means to a given person or group must always be to some extent indirect. Especially in church settings, where many of those involved lack formal musical training, it can be helpful to arrange sessions in which people representing different "taste groups" are invited to share percep-tions, reactions, and provisional judgments.

One kind of exercise—and one of these will suffice to illustrate the point—is to arrange for church members with different musical tastes to meet in a group at regular intervals to share examples (probably in recorded form) of music they find worshipful. In this exercise, a leader will ask a specific person or group to play their favored selection while they begin to imagine the music as a soundtrack for a film. They are to indicate what sorts of images, actions, feel-ings, or scenes might fit with the music as they hear it. Going on to imagine the film as in some sense specifically religious or spiritual, they then describe a range of religious themes or symbols or events that would accord with the traits they perceive in the music they have identified and offered as worshipful.

With others in the room now asking questions, but making no judgments, our musical "film directors" reconsider the music itself: Does the music resist or work against certain kinds of religious topics or moods? Does it seem, after all, more evocative of settings outside church, even if somehow still "spiritual"? Is the music possibly more fulfilled when pictured as accompanying a film that has nothing to do with religious love and moral commitment, for instance, and more to do with adventure or romance? In answering such questions, the par-ticipants evaluate what they expect from worship itself, and why.

In the last part of the conversation, everyone involved in the exercise is per-mitted to discuss what they themselves perceive, enjoy, and judge regarding both music and worship. If it turns out that a person or group hears a particu-lar kind of music as meditative but many others hear it as merely depressing, there is ample room for a fruitful conversation. Often people hear a work differ-ently when they attend to how others are hearing it—which is crucial for wor-ship, since it is important for different people to find something like the same "wavelength." The leader guiding the discussion can make sure that it touches on the possible aims of worship itself, as approached musically. The group will naturally come to consider different norms and paradigms: worship as essen-tially casual and earthy in tone, or full of vitality; worship as something intensely quiet and "reverent" or else exuberant and ecstatic; worship as intensely personal or else public and formal; or as either ethical or mystical (or perhaps ethical and mystical both). The whole structure of liturgy, and its variations, can come into view, along with criteria that the leader can help articulate, largely on the basis of what different liturgical practices themselves teach.[76]

The purist will object that music and musical style are not to be reduced to pictures and programs. We are supposed to have outgrown such treatments of music in elementary school. Working with the exercise I am describing demonstrates, nonetheless, how even abstract music can work as metaphor. Moreover, this approach is adaptable. It can be used in an intergenerational setting. It uses a familiar art medium (film) to help interpret the latent meanings of music and worship—although there is some minimal risk of feeding the current tendency to think of worship in terms that are already excessively cinematic. Despite that risk, imagining worshipful music as adapted to a film makes sense as a way of thinking about music in worship. That is because, in worship, musicians need to tailor their music to fit the larger needs of the liturgy, just as a composer of film music must serve the larger purposes of a film. While the film can be made in such a way as to respond to the music, one naturally thinks of the whole film as taking precedence over its sound track, just as liturgy finally takes precedence over its musical component. All in all, participants in the exercise begin to notice more clearly what they and others are listening to, and how they are listening, and why they would suppose their favored music could ever fit or enhance acts of worship.

Not incidentally, that kind of "spiritual exercise" in practicing musical taste could be pertinent to various modes of religious practice in our day. Many churches, in their worship services, have begun to experiment with multiple services, each in a different style. There is much to commend such an approach, particularly while people are just beginning to learn new languages of music and new dimensions of worship. But it requires learning to distinguish between personally liking a kind of music and judging it appropriate for worship in a particular community. It also requires learning a degree of discipline to match enthusiasm. Nothing is more jarring than incompetently presented and unfamiliar music forced into a service that is poorly interpreted and in no way modified to accommodate the change. And that is what can easily happen as clergy, musicians, and congregants are all feeling their way into new idioms. Better to gather together those who are especially committed to a new mode, thereby allowing them freedom to discover what can be said in an alternative style using alternative forms of music.

Most liturgists would recommend that in general the ultimate goal be the enrichment of a united worship that is structured in a theologically, aesthetically, and liturgically artful way—one that can encourage relatively diverse styles and voices within a whole service that achieves its own kind of integrity. Many churches are accordingly committed to what has been called "blended worship"—a "creative mixture of old and new."[77] There is no formula for success, however; and such a blending of patterns must be carried out with considerable artistry if it is not to result in something like a variety show in the arena of worship. Up to this point, many proponents of blended worship have relied too heavily on an approach that treats each element or style as one component simply to be inserted (more or less interchangeably) into a designated worship slot, with minimal attention to the aesthetic character of each element, and therefore with relatively little consideration to creating a variegated yet integral liturgical and aesthetic structure out of multiple styles.

Even at its best, the large-scale blending of styles (contemporary, popular, ethnic, traditional Euro-American) is not a global answer. A kind of religious service that depends on prolonged periods of silence with intervals of chant cannot readily be "blended" with a kind of service that is animated by periods of dancing and clapping, after which neither the mind nor the body can calm down or focus. Nor can a style of worship that has become a kind of ethnic or minority classic in itself easily be "blended" on a regular basis without serious compromise. I once attended a service at St. Francis de Sales Catholic Church in New Orleans—a church that is almost exclusively African American—at which most of the music used in the nearly three-hour period was New Orleans jazz and contemporary gospel. It would rarely be desirable to "blend" Euro-American elements into such a service—a portion of a Bach cantata, for instance.

One alternative or supplement to blended worship is in fact something completely different. It consists in the cultivation of church gatherings that center around religious music itself (or some other art, such as drama), with special attention to alternative and minority music styles. Indeed, in churches where "classical" European-style music is no longer primary fare, and where cantatas or full-length choral masses are no longer practical or permitted, "sacred concerts," for example, would give those traditions, too, a new lease on their spiritual life, without forcing any of the music to conform (and properly so) to the aims and structure of a worship service as normally conceived and conducted.

We have been paying special attention to these matters of ecumenical taste partly because, as we have seen, even informed preferences and judgments in taste are not so universal in scope as people have often thought. They develop differently within different communities (many of which may overlap); and their standards of excellence vary, even though a cultivated taste in one kind of music can equip one at least to notice more about music of another kind. All of this has definite consequences for church life and for the norms and patterns of worship.

In a diverse culture with increasingly competitive tastes, churches cannot assume that everyone is readily acculturated to any one predominant style. Even if a church community has strong reasons for wanting to retain relative uniformity in musical and liturgical style—perhaps because of the richness of its heritage and its overall commitment to tradition (as in much Eastern Orthodoxy)—it cannot assume that its musical language will be transmitted fully and naturally without special attention to the education of newcomers.

Nevertheless, we must add that the extent of a person's initial affinity for the worship styles preferred by certain other Christians does not determine in any absolute way whether that person can worship with them. Indeed, part of what I have been arguing is that Christians in every position, whether inside or outside a given tradition, would do well to develop a more extensive taste for difference and diversity, along with more penetrating powers of discernment and discrimination. Quite apart from the dictates of worship, that is an important dimension of learning to love the neighbor. The willingness (and not merely the ability) to love both wisely and expansively, in the sphere of aesthetics, is indeed something learned, however, and not spontaneous. It is an acquired taste. I have endeavored to examine, therefore, how such a taste might be cultivated more broadly and exercised more critically.

Time and again the critical question of the quality of a particular taste in music has converged with the question of its appropriateness for worship. Yet in our era, as we have noticed, the question of appropriateness often prompts, in turn, a reexamination of the relationship between sacred and secular, because of the extent to which secular styles are being raided for sacred purposes. In the chapter that follows we explore the relationship between secular and sacred in the sphere of architecture and in the context of cultures far removed from the "West," and generally from Christianity as well. That distance may provide a fresh perspective on the whole issue of making sacred art and of making art sacred within the wider ecumenical world—a world in which Christians encounter faiths and arts both like and unlike their own.

Making Sacred Places, and Making Places Sacred

Architectural and Ecumenical Taste

In the course of reflecting on new possiblilties for Protestant architecture, Paul Tillich remarked in 1962 that the great periods of Christian visual art and architecture have all been Catholic—in large part because of the greater Catholic emphasis on sacrament. By contrast, he said, Protestant worship has almost always emphasized Word over art and sacrament, and "ear" over "eye." It has also emphasized the congregation over its liturgical leaders and artistic specialists. Protestants, moreover, have been especially worried about idolatry when dealing with material things. Without trying to jettison all that, Tillich argued that it is time for Protestantism to pay far more attention to architecture as integral to religious practice and worship—as what we might term a genuine medium of the sacred rather than a mere housing for it. When that is done, Tillich thought, "genuine Protestant church architecture is possible, perhaps for the first time in our history."[1]

Tillich's agenda as a Protestant theologian clearly entailed, in part, reeducating Protestant taste by taking into account Catholic aesthetics. Whether he was sufficiently appreciative of what Protestants had already accomplished in some of their historic and modern architecture is debatable. Yet Tillich did not naively suppose, in any case, that Protestants should adopt new styles without first being attuned to their own identifiably Protestant aesthetic and religious sensibility—to their own distinctive sense of the sacred and of how the sacred is mediated by human artistry. Although he encouraged the critical appreciation of multiple traditions and styles, and was in that sense a proponent of ecumenical taste, Tillich was aware of the importance of particular traditions of marking and mediating the sacred.

Such an awareness may be even more imperative now, as cultures increasingly meet and mix throughout the world, and as sacred styles interact more than ever with secular. We therefore continue our study of ecumenical taste by examining the possibilities and ambiguities of sacred architectural styles as seen in relation to particular traditions, both religious and secular. To broaden our cultural and religious perspective, we will turn to non-Christian traditions, and to the ways of sacred making associated with Chinese culture in particular. In reflecting on worldwide patterns of sacred artistry and architecture, however, the thinker most relevant to our discussion will not be Paul Tillich but the late historian of religions Mircea Eliade (1907–1986), whose ideas we will examine after we first consider briefly the various factors involved in sacred making.[2]

Sacred Making, and Making Sacred

However complex or vaguely defined the relationship may be between sacred and secular in any given culture, people who practice and appreciate religious artistry must learn to discern and design things that can rightly be regarded as sacred. In the realm of religious architecture, therefore, one is bound to ask at some point: How is a sacred place *made*? And how is a place made *sacred*?[3]

People who plan, design, and build sacred places are likely to dwell on the first question, the question of *making*: What materials and structures can best serve sacred purposes? Not that this question must be asked in every instance. Someone authorized by a religious tradition can simply erect a building along conventional lines and have it dedicated to what is perceived to be holy. By definition, that becomes a sacred place. But in practice, more is typically involved in sacred making—much more. In addition to drawing on the wide array of architectural skills that come into play in all sorts of building, makers of sacred places must keep in mind specific traditions, purposes, and problems. An architect cannot just whimsically decide, for instance, to design a synagogue in the style of a Sukkoth booth, simply because the latter structure is likewise sacred and Jewish. While a small shelter with a thatched roof that lets in starlight is entirely appropriate for Sukkoth, it would obviously be entirely inappropriate for the synagogue.

The requirements of sacred making vary widely even for the same sorts of religious building. An urban architect may often be asked to design Christian churches that will be contemporary in style, equipped with modern media, resistant to pollution and to noise, and physically comfortable in all seasons. Outside of metropolitan areas architects may need to design certain churches using materials and forms that will be compatible not only with local vernacular styles but also with natural environments such as forest groves, highland meadows, or riversides. People charged with making sacred places may have to consider, also, whether it is possible to provide beautiful and durable buildings that are economical, so as to serve less affluent religious communities. Or they may want to figure out how to counteract the tendency of newer sacred buildings to look increasingly dated and mundane as they age (prior to the stage at which they can be regarded as venerable and seemingly timeless). In designing worship spaces in a pluralistic and largely secular society, architects should surely attempt to anticipate what forms are likely to be perceived as sacred or not, and by whom—a question particularly relevant at a time when formerly secular styles of art and music are being imported on a large scale into various sacred settings such as churches, Buddhist temples, and Hindu home shrines. Finally, those involved in making sacred places may wonder how to make room for the sacred at all in an era preoccupied with profane pursuits.

Such questions about how a sacred place is *made* begin to merge with questions of the second sort: the more philosophical or theological questions having to do with how a place is made *sacred*. To answer the latter questions, which are in some ways even more crucial to religious artistry and architecture, we must reconsider the whole framework of sacred and profane as it has been elaborated by modernist theorists of culture and the sacred, and most notably by Mircea Eliade.

Sacred and Profane Revisited

The concept of the "sacred" maps a large terrain bounded by the "profane." It includes, in principle, everything that is specially devoted to something holy, or that is holy in itself. Useful as this notion is for theology or religious studies, people practicing religion seldom think about the sacred per se. When one worships and serves Guanyin or Allah or Jesus Christ, and does so at particular sites and with specific rites, the notion of the sacred as something invoked in virtually all societies may not even cross one's mind. And even if it does, one will normally regard some of the world's purportedly sacred acts and objects as inappropriate, inferior, or profane. Thus, at the level of particular religious traditions, there are distinctions made among available religious perceptions and practices; and always there are insiders and outsiders. That is part of what it means to have an identity and a tradition. That is also why matters of making sacred can be addressed satisfactorily only if one pays attention at some point to different kinds of sacrality, and to the manner in which different places and experiences of the sacred are made accessible or inaccessible to different people, whether by design or default.

Yet in the modern study of religion and culture—modern as opposed to postmodern—questions about different kinds of sacrality, and about the politics of inclusion and exclusion associated with them, have largely been treated as of peripheral interest. A great many modern religion scholars, drawing much of their ideology from the Enlightenment and much of their residual religious inspiration from Romanticism, have (understandably) been both wary and weary of sectarian divisions, leery of dogmas, and more than a little suspicious of narrow notions of religious devotion and duty. In reaction they have looked for something deeper, more essential, focusing on what they have seen as the universal dimensions of the sacred as such even as they have studied different patterns of belief and practice. Thus they have sympathized with those theorists of mind and culture who have seen different cultural patterns either (in religious terms) as ways to the same sacred center; or (in psychological terms) as myriad imaginative expressions of what are, at core, a very limited number of archetypal patterns; or (in literary terms) as innumerable versions of what amount to but three or four basic types of story, which in turn may even be reduced to one primary saga: a monomyth of spiritual quest and conquest.

In connection with such theories, one thinks of scholars such as Rudolf Otto, James Frazer, Carl Jung, Northrop Frye, Joseph Campbell, Claude Lévi-Strauss, René Girard, and most recently a popular exponent, Ken Wilber. However real their differences, these students of mind, culture, and society have all emphasized universal patterns of language, art, and imagination, including the religious.

For students of religion itself, however, the name most likely to come to mind in this regard is Mircea Eliade. In his voluminous writings on religious phenomena, Eliade attempted to show how different religious stories, rituals, places, and artifacts—especially in premodern settings—share a common concern for establishing a sacred center, distinguished from the profane space outside. According to Eliade, the sacred is perceived in traditionally religious societies as something set apart, although potentially pervasive in influence. As such, the sacred provides access to that which is higher, eternal, and ultimately real. In hallowing space and time, for instance, religious leaders and representative devotees narrate sacred myths and they ritually reenact primordially creative deeds from the mythical past. In that way the sacred tradition periodically renews the community and its world, recreating a viable present that is patterned on the timeless source and ultimate paradigm of cosmic order.[4]

Eliade claims that almost anything can become sacred or numinous; virtually anything can serve as the site of a theophany or a hierophany. But to do so it must be chosen by the divine, the holy. In Eliade's words, human beings "are not free to *choose* the sacred site"; rather, "they only seek for it and find it by the help of mysterious signs."[5] They elaborate "techniques of *orientation*, which, properly speaking, are techniques for the *construction* of sacred space."[6] But, Eliade insists, "we must not suppose that *human* work is in question here," that humans can consecrate a space through their own efforts. In reality the ritual by which human beings construct a sacred space "is efficacious in the measure in which *it reproduces the work of the gods.*"[7] Outside the sacred lies the fragmentation and chaos of the profane, with its empty time and state of disorientation. In Eliade's view the latter state is not unlike the modern condition as a whole; for he judges that life today has become profoundly impoverished as it has largely confined the sacred to the realm of art and dreams.[8]

Theorists and historians of art, architecture, and sacred geography have been influenced more by Eliade than by any other single historian of religions.[9] Moreover, in reading Eliade's work, living artists and architects have often been encouraged to see themselves as unconventional custodians and transformers of sacred tradition elsewhere under dire threat. Some artistic practices can reasonably be compared to some of the sacred yogic practices discussed by Eliade;[10] and certain artists do seem rather like shamans—the religious visionaries and healers from those archaic cultures that Eliade examines so extensively.[11] It does seem, moreover, that when the desire for the sacred is repressed in intellectual circles, and when it is commercialized and commodified in much of culture at large, the sacred may find some of its more authentic expressions in disciplined and daring artistry.[12]

Nevertheless, there are significant questions about how, in Eliade's scheme, sacred artistry can or should occur, and what it is supposed to accomplish, given Eliade's view that, at least from a traditional perspective, the divine simply chooses the sacred place, time, or object, becoming known through a special irruption into—or manifestation within—the ordinary. For one thing, whether authorized to do so or not, religious artists often engage in a far from passive spiritual quest; although the sacred is not thought to be of their own making, their art is often experienced by themselves and others as a process of genuine discovery without which the sacred could not manifest itself in precisely the same way. Such artistry goes well beyond the process of sacred discernment and detective work entailed in the use of auguries to reveal sacred places, which Eliade himself is happy to acknowledge. Like the work of theologians and prophets in relation to divine revelation, the work of artists can constitute a creative contribution to the manifestation of the sacred. Religious artists may be deliberately innovative even when they follow basic ritual instructions or tap into unconscious depths for signs and directions. Evidently artists can be both consciously crafty and unconsciously creative in the realm of the sacred.

Again, if artistry includes the traits just described, it is not clear how Eliade could accord it a legitimate place in sacred making. If only the gods can make something sacred, and if the instructions for imitating their patterns are permanently established in myth and ritual, this appears to rule out imaginative critique and artistic innovation from the start.

In this regard, Eliade offers an excessively conservative paradigm for sacred making and religious art—and this despite his own experiments with Surrealist techniques in writing fiction, and despite his admiration for artists such as Brancusi, who embraced both the modern and the "primitive." In limiting the active role of the religious artist (not to mention the theologian), Eliade is doubtless trying to honor the self-understanding of many sacred traditions. The makers of icons in the Orthodox Church, for instance, follow specific guidelines and are not seen, traditionally, as artists per se or as innovators, though sometimes innovation occurs. Yet it seems plausible that religions habitually obscure the level of human involvement in the creation of sacred places and patterns, just as they habitually obscure the human factors in divine revelation and likewise obscure the extent to which religious practices and beliefs evolve in human history instead of remaining what ostensibly has "always" been believed and practiced. If that is so, sacred making may simply stand as another instance in which religions should not be taken completely at their own word, or at least not literally.

In point of fact, Eliade's image of making or discovering sacred places and structures, framed in the first place primarily in terms of archaic religions, shows up as manifestly flawed when taken as a universal paradigm. From the newly naturalistic sacred arts sponsored by the revolutionary pharaoh Akhenaton (14th c. B.C.E.) to the often playful, conspicuously figurative Jewish paintings and stained glass of Marc Chagall (1889–1985), the arts have repeatedly contributed something new under the sacred sun. Indeed, they have contributed to the evolution of sacred traditions themselves, as one sees in the development of Protestant hymnody, which, as Max Weber argued, played a major part in energizing and shaping the Reformation. Such sacred making, identifying and creating a particular kind of religious community, is also a preparation for encountering the Holy and a mode by which that Holy Other is made manifest and interpreted.

To point this out is in part to echo, from the artistic side, an objection recently raised elsewhere from a distinctly postmodern perspective—namely, that when Eliade depicts the creation of sacred places and spaces as primarily a matter of irruption and manifestation, this finally "obscures the symbolic labor that goes into making space sacred. It erases all the hard work that goes into choosing, setting aside, consecrating, venerating, protecting, defending, and redefining sacred places."[13] And that is not all, according to this line of critique; for Eliade's account of the sacralization process also "covers up the symbolic violence of domination or exclusion that is frequently involved in the making of sacred space."[14] To which I would add the criticism that Eliade's approach by and large fails to recognize the distinctive religious value of neutral or profane space, space that makes room for criticizing sanctified ideas and images, for resisting abuses of sacred power, and for helping to generate alternative approaches to the holy.

But there is a more general problem with Eliade's account of sacred making and of the sacred as such. This has to do with the issue with which this section began—the danger of homogenizing the sacred. Eliade brings into view exceedingly diverse means by which cultures demarcate the sacred; and he discloses what is common to these diverse sacred places, objects, and acts. Furthermore, in contrast to some of his postmodern critics, Eliade resists reducing issues of sacred making to matters of politics or sheer ideology, and in this way avoids one kind of monolithic interpretation. But Eliade's preoccupation with underlying patterns—and, even more, with the basic contrast between the sacred and the profane—leads him to minimize the extent to which the sense of the sacred must itself vary according to differences in style, social location, and cultural context, and to overlook how fiercely contested places can be when they are claimed for the sacred.

Thus it seems clear that Eliade's discussions of the sacred and the profane need to be corrected and supplemented, and not least by accounts of sacred artistry attentive to the issues I have been highlighting. In the remaining discussion, therefore, I want to examine briefly a tradition of sacred architecture that suggests how perceptions of the sacred are indeed shaped by different material forms, how this shaping process affects religious identity by including and excluding, and, last, how the enterprise of sacred making itself often involves commerce between the sacred and the mundane or even the profane.

In What Way Sacred, and for Whom?

To gain a fresh perspective on questions raised in the course of our discussion of Eliade, I want to turn to a distant cultural setting about which he wrote relatively little—acknowledging that its relative unfamiliarity will mean that we will miss many subtleties. These particular observations are an outgrowth of recent travels I undertook with a small delegation visiting religious teachers and sacred places in China: Beijing, Xi'an, Nanjing, Suzhou, and Shanghai.

The starting point for my reflections is the simple observation that in much of China the majority of the temple complexes and monasteries, whether Taoist, Buddhist, or Confucian, are built in a similar style and utilize similar ground plans—an observation confirmed by any of the relatively few texts published in English on Chinese religious architecture.[15]

Upon visiting a Chinese temple complex of almost any sort, one can normally expect to encounter a high outer wall marking and protecting the outer edge of the sacred precinct (Figure 6). This wall almost always has a main gate opening to the South, which is the auspicious direction of *yang* forces, and therefore the orientation of many major Chinese buildings as dictated by the principles of *feng shui* (or geomancy). In passing through the tall, decorated gatehouse, which leads one over a high sill and sometimes around a false wall (to ward off evil spirits), one moves past sculpted images of guardian deities or kings. Once inside the compound the visitor stops, perhaps, at shops for incense and religious paraphernalia, then progresses along an architectural "path" that presents a series of focal points, or "nodes,"[16] consisting of incense burners, stalls for votive candles, and (more important) a succession of several halls that house sacred images.

The entire inner space of the compound, which usually takes the shape of a long rectangle, is organized symmetrically along a strong central axis that guides one from South to North. Along the way, open spaces form courtyards that invite one toward each locus of devotion.

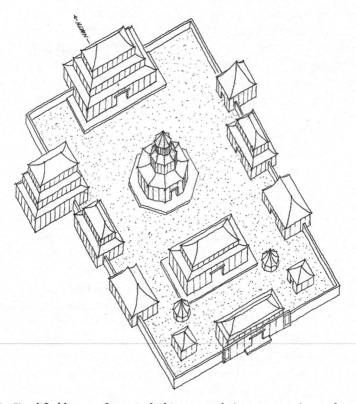

Figure 6. *Simplified layout of a typical Chinese temple (or monastery) complex—in this case Buddhist, as indicated by the pagoda. (Drawing by Bruce Loewenthal.)*

There are frequently several halls along the median axis—as many as four or five. (Figure 6 shows a smaller number for the sake of clarity.) These halls are usually modest in height, and oblong (much wider than they are deep). Built of wood, with glazed tile roofs supported by a system of brackets at the top of columns, all of these halls stand at right angles to the main axis and rest on brick or masonry platforms that one ascends by way of steps. Because the halls tend to be visible only one at a time, it is only as one reaches each worship "stop" along the central axis that another appears. Subsidiary halls line either side of the space, oriented lengthwise to form a border. Whereas the halls along the central axis are used for prayers, offerings, and divinations—the latter especially Taoist (Figure 7)—the side halls may include work spaces, study rooms, lesser shrines, or (in Buddhist temples) prayer halls for monks.

Figure 7. *In front of the Hall of the Three Pure Ones, with incense burner, White Cloud Taoist Temple, Beijing. (Photograph by Frank Burch Brown)*

Even though the avenue that one travels in moving forward from building to building is typically longer than it is wide, it never seems constricted except when one comes to the doorways to the halls, which make for a sense of passage. In time, one will inevitably come upon a hall that is somewhat larger than the rest, or more richly decorated. It will house more splendid images, or a greater number of them, or the most important ones—the powerful Three Pure Ones of Taoism, for instance, or a huge Buddha reclining in the pose of his *parinirvana* (final decease and release). Such a hall may be the last of all, or it may literally be the central one. Here there is a sense of focus and of culmination, calling for special prayers and offerings. But even upon arriving at the most important hall in the complex, one usually sees only a moderate change in scale, and no tremendous surge in height. In a Buddhist compound the highest point, in fact, may be a pagoda, standing at the side or front, or near the center, but seldom where the worshiper ultimately "arrives." Consequently the sense of climax, while real, is seldom terribly dramatic. The process has had rewards all along, with multiple sacred places. Everything is subtly balanced and (especially in Buddhist complexes) tends quite often to be symmetrical, so that the space symbolizes and manifests the order ascribed to the larger cosmos.

For most who visit them, these places conduct one on a kind of sacred journey, a little pilgrimage with various significant moments. In such places the experience of the sacred has many sources. The sense of multiple foci is reinforced by the fact that these sites are not mainly for joint public worship. Only on special occasions are there large groups of people joined together in simultaneous song, prayer, or devotion. Most of the time the space accommodates a diffuse flow of worshipers, each focusing on different acts and objects at different moments, with the result that the whole area is permeated by gazes and movements directed toward multiple sacred points at any given instant.

This profusion and diffusion of activities and focal points within the sacred precinct contrasts markedly with the spaces most characteristic of Christian (especially Protestant) worship—even in China, where Catholic and Protestant churches alike strongly resemble their European and American counterparts. Christian houses of worship collect all the faithful inside, where the typical rectangular hall creates a processional space or path that leads to a definite focus and climax at the front, or liturgical East end. There, at a dramatic termination point of the architecture, one sees either the communion altar (associated with Christ's atonement and redemptive presence) or else a pulpit (where the Word is proclaimed, encountering the hearer with the gospel). In recent years Christian churches in many parts of the world have made more use of a central plan, which historically has been more prominent in Eastern Orthodoxy. But here, too, there is a definite center of attention. And though many Catholic churches have side chapels and a proliferation of images, there is rarely if ever much doubt about the center of worship, architecturally speaking, and especially when the faithful gather as a whole.

Unlike Christian churches, the typical Chinese temple complex seems especially evocative of, and accommodating to, a spirituality that finds many sources of the sacred or that, alternatively, emphasizes awakening to an overall sense of sacred presence. And this readily fits, of course, with religious Taoism and its many deities, with Mahayana Buddhism and its innumerable buddhas and bodhisattvas, and even, historically, with Confucian ritual, which likewise honors multiple sages, gods, and ancestors. While those Chinese traditions are all concerned with an array of holy beings and powers, the more mystical forms of Taoism and Buddhism in particular may cultivate a sense of ultimate harmony and omnipresent holiness (the Buddha nature, for instance) that is potentially to be found everywhere and in every moment of sentience. That overall awareness is likewise accommodated or encouraged by the meditative pace and breadth of attention invited by traditional Chinese sacred space.

By the same token, such a disposition of sacred space seems less conducive to a spirituality that focuses on one particular transcendent goal toward which all other sacred things point (as in many forms of Catholic spirituality), or on one Holy Other compared to which there is nothing else truly sacred (as in much Protestant spirituality and in much of Islam). It therefore seems more than likely that Christianity's characteristic distance both from traditional Asian spiritualities and from Chinese eclecticism may provide one significant reason why, even today, Christian churches in China rarely adopt the more-or-less standard East Asian temple plan. Clearly, a tradition's dominant sacred space shapes its characteristic perceptions of the sacred and the very identity of those who worship in a particular way.

This is not to suggest that the traditional Chinese ways of organizing sacred architectural space are strictly uniform. It is possible, in fact, that on the Chinese mainland today the similarities are somewhat exaggerated and the differences obscured.[17] Nor is it to suggest that these patterns of building and of organizing space always reflect precisely and only such concerns and perceptions as I have described. Every style has variations, and multiple reasons for existing. We will be noting, for instance, that classic Chinese temple architecture is closely related in style to palace designs that date back as far as the early years of the Han dynasty (from around 200 B.C.E.). The reasons for using such a design must not all be purely spiritual, therefore.

Nor do I mean to say that the spaces and places associated with Chinese temples could never be made to accommodate strictly monotheistic traditions. In fact the famous Great Mosque at Xi'an adopts such a plan—but not without introducing differences. At the Great Mosque, the central axis is not from South to North but from East to West, which in China points one toward Mecca. And the lengthy path of one's progress toward the great Prayer Hall at the end of the way is relatively direct. There are small pavilions, to be sure, and rock gardens, and a tall minaret in the shape of a pagoda (Figure 8). One even pauses to gaze at dragon figures on the eaves of the minaret (a departure from the geometrical or vegetal designs often associated with Islam). Yet there is only one place set apart for prayer, only one real goal, one center of devotion—with its single prayer niche, the *mihrab*, set in the *qibla* wall, orienting worshipers together and throughout the world toward a single Center, chosen by the One God. In short, the traditional, multifocal Chinese temple space has here been converted to distinctly monotheistic purposes.

Figure 8. *Pagoda-like minaret at the Great Mosque, Xi'an. (Photograph by Frank Burch Brown)*

If places can be made and used in such a way as to mediate a particular sense of the sacred, this means that the sacred is partly defined and created by material making, which also makes for a particular sense of religious identity and power.[18] It is no accident that religious zealots often destroy the worship places of their opponents. Nor is it an accident that when Christians in the Roman Empire first began to build large churches in the fourth century, they rejected the alien form of the pagan temple and adopted, instead, a more neutral building. This was the civic basilica, which they converted from a place governed by the Roman emperor to a place governed by the Lord Jesus Christ, emperor of the universe.

But if religious identities, and spiritual and social realities, are typically mediated by sacred places, why should Chinese temple complexes representing different traditions—Taoist, Buddhist, and Confucian—all share many of the same formal features? Why would they not be more distinct? Surely part of the answer is that a great many Chinese, past and present, have long combined in their practices aspects of different paths—Taoist, Buddhist, Confucian, and traditional folk religion. These ways are more complementary than antagonistic.[19] This is not to deny that, even for the average worshiper, it makes some difference whether one is honoring the Jade Emperor of Taoism or the Buddhist bodhisattva of mercy, Guanyin. Even if both are regarded as powerful and helpful, they tend to serve rather different functions, and in different spheres of life. One turns to Guanyin in childbirth or sickness (for example); one goes to the hall of the Jade Emperor in search of physical immortality. For most Chinese, this has been more a matter of seeking out the right specialist than of pursuing the one true way. Small wonder, then, that the sacred places made for these traditions are externally similar, even though the specific powers that the traditions honor do differ, as seen in the different images in the respective halls.

At this point another question arises, which has to do with the relation between secular and sacred. What can be perplexing is that the style of buildings and grounds traditionally associated with temples and monasteries in China is approximately the same as that found in traditional palaces and imperial buildings, from the Han dynasty up to the recent past. Even today, many Buddhist, Taoist, and Confucian temples are designated by Chinese terms meaning "palace." A number are in fact former palaces that were donated for religious purposes. Some architectural historians go so far as to claim that the religious style from its very beginning was taken over from the palatial and the political. Others suggest that there was simply a generic style of monumental Chinese building that has continued with a limited number of variations. Either way, we must ask whether we were wrong to think that the style we have discussed in relation to Chinese temples can have genuine religious significance.

It must be acknowledged that few studies of Chinese architecture explore ways in which the common traditional style could ever foster religious perceptions and accrue religious meanings of the sort I have described here. Since the style is not exclusively religious, there is a tendency to suppose that it cannot function as particularly sacred.[20] That assumption is not shared by certain scholars writing about the closely related religious architecture of Japan, however, who do see a connection between such a style and religious or spiritual significance.[21]

An analogy from Christian history may help show why the religious line of interpretation may be called for. Recalling that Christians in the era of Constantine adapted the secular Roman basilica for liturgical purposes, one realizes that this became politically and spiritually possible partly because the Roman government was no longer a hostile force. And architecturally it was possible because a certain kind of civic building could readily be converted to the purposes of Christian worship. Unlike pagan temples, which had all the wrong associations and which, in any case, were worship sites designed to be experienced mostly from the outside, the basilica was relatively neutral and allowed ample space inside for congregational worship. When turned longitudinally so as to focus attention on the altar for the Eucharist, and when modified by inserting at the end of the nave a triumphal arch framing an apse (usually with a mosaic image of Christ), the basilica became an exceptionally apt form for Christian worship.

Similar processes can be seen at work, for example, in the Buddhist adaptation of the palace and civic style of building. Buddhism, as an import from India at roughly the time that Christianity came into existence, struggled for many centuries in China to win and then maintain imperial approval and support, even while resisting complete imperial control. That the need for both approval and freedom was real is indicated by the fact that in the ninth century the Taoist emperor Wu-tsung tried to wipe out Buddhism from China, or at least to eradicate its economic influence. In the attempt, he managed to destroy some 4,600 temples, along with 40,000 shrines.[22] It is understandable that Buddhists establishing themselves in China would have chosen to adapt for their own purposes a building style that was not only spiritually compatible but also already recognized in the political and religious spheres as worthy, acceptable, and indigenous—but not the exclusive property of any one tradition.

The fact that the style chosen was not exclusively Buddhist or even exclusively sacred did not mean that it could not be highly amenable to specific sacred purposes, especially when modified from within. During the Tang dynasty, for example, Buddhist image platforms in the halls of the temples came to resemble royal audience halls, with all the statues facing the worshiper in much the way that the emperor and his entourage would have faced their subjects.[23] Just as Christians had installed in their basilicas the image of Jesus (and the throne of the Bishop) in the place of the Roman Emperor, so Buddhists installed buddha(s), lohans, and bodhisattvas in the place of the Son of Heaven and his associates. Without insulting the emperor, this arrangement honored still higher powers.

Meanwhile, Buddhists had already created their own identifying sign by adapting the Indian stupa, which had been a reliquary mound, and turning it into a new form based on the traditional wooden Chinese watchtower—thereby making a pagoda. Subsequently any temple accompanied by a pagoda would be recognized as Buddhist (though eventually the pagoda itself diminished in significance).

The fact that the style of imperial architecture could be put to good sacred use is nothing surprising in itself, since the synthesis of residential, palace, and sacred architecture is one that is found intermittently throughout the world.[24] That does not eliminate potential ambiguities regarding secular and sacred, however. For one thing, from a traditional Chinese point of view (which, again, is one shared by many societies) the division is not clear-cut. Historically the political ruler himself had sacred functions and responsibilities. As Son of Heaven, the emperor could rule only by the mandate of heaven. He was thought to be governing properly only if he acted according to heaven's moral laws and if he carried out important ritual acts on behalf of his whole domain—the realm "all under heaven" that constituted the center of the world. In this capacity the emperor provided a vital link between heaven and earth, between the *yang* and *yin* forces of the cosmos, which in turn made the difference between prosperity and hardship for the whole realm. Thus, when ruling from Beijing during the Ming and Qing dynasties, the emperor would seasonally leave the vast imperial palace (the so-called Forbidden City) and perform sacrifices—sometimes at the great Temple of Heaven complex (Figure 9), at other times at the smaller Temple of the Earth. In addition, many emperors patronized each of the "Three Teachings"—Confucianism, Buddhism, and Taoism—by building temple halls, commissioning images, sponsoring publications, and so forth.[25] The political was by no means the same as the profane, in this scheme, unless the emperor failed in his duties and so fell into profanity.

Even so, one cannot say that the emperor's home base, as it were, either established or defined the sacred as such. After all, to perform his most important sacred acts, the emperor not only had to leave the imperial palace and the political center of China—the Forbidden City—but also, with great ceremony, proceed with his entourage to the temple precincts in order to make sacrifices. It was the Altar of Heaven at the Temple of Heaven that was situated at the most sacred spot in the universe, the line of direct connection between heaven and earth (Figure 10). Significantly, that was not where the emperor dwelled but where, at the winter solstice, he sacrificed.

Our inquiry has led us to question Eliade's idea (or implication) that the sacred is experienced in much the same way in all times and places, and for different kinds of communities. Differences in form do make a difference in experience, in one's very conception of the sacred itself, and in the very activity of making

Figure 9. *Hall of Prayer for Good Harvest, Temple of Heaven, Beijing.* (*Photograph by Willard G. Oxtoby*)

sacred places. An architect convinced of the ultimate oneness of the sacred could not on this basis simply decide to build a Christian church in the style of a Buddhist temple, or to replace a statue of the Virgin with a statue of Guanyin (though the two resemble one another in function). However interesting as a religious and artistic statement, that stylistic choice would certainly desecrate sacred space for most Chinese Christian worshipers.

Ironically, this line of thought lends some credibility to Eliade's claim that sacred forms are given, not made. We can say that they are given, because they are typically identified and transmitted by traditions and communities that have

Figure 10. *Circular, terraced Altar of Heaven at the Temple of Heaven, Beijing.* (*Photograph by Willard G. Oxtoby*)

already marked them as pertaining to a special sphere—higher, more real. Beyond that, religious people and groups experience something sacred as given because they do see it as chosen, authorized, or inspired by the Holy, which is beyond what they know themselves to be.

That is by no means the end of the matter, however, though here is where Eliade would normally have us stop. Once objects and styles are identified as somehow sacred, there are choices as to their use and arrangement—choices that distinguish and divide one tradition from another. Every tradition has areas in which it typically restricts choice and others in which it elects to create in fresh ways. The use of a certain architectural plan for sacred purposes did not simply come about without human agency, nor did the religiously important invention of the pagoda. Sacred objects and places, however inspired they may be, are in a very real sense creative, cultural products.

But to admit human involvement in making things sacred is also to admit that sacred objects may share human frailties and limitations, not to mention ambiguities. One such ambiguity is evident in the act of religious inclusion and exclusion that, while in some ways inevitable, can signify hostility and the abuse of creativity and power. Another ambiguity is the frequent blurring of the very distinction between sacred and secular. That, too, is inevitable, since the sacred, if it is culturally embedded, must always make use of materials and powers that can otherwise be used for mundane purposes. Such a process clearly can result in the sanctification and renewal of the mundane—in making the ordinary sacred. The watchtower can be converted and reworked into a pagoda. But the process can also end in making the sacred ordinary. Thus, if the state at one point sacrifices its goods on the altar of heaven, that can degenerate into a situation in which the state sacrifices heavenly goods on the altar of politics.

Such alternative possibilities lead me to a theological conclusion. If religious power and sacred making are prone to serve ambiguous purposes, or to serve good purposes ambiguously, it is not enough simply to be content with making sacred places, knowing in advance what will count as sacred. One must also be ready to make places sacred where what will count as sacred is very much in question. That is to say, there must be places where the sacred itself can not only question but also be called into question, and through reformation create a larger and more penetrating vision—one that better honors or more fully manifests the holy for a particular situation and time. As Tillich was fond of pointing out, any cultural form, however secular, can potentially be made sacred; yet no cultural form, however sacred, should be seen as utterly above criticism. Oddly enough, those places of criticism, reflection, and re-creation sometimes appear from conventional perspectives to be secular or profane, because their modes or styles of sacrality are as yet unnamed. The Holy is that to which sacred making points at its truest and fullest, in dialogue with the mundane and the profane. But the Holy is never attained, only glimpsed. The Center that is genuinely central defies permanent fixation and must always be approached, and approached again.

In an increasingly heterogeneous yet "blended" society and interconnected world, making places sacred may mean designing them in such a way as to welcome the new and the diverse, yet without becoming utterly estranged from those practices that the community has cultivated as its own. It may mean making an opening, a middle ground where sacred and profane can mix; that, too, can be a sacred act. Finally, it may also mean standing attentively before or within a place that others find sacred (church, synagogue, mosque, or temple) to learn what it is that draws some people in—and what it is that leaves others out.

To be inside a religious tradition means, in part, to find accessible its particular modes of sacred making and of making sacred. Some of those modes are designed to make the sacred accessible to the widest number of people—to those on the threshold of the tradition, or to those who have just entered. Other modes are designed to take one farther, or higher. In the final two chapters we look more closely at religious artistry and taste that humbly aspires not only to invite guests and newcomers but also to serve those seeking more advanced stages of religious—and specifically Christian—development.

EIGHT

Styles and Stages of
Faith and Art I

The Next Stage

Preparation

Since I am coming to that Holy room,
  Where, with the Choir of Saints for evermore,
I shall be made thy Music; As I come
  I tune the Instrument here at the door,
  And what I must do then, think here before.
—John Donne, from "Hymn to God My God, in My Sickness" (1631)

. . . Some to church repair,
Not for the doctrine, but the music there.
—Alexander Pope, from *Essay on Criticism* (1711)

Most Christians would assume, along with Alexander Pope (1655–1744), that there is something dubious about going to church for the music instead of for the doctrine. But the Anglican preacher and poet John Donne (c.1572–1631), gravely ill eight days prior to his death, pictures coming into the ultimate House of Worship precisely in order to make music—indeed, in order to become part of the music, himself. And since he is to become an instrument of God's praise, he contemplates the necessity of tuning his instrument, his very soul. He prepares himself to become more musical, not because he cannot rely on God's grace, but precisely because God is gracious and greatly to be praised. The process evidently requires discipline—better learned late than never.

Of course, Donne as a poet is making the most of music as a metaphor. But if glorifying and enjoying God forever is best imagined as a kind of music-making, we should doubtless think twice before slighting the taste and art required for actually making music, as though artistry and a love of beauty would be inconsequential within any realm where God reigns.

217

Even so, we should not suppose that all kinds of music-making are equal in religious value, or affect the soul in the same way regardless of the situation. As Christmas approached this past year, when my father was within weeks of dying, he briefly enjoyed listening to a new recording of Christmas tunes in light and lively jazz arrangements by the pianist George Shearing. In his weakened condition, he lay in bed listening with headphones, tapping his toes to the music. But he decided before long that the music he was listening to was inappropriate under the circumstances. It was good music, in its way; but it was not music that helped him tune his soul properly as he was preparing to die; it did not enhance his life-and-death conversation with God. In the end he chose, instead, to ask family members to sing hymns for him, and with him, up until the long night before the morning when he would find out, I suppose, whether Karl Barth was right about angels and Bach and Mozart.

The Path from Here

From the very beginning, one of our aims has been to discern how aesthetic taste (inside the church, and outside) can be disciplined in such a way as to become inclusive and yet discriminating; appreciative and yet critical. In these last chapters we focus as well on the question of how taste can be humble and yet aspiring. But none of that would matter from a religious and Christian point of view if it were not possible for taste to be aesthetic and religious, both. To envision that possibility—a special concern of the earlier chapter connecting the taste for art with the desire for God—we have needed to perceive how taste can be bodily and yet spiritual, and in some way worldly or ordinary and yet sacred.

As we saw in the preceding chapter, there must indeed be some connection between ordinary reality and sacred reality, and therefore between secular art and sacred art; otherwise, the sacred could not be perceived at all. It would be utterly and unbridgeably transcendent. But if ordinary reality and art were already sacred through and through, they would never be thought simply ordinary, however common. At that point there would be heaven on earth. As it is, we might do well to imagine the boundary between secular and sacred as real for us but not for God, and in any case shifting and permeable. As we were reminded by Paul Tillich, any aspect of secular culture, including worldly art, is potentially made sacred by the grace of God. Conversely, any aspect of sacred culture, including religious art, can eventually fossilize or erode into something that is sacred in name only. Then, effectively, what was formerly sacred becomes secular.

Even arts that remain essentially secular can sometimes have sacred or "spiritual" overtones or import. And even arts that are recognized as sacred can differ greatly in kind and purpose, from modest to lofty. Accordingly, in the early portions of this chapter, we will try to understand more clearly the possible range of artistry that is conducive to the sacralization of life and to spiritual development, or what Christians have liked to term "sanctification." In the process we will find ourselves questioning the widespread teaching that whatever spiritual progress is possible through art is bound to stop short of the higher reaches of sacred reality and spiritual growth. Then, in the remaining two-thirds of the chapter, we shift the focus and tone of the discussion by reflecting on the prospects of present-day Christian art. We do so primarily by considering in detail one prevalent contemporary trend in worship and music—one that in fact sets aside most of the elements of an identifiably sacred style. That approach and its theological rationale will prompt us to examine once again the matter of the relation of sacred to secular, and of vernacular to "classical." It will also cause us to test and clarify our hypotheses regarding how to address aesthetic conflicts within the realm of Christian practice. In conclusion, we extract from our study as a whole twelve principles that might guide the practice and discussion of Christian art and taste in the present day. That will return us in the final chapter to our effort, begun here, to discern what is required of Christian artistry and taste if it is to have hopes of progressing from minimally spiritual exploration to maturely Christian transformation.

Poet's Progress—or Regress

Our immediate concern is to reflect on the potential religious value of certain kinds of artistic exploration that do not profess to be Christian at all. We begin, therefore, with a pair of poems that, in sequence, might be said to mark something of a spiritual progression. Yet there is nothing stable or linear about that progress, since both poems vacillate or reverse directions as they crisscross the outer boundaries of the spiritual or religious life. Whereas the second poem discovers a fleeting yet transforming sense of the sacred and preserves a hint of hope (however lacking in trust), the poem with which we begin recounts a kind of religious deconversion. From the volume *Crow* (1971), by the eventual poet laureate of Britain, Ted Hughes (1936–1998),[1] it voices—somewhat raucously, we could say—a challenge to any traditional theology or spirituality.

> Crow's Theology
> Crow realized God loved him—
> Otherwise, he would have dropped dead.
> So that was proved.
> Crow reclined, marvelling, on his heart-beat.

And he realized that God spoke Crow—
Just existing was His revelation.

But what
Loved the stones and spoke stone?
They seemed to exist too.
And what spoke that strange silence
After his clamour of caws faded?

And what loved the shot-pellets
That dribbled from those strung-up mummifying crows?
What spoke the silence of lead?

Crow realized there were two Gods—

One of them much bigger than the other
Loving his enemies
And having all the weapons.

The slightly smug natural theology that Crow initially sets forth as proof of God's existence and love actually parodies, of course, certain arguments used by theologians over the centuries. Augustine, for example, reassured himself by means of both reason and revelation that nothing could so much as exist without having an origin and goal in God, who works to the everlasting bene- fit of trusting and faithful human beings. To hear that kind of theological argument uttered by Hughes's Crow is already to hear it differently, darkly, with an ironic edge. The irony sharpens as Crow ponders the power behind shot-pellets and the stony silence into which his caws fade—discovering thereby the pervasive hostility of the universe, and of human beings in particular. Far from having anything like a mutual, "I-Thou" encounter with the Other, he ends up with a kind of Manichean dualism. And in his case it is a dualism in which the more powerful God is revealed as the Enemy.

Although Crow sees human beings as antagonists, it will doubtless occur to most readers that humans can experience their own lives as similarly crow-like— besieged by greater forces, and possibly opposed (or ignored) by some inscru- table Force overshadowing whatever appears to sustain and befriend. Crow's voice has a certain harsh resonance.

Whereas, in Hughes's poem, Crow's sardonic anti-theology argues against any sense that the Force is with us, in our second poem a black rook's shining appearance provides a moment of aesthetic epiphany, a hint of transcendence, however obscure. Sylvia Plath (1932–1963) wrote "Black Rook in Rainy Weather" in 1956, around the time of her marriage to Ted Hughes. To discern the poet's larger design in this poem is something of a spiritual exercise in itself—one that will require and reward our persistence.

Black Rook in Rainy Weather

On the stiff twig up there
Hunches a wet black rook
Arranging and rearranging its feathers in the rain.
I do not expect miracle
Or an accident

To set the sight on fire
In my eye, nor seek
Any more in the desultory weather some design,
But let spotted leaves fall as they fall,
Without ceremony, or portent.

Although, I admit, I desire,
Occasionally, some backtalk
From the mute sky, I can't honestly complain:
A certain minor light may still
Leap incandescent

Out of kitchen table or chair
As if a celestial burning took
Possession of the most obtuse objects now and then—
Thus hallowing an interval
Otherwise inconsequent

By bestowing largesse, honour,
One might say love. At any rate, I now walk
Wary (for it could happen
Even in this dull, ruinous landscape); sceptical,
Yet politic; ignorant

Of whatever angel may choose to flare
Suddenly at my elbow. I only know that a rook
Ordering its black feathers can so shine
As to seize my senses, haul
My eyelids up, and grant

A brief respite from fear
Of total neutrality. With luck
Trekking stubborn through this season
Of fatigue, I shall
Patch together a content

Of sorts. Miracles occur,
If you care to call those spasmodic
Tricks of radiance miracles. The wait's begun again,
The long wait for the angel,
For that rare, random descent.

This is not an instance of everyday bird watching. As the rook arranges and rearranges its feathers, its blackness shines almost miraculously in the midst of a darkened, rainy day. Noticing that, the one watching is prompted to reflect on what, if anything, can suffice in the arrangement of life—suffice by hallowing briefly and incandescently what otherwise seems a "dull, ruinous landscape." Where religious faith belongs in this poetic landscape, with its hints of dark angels, is very much a question, though the question becomes visible only in brief flashes. That the poet was soon to take her own life, as is now well known, cannot easily be bracketed out, and perhaps should not be; but it is less important to the reading than the act of looking, ours and hers—the attentiveness to what is mutely random or inexplicably miraculous in experience, or somehow part of a pattern beyond our knowing.

The poet denies, at one level, that she is looking for a miracle or any sort of meaningful design in the pattern of things, professing a willingness to let leaves fall as they fall, without ceremony or portent. She "can't honestly complain"—a sure sign of the inclination, however—and professes to be prepared to rest content with those unexpected "tricks of radiance" that happen from time to time in daily life, bestowing something one might call love (but why?), allowing her to patch together a content of sorts. Yet she gives us clues, throughout, that she is alert to patterns and meanings after all. For one thing, more than halfway through, she says she now walks "wary" (both attentive and cautious); though ignorant of any angel that might appear at her elbow, she is aware of how a bird might order its feathers in a specially shining sort of way. The bright descent she looks for may be "random," but she is waiting. And the poem has got us looking, as well.

What we find ourselves looking for, partly, is some sign that what seems random about these minor, miraculous occurrences is not so random after all. So we readers begin looking, "wary" ourselves, though apparently "ignorant." The fact that the poem is divided into eight stanzas of five lines each does give, in itself, some sense of order, but nothing striking—particularly since the number of the syllables and stresses fluctuates from one line to the next within each stanza.

It turns out that there is a hidden and surprising order to the poetry, after all, drawing our attention randomly, like the rook ordering its feathers. It does not take too much effort to see that each line within a given stanza has roughly the same number of syllables and stresses as its corresponding line within every other stanza. But one can read the poem any number of times before noticing (while thinking about the matter of order) that there is a hidden rhyme scheme. The last word of each of the lines within each of the eight stanzas rhymes, or half-rhymes, with the last word in the corresponding line in every other stanza. Thus, lining up the last words of the first lines, we find: there, fire, desire, chair, honour, flare, fear, occur. Or, looking at the last lines: accident, portent, incandescent, inconsequent, ignorant, grant, content, descent. That last series of terms seems, in particular, almost a code for questioning and discovery. This is not the sort of thing that a poet does to create a strong feeling of coherence in a poem, because the rhymes are too loose and too widely separated. It is, rather, what a poet does who is designing an order that is meant to be barely perceptible, hinted at but caught only by accident. The hidden rhyme scheme will never be noticed by someone not on the lookout. Yet being on the lookout guarantees nothing, so unusual is the scheme. One could be a veteran poetry reader and never notice it.[2]

Plath's poem could be said to be about "ordinary transcendence" and discernment—about whether there is anything miraculous to be discerned in life, or any underlying pattern or purpose, aside from brief moments of "respite from fear of total neutrality." Perhaps there is, "with luck." Or should we say, with grace?

Despite the fact that most criticism attempts to assume the stance of a relatively neutral or generic reader, no reader is in fact so neutral. And though criticism of the usual sort might think it almost in bad taste to go so far as to picture how a Christian reader might respond to the poetry we have been discussing, there are many such readers. And in truth the poetry is hardly uninteresting from various Christian—or broadly religious—points of view.

What is most immediately striking from a religious standpoint is that artistry like that of Hughes and Plath imaginatively exposes fundamental fears and anxieties while also exploring fugitive spiritual longings and moments of transfiguration, however ephemeral. Theologians in our time have by and large welcomed such quests and questionings as at least signaling the restless stirring of the soul at its depths.[3] But, finally, the religious significance of such poetry does not consist merely in the fact that one can find in it a revealing expression of the human condition, or even some marginally religious "ultimate concern."[4] There is something that relates this poetry more intimately and internally to a life of faith—of genuinely affirmative faith. As James Fowler's work suggests, a contemporary faith whose affirmations exclude such questions and ambivalences is a faith that is likely to be in some respects spiritually immature, itself.[5] In a volatile time, anxious questionings and ambiguous epiphanies play a significant role in religious experience, which is seldom linear in its progress or univocal in its truest confessions and beliefs. Besides, it is not as though Crow's voice itself were one that an attentive and honest Christian theology could treat with condescension, given the massive amount of inexplicable suffering in the world, or could presume to answer neatly and dogmatically.[6] And this again indicates that—as we noted in the previous chapter—art can sometimes be of special religious value precisely when its voice comes from outside the religious community proper and when its vision is not perceived as sacred at all but as profane, and possibly grotesque. Compared with identifiably sacred art, such "secular" art is freer to probe and question. Its illuminations, when they occur, are less likely to be stereotyped in conventionally religious ways. And its ironies or agonies can show why the ways to the sacred are blocked for many, unless those paths can be re-created or re-routed. Even for the professing Christian, the path toward the sacred center may circle back through such dark reversals and frustratingly fugitive epiphanies. Easter never forgets Good Friday. And faith cannot claim, as yet, to see face to face.

The Next Stage

Art in Its Place

Strange to say, it is often easier for Christians to picture art as posing questions from the abyss or as expressing longings on the verge of faith than it is for Christians to think about creative imagination as a vital and ongoing means of theological affirmation, or about art as a potentially advanced spiritual exercise. That is not only because art in the modern era so often hesitates to venture overtly into the realm of the sacred. It is also because so much theology has insisted on treating art even at its highest as a relatively elementary religious activity, to be surpassed as one matures spiritually.

In the last book he wrote, the Trappist (Cistercian) monk Thomas Merton (1915–1968), who by then had discovered an affinity for Zen Buddhism, pointed out the far from negligible importance of "image, symbol, art, rite, and of course the sacraments above all."[7] He observed that "the greatest mystical literature [such as the English *Cloud of Unknowing*] speaks not only of 'darkness' and 'unknowing' but also, and almost in the same breath, of an extraordinary flowering of 'spiritual senses' and aesthetic awareness underlying and interpreting the higher and more direct union with God 'beyond experience.'"[8] He acknowledged, as well, that such poetry as that of St. John of the Cross translates the "savor of eternal life" into symbolic terms. In the same passage, however, Merton deflated the role of the senses, sacraments, and arts by going on to say, in a condescending way: "Even if these human and symbolic helps to prayer lose their usefulness in the higher forms of contemplative union with God, they still have their place in the ordinary everyday life even of the contemplative." They form part of the contemplative's "environment and cultural atmosphere."[9]

Merton, to be sure, had just noted that we are "barely recovering from an era of abomination and desolation in sacred art, due in part to a kind of manichaean attitude toward natural beauty on the one hand, and a rationalistic neglect of sensible things on the other."[10] He was trying to sound encouraging about a renewal of artistic and material spirituality. It is just that Merton thought he knew full well that the "higher forms of contemplative union with God" are bound to do without such things. Many a Buddhist monk would have agreed.

Aesthetics on the Ascent

There is no denying that a host of religious thinkers and believers—many of them Christians—would expect to set aside artistry and aesthetic experience as they reach the higher slopes of their spiritual ascent. But is that religious sacrifice of the aesthetic inevitable? And at what stage, exactly? According to the redoubtable Samuel Johnson (1707–1784), one must give up on the poetical path almost from the start. In his words, "Contemplative piety, or the intercourse between God and the human soul, cannot be poetical. Man admitted to implore the mercy of his Creator, and plead the merits of his Redeemer, is already in a higher state than poetry can confer."[11]

It is perhaps not surprising that the most vivid evidence to the contrary is offered by a poet, and in poetry of a high order indeed. In the highest region of Paradise (Canto XXXIII of *Paradiso*), Dante the pilgrim—who has journeyed down to the depths of Hell, up through Purgatory, and finally through the concentric Heavenly spheres—approaches the moment when he will be granted a vision of the reality of God. Using his painfully acquired and newly strengthened power of sight, he can already behold, within one exalted Light, three superimposed and luminous circles with three different colors, and with a human image "painted" ("*pinta*") within the second circle of Living Light. He is thus beginning to attain a vision of God as the Holy Trinity:

> . . . In the deep and bright
> essence of that exalted Light, three circles
> appeared to me; they had three different colors,
> but all of them were of the same dimension;
> one circle seemed reflected by the second,
> as rainbow is by rainbow, and the third
> seemed fire breathed equally by those two circles.
> (*Par.* XXXIII, 114–20)[12]

Given that the poetry is allegorical, we must recognize that such a vision is not meant to be taken as a matter of literal sight. "Vision" here is meant to be a metaphor for a kind of knowledge, indeed a kind of intellectual knowledge, as the medieval scholastic tradition would insist.[13] We might suppose, therefore, that what Dante is depicting is simply a gradual increase in understanding. But, whatever Dante would have said in person, the poetry does not convey that impression. What the poem apparently depicts at this stage is an increase of "sight" that exceeds the pilgrim's intellectual insight. It registers that some more intuitive power, a certain kind of seeing, exceeds the grasp of his current knowledge as such, and precedes the knowledge to come. That power is at work when Dante is just beginning to make out the circular forms and colors and when he begins to discern a rainbow-like reflection of the first circle (the Father) in the Second (the Son), and a fire of love that both circles together exhale to form the third (the Spirit). Dante as pilgrim "sees" all this, but as yet lacks understanding. He has not reached his final goal. We should not, however, think of such fantastic "seeing" as merely a lack; what it lacks in conceptual clarity, it partly makes up for in the vivacity of the luminous images and forms that it apprehends. Beholding these, "sight" reaches beyond knowledge per se and prepares the way. That extension of "sight" we could call a religious form of aesthetic imagination.

Suddenly, by the grace of God, a flash of light illumines Dante's mind. Instantaneously, we are to believe, he has a true vision of God in which he experiences a foretaste of the Beatific Vision:

> But then my mind was struck by light that flashed
> and, with this light, received what it had asked.
>   Here force failed my high fantasy; but my
> desire and will were moved already—like
> a wheel revolving uniformly—by
>   the Love that moves the sun and the other stars.
>
> (*Par.* XXXIII, 140–45)

Once again, with Dante's own sanction (*Par.* IV, 124–29), and perhaps with additional help from Thomas Aquinas, one could manage to stretch language enough to call that experience intellectual, remembering, however, that this is knowledge *of* God, not merely knowledge *about* God. Yet we have even more reason to call it a satisfaction of the whole being. Saint Bernard has introduced this culminating canto of the *Divine Comedy* with a prayer to the ever-loving Virgin Mother, humble and sublime, asking that she, through her prayers, make it possible for Supreme Joy to be disclosed to Dante. As Jean Leclerq reminds us, Bernard had spoken in his writings of knowing through love and of "savoring and relishing the Divine realities."[14] It is that sort of enraptured and transfigured satisfaction that Dante describes poetically (aesthetically) and that his poetry to some degree preserves, upon his "return" to earth, in a form that evokes not only joy but an indescribable yearning, blinding in its bright ineffability. The poetically wrought sense of divine light, so splendidly and sublimely imagined, endures as an after-image that is never reduced to anything we would ordinarily call intellectual, or merely so. Indeed, in the eyes of some readers—perhaps especially those who seem well beyond spiritual infancy—the art of Dante's poetry comes closer than any purely intellectual theology to conveying a sense of the mystery of the Trinity and of beatific bliss.[15] If the poetry still cannot contain all that it invokes and betokens, neither can thought. As John Donne's "Hymn" likewise testifies, the soul's poetic art is ultimately to be transformed, but by becoming still more "musical," not less. In the end, just as the ultimate Beatific "Vision" of God can be regarded as at once the fulfillment and transfiguration of knowledge, so can that highest "Vision" be regarded as at once the fulfillment and transfiguration of love and aesthetic delight.

What's Next

The symbol gives rise to thought, as philosophers such as Immanuel Kant, Karl Jaspers, and Paul Ricoeur all say.[16] Perhaps we should also acknowledge that thought and further experience can, in turn, give rise to the symbol—the aesthetic and artistic symbol that, even as words begin to fail, is lifted up by illumined imagination, however imperfect, or by what has traditionally been called inspiration. To follow Merton and numerous other religious thinkers in looking on poetry and art as necessarily and merely a lower-level "help" to higher contemplation is surely, itself, to perpetuate attitudes and biases we have been trying hard to dispel. From another point of view, nothing could be more poetical or musical than the beatific vision. Augustine pictures that, in the eternal City of God, the "harmonies" of the transformed body itself will contribute to the eternal song, "the praise of the great Artist by the delight afforded by a beauty that satisfies the reason"—and satisfies, moreover, one's whole being.[17]

Yet even as we say that, and say it on the basis of both artistic and theological evidence, the pluralism we have needed to employ all along insists on hearing the other side once again. We must acknowledge, with Merton, that mystic and contemplative traditions, worldwide, testify to a kind of ascent (or else a profound descent) that, in the moment of supreme union or communion, leaves one blissfully in the dark, so to speak, rather than in superabundant light.[18] One also recalls Derrida's not-so-mystical tears that nonetheless blind faithfully: "—I don't know, one has to believe." It would be foolish to deny that there can be a transcendent emptying of thought, sense, and feeling that makes for a major form of religious "peak experience," however great our eagerness to insist on the possibility of aesthetic plenitude at the top.

It would likewise be foolish to presume that sages and theologians can never have anything valuable of their own to say, once art has spoken its best—as though "best" could be defined as something artistic alone. And theologians have surely not been completely mistaken in their suspicions and criticisms even of certain religious art that aims very high indeed.

Thus, it is not hard to imagine Kierkegaard's brow furrowing were he to stand before a painting referred to earlier in our study: *Morning in the Riesengebirge* (Figure 11), by the German Romantic artist Caspar David Friedrich (1774-1840). The setting depicted in this painting could not be more sublime, to be sure, with the cross implanted on a dark, craggy peak, silhouetted against a sky washed with emerging sunrise light, and waves of misty mountains behind, fading—ever brighter yet ever less distinct—into a scarcely visible horizon line that seems to merge the whole scene with infinity. Upon closer inspection, one sees in the foreground two figures climbing the peak and approaching the cross. They are a man and a woman, both clad in city clothes, with the woman's raiment being light in hue, in contrast to the dark clothing of the man. The woman, in fact, is interposed between the man and the cross itself, standing with one hand on the cross, and reaching back with the other hand to draw her male companion upward toward his destination. And the cross is not just a cross, but a crucifix, with the corpus of Christ. Or might it not be the case that the scene is more symbolic, the mystical body of Christ becoming a meeting place between heaven and earth, eternity and time? Love, it would appear, is drawing the man to Christ, or to whatever reality Christ embodies; indeed, the immediate attractive force is a woman's love—the Eternal Feminine, no doubt, like Dante's Beatrice.[19]

Friedrich's unconventional use of traditional Christian iconography was not without controversy in his own time. Kierkegaard would surely have found in this painting a dangerous confusion of aesthetic, erotic, and religious yearnings. And one can speculate that, in our own era, even the late Henri Nouwen, whose meditation on Rembrandt's *Return of the Prodigal Son* pays homage to the spiritual value of art, might have had doubts about Friedrich's imagery and symbolism. Whereas the Rembrandt work prompted Nouwen to recognize the love of God at the gracious center of things and to confess, "I am the prodigal son every time I search for unconditional love where it cannot be found,"[20] the painting by Friedrich might have struck him (as it certainly would have struck Karl Barth) as ambiguous in its treatment of the nature of redemptive love itself, and of the goal of the spiritual journey. Are the Cross and Christ being absorbed here into some sort of nebulous pantheistic mysticism? Or are they to be seen, rather, as functioning as a Christian cosmic principle of the sort Teilhard de Chardin embraces in his meditative "Mass on the Earth"—in that part of *Hymn of the Universe* where he writes: "Now, Lord, through the consecration of the world the luminosity and fragrance which suffuse the universe take on for me the lineaments of a body and a face—in you"?[21] Is there any way of deciding? Meanwhile modern feminists might worry about the role of the woman (or the Feminine) in mediating between two men, one lower and one higher—between her male companion and Christ, or humanity envisioned as

Figure 11. *Caspar David Friedrich (1774–1840). Morning in the Riesengebirge (1810–1811). Schloss Charlottenburg. Gallery of Romanticism, Berlin. (Courtesy AKG London)*

an ordinary male and God envisioned as a supreme male. Finally, Friedrich's painting, wonderful as it remains in the eyes of many of us, reminds us again that much art that aims at sublimity borders on kitsch. That is because the means of such art, as it strives to be somehow "inspirational," are so likely to seem "cheap" compared with the Infinite towards which they reach or point. Inspirational religious art is not always (to say the least) an unmixed blessing.

Accordingly—in calling for a fuller Christian critical appreciation and practice of the whole range of artistic possibilities at various stages of the religious journey—I am not supposing that we have completely left behind either Kierkegaard or Blake, our old friends whose contrasting views set the stage for much of our discussion. We cannot afford to forget Kierkegaard's concerns about the seductive allure of the aesthetic, whereby the legitimate desire to enjoy art (or life) freely and sensuously can be lured into an illegitimate desire to enjoy freedom from responsibility and commitment, and a refusal of enjoyment "in God" (as Augustine would say). And we cannot forget Blake's insistence, on the opposite side, that a Christianity without artistic imagination is a paltry and unchristian thing, especially considering that the Bible itself is artful and aesthetic in making its religious and ethical appeals.

The claims of Kierkegaard and Blake represent something approximating a thesis and antithesis in our dialectic. But now we need also to recall that earlier, when reworking Augustine's aesthetics to formulate a new synthesis, we spoke of a mutual conversion of the ordinarily artistic and the ordinarily religious. That possibility envisioned a transformative reconciliation between Kierkegaard and Blake and, theoretically, opened up the prospect of a fuller religious artistry, and of enjoying even secular art more fully "in God."

The Next Church

The Situation: An Overview

In arguing for a wide-ranging understanding of the place of the arts and aesthetic taste within the Christian life, I have ventured to suggest that artistic discernment and aesthetic imagination are potentially vital to faith at every stage, from the most tentative and doubtful to the most ecstatic and beatific. If artistic resources and aesthetic sensibilities can make such a difference to Christian faith, however, it is surely appropriate to ask how they are being engaged in our own time, and particularly in Christian worship. In exploring that question, we are in effect exploring how to practice Christianity in diverse ways, traditional and nontraditional, some of which qualify as "entry level" practices, and some of which dare to aspire to a high degree of "sanctification." Already we can say that, contrary to what is commonly believed, even the earlier stages of religious exploration can make progress by way of art that is challenging—such as the poems of Hughes and Plath. By the same token, even the higher phases of disciplined Christian exploration can be "inspired" at times by accessible art, verging on kitsch—such as the painting by Friedrich.

The whole question of how the powers of art and music can be summoned to meet a wide range of emerging religious needs is certainly not without precedent. In 1834, Franz Liszt (1811–1886) felt compelled to publish an article calling for a new church music that would transcend the tawdry products of his time by being at once broadly democratic and inspiring, "mystical, forceful, and readily intelligible," uniting "theater and church in one great synthesis which is at once dramatic and holy, solemn and plain, joyful and serious, passionate and restrained, stormy and restful, clear and mystical."[22] This new church music would be part of a whole new age in which music would be "composed *for* the people, taught *to* the people, and sung *by* the people" and in which "all great artists, poets, and musicians" would make their contribution. Then, Liszt wrote, "*all classes* will at last melt into one religious, magnificent, and lofty unity of feeling." And "art will unfold and complete itself in all its forms, soaring up to the highest perfection."[23]

Liszt was writing in a Romantic and revolutionary age. His hopes for a newly invigorated—and newly educated—music for the Church and for society at large, while not fruitless, were certainly never fulfilled in the manner and degree he had envisioned. Yet the dream of a new, accessible, and nonetheless high-quality artistry for the Church has been renewed time and again, albeit more modestly expressed.

I have dared to express a certain kind of hope, myself. At the conclusion of the chapter on kitsch, I ventured to suggest that the long-term viability of Christianity in its more adventurous and aspiring modes would be enhanced by a new and renewed artistry and (by implication) a more thoroughly artful approach to the arts of worship, which are not, of course, only aesthetic. Both of those things would require a new and renewed aesthetic imagination and taste. Christian artistry and taste, I proposed, would do well to find new ways to be popular without being cheap; and Christianity would benefit, as well, from cultivating further a capacity for intelligent and imaginative religious exploration that is demanding enough to be unpopular.

The obstacles, we must now admit, are considerable. It is sobering to realize that Liszt was already conscious, in 1834, of a serious decline in the arts created for ecclesiastical use. It seems plain that the majority of dedicated and disciplined artists and musicians long ago ceased to think of the institutional church as a major patron or ally, even when they proceeded to create works that were theologically searching or spiritually celebrative or socially prophetic.

A case could be made that, ever since the early nineteenth century, if not before, much of the finest art and music of spiritual and theological import—whether popular or highly cultivated—has been created without the Church's blessing or, indeed, the Church's knowledge. For close to two centuries (and perhaps longer), many of the most powerful and moving artistic "sermons" have been "preached" outside the church. That is not altogether a bad thing, but the fact that most Christians have been but dimly aware of any possible loss only underscores the point.

Even so, there are signs that some of this has begun to change, partly due to changes in culture overall. In virtually every artistic medium, new and old, one sees a resurgence of interest in spirituality, not only of the vaguest sort but also of a kind willing to enter into traditional religious practices as those meet the contemporary world. And in the arts of worship, especially, our era is once again witnessing considerable ferment. Whether such ferment is likely to produce, in some of its present forms, a truly wide and encompassing range of Christian artistry is what we want next to consider.

In Particular

In much of the world today, Christian traditions are undergoing transformation, including new styles of Christian self-expression—Christian fashions, Christian videos, even Christian skate nights (primarily roller-skating) and Christian mosh pits, where bodies surf on the uplifted hands of the throngs attending Christian rock concerts. As one might expect, the greatest changes often are occurring without benefit of anything more than a relatively modest understanding of the multiple traditions of theology, art, and worship that have conveyed and recreated Christian faith in all its depth and height. A number of churches in various parts of the world are undertaking, in effect, a sort of Christian cultural revolution—not to sensationalize the matter by borrowing a term from recent Chinese history. Many of the more remarkable trends are especially conspicuous in church life as experienced in the United States.

Charles Trueheart, in a widely noticed article in the *Atlantic Monthly* (August 1996), describes what he calls the "Next Church."[24] The blurb on the front cover of the magazine catches the drift: "Giant 'full-service' churches are winning millions of 'customers' with pop-culture packaging. They may also be building an important new form of community." The first paragraph of the article itself continues:

No spires. No crosses. No robes. No clerical collars. No hard pews. No kneelers. No biblical gobbledygook. No prayer rote. No fire, no brimstone. No pipe organs.

No dreary eighteenth-century hymns. No forced solemnity. No Sunday finery. No collection plates.

The list has asterisks and exceptions, but its meaning is clear. Centuries of European tradition and Christian habit are deliberately being abandoned, clearing the way for new, contemporary forms of worship and belonging.[25]

Given that the "Next Church" and its myriad smaller (and typically suburban) relatives are often held up as paradigmatic of the options available to Christians wanting to catch the next wave, it seems legitimate to ask, in thinking about Christian aesthetic aspirations, just how such Christians are making decisions regarding the arts, and about music in particular. How are Christians who understand themselves to be on the "next wave" carrying out theological aesthetics at a practical level? Music provides the clearest indication.

The Next Music

The musical idioms of the "Next Church" are unmistakably contemporary (nothing dating from before 1990 in many cases). One twenty-four-year-old pastor characterized the predominantly rock music of his university-related church as "a cross between Pearl Jam and Hootie and the Blowfish"—in other words, somewhere between angst-ridden "grunge" and upbeat pop.[26]

Yet, as it happens, in many of these "Next" churches the spectrum of styles being offered is actually quite narrow—just as it has been in most churches throughout history. Country music is usually out of the question, as is religious jazz in the style either of Duke Ellington (in his "Sacred Concerts") or Wynton Marsalis (*In This House on This Morning*, 1994). Nor is there world music like that of Sister Marie Keyrouz, a Lebanese nun who has begun singing the chants of her tradition in an appealing, "secular" style that utilizes colorful instrumental accompaniments. The typical "Next Music" sound is club-style soft rock.

Appraising still further what is included and what is left out, one could observe that it would be unusual (though by no means impossible) to hear anything so morally daring as certain of the songs of the Grammy award–winning Indigo Girls, or anything so ironically and astutely probing as a song on ecological spirituality by James Taylor ("Gaia," *Hourglass*, 1997), or music as alert to alternative spiritualities—African and South American—as Paul Simon's *Graceland* (1986) and *The Rhythm of the Saints* (1990), or yet as achingly yearning in overall effect as k.d. lang's "Constant Craving" (*Ingénue*, 1992) or U2's "I still haven't found what I'm looking for" (*Joshua Tree*, 1987). And that is just to mention a smattering of widely accessible, equally white, and mostly middle-class alternatives.

The more ritualized yet contemporary music from Taizé (composed by Jacques Berthier) and the newly composed yet folk-based songs of the Iona Community apparently smack too much of traditional religion to find wide acceptance in the Next Church. Certainly little of what is currently heard in the typical new megachurch, or in the smaller suburban churches providing casual and contemporary worship "options," would resemble contemporary classical "spiritual minimalism." Nothing in those settings sounds much like Arvo Pärt, Philip Glass, John Tavener, John Adams, Giya Kancheli, or (more Romantic in idiom) Einojuhani Rautavaara. Nor would such churches, which often make use of recordings, be tempted to venture into the recorded repertoire of more avantgarde classical composers such as Igor Stravinsky (by now virtually a classical icon), Olivier Messiaen, Krzysztof Penderecki, Sofia Gubaidulina, or James MacMillan—all certifiably contemporary and almost shockingly spiritual, and frequently explicitly theological. Such selectivity in church music, because it is more the rule than the exception in virtually all worshiping communities, would be unremarkable except for the fact that the image constantly cultivated by the Next Church and its more conservative Contemporary Christian relatives is that theirs is the truly contemporary alternative for Christian music today.

Meanwhile, church music that derives from the past is treated by most of the intensely growth-oriented churches as quite obviously dead. In a book called *Dancing with Dinosaurs: Ministry in a Hostile and Hurting World*, one outspoken yet representative proponent of the church-growth movement (by no means only for megachurches) has much to say about worship today and its music. A former United Methodist pastor and director of 21st Century Strategies, William Easum spends almost every day of the year as a consultant to countless different congregations and religious organizations. Describing major changes in worship that amount to what he and a good many others think of as the "second stage" of the Reformation, Easum states: "The shift in the style of worship is the most obvious and divisive [of the changes]. This divisiveness is over the *style* of worship rather than doctrine or theology."[27]

Easum insists that the generations that are most vital to church growth—usually identified as the midlife "(baby)boomers," followed by "busters," born after 1964—do not want to be reverent or quiet during worship. Looking to African American congregations for inspiration in dealing with high-energy worship, Easum encourages clapping, among other practices (though, one might note, clapping has not been traditional among all African Americans). In any case, music is what Easum singles out as the "major vehicle for celebration and communication." Few movies, he observes, make a profit without a "solid sound track" (recall my discussion in chapter 6). And what sort of "sound track" should a church choose, given the variety of options? Easum claims that the right method for arriving at a suitable style for church music is to determine which radio stations most of the "worship guests" listen to. "Soft rock" is usually the answer, he declares (p. 84)—something that the survey we cited in chapter 6 would apparently dispute.

For pastor-consultant Easum, classical music—and traditional church music in general—is a relic of a dying past. If you want life and growth, he says, make use of music, art, and media that are "culturally relevant." "Classical music was rooted in the native folk music of the time," he assures us. "That world is gone" (p. 84). At this point Easum quotes John Bisagno, pastor of the First Baptist Church in Houston, Texas, who "minces no words when he describes the debilitating effects that classical music has on worship in most settings":

> Long-haired music, funeral-dirge anthems, and stiff-collared song leaders will kill the church faster than anything in the world. . . . There are no great, vibrant, soul-winning churches reaching great numbers of people, baptizing hundreds of converts, reaching masses that have stiff music, seven-fold amens, and a steady diet of classical anthems. None. That's not a few. That's none, none, none. (p. 85)

Easum repeatedly emphasizes the importance of what he terms "quality music." But today, he insists, quality music is less likely to be produced by choirs and organs than by praise teams, soloists, a variety of instrumentalists, and small ensembles that use synthesizers, drums, electric guitars, and so forth. Quality music, in the context of youth evangelism in particular, needs to be entertaining (p. 89). As for cultivating some sort of developed and mature taste for quality in worship music, he states curtly: "Worship is not the place to teach music appreciation" (p. 86). In fact, according to Easum, it turns out that there is only one question that worship communities in the new paradigm need to ask about music: "Does it bring people closer to God?" Music is never "the message itself." Indeed, "No form is inherently better than another. Music is good if it conveys the gospel; it is bad if it does not" (p. 86). Easum is willing to cite historical precedents, if he thinks they serve his purpose:

> Spiritual giants such as Martin Luther and Charles Wesley showed us the importance of culturally relevant music [by] taking the tunes out of bars, putting words to them, and using the songs in worship. They accommodated the needs of people in order to reach them with the message that would eventually change their lives. They did not conform the message, just the package. (p. 86)

Easum does make one concession to the music of the past. In cases where a congregation is aging and possibly declining, he says, it may be best to create two kinds of service, one of them using a style that is still able to validate the cultural needs of the older generation. But, according to Easum, that will not be the service that is "culturally relevant" (p. 89).

Facing the Music

Putting Theory to the Test

The views and developments we have been examining present a significant test for the theories I have been sketching and fleshing out. Leaders like Easum are not bashful about advocating the sort of Christian artistry that they see as crucial to the second stage of the Protestant Reformation. And there is little doubt that much of what motivates the largely nondenominational "Next Church" and its close denominational relatives—including what Easum himself discusses and proposes as promising church music and worship style—could fall under the category of taste, in the expanded sense articulated in the present study. The issues have everything to do with what Christian individuals and groups perceive to be the traits of the available arts and styles of worship, what they enjoy, and what they judge to be good or bad.

Easum's claims, in particular, are representative of much that is being said and done among Christians at the present time. Although directed to churches in the United States in particular, his comments are not unrelated to issues that increasingly arise these days in Great Britain, in Western Europe, and (with important variations) in many other parts of the world, as secular and sacred styles mix and collide and as contemporary arts and modes of worship vie with older traditions. He presents his ideas, moreover, in a clear, succinct, and urgent kind of consulting vernacular—not much given to philosophical honing or theological polishing, but charting the direction in which he is convinced the churches need to move if they are to be vital in their congregational life and artistry. If the sort of inclusive, critical, ecumenical, and aspiring Christian taste I have called for is to be possible at all, it must be able to respond both constructively and critically—and specifically—to just such arguments as the ones Easum sets forth. Whatever we may initially assume about the plausibility or implausibility of Easum's position, it is important to move through our response step by step, so as to clarify our methods of evaluation and our guiding principles.

If taste is a matter of apperception, appreciation, and appraisal, and if it is always influenced by context and community, the first step in assessing claims regarding religious aesthetic taste is a move that is no less important for being almost a cliché. It is to try to listen to and through the rhetoric and sometimes curious logic of particular claims regarding music and worship so as to discern the underlying musical and religious perceptions, values, and judgments. Taking the personal and cultural context into account is integral to that process.

There can be little doubt that Easum is a passionate advocate of the Church and its ministry. It appears that he is most at home in evangelical churches that are relatively conservative theologically and socially; that he believes growing churches minister the best; that he is moved, touched, and excited by churches he finds alive with a sense of future possibility; that he himself perceives a kind of vitality in popular music, as expressive of modern experience and feeling; and that he is personally able to appreciate soft rock as a specifically religious medium, at least when combined with religious words. Encouraged by the large number of people who share his opinion, he has reached a judgment that pop and rock music is not only good for worship but is also the medium of the future for growing churches.

Although Easum does not say so, it seems pertinent to understanding his stance that, in the sorts of church communities with which he works most often, grass-roots support for what is usually considered classical music has rarely been intense. The traditional music of many such churches has long included hymn-based anthems and a generous helping of revival and old-time gospel hymnody closely akin to, or borrowed from, nineteenth-century American popular song. In such settings, therefore, the idea of singing church music that borrows from popular secular culture is nothing new. Furthermore, an element of distrust of "high" culture is not uncommon even among those church members interested in "cultivation" and higher social status. That is not surprising, since American culture in general has a healthy populist and anti-intellectual streak. At the same time, however, opposition to rock music as a medium of worship has indeed been intense among a wide spectrum of such churchgoers, some of whom have associated that music with worldliness of the worst sort.[28]

Any Christian sensitive to the necessity for addressing people within their particular cultural situation should be able to sympathize with most of Easum's pastoral and musical concerns. They are consistent with the need for what in Catholic circles has been known as the indigenous "inculturation" of the gospel—something that missionaries to foreign cultures have for some time now encouraged and attempted. Importing Vivaldi or Brahms or William Mathias into a church community whose native musical languages are closer to those of Madonna, Jimmy Buffett, or John Tesh might be compared with earlier missionary efforts to impose European or American religious styles on drastically different cultures, out of an imperialist or colonialist mentality. (Not that converts do not sometimes need and welcome a sharp alternative to their native cultural vocabulary. Westerners learning to follow a Buddhist path would probably be disappointed to be presented with Western-style sculptures of the

Buddha or with gospel-style Buddhist songs. By the same token, Chinese Christians have in fact widely treasured the gospel hymns brought to them by nineteenth-century missionaries, privileging them over the songs using Chinese folk tunes or composed later by Chinese Christians and in a Chinese idiom.)

Easum makes a valid point, moreover, in claiming that music that was originally secular has repeatedly found its way into church. The boundary between sacred and secular has repeatedly been blurred or transgressed. No one style is unalterably sacred, nor another unalterably secular. And Easum is probably on solid ground when he assumes that much of the soft rock or pop music that he advocates for worship has by now, in many parts of the world, become a kind of generic musical product, with no set of specifically worldly associations that would in themselves prevent its use in worship. One could make a similar observation regarding the Baroque and early Classical musical styles of the seventeenth and early eighteenth centuries (roughly from Handel to Haydn), which crossed rather freely from the operatic stage and concert hall to the church and back again.

Again, Easum is surely correct to think that matching religious words with neutral or nonspecific popular music can bring out a suitable range of meanings that the music might not have on its own. That possibility is borne out by the way in which Amy Grant, Petra, and countless others can now adopt and adapt rock as a Christian musical style that their listeners hear as entirely consonant with their sense of Christian life and proclamation.

Finally, as I have already argued, one can agree with Easum's implicit claim that church music has sometimes been unduly limited by traditional suspicions of pulsing or lively rhythms, "irreverent" instruments, and entertainment—as though levity, syncopation, and a pronounced beat were always inappropriate for church. (Religious music would be in trouble in much of the world, if it could never be rhythmic or animated.)

I have been recasting some of Easum's central claims, particularly those that I find most plausible and promising. But now we need to look more closely at the argument as Easum presents it, himself, examining his rhetoric as well as his logic. This will suggest how religious controversies over taste get tangled up, both with themselves and with other issues. It will also help us assess the larger implications of Easum's claims about the future direction of musical aspiration for Christian communities.

In Time but Out of Tune

William Easum claims nothing for himself if not that he is attuned to the times and to the needs of contemporary Christians. Yet, in reading Easum's argument in the manner in which he sets it forth, many readers will find that his assertions regarding church music are not only uncompromising but also discordant and at points uninformed and misleading.

Easum advances his argument in terms that are evidently meant to rally support on the part of people who, whether or not they have realized it, are tired of the status quo in the church music of their own traditions. He does not couch what he says in terms meant to invite or encourage change on the part of people whose faith has been fed, and continues to be fed, by much of the more traditional music—except insofar as Easum can persuade them to see themselves as "dinosaurs" standing in the way of vital change. People who love Jesus, he insinuates, would not want to be guilty of standing in the way of using pop and rock music in church.

Although one would think that the primary target of Easum's assault on traditional church music would be professional church musicians (to whom we are coming momentarily), it seems likely that Easum is operating out of an intuitive sense that an attack on classical music will accomplish two things at once. If he can depict the advocates of classical church music as both elitist in taste and disloyal to the gospel, he will not only discredit them in the eyes of popular music lovers; he will also gain the sympathy of those many Christians who, while populist in taste and sentiment, have tended to accept "classical" styles because they associate rock 'n' roll with worldly activities and feelings.

Be that as it may, for the many professional musicians whose livelihood is based in large part on their training and competence in more traditional church music, no way of raising the issues could be more threatening or alienating than this. Easum insists that churches that want to survive and grow have no choice but to change the music they use in worship. And, as we have seen, he argues that the new music should be the same music that the "worship guests" most enjoy on the radio, which he assumes will normally be "soft rock." The number of musicians in the American Guild of Organists who are both proficient in playing soft rock and eager to use it as the basic musical style for worship is miniscule. That is to be expected, in view of the fact that it takes great amounts of time, skill, and dedicated training to become even moderately competent as a traditional organist. Easum is providing a recipe for getting such people fired or retired.

Then there is the matter of how Easum states his own aesthetic claims with regard to church music. One might have thought that a person who began his discussion of style and worship by remarking on the divisiveness of the issue would take considerable care with how he phrased his own judgments. Unfortunately, Easum exemplifies just how prone we all are to take our own judgments of taste, or the judgments of our own group, as universally valid. Kant was right, at a psychological level: Most of us tend to think that our judgments in matters of taste ought to be shared universally, even if we know they won't be. In this case, Easum is unhesitating in his sweeping rejection of certain music (classical) and completely confident in his endorsement of certain other music (particularly soft rock). Yet, aside from alluding to radio listening habits and referring to the importance of popular music in film soundtracks, Easum offers minimal evidence that classical music is virtually fossilized as a worship medium or that pop music is ideal. The primary proof that he offers is that no big, soul-winning churches use classical or related music. While he recognizes that many professional church musicians resist the change-over, he contends that they are letting their own private taste stand in the way of the gospel: "The source of . . . conflict comes primarily from trained musicians who often find these concepts repugnant and resist any change in the style of the music. . . . Many are more interested in music appreciation than in helping people find new life." In short, such musicians supposedly think that "making disciples is not as important as making good music. It is time we recognize this problem and deal with it accordingly" (p. 88).

We have had occasion to see that professional traditional church musicians are not always pluralistic, themselves, and are seldom the best judges of the worship potential of popular music. But Easum, instead of encouraging dialogue, simply turns the elitism of David Hume on its head. A musical elitist assumes that any music that is popular must be bad. A musical populist, on the contrary, assumes that only popular music is good and that the most popular music is necessarily the best music—and indeed, the best music for worship. Operating on the basis of that populist principle, Easum argues that the best music for church is nothing other than the music that the greatest number of people like; and since we cannot formulate precise rules and concepts that will fully describe or guarantee high quality in music (on this point Easum, Kant, Hume, and I would all agree), Easum asks us to look only at the results. The music that wins his contest is bound to be the music of those churches that grow the fastest.

Needless to say, Kierkegaard would have no sympathy with Easum's claims, since Kierkegaard was highly suspicious of any form of Christianity that might be thought compromising or popular. But we do not need to resort to Kierkegaard to suggest alternatives. With previous chapters in mind, a little further reflection would suggest that, despite the merits of some of Easum's claims, his argument makes a number of highly questionable assumptions: that religious quality and musical quality are both reliably indicated by numerical success; that liking a certain kind of music for light entertainment is necessarily the same as liking that very music for all the purposes of worship; that the key to musical quality, religiously and aesthetically, is immediate accessibility; that religious music is never, therefore, a medium one might expect to grow into and grow through as a part of Christian formation and development; that worship music today must always be upbeat and animated if it is to be "culturally relevant"; that classical music in general is stodgy and fossilized; that religious words guarantee genuinely religious music, as long as the music is likeable; and that music can be treated simply as a "package" that contains the gospel message instead of being treated as an art that embodies and interprets the gospel message by its structure and by the very way it sounds. Finally, Easum assumes that he is competent to make judgments about the viability of particular kinds of music without engaging in genuine dialogue with musicians trained in those traditions. Thus, far from exhibiting ecumenical taste, he takes a quite selective and dogmatic position disguised as welcoming obedience to a gospel imperative to spread the Word.

In fairness, it must be said that the musicians Easum has generally dealt with might not have been open to much dialogue on these points. Traditional and classical musicians in the employment of churches have all too often waved off pastoral and worship concerns as irrelevant to their music-making. Not long ago a prominent New England composer of church music declared before a society devoted to religion and contemporary arts that he had a profound *disin*terest in anything having to do with religious doctrine. "Music is my religion," he avowed—not proudly, but truthfully, without supposing for a moment that, when composing for churches, even an agnostic composer might want or need to find musical ways of enlivening doctrine itself. (One thinks of the contrast with Ralph Vaughan Williams, whose private agnosticism transcended itself in the very act of imagining faith in musical terms.) Still more recently, in a prominent classical music magazine, a young classically trained organist recounted how he had always been accused in English churches of playing too fast and too loud. With pleasure he recalled how he responded when he was told by the Dean of Worcester Cathedral that, as guest organist, he should tailor his voluntaries to the more subdued tastes of people in Elgar country. His answer was to let forth a "torrent of Widor." Asked by the bemused interviewer about his religious convictions, the organist replied: "Well, I spend a lot of time in church, but . . . let's put it this way: I would never go to church to hear a said Mass. No, music is my religion."[29]

Faced with the narrowly musical mindset and unchristian arrogance of certain professional "classical" church musicians, Easum and numerous others have evidently taken matters into their own hands. They have discerned and reacted to a level of congregational restlessness and dissatisfaction—which is something that the more traditional musicians have been slow to notice and understandably reluctant to treat as relevant to their work.

That still does not mean, however, that Easum and others taking his approach exhibit the sort of taste and informed judgment that would make them reliable guides to Christian growth (or even church growth) in the sphere of music and the arts. Let us return to two points in particular: (1) the current status of classical music—and of certain other "minority" styles—in church and out; and (2) the use of "secular" musical styles in church, and hence the relationship between medium and message in worship.

A Closer Listen

Dinosaur or Phoenix?

The argument that traditional church music, particularly classical, is either extinct or well on the way toward extinction may seem to be a historical and cultural question that is of relatively minor theological consequence. Yet it is highly charged from the perspective of those Christians whose faith is significantly shaped through such music; it has a direct bearing on the whole question of assessing "cultural relevance"; and the way the argument is usually deployed (whether true or not) reflects a highly questionable understanding of the range of art needed for the whole of the Christian life.

Without pretending to have William Easum's clairvoyance regarding the future—he predicts, for example, the quick death of all symphony orchestras that do not soon begin to feature a significant amount of pop and rock music (pp. 84–85)—we can make a number of observations that run counter to his suppositions. They constitute the very sort of evidence regarding "cultural relevance" that he, as a consultant, treats as pertinent.

First, it is worth pointing out that opera has experienced a tremendous revival of late, and not only among the senior generations. At present, opera houses in many parts of the world (including Easum's own United States) are filled to capacity and are adding series rather than trimming back. Second, the number of people in North America who say they very much like classical music stands at a comparatively substantial 14 to 20 percent across the generations (see the survey cited in chapter 6), which constitutes a more consistently favorable cross-generational response than most other styles elicit. Although the sale of classical recordings is a relatively small percentage of total audio sales, that can partly be explained by the fact that classical music is much less oriented toward the currently fashionable and the new, which is of course also quickly unfashionable and must therefore be replaced. As Mark C. Taylor remarks, in the course of rejoicing in the "profoundly superficial" surfaces of postmodern life, fashion—being "forever committed to the new"—speaks only in the "present tense."[30] That hardly argues against incorporating classical styles in many church settings, where riding each successive wave of fashion seems neither desirable nor even possible.

Third, it is well known that, for the past quarter century, "early music" (roughly, European "classical" music before the eighteenth-century Classical period itself) has attracted a significant and ardent audience, young and old. That audience augments the already considerable following of Baroque music in particular, whose popularity is indicated by the enthusiastic reception accorded to Pachelbel's "Canon in D," Bach's *Brandenburg Concerti*, and Handel's *Messiah*. A concert by the women's medieval quartet Anonymous 4, by the Monteverdi Consort (directed by John Eliot Gardiner), or by the Tallis Scholars (directed by Peter Phillips) is normally "packed" almost anywhere these and comparable groups sing, be that in Rome, London, or Indianapolis.

Fourth, recent years have seen a surge in the popularity of chant among people of all ages. The widespread introduction of religious services using music from the religious community at Taizé, France fits with this trend, since much of it tends to be rather contemplative and in harmony with the moods if not modes of chant. The attraction of such "boring" ritual music certainly challenges Easum's notion that "culturally relevant" music must be lively and entertaining. Fifth, such trends have themselves been accompanied by rising interest in "spiritual" classical music of all sorts, both ancient and contemporary—a development that classical musicians and record companies have been quick to exploit.

Sixth—and this most of all should have caught Easum's attention, given his interest in the "sound tracks" needed for worship—a great many scores for films that feature high drama, serious feeling, or intense introspection still make use of music that draws primarily on classical idioms. A whole array of recent movies, even popular ones, use music indebted to classical traditions. The music that John Williams has composed for the immensely popular *Star Wars* series of George Lucas often sounds like something one might expect from Sergei Prokofiev or Gustav Holst. One could also single out the film *Shine*, featuring the Rachmaninoff Third Piano Concerto, or John Corigliano's largely classical score for *The Red Violin*, the contemporary classical music for Terrence Malick's much-discussed war movie *The Thin Red Line*, the equally fascinating and contemporary sound tracks for the morally complex films of Krzysztof Kieslowski, and Ennio Morricone's score for *The Mission*, not to mention music for "period" films such as the crowd-pleasing *Shakespeare in Love*. One could go on indefinitely, except that there is really no need.

The variety and ubiquity of film music that is closely allied to classical styles should be sufficient to suggest that not only is "classical" music still very much alive, though evolving, it is also enormously varied, itself—and in fact more varied than one would ever guess on the basis of the so-called classical music typically heard in churches. The historical and cultural evidence seems to indicate that, instead of being the dinosaur that some consultants to churches judge it to be, what we term classical music has, over the centuries, been very much a phoenix, albeit an evolving phoenix, consumed by cultural fire in one form only to be resurrected in another.

Clearly, before judging which kinds of music are culturally relevant—and, more important, relevant to the transformation of values appropriate to Christian culture and growth—it is important to attain a theologically adequate and aesthetically informed picture of the musical options. I would argue that, out of those many legitimate options, the Euro-American classical tradition remains among the most varied, profound, and adaptable, and perhaps in ways churches have yet to imagine.

But there is a larger issue here than simply whether classical music per se is still "culturally relevant" and thus of use to churches. It is that the range of "culturally relevant" music in general is altogether more diverse than many promoters of church vitality recognize. In fact, given what we have just observed regarding classical music, it would be surprising if the candidates among popular styles were not, themselves, more varied than we are usually urged to believe. In his book *Virtual Faith: The Irreverent Spiritual Quest of Generation X*, Tom Beaudoin argues convincingly that theological ambiguity and an acute awareness of suffering are central to those forms of faith and culture that are most characteristic of the members of "Generation X" (born between the early 1960s and the late 1970s).[31] It is his observation that Generation Xers (of whom he is one) often seek out forms of contemplative spirituality, albeit eclectic and heterodox, and would frequently prefer *more* silence in church services rather than less. These are things that church consultants and others ignore when they prescribe a steady diet of peppy music for the younger generations of the church and when they suppose that the gospel message itself needs no reinterpretation, only a new package.

If all churches interested in survival and growth were to follow the advice being urged on them by those pushing hardest for "cultural relevance"—and many churches are doing just that—Christian churches would be put in the ironic position of refusing to make use of music as serious (or exalted) as what one can still hear on a regular basis in the movie theater, on television and radio, in the opera house, symphony hall, and (indeed) the local restaurant. And that would be, in no small part, because the churches would have misunderstand their cultural situation. Still more, it would be because they would have defined their mission primarily in terms of misplaced marketing values— values that, if followed consistently, would seriously undervalue the spiritually transformative potential of challenging artistry (both "classical" and vernacular) and that would surely have had Jesus popularize his image and simplify his message before it was too late. Similar misunderstandings can be found behind common assumptions about the viability of simply "packaging" a sacred message in an appealing secular style.

From Sacred to Secular and Back

On several occasions we have noted that Protestants and other Christians have made wide use of secular sources for their hymn tunes and other religious music. J. S. Bach borrowed from his secular cantatas and even from harpsichord concerti when composing his sacred works, including his B Minor Mass. Martin Luther, moreover, has been credited with saying, and acting as though, he did not want the devil to have all the good tunes.[32] Yet secular and popular music was not the only sort that Luther wanted to raid. He was openly jealous of "the fine music and songs" and "precious melodies" that the Catholics got to use at masses for the dead, and thought it would "be a pity to let them perish."[33] In fact, he said, the Pope's followers in general possess "a lot of splendid, beautiful songs and music, especially in cathedral and parish churches," which he thought ought to be divested of "idolatrous, lifeless, and foolish texts" and reused for the sake of their beauty.[34] For that matter, Luther also expressed admiration for the Roman church's "beautiful services, gorgeous cathedrals, and splendid cloisters."[35] He was hardly the advocate of strictly casual and vernacular styles.

John Calvin (1509–1564), for his part, was extremely cautious about the music he sanctioned for use in worship, which he thought should exhibit moderation, gravity, and majesty. Martin Luther and, later, John Wesley (1703–1791) could both be very particular about the specific tunes they wanted to use with hymn texts. John Wesley (more often than his brother Charles) ordinarily designated which tunes he judged to be suitable; and Luther would not, in fact, sanction the free use of music from bars and brothels.[36]

Now, why might any Christian theologian, pastor, or musician want to make such discriminations? It is doubtful that such people would, if they thought that music provides nothing more than a "package" for the gospel message, and one that is adequate as long as it is appealing. But that is not what any of the major Reformers thought, or a good many of their successors either, even though most were sure that some secular music could legitimately be borrowed and adapted for religious purposes.

It seems evident that Christians today likewise need to be thinking more carefully and deeply about sacred and secular in the realm of music. Art, and certainly musical art, may have a special religious calling; because art, more than most other things, tends to come from the heart and go to the heart—to paraphrase again what Beethoven said of his *Missa Solemnis*. But perhaps not all art is meant to touch the heart, let alone the soul; and perhaps even the music that touches the heart does so in quite different ways. A clever piano sonata that Mozart composed in his head is not likely to be perceived as any more religious or "spiritual" than David Hume's wittily composed theory of taste, although the one is artistic and the other is philosophical. However justified Karl Barth's conviction may have been that Mozart's ostensibly secular music is possibly even more significant, religiously, than his masses, a lover of Mozart's music may "adore" Cherubino's adolescent and flirtatious songs in the *Marriage of Figaro* without needing to regard them as even remotely religious, let alone as generally well suited for worship. As for the masses themselves, reservations about their more operatic traits have been expressed by a great many clergy and musicians from Mozart's time to the present—the religious admiration of Barth and Hans Küng notwithstanding.[37] One does not have to believe that certain styles of music are inherently religious in order to be convinced that some kinds of music are more suitable for worship in general than are other kinds. In our own day, the pianist and musicologist Charles Rosen has articulated a number of cogent reasons (whether or not one agrees with them) for regarding the Classical style, proper, of Haydn, Mozart, and Beethoven as peculiarly handicapped in the realm of sacred music.[38] In Rosen's view, those composers wisely departed from the more "Classical" conventions to become more "archaic" in style (modal, contrapuntal) when writing their most serious church music—Haydn's oratorio *The Creation*, for instance, or Mozart's Requiem and Mass in C Minor, or Beethoven's *Missa Solemnis*.

There is also good reason to believe, in any case, that some musical styles are more flexible than others. Both Baroque music and African American gospel music have roots within the churches as well as within secular settings, permitting composers and performers in these idioms to make relatively minor stylistic adjustments that will readily put into play the appropriate range of associations, thoughts, and feelings. Often, with such adaptable styles, a change in the performance context is enough to serve that purpose.

That cannot be said regarding certain other music, which today may be designed and adapted primarily to do such things as create highly cerebral conundrums (in the case of some avant-garde classical works) or energize sporting events, entertain at parties, reduce stress, or enhance bedroom desires. As Martha Bayles argues in her book *Hole in our Soul: The Loss of Beauty and Meaning in American Popular Music*, early rock 'n' roll, for all its undeniable sexual energy, originated out of a milieu deeply influenced by a white Pentecostalism that borrowed African American musical styles (mainly rhythm and blues) while remaining defensively segregated. Elvis Presley, Jerry Lee Lewis, and Little Richard all grew up in the Pentecostal church and sometimes made highly conflicted, guilt-ridden alterations of its music. But, Bayles argues, a multitude of influences—not least the impulses of artistic modernism—conspired to push moral and religious associations and tensions out of much subsequent popular music. Her claim may be overstated, but it finds a certain amount of agreement among popular musicians themselves.[39]

In point of fact, some musical styles, far from being flexible or neutral, seem quite specialized in character—something made exceptionally clear in the following passage from a novel by Robertson Davies entitled *The Cunning Man* (1994). Describing his first encounter with plainsong (chant) at St. Aidan's Church, the narrator says:

> At first I did not know what it was. At intervals the eight men in the chancel choir, or sometimes Dwyer alone, would utter what sounded like speech of a special eloquence, every word clearly to be heard, but observing a discipline that was musical, in that there was no hint of anything that was colloquial, but not like any music I had met with in my, by this time, fairly good acquaintance with music. My idea of church music at its highest was Bach, but Bach at his most reverent is still intended for performance. This was music addressed to God, not as performance, but as the most intimate and devout communication. It was a form of speech fit for the ear of the Highest.[40]

Gregorian chant would serve poorly for purposes of inebriated celebration; by the same token, the latest Ricky Martin hit would serve poorly for purposes of meditative prayer.

Thus, in response to any uncritical willingness to adopt for worship whatever music people favor in their radio listening, one might ask: Is it possible that musicians in our notably secular era have become especially adept at shaping music to specifically erotic, recreational, and commercial purposes? If so, might it not be the case that regularly bending those sorts of music to the ends of worship would be rather like regularly choosing to praise or thank God in the tone of voice one would ordinarily use to order a pizza or to cheer a touchdown—or perhaps even to make the most casual sort of love?

No doubt part of the meaning we hear in a given kind of music is "socially constructed," which raises the possibility that an alteration in the construct will alter completely how the music sounds. Simon Frith makes such an argument, in effect, when he proposes that "cultural ideology," rather than anything within the music or its beat, produces most of the sexual and bodily associations of rock 'n' roll; but, despite his elaborate and brilliant defense of that claim, it is surely too clever by at least half.[41] Nothing one can do will convert Gregorian chant into a style as bodily and erotic in its center as various kinds of rock; nor can rock be made to sound as contemplative or as ethereal as chant, though it can indeed take on an aura of ecstasy.

The whole question of meaning in music (whether sacred or secular) is of course extraordinarily elusive, and in many ways a matter of intuitions that we cannot fully explain. Nonetheless, music does have meaning, as the literary and cultural critic George Steiner insists: "It is brimful of meanings which will not translate into logical structures or verbal expression. . . . Music is at once cerebral in the highest degree—I repeat that the energies and form-relations in the playing of a quartet, in the interactions of voice and instrument are among the most complex events known to man—and it is at the same time somatic, carnal and a searching out of resonances in our bodies at levels deeper than will or consciousness."[42] Indeed, Steiner says, because of the virtually sacramental "real presence" of its meaning, music has "celebrated the mystery of intuitions of transcendence."[43]

Although Steiner is prone to talk about the powers of music as such, apart from specific cultural mediations and cultural conventions, it may be best to see particular sorts of music as having a range of possible nonverbal meanings that verbal language and cultural context can then shape and construe in more specific ways.[44] One can then distinguish, by and large, between religious music most appropriate for the inner sanctuary (to use the place name both literally and figuratively), and that which is best for the nave of the church, or for the courtyard, recreational hall, or concert stage. One can fittingly choose to use religious music in any of these settings; but its character and purpose will shift accordingly, with convention playing a part in shaping those choices.

Coming back to the question of sacred and secular styles, none of this means that worship services should never make use of rock, or perhaps even heavy metal and "grunge." One scholarly interpreter and performer of heavy metal, for instance, argues that this notoriously "diabolical" genre of music can be converted into a credible and creative force with a Christian evangelistic message. Thus, according to Robert Walser, the Christian heavy metal band Stryper uses heavy metal to communicate "experiences of power and transcendent freedom" in which a new sort of meaning emerges from the sounds and gestures, which begin to serve as religious metaphors: "The power is God's; the transcendent freedom represents the rewards of Christianity; the intensity is that of religious experience. . . . Stryper presents Christianity as an exciting, youth-oriented alternative."[45]

That said, it must also be said that, because religious meanings cannot simply be imposed on every sort of musical medium, regardless of its style, considerable musical and liturgical experimentation could be required to find out which forms of rock and pop permit or invite stretching for religious purposes. Christians probably need musical "laboratories," involving both clergy and musicians, as well as adventurous congregants.

In the meantime, people for whom rock, pop, and Broadway musicals are nothing like their native language for serious celebration and for soul-searching expression cannot be expected to worship freely and often in a worship atmosphere dominated by such musical styles. For such people (perhaps still the majority of Christians), an identifiably sacred style can mark a difference that allows them to regard some music as specially consecrated for enjoyment "in God." They will resonate with Edward Farley's observation that, at present: "To attend the typical Protestant Sunday morning worship service is to experience something odd, something like a charade. . . . Lacking is a sense of the terrible mystery of God, which sets language atremble and silences facile chattiness. . . . If the seraphim assumed this Sunday morning mood, they would be addressing God not as 'holy, holy, holy' but as 'nice, nice, nice.'"[46] Similar observations are made from time to time on the Catholic side as well.

No doubt some of the worship services that have undergone renovation through popular and casual idioms were not, to begin with, so awe-filled as they were awful: bland, stiff, and stifled. Furthermore, it is important to be pluralistic enough to recognize that Christianity knows more than one sacred manner of approaching God. In the interests of ecumenical taste, for instance, we could note that, whereas most Javanese Christians address God using only the most formal personal pronouns, reserved for someone of higher status, the Amharic-speaking people of Ethiopa use only the most intimate personal pronouns for the same purpose. As they see the matter, God already knows our hearts, motives, and intentions and is therefore too intimately acquainted with us to require (or be flattered by) formal modes of address.[47] Each approach has its theological reasons, and in fact a good many cultures figure out ways to address God both formally and informally, though in different media and contexts.

Nevertheless, if the medium of religious practice and expression is not only predominantly casual in style but also artistically "flimsy" (a complaint lodged by Kathleen Norris),[48] perhaps even kitsch (which is not to say worthless, or equally cheap in everyone's ears and eyes), then one must ask: What sort of God are worshipers envisioning as they sing or look or move? To what sort of life and growth do they suppose they are being called? The possibility that a relatively casual and unchallenging style might be all there is to a given community's worship life or musical language is bound to be deflating to those whose call to discipleship causes them to yearn for something more by way of aesthetic formation and development.

As for the uncritical religious adoption of "secular" styles themselves, there is no denying that the act of giving ordinary, secular-sounding expression to extraordinary reality can work miracles, transforming the ordinary and secular into something sacred. Nevertheless, marrying gospel insights and liturgical actions to a musical or linguistic medium that was originally secular in sound and purpose is an art in itself. Carelessly done, it can inadvertently convert the sacred into something quite ordinary.

Testing Christian Taste: Twelve Assumptions

Mindful that in *Dancing with Dinosaurs*, William Easum helpfully spells out twelve of his underlying assumptions, let me conclude this penultimate portion of our study by setting forth twelve assumptions that I hope could fruitfully guide discussions of aesthetic taste as they arise in the next stage of religious, and specifically Christian, development in relation to the arts. None of these should come as a surprise to readers who have come this far in the present book. I regard them as assumptions or premises rather than as goals; but one could also look on them as habits of mind useful for exercising Christian taste in healthy ways. By calling them assumptions I do not mean that they do not require support (which the rest of the book has been intended to provide), only that such points cannot immediately be argued from the ground up when matters of Christian taste are in dispute.

(1) There are many kinds of good taste, and many kinds of good religious art and music. In view of cultural diversity, it would be extremely odd if that were not true.

(2) Not all kinds of good art and music are equally good for worship, let alone for every tradition or faith community. In terms of worship, therefore, it is not enough that a work or style of art be likeable; it must also be appropriate.

(3) There are various appropriately Christian modes of mediating religious experience artistically—from radically transcendent to radically immanent in a sense of the sacred; from exuberantly abundant to starkly minimal in means; from prophetic to pastoral in tone; from instructive to meditative in aim.

(4) Every era and cultural context tends to develop new forms of sacred music and art, which to begin with often seem secular to many people.

(5) Because every musical/aesthetic style calls for a particular kind of attunement, no one person can possibly be competent to make equally discerning judgments about every kind of music or art. Yet almost everyone is inclined to assume or act otherwise. That impulse is related to the sin of pride.

(6) It is an act of Christian love to learn to appreciate or at least respect what others value in a particular style or work that they cherish in worship or in the rest of life. That is different, however, from personally liking every form of commendable art, which is impossible and unnecessary.

(7) Disagreements over taste in religious music (or any other art) can be healthy and productive; but they touch on sensitive matters and often reflect or embody religious differences as well as aesthetic ones.

(8) The reasons why an aesthetic work or style is good or bad, weak or strong (and in what circumstances), can never be expressed fully in words; yet they can often be pointed out through comparative—and repeated—looking and listening.

(9) Aesthetic judgments begin with, and owe special consideration to, the community or tradition to which a given style or work is indigenous or most familiar. But they seldom end there; and they cannot, if the style or work is to invite the attention of a wide range of people over a period of time.

(10) The overall evaluation of any art used in worship needs to be a joint effort between clergy, congregation, and trained artists and musicians, taking into account not only the aesthetic qualities of the art itself but also the larger requirements and contours of worship, which should at once respond to and orient the particular work of art or music.

(11) While relative accessibility is imperative for most church art, the church also needs art—including "classic" art of various kinds—that continually challenges and solicits spiritual and theological growth in the aesthetic dimension. This is art that the Christian can grow into but seldom out of.

(12) Almost every artistic style that has been enjoyed and valued by a particular group over a long period of time and for a wide range of purposes has religious potential. That is because life typically finds various and surprising ways of turning religious. As Augustine said, our hearts are restless until they rest in God.

Those twelve assumptions, or premises, when supported by the arguments of this study as a whole, may be able to help guide the fruitful exercise of Christian taste—apperception, appreciation, and appraisal—as it moves through successive stages. In the final chapter we pursue further the idea of practicing Christianity artfully. And we contemplate several exceptional examples of Christian artistry and imagination that one could fairly regard as fulfilling, with all due humility, a high degree of artistic and religious aspiration.

NINE

Styles and Stages of Faith and Art II

Practicing Christianity Artfully

With Difficulty and Delight

Perhaps because Protestant Christians have been particularly emphatic about salvation by grace through faith, as opposed to works, they have often been wary of trying to spell out the requirements for Christian maturity or "progress." Most Protestants have jettisoned the notion that, among past Christians, some merit special designation and veneration as saints. They have not accorded any special religious status to the monastic life, let alone regarded the cloistered "religious" as in any way fulfilling a calling higher than that of the clergy who serve in the world. And in their various interpretations of the priesthood of all believers, Protestants and evangelical Christians in general have taken special care to treat clergy as the spiritual equals of all other Christians.

Furthermore, under the influence of Martin Luther in particular, Protestants have held a broad view of the range of possible Christian vocations. But exactly what could be Christian about a good many of those vocations, and exactly how all of life might be ordered, proportioned, and cultivated in maturely Christian ways, has for many Protestants been something of a puzzle—particularly for those who stress that the climactic step in the Christian life is, in effect, initiation: one's profession of faith and baptism.

To be sure, Protestants have generally been enthusiastic supporters of Christian education, not only through Sunday schools but also through institutions of higher education. Moreover, various Protestant groups—and particularly Methodists—have paid special attention to the gift and task of sanctification, daring even to envision a path toward "Christian perfection." It is probably no accident that James Fowler, well known for his psychological work in describing and documenting seven developmental stages of faith, works out of the Methodist tradition.[1] Indirectly this emphasis on sanctification has allied Methodists with the otherwise quite different Eastern Orthodox Christians, who are dedicated to the idea of the gradual "theosis" or, in a certain sense, "deification" of the believer. In that process, through God's grace and the power of the Holy Spirit, the believer is to become Christlike by being remade into the image and likeness of God. Even without highlighting that theme in so many words, virtually all Christians have acknowledged that Christ calls for disciples to learn to pray, minister, and love better, and in a more disciplined and Christlike way.

Nevertheless, there remains a certain Protestant reluctance to adopt an agenda for spiritual growth. And when one combines that reluctance with the commonplace assumption that art is naturally a matter of leisure and immediate delight, the very idea that art could be practiced or appreciated as an important Christian exercise and discipline can sound strange indeed to various members of the Christian flock.

To be sure, Christian theologians were once well acquainted with the idea that the best art often delights only with difficulty, and through difficulty. Jonathan Edwards wrote, "Hidden beauties are commonly by far the greatest, because the more complex a beauty is, the more hidden is it."[2] Augustine, likewise, in *The Trinity* and *On Christian Teaching*, celebrated the aesthetic rewards of difficult art, including sacred allegory and scripture, whose veiled meanings in the harder passages both ward off the undisciplined and attract the devoted.

But in the minds and hearts of many Christians—and not only Protestants— art that is Christian should be easily accessible. Music in particular is supposed to be the easy part of Christianity. It is expected to be heart-warming and instantly gratifying. From a purely artistic perspective, it might be all right for Cornel West to insist that "the best of the black musical tradition," especially spirituals, blues, and jazz, is music that, "like all serious art," requires of its practitioners "high levels of discipline and quality" and makes tough demands on its audience—demands that West worries some young black people may tend to avoid "in this moment of the pervasive commodification of art and the vast commercialization of music."[3] What many Christians would have more trouble accepting is the notion that the specifically religious rewards of that music, or any other, could be closely correlated with the extra discipline needed either to make it or to enjoy it.

For similar reasons, Christians sometimes have trouble taking seriously the idea that artistry can become a high calling, a genuinely Christian vocation. Kierkegaard, for example, struggled when approaching the idea that the poet and artist could ever have a fully Christian vocation, not as simply preparatory to discipleship (which he sometimes allowed) but as vital to some form of discipleship at its highest and most committed.[4] And even Blake could recall a time when he hid his face in shame for being unable to force himself to abandon his passion for art, which at that time seemed to him a kind of "criminal dissipation" that was "forbidden by Law & Religion."[5]

And when it comes—if it ever does—to thinking about their own artistry, taste, and imagination, Christians today are usually quick to reassure themselves by citing Eric Gill's remark: "Every artist may not be a special kind of person. But every person is a special kind of artist."[6] If we are all artists already, perhaps that is already enough.

Gill's saying has become something of a mantra among groups seeking to inspire artistry among spiritually and theologically motivated amateurs. Rightly interpreted, it provides a needed recognition that every person is artistic to some degree, simply by being human. But Gill's observation is meant to encourage artistic growth, not to encourage complacency. And we are not, without training, already the artists (and theologians) we could or should be. The whole meaning of a religious and artistic life is compromised unduly if we simply equate (as is popularly done) both spirituality and artistry with lightly guided spontaneity and with "opening up" to feeling and creative intuition, in the belief that "creative expression is the natural direction of life."[7] Becoming what we are meant to be by nature (or by God) does not usually come so naturally.

Far from being a sign of excessive pride, therefore, submitting to artistic training and discipline can show a degree of humility that is all too often missing from programs of self-expression and from those kinds of artistry that consistently settle for easy or splashy effects. That is one reason why highly trained artists and critics thrive on puncturing what they perceive to be the pretensions of art that aspires to move us without exhibiting the creative discipline that usually comes only with difficulty. Janet Maslin, in the course of a *New York Times* movie review, pronounces Robert James Waller's best-selling novel the *Bridges of Madison County* to be "arguably the world's longest greeting card," full of curdling sentimentality.[8] Again, critic and reviewer Jim Svejda applies to Henryk Gorecki and his terribly popular yet terribly serious Symphony No. 3 (the *Symphony of Sorrowful Songs*) a comment that Dr. Johnson originally made regarding the popular poet Thomas Gray: "He was dull in a new way, and that made many people think him great."[9] Then there is Flannery O'Connor's wickedly clever aperçu: "Everywhere I go I am asked if I think the university stifles writers. My opinion is that they don't stifle enough of them. There's many a bestseller that could have been prevented by a good teacher."[10] Behind all of these comments (fair or unfair) is something approaching disgust for the popular, a prejudice that we have already questioned in a variety of ways. But no thoughtful Christian, recognizing the twin obstacles of sin and finitude, should be surprised at the thought that artistic aspiration can actually spring from humility and is normally fulfilled only with difficulty—which is not inconsistent with play and delight.

That idea becomes even less surprising when one realizes that artistry involves not only intuition, skill, and inspiration but a kind of intelligence. Howard Gardner, in a study entitled *Frames of Mind*, has argued that there are multiple kinds of intelligence, and not merely one kind of intelligence served by multiple faculties and accompanied by multiple kinds of talent. Among the multiple intelligences he studies are ones Gardner designates as linguistic, musical, spatial, and bodily-kinesthetic. All of these can be considered intelligences by virtue of the fact that they all involve "the ability to solve problems, or to create products, that are valued within one or more cultural settings."[11] Moreover, several of these intelligences have an artistic component that can respond and contribute to different domains of culture: disciplines, crafts, the arts themselves. Whether or not one agrees with all Gardner's specific claims, or even with his specific ideas about what constitutes intelligence, he provides considerable evidence that the arts are domains for genuine education and learning. They exhibit various mental and imaginative powers that must be cultivated to be truly fulfilled, while simultaneously feeding into other advanced modes of knowledge.

To take artistic intelligence seriously, from a Christian perspective, would surely mean, in part, to see art as both a subject and a means of disciplined religious practice and strenuous education—indeed, *higher* education, including theological education itself (where the study and practice of the arts is still in its relative infancy).[12] It is of course true that not all Christians are called to exercise their faith and spirituality primarily in aesthetic modes, let alone in a highly schooled fashion. Christianity has traditionally recognized the legitimacy of both the active life and the contemplative life, and there is no requirement of formal artistry within either. Yet artistic craft and aesthetic discernment seem germane to a responsive, responsible, and "intelligent" Christian life and ministry—not least in the more artistic modes of preaching. If one agrees, for instance, with narrative theologians that the Christian *story* is crucial to Christian faith, there would seem to be considerable value in cultivating precisely the ability to tell, take in, and interpret religious and biblical narrative as either "realistic" or "symbolic," or some blend of the two.[13]

Christians would do well, in any case, to recognize artistry more explicitly as a significant and potentially advanced mode of Christian practice, and as potentially a Christian vocation. Within Hinduism, there is a belief that different types of religious practice can lead to *moksha*—final liberation, or salvation. The types most commonly mentioned are the path of dutiful action (*karma*), the path of knowledge (*jnana*), the path of devotion (*bhakti*), and a path combining meditation and spiritual discipline (a path sometimes referred to as royal, or *raja*). While not necessarily required, and often carefully controlled, artistry can fit with one or more of those paths (particularly *bhakti*). The freedom of the

Christian surely includes an equally wide variety of legitimate modes of practicing Christianity, even though they have never been identified so clearly. In point of fact, several approaches to artistry that could become fully and maturely Christian (even when not practiced professionally) are described by Deborah Haynes in *The Vocation of the Artist*. These include the more traditional crafts of "theocentric mimesis" (usually following a set pattern in service of a religious community), socially prophetic artistry (engaged, risky, answering to a particular moral need), and artistry which is imaginatively visionary, sometimes even utopian.[14]

Practicing Christianity Musically

Nicholas Lash once wrote: "Theologians are often accused of making things difficult."[15] But the theologian, he insisted, does not *invent* the complexity that makes for the difficulty. "Serious theological reflection is always hard work," and much of that work is to avoid oversimplification.[16] I have been claiming something like that about the making of art and about the cultivation of the taste required to take in, enjoy, and criticize its religious goals. I have not been meaning to suggest, of course, that the only legitimate modes of practicing Christianity artfully are the difficult ones. I have only meant to claim that the idea of combining disciplined artistry with disciplined training in Christianity has rarely been given its due. For many of us, in fact, it is difficult to imagine.

In bringing our study to a close, therefore, I offer a cluster of musical *exempla* illustrating what such a practice might entail. While providing commentary as needed, in most of these cases I intentionally keep critical analysis to a minimum—and forgo technical musical analysis altogether—hoping, instead, to coax the pertinent ideas and perceptions to unfold more or less of themselves.[17] In due course I introduce the Indian concept of *rasa*, along with Iris Murdoch's response to Plato's ideas of the aims and limits of art, in order to help interpret philosophically the potential religious virtues of cultivated art and taste. Finally, I give an account of the film *Babette's Feast*. Encompassing taste as exercised at many levels of appreciation and practice, this film exemplifies, in the process, virtually every kind of good taste that has been pertinent to our study—taste that is sensory, aesthetic, moral, religious, and indeed Christian.

As we set out to think, now, about ways of practicing Christianity musically, and in modes that are difficult (however delightful), we need to be sure to acknowledge that some sorts of artistic difficulty are extraneous to religious ends. Only the most technically advanced violinist can play the twenty-four brilliant but musically slight Paganini *Capricci*. One can, just barely, imagine such artistry as being dedicated in some fashion to God, just as football players sometimes dedicate their most astounding and virtuosic victories to the deity. In that sense both the violin virtuosity and the football players' skills can be enjoyed "in God." But there is nothing about such activity itself, beyond its transcendent difficulty, that particularly brings God to mind or that serves either God or neighbor in a strikingly religious or moral fashion.

On an altogether different plane is the youthful but accomplished artistry described by Friedrich Schleiermacher in the dramatic dialogue I first mentioned in the Prologue—a brief work entitled *Christmas Eve: Dialogue on the Incarnation* (1806/rev. 1826). Early on, Schleiermacher provides a memorable image of a way of practicing Christianity musically. He describes how Sophie, a precocious girl of ten or eleven, enjoys practicing certain church music in the "grand style"—a clear sign that her "taste was not at all limited." Although Sophie might casually warble to herself some "light and merry song," that was not what was indicative, in her experience, of a "purely joyful mood." Pure joy became audible, rather, when she would sit down at the piano and sing that "grand style" of church music:

> Here she knew how to treat each note aright; her touch and phrasing made each chord sound forth with an attachment which can scarcely tear itself from the rest but which then stands forth in its own measured strength until it too, like a holy kiss, gives way to the next. . . . Such performance can hardly be otherwise described, quite apart from the particular music, than that she sang with reverence, anticipated and cherished each successive tone with humble caring.[18]

Schleiermacher is describing a Christian artistic practice that is still budding, as it were, though already exceptional. More mature is the utterly transforming—though far more pain-filled—blues piano artistry of Sonny in the story by James Baldwin (1924-87) entitled "Sonny's Blues."[19]

Raised in Harlem and quickly involved in using and peddling heroin, Sonny had accumulated a lot of experience, much of which made him feel ashamed. He came to feel glad that his parents, who had died, could not see what he had become. As a teenager he had wanted to go to India for spiritual wisdom, but that had come to nothing. Sonny grew up hearing church songs his mother sang: "Lord, you brought me from a long ways off." Even now they stuck with him.

Dropping out of school, Sonny decided to become a musician, to play the piano—to play jazz. His brother thought it was a waste, playing music with what their dad had called "goodtime people." But Sonny admired Charlie Parker, and that was jazz of a different caliber. He practiced the piano endlessly and seriously. Music became "life or death to him." Although his brother, who narrates the story, had suspected that Sonny was wasting both his life and time, he found out differently one night when he went with him to a nightclub. When they came in, a bass fiddle player named Creole referred to Sonny as "a real musician." Listening to Sonny begin playing the piano with Creole and a nameless horn player, Sonny's brother remarks: "All I know about music is that not many people ever really hear it." And on the rare occasions when we do hear it, he says—when "something opens within"—we begin to realize that for the real musician who is making the music, what is evoked "is of another order, more terrible because it has no words, and triumphant, too, for that same reason. And his triumph, when he triumphs, is ours."

That night Sonny and Creole and the horn player played it safe at first, not venturing out, musically, into deep water. The piano and Sonny were not getting along; it was as though Sonny was being tortured by his life even as he played. Yet near the end of the first set, Creole's face showed that something had happened, something Sonny's brother couldn't hear. They started playing "Am I Blue," and it seemed as though the group had become a family and as though Sonny was playing "a damn brand-new piano." Then they got deep into the water. Creole was wishing Sonny "God-speed." The music began to sound like ruin, destruction, madness, and death—all the things blues is supposed to be. But when Sonny began to take the lead, he went back to the opening phrase of the song and began to make it his. It was very beautiful, and it was no longer a lament. The brother comments: "I understood, at last, that he could help us to be free if we would listen, that he would never be free until we did."

Then Sonny took the musical line, and the long line of suffering in everyone's lives around him, "and he was giving it back, as everything must be given back, so that, passing through death, it can live forever." It was only a moment in the troubled world all around. But after Sonny had stopped, and then resumed playing again—putting down his glass of Scotch and milk on top of the piano—he nodded to his brother. The brother testifies: "For me, then, as they began to play again, [the glass] glowed and shook above my brother's head like the very cup of trembling"—the cup we are to recall from Isaiah 51:22: "Thus says your Lord, the Lord your God, who pleads the cause of his people: 'Behold, I have taken from your hand the cup of trembling; the bowl of my wrath you shall drink no more.'"

The redemptive process entailed in that sort of music-making has its spontaneous side and its unpredictability; but the inattentive and undisciplined listener cannot grasp what is going on. And the musician who is unpracticed and careless cannot begin to approach that level of musical creation, a genuinely spiritual exercise for everyone involved.

No doubt closer in style to Sophie's music, yet with surprising points of connection, *The Goldberg Variations* of J. S. Bach likewise seems to invite the keyboard artist and listener, both, to turn a musical exercise into a spiritual practice. And this music, too, is nominally secular—allegedly composed to address a patron's insomnia, though by making the wakeful hours rewarding rather than by inducing sleep. As the musicologist Wilfrid Mellers puts it, acknowledging the inevitable poverty of words before music: Bach's harpsichord student Johann Goldberg played the variations of this immense passacaglia to the sleepless patron, a count; "Bach played, or at any rate composed, them to his God; and their mathematically preordained features encourage us to hear them within an eternal silence. . . . Though the unity isn't religious in affirming dogma or creed, it might be called such in a philosophical sense."[20] Of the crucial Variation 15, at the midpoint of the work, Mellers observes: "From the quiet content of the first variation we have reached [a] tragic statement, which resolves an infinity of suffering into calm. . . . Despite the pathos, this is no subjective lament; there could be no sublimer image for the whole that makes [a human being] hale and holy."[21] To characterize a later variation, Mellers quotes Blake: "He who catches a joy as it flies Lives in Eternity's sunrise."[22] And, according to Mellers, when the opening aria-sarabande returns at the very end, "in context, in the timeless stillness of the night, the effect of this da capo is indeed out of this world: for although it brings us back to the immediate moments of Goldberg's (or Bach's, or our) performance, we now hear this gracious sarabande—originally composed for an eighteenth-century wife, later offered to an eighteenth-century count—as it 'intellectually sounds in the Ears of God.'"[23]

The accusation that all this is sheer romanticism is almost inevitable. Karl Barth said similarly "outlandish" things, however, regarding his encounters with Mozart's music, in which he professed to hear parables of the Kingdom of God. Mozart's art, according to Barth, provides "music which for the true Christian is not mere entertainment, enjoyment, or edification but food and drink."[24] The height of theological art, this music with its gracious, many-sided qualities transmutes the darkness of tragedy into deep shadow from which light breaks. At least for "those who have ears to hear," it provides, better than the theologians do, a genuine theodicy.[25] Mozart's music, Barth asserts, allows one to hear the goodness of the created order of the world,[26] to "hear" God's *lux perpetua* that shines even in the midst of unspeakable loss and devastation (like that of the Lisbon earthquake in Mozart's own time), and thus to perceive the whole world with all its death and "nothingness" finally "enveloped by this light."[27] Barth says all this, and yet Barth is rarely accused of being a Romantic.

Such accounts and experiences of the religious power of music, including music without words, remind us that perhaps the Church has been overly guarded in constantly providing a verbal hedge about its music.[28] It has surely been overly rationalistic in claiming that the words of its songs must always be clearly understood. Schleiermacher made much the same point in *Christmas Eve*, where young Sophie's father, Eduard—who is identified from the start as "theologically astute"—asserts that sacred music does not depend on particular words for its power. Indeed, Eduard suggests, "No one would say that anything of gross importance was lost even if he didn't get the words at all." It is true that music "attains its perfection only in the religious sphere" (as one of Eduard's guests declares); it thus benefits from the context of worship and from what Eduard calls the "concrete reference that religion can provide." But religion, for its part, penetrates the heart best when set to music and when practiced as a "singing piety"; for "what the word has declared the tones of music must make alive, in harmony conveying it to the whole inner being." So it is that Christianity and music are able to "elevate and give radiance to each other" (pp. 46–47).

There is no way, of course, for any music to coerce a religious hearing or a religiously attentive performance. How could it? And the more demanding the music, the less assured the response (religious or otherwise), however rewarding potentially. But for that very reason, art that has religious designs must be complemented by a taste that is both spiritually astute and aesthetically attuned, or that learns to be.

The idea that art of spiritual consequence could make such demands on taste is by no means unheard of in Western aesthetics and religious thought. A certain kind of disciplined attention, for instance, is implicitly required in the metaphysical poetry that Louis Martz has studied under the rubric "the poetry of meditation."[29] But the disciplining and cultivation of religious aesthetic taste appears to be a much more familiar idea in Indian aesthetics than in Western. Indeed, there is perhaps no tradition of thought more emphatic than is classic Indian aesthetics about the necessity of cultivating a certain aesthetic capacity, or taste, if one is to be able to savor the artistic essence (*rasa*) of a work in a way that can be both spiritual and aesthetic. Without in any way abandoning our concern with Christian aesthetics, therefore, we need to look briefly at Indian traditions of thought concerned with this very point.

Rasa and Aesthetic Discipline

Indian aesthetics has very much stressed the bliss dimension of perception. The consciousness of the human arising from an inner being, is itself pure bliss. How then does this joyful awareness of the artist view the suffering (*dukkha*) of everyday experience? I feel that in this very dialectic of fundamental joy (which is the very nature of our human consciousness) and perceived imperfection and suffering in the world, lies the mystery of our Resurrected body. . . . Through our Faith we come to a new understanding of the essential body of humanity, which is the aesthetic body, the creative, imaginative body. This body is the risen body, a body which rejoices in the reality of the risen Christ. It is the realisation of this reality which is the ultimate vision to which all Christian art aspires.

—Jyoti Sahi, "Christian Art and the Image of God in the Human Person"

Jyoti Sahi, a Christian artist from Bangalore, India, sounds rather like William Blake when he links artistic taste and imagination with religious vision and experience. Yet Sahi is actually drawing on a venerable tradition of Indian aesthetics known as *rasa* theory. The passage quoted above reiterates, in its own way, our now familiar theme that art and its enjoyment can reveal a joy deeper than woe, in a process of aesthetic and religious conversion, or what Sahi terms "resurrection." But it is *rasa* theory, and not the specific theology proposed by Sahi, that is of special relevance at this point in our study.

In the ancient Indian religious texts known as the Upanishads, the term *rasa*, which came to mean the essential aesthetic savor or taste of a work of art (drama, literature, music), was on occasion used to refer to "the highest Taste or Experience accompanied by a sense of joy." In that sense, *rasa* stands for experience of the "one Supreme reality of the Universe," the attainment of which results in perennial bliss.[30] The term *rasa* was also used to refer to the perfect joy that the sage experiences when perceiving the highest truth. It is possible that the earliest thinkers in Sanskrit literary criticism tapped into this use of *rasa* when they applied the term to that aesthetic pleasure which the *rasika* enjoys as the "cultivated spectator with a responsive heart."[31]

Rasa theory became highly developed and refined under such thinkers as the great Kashmiri philosopher and drama theorist Abhinavagupta (c. 10th–11th cen.). It came to be understood that the *rasas* were either eight or nine in number—the erotic (*shringara*), the comic (*hasya*), the pathetic (*karuna*), the furious (*raudra*), the heroic (*vira*), the terrible (*bhayanaka*), the odious (*bibhatsa*), the marvelous (*adbhuta*), and (last to be added) the quiescent (*shanta*).[32] Analogous to the unique flavor produced by a specific blend of spices in a basic food, a *rasa* was thought of as "a relishable 'sentiment' or 'mood' awakened in the reader or spectator through the combination of elements in a given poem or drama."[33] Although there usually was no separate *rasa* designated as religious, Abhinavagupta described the *shanta rasa* as characteristic of the drama that depicts the endeavor to attain *moksha* (final liberation, salvation).[34] Indeed, one theorist spoke of a separate Brahma *rasa* specific to the regular activity of pursuing *moksha*.[35] In any case, Abhinavagupta, as Donna Wulff has pointed out, was clear that the utter bliss (*ananda*) of aesthetic experience—experience denoted by the term *rasa*—could be both akin to and preparatory for the ultimate salvific experience.[36] It is true that, according to Abhinavagupta and numerous other classical Hindu and Buddhist traditions, the very highest state of religious experience employs no medium whatsoever. In that respect, however, the ultimate religious state differs not only from religious experience that is aesthetic but also from every other kind of religious experience.[37]

Abhinavagupta's theories influenced the medieval forms of North Indian devotional poetry that explored *bhakti* itself (religious devotion and love) as a state of *rasa*. These and other traditions linking *rasa* with religious experience continue in various ways to the present time, and not only in India itself. It is probably not by chance when a Christian Indonesian sculptor who is familiar with Indian aesthetics encourages Christian artistry and art appreciation by saying: "Seeing something that touches our inner feeling is like eating delicious food," enabling one thereby to "touch the mysteries."[38]

The intricacies of *rasa* theory need not detain us here. What is apparent from all of them, and more so than from most Western theory, is that the work of art alone does not automatically bring about any special sort of aesthetic or religious state on the part of the reader, viewer, or listener. One must be a genuine and disciplined sort of connoisseur, or *rasika*, for that transformation of feeling and understanding to happen. As Ananda Coomaraswamy puts it, "criticism repeats the process of creation."[39] Because it is the spectator's own energy that is the cause of the tasting, aesthetic competence at this level is more than the requirement that one have taste in the ordinary sense. It is that one have a certain purity of heart and inner character and sensibility.[40] (No one would ever accuse Indian aesthetics of being excessively egalitarian.)

In demanding aesthetic and religious cultivation (or developed religious taste) on the part of both artist and viewer, *rasa* theory and the accompanying ideal of the specially attuned taste of the *rasika* seem compatible with what Eastern Orthodoxy has expected of the painter of icons: "To paint an icon is to bring about a transformation of matter that is only real as a result of a transformation in the inner being of the painter."[41] Again: "[Icon painters] are engaging in a 'heavenly task given by God' as they learn the art of painting the holy icons. . . . The true iconographer has to master the 'science of sciences and arts of arts': he has to be adept in the art and science of prayer of the heart, to be engaged in the work of pure prayer so that his iconography may stem from both the holy tradition and his own experience of the work of grace restoring him in the image and likeness of God."[42] The Eastern Orthodox tradition does not normally apply the ideal of the iconographer's artistic and religious discipline to the sacred arts in general. Nor does the Orthodox tradition parallel Indian *rasa* theory when the latter places an equal emphasis on the discipline of viewing or "tasting" the art spiritually. Even so, there is no disguising, from the standpoint of Indian *rasa* theory and its Eastern Christian parallels, that extraordinary art and its spiritual enjoyment usually asks for exceptional discipline and spiritual discernment. It requires a kind of intelligence and taste, even as it requires more than intelligence alone, and more than ordinary taste.

Transformation: Uncommon Art and Common Taste

Considering such disciplines of taste, in an extraordinary sense, it is all the more remarkable that some of the greatest works of art do, after all, spiritually "energize" a wide range of tastes, from the ordinary to the expert. The conductor Joseph Krips always heard Beethoven's Ninth Symphony as essentially a religious work, even in the purely orchestral movements that precede the famous choral finale. In that regard he was like a great many other people, whether musically literate or happily untrained. The finale of the symphony, in his way of hearing it, brought out the religious meaning decisively. As Krips wrote: "For me the finale simply does not take place here on earth. It is dangerous to talk so specifically about one's personal vision, but in my mind's eye I see quite clearly the instant in which Beethoven enters Heaven." Then one realizes, Krips said, that the theme is our redemption, our deliverance "through joy."[43]

It is safe to say that many an ordinary listener has been able to perceive the religious quality inherent in the joy of that finale. After all, the most familiar tune from the finale—its leading theme—finds its way into church in the form of the hymn, "Joyful, Joyful, We Adore Thee!" The hymn, however, sounds more mundane. It is also typically less moving and in that sense less accessible—a pale reflection of the fully symphonic choral music which, in itself, becomes something like a liturgy for a broad range of humanity.[44]

Precisely in its greatness as a work of art, Beethoven's Ninth offers to a wide array of us listeners a musical language for what they cannot otherwise say or know so fully. That kind of expressive gift, found in art at its highest (and for all its limitations), is described aptly in a dialogue by Iris Murdoch called *Acastos*, which is patterned on the Platonic dialogues. Here Murdoch depicts a conversation between Plato, Socrates, Callistos, and Acastos. Plato, characteristically, objects to art as offering seductive half truths that are second best, as stopping short of the highest, and as gratifying one prematurely. Near the end of the dialogue Socrates gives his response, speaking more directly than usual. Addressing Plato, he says:

> It may be that human beings can only achieve a second best, that second best is our best. Perhaps not only art but all our highest speculations, the highest achievements of our spirit are second best. Homer is imperfect. Science is imperfect. Any high thinking of which we are capable is faulty. . . . [Nevertheless] it may

[also] be that, as Acastos says, good art tells us more truth about our lives and our world than any other kind of thinking or speculation. . . . We are mixed beings, as you said yourself, mixed of darkness and light, sense and intellect, flesh and spirit—the language of art is the highest native natural language of that condition. . . . We are all artists, we are all story-tellers. We all have to live by art, it's our daily bread. . . . And we should thank the gods for great artists who draw away the veil of anxiety and selfishness and show us, even for a moment, another world . . . and tell us a little bit of truth.[45]

If Murdoch's Socrates is right, the practice of art at its highest speaks in a fallible yet often truly encompassing manner to the "mixed" creatures we are, who are embodied even in our spiritual being. But still more can be said, and must be said before we are through. As not only a special language but also, in a way, our "daily bread," art is ultimately more than a matter of skill and understanding or even of joy and ecstasy. It is also a matter of love. The native language of love has always been preeminently artistic and aesthetic, moving the self and will to envision that which is to be desired, to discern how to reach toward it, and to *want* to reach, and to be reached. That is why, as Murdoch knew, Plato's dialogue "The Symposium" is able to take up so naturally the themes of love and desire and beauty in the same conversation—and all at a communal meal.

But Plato's Socrates was in many ways a philosophical elitist, and certainly never envisioned a common sharing in the joy and love of the highest beauty. How on earth, then, can the highest art or taste ever come to be shared communally? Only through a strange and mysterious transformation. Here we come to what is perhaps the greatest enigma having to do with art and taste at their highest. Without in any way denying the artistic aspirations and gifts just now invoked and examined, we must consider, at this last stage of our study, the following paradox: One cannot aspire toward the most developed and discerning taste without recognizing that taste must be discriminating—that not everything is beautiful and not all beauties are equal. Yet there comes a moment or state in which taste at its very highest, and the art associated with it, allows one to relish all that one hears and sees and touches, perceiving it as blessed in the eyes of God, and so to take delight in the whole world as beautiful and entirely enjoyable "in God." For some listeners, that seems to happen in the course of listening to the Ninth Symphony, especially when the choir comes to the moment of singing: "*Seid umschlungen, Millionen*"—urging all the millions of human beings to embrace each other, in God. (The fact that many listeners are blissfully unaware of the text at that very moment seems not to matter.) It can also happen, evidently, in the moment of mystical communion or union, where ugliness and evil seem somehow taken up into a beautiful, unified whole (as Augustine himself asserted). But it can transpire at a more practical level as well. It can occur when love—and when the someone exercising art and taste as a form of love—looks upon things and beings that are defective and imperfect and in some way regards them as lovable—indeed, makes them lovable by the very act of loving them. As Kierkegaard wrote:

> Let us understand each other. It is one thing fastidiously to want to eat only the choicest and most delectable dish when it is exquisitely prepared or, even when this is the case, fastidiously to find one or another defect in it. It is something else not merely to be able to eat the plainer foods but to be able to find this plainer food to be the most exquisite, because the task is not to develop one's fastidiousness but to transform oneself and one's taste.[46]

It is a mystery, this transformative taste and love, which in the moment of becoming most developed and discriminating becomes most inclusive and all-accepting. Perhaps it is related to the mystery of divine grace in relation to divine judgment, where judgment has its necessary place but where redemptive grace nonetheless is more encompassing.[47]

Conclusion: Taste, Babette, and the Artistic Feast

All of what we have been discussing is pertinent to our last artistic example, which it seems again better to describe than to dissect. It is a story that not only ponders but in many ways exemplifies the prospects for a kind of Christian artistry and taste that is genuinely ecumenical and yet discriminating; a transformative art that is humble and nevertheless filled with aspiration. Like Mozart's music as perceived by Barth, such artistry "for the true Christian is not mere entertainment, enjoyment or edification, but food and drink."[48]

Awarded an Oscar as best foreign-language film in 1987, *Babette's Feast* (Gabriel Axel, 1987) sets up a polarity between religion and the world, between spiritual taste and physical taste, and hence between faith and art—not unlike the polarity we discerned early on in the contrasting views expressed by Kierkegaard and Blake. Here the polarization is manifest in the lives of a community of devoted Lutherans living on a remote coast of Jutland, Denmark (or Finland, in the story on which it is based). Yet the film—faithfully following the original story by Isak Dinesen (Karen Blixen)[49]—discloses that polarity only to transform it. This it accomplishes by developing its image of the feast. Not an ordinary meal by any means, the feast depicted here is at once a work of "worldly" art and a communal sacrament, with the chef Babette playing the part of the artist and, at points, of the unseen and self-giving host in the pattern of Christ (though never exactly or woodenly so).

In the film—the artistry of which exceeds, at points, even that of the written story—we see over and over again how these rigorous Christians from Kierkegaard's own Denmark, and from a time in the nineteenth century only slightly later than his own, make sacrifices that the world at large would never understand. Although the feast itself, which is not their own doing, occupies the last twenty minutes of the hundred-minute film, the scenes from the years leading up to the time of the feast reveal what it means to practice Christianity from a certain ascetic perspective. It is a style of life established when the community was founded by the prophet-like father of the two sisters who play a central role.

The sisters' names are themselves telling: Martine and Philippa, after Martin Luther and his close associate Philip Melancthon. Their dwelling, like all the others in the village, is very humble, the style of clothing and food austere. The church itself lacks ornament; its bare interior shows no sign of ever having been painted. Altogether, in word, deed, and song, the whole community makes it clear that Jerusalem is their one true home—the Heavenly Jerusalem, that is.

In their youth, Martine and Philippa were exceptionally pretty, as we see in the film's lengthy flashback; and in successive years each received the attentions of some man from the outside world who would have married her. In Martine's case, a young and handsome military officer named Lorens Loewenhielm came to visit, because of an aunt who lived nearby. To put it simply, he fell in love. Yet after a short time, observing this Christian life and its austerities, in which the only love that could thrive must be purely spiritual, he departed, kissing Martine's hand and telling her that he had learned how in this world "there are things which are impossible." He had heard the community's motto (taken from Psalm 85:10): "Mercy and truth have met together; righteousness and bliss shall kiss one another." But he could perceive no room there for woman and man to kiss and to enjoy a more earthly sort of bliss. Loewenhielm chose instead a life in the world, where he could and would marry well and be successful.

A year after that, a great opera singer Achille Papin happened to come to the region on the recommendation of a Romantic admirer who had praised the sublime scenery in that remote spot. His life was transformed when he went to church in the village and heard Philippa sing, along with others. What they sang was this: "God is God even if the whole world vanishes." Although, when asked, Papin confessed to being a Roman Catholic (a worldly and pagan thing, in those Protestant eyes), Philippa's father accepted Papin's offer to give voice lessons to Philippa for the glory of God. Papin, however, proceeded to teach Philippa seductive duets from Mozart's *Don Giovanni*, during which he could see her heart beginning to melt. Papin's own heart was soon brought low, however, as Philippa decided she could not give herself over to such singing, let alone to anything more.

The sisters never married, continuing to live together after their father's death. That is how Babette found them, when fifteen years later she came to their door during a great storm, seeking a shelter in return for service, having fled Paris upon threat to her life as a consequence of the Franco-Prussian War of 1870–71. It was Achille Papin who had directed her to Philippa, his "lost Zerlina," conveying in writing his assurances, moreover, that in Paradise he would hear Philippa sing again as the great artist God had meant her to be.

Noting merely that "Babette can cook," Papin's letter of introduction gave no hint of the great chef that Babette had been in Paris. But Babette, now provided with a place to stay and the chance to labor in the house and prepare meals for the two sisters, contented herself with gradually transforming the formerly ascetic meals of dried fish and ale-bread into something at least palatable. Babette earned the respect, too, of the whole community as she drove a hard bargain for goods.

After a long time, and quite out of the blue, news came to Babette that a lottery ticket she had bought many years before in Paris had just won her the grand prize of ten thousand francs. Although Babette did not take this opportunity to leave her adopted life, as the sisters expected, she did finally ask them a favor. She requested to be allowed to prepare a special French dinner on the occasion of the hundredth anniversary of their deceased father's birthday. Reluctantly the sisters gave in. Members of the community, despite an increasing level of internal discord and dissention, would also be invited. Babette took a journey and arranged for her nephew to bring her all the goods she needed from France.

At this point the film, emerging from its tone of retrospection and rumination, takes on a greater sense of anticipation. When what is needed for the meal finally arrives, we see a veritable liturgical procession of the makings and "offerings." These include a live sea tortoise, quail, and the like. Babette even arranges to have exquisite wine. All this alarms Martine; at night she dreams of bloody pagan sacrifices and a witches' sabbath. When she wakes, she summons her invited guests, who vow that they will join in the meal but remain silent regarding the food. It will be as though they never had the sense of taste, they say.

Quite by chance, or else by Providence, the officer who had courted Martine, and later married, is back visiting his elderly aunt. It is she who asks if he might come to the meal as well. The sisters accept, telling Babette that there will now be a total of twelve for dinner—hardly an insignificant number in a Christian context, and in connection with a meal, no less. After singing hymns directing Christians to give no thought for food and raiment, the group welcomes General

Loewenhielm. He has learned the ways of the world, including the gourmet arts; but he has recently been aware of a certain emptiness of soul. Indeed, he has been thinking to himself that when he earlier abandoned Martine for a life of success, he may have made a poor bargain, though he gained the whole world: "Vanity, vanity, all is vanity!" He seems to know his Ecclesiastes, at any rate.

While it snows outside, Babette finishes preparing the meal, assisted by a lad who helps set the table in a fine manner never seen there before. Meanwhile, General Loewenhielm has the opportunity to admire Martine, whom he has not seen for thirty years. She still has trustful eyes and a sweet mouth. Following a blessing that speaks of food as a bodily necessity for the good of the soul, the meal commences.

General Loewenhielm, presiding over the meal, notices every detail and savors it, commenting in a manner that might remind one of the various ritual words of a celebrant at communion.[50] It is a memorial meal, after all. But Loewenhielm is not engaged in religious commentary. He is noticing each tasty, well-crafted dish, and the quality of the various wines, which he can identify exactly. He seems only mildly perplexed when others at the table deflect every remark on the food and say nothing to the point, remembering their vow to act as though they had no sense of taste. For our benefit as viewers, the camera lingers over the meal's colors and shapes, and we hear all the little sounds of eating and sucking and crunching, which the microphone treats as something delectable as well. All are beginning to relish each dish as it is brought out and presented beautifully and ceremoniously. Perhaps the best of all is "Caille en Sarcophage"—the quail dish. Each serving is given a pastry "sarcophagus" and reshaped into a form that mimics the appearance of the living bird; and the name itself reminds the partaker of the sacrifice of life that makes the meal possible. This dish is so miraculous and unique that the General recognizes it as a specialty of the woman who was a famous chef at the Café Anglais in Paris. As he recalls, she could transform a dinner into "a kind of love affair" in which one no longer distinguishes between bodily and spiritual appetite.

When the meal is well advanced, and some of the guests are actually a little tipsy—one of many slightly humorous touches—the General stands to give a speech, beginning with the words familiar to the community: "Mercy and truth have met together; righteousness and bliss shall kiss one another." The General sounds like himself, but different. It is not just the wine. He is seeing things in a new way and begins talking about how God's grace is not the finite thing that humans keep imagining it to be, but infinite. We tremble at making wrong choices, he observes; but that which we have chosen is given to us, by the grace of God, and that which we have refused is also granted in the end.

It is not a speech that the gathered Brothers and Sisters can altogether understand; possibly the General does not quite understand it, either, or its eschatological promise. But for the rest of the evening it is as though a benediction has fallen on the whole lot of them; time and eternity merge, says Dinesen in her story, and the film shows that in numerous ways. In the interaction that follows, people forgive each other old wrongs they have harbored for many years. The General takes an opportunity to hold Martine's hand: "I have been with you every day of my life. You know, do you not, that it has been so?" And Martine acknowledges that. Stumbling out under the stars, the departing guests move in a circle dance, singing how the stars have drawn near, how eternity has drawn near. One old man who, being nearly deaf, always says "Hallelujah" when he is not sure what else to say, says it once again, only now with a voice full of feeling.

Babette has remained behind the scenes, in the kitchen. We see her quietly sip her wine appreciatively after the meal is over and the guests have gone. In conversation with the two sisters, who finally express their thanks, assuming that Babette will now return to Paris, it comes out that Babette had spent the entire ten thousand francs on the meal—had sacrificed all she had. She informs the sisters, not without some sense of dignity, that she had been the chef at the Café Anglais whose artistry the General had recognized this very night. And an artist, she says, is never poor. She had stood up for the poor in Paris, during the conflict; she had done her best for them all, as she had done for those who dined on her food in Paris and recognized her artistry. Philippa puts her arms around Babette, pauses a moment, and tells her quietly but fervently: "Yet this is not the end! In Paradise you will be the great artist that God meant you to be! . . . You will enchant the angels!" Those closing words repeat, but in a new key, what Papin had written to Philippa years before in the note that accompanied Babette's arrival. In a sense, it is what the General as the meal's Celebrant had said when declaring that grace exceeds our finitude and grants more than we had dared hope.

Many a critic treats the tale as a kind of parable in which the church folk are blessed despite themselves, and by an art they cannot fully appreciate. But that interpretation is of course one-sided. To be sure, the film implies, as does Dinesen's story, that a church with no roots in the world, with no world to love, with no body and no taste, with only eternity in its heart, gradually starves the body of faith itself in an attempt to feed the soul. But the film also implies that a world that has only itself in mind—devoted only to success and to erotic love devoid of depth, and in its dining discerning only in its taste for the food as such—that world could not, on its own, create such a meal as the artist Babette provides, with its sacramental qualities and community-transforming grace.

Hers is an extraordinary art that makes a banquet for body and soul, providing a foretaste of the Heavenly Banquet. It thus comes to symbolize the kind of art that the film itself evidently aspires to emulate. And it represents the sort of art that the Church would do well to cultivate, along with the taste—sensory, aesthetic, and spiritual—that is needed to savor it fully.

Notes

Prologue

1. Friedrich Schleiermacher, *Christmas Eve: Dialogue on the Incarnation* (1806), 2d edition, 1826, trans. Terrence N. Tice (Richmond, Va.: John Knox, 1967), p. 47.

2. See David B. Morris, *The Religious Sublime: Christian Poetry and Critical Tradition in Eighteenth-Century England* (Lexington, Ky.: Univ. Press of Kentucky, 1972).

3. For a comparable attempt to retrieve a complex notion of taste for contemporary use, see Charles Wegener, *The Discipline of Taste and Feeling* (Chicago: Univ. of Chicago Press, 1992), p. 29.

4. One could, of course, still object to such a rendition of the song on strictly musical grounds. My brother has pointed out, for instance, that the song does not "work" at a very slow tempo. The repeated notes of the fourth phrase turn into monotonous plodding and the "harmonic rhythm" of the chord progressions bogs down.

5. See Hans-Georg Gadamer, *Truth and Method*, 2d ed., revised, trans. Joel Weinsheimer and Donald Marshall (New York: Crossroad, 1989), pp. 19–40.

6. Joseph Addison, "The Pleasures of the Imagination," *The Spectator* (June–July 1712): nos. 409–21.

7. See Scott L. Marcus, "On Cassette Rather than Live: Religious Music in India Today," in *Media and the Transformation of Religion in South Asia*, ed. Lawrence A. Babb and Susan S. Wadley (Philadelphia: Univ. of Pennsylvania Press, 1995), p. 175.

8. Frank Burch Brown, *Religious Aesthetics: A Theological Study of Making and Meaning* (Princeton, N.J.: Princeton Univ. Press, 1989).

9. Matthew Zyniewicz, ed., *The Papers of the Henry Luce III Fellows in Theology*, Vol. 3 of the Series in Theological Scholarship and Research (Atlanta: Scholars Press, 1999), pp. 33–56.

10. *Companion Encyclopedia of Theology*, ed. Peter Byrne and Leslie Houlden (London: Routledge, 1995).

11. Frank Burch Brown, "Making Sacred Places, and Making Places Sacred," Festschrift Issue for Richard Dickinson, *Encounter* 59, nos. 1–2 (1998): 95–117.

12. Frank Burch Brown, "Characteristics of Art and the Character of Theological Education," Issue on Sacred Imagination: The Arts and Theological Education, *Theological Education* 31(Autumn 1994): 5–11.

Chapter 1

1. Bob Roehr, "Cheap Shots: A Talk with Andrew Sullivan," *Christian Century*, Sept. 13–29, 1995.

2. An otherwise perceptive book by Terrence Erdt, *Jonathan Edwards: Art and the Sense of the Heart* (Amherst: Univ. of Massachusetts Press, 1980), is clearly mistitled. There is much in the book, and in Edwards, about beauty; there is very little about art. Even then it is mainly the rhetorical art of sermonizing, which justifies being considered artful, but is rarely art in the modern, aesthetic sense of the term.

3. For pioneering—if also partial—insights into the social influences on art and art theory, see Arnold Hauser, *The Sociology of Art*, trans. Kenneth J. Northcott (Chicago: Univ. of Chicago Press, 1982).

4. On spiritual taste, see Karl Rahner, "The Doctrine of the 'Spiritual Senses' in the Middle Ages," in *Theological Investigations*, vol. 16, *Experience of the Spirit: Source of Theology* (New York: Seabury, Crossroad Books, 1979), pp. 104–34; and Jonathan Edwards, *Religious Affections*, ed. John E. Smith (New Haven, Conn.: Yale Univ. Press, 1959), pp. 281–84.

5. The theological or religious analysis of the various arts, usually studied independently of one another, has by now become a minor industry. Yet it is widely recognized that the institutions of the Western "art world," and the dominant schools of modern scholarship and criticism in the arts, long found art's continued involvement with religion to be an embarrassment or anomaly that would best be ignored. At present the trend seems to be reversing itself, with publishers, galleries, museums, film producers, and record companies often eager to interpret or promote (and exploit for commercial purposes) forms of artistic expression that are identified as religiously significant or else as somehow "spiritual." In the latter category they tend to prefer, to be sure, something unconventional or exotic, perhaps invoking ancient and esoteric traditions.

6. Hans Urs von Balthasar, *The Glory of the Lord: A Theological Aesthetics*, 7 vols., various translators (San Francisco: Ignatius, 1982–89).

7. Herman Bavinck, quoted in an extensive discussion of Dutch Neo-Calvinists in Jeremy Begbie, *Voicing Creation's Praise: Towards a Theology of the Arts* (Edinburgh: T. & T. Clark, 1991), p. 100.

8. The image of Bach as the "Fifth Evangelist" can be traced in a long line from Philipp Spitta to Albert Schweitzer. See John Ogasapian, "Bach: The 'Fifth Evangelist'?" *Journal of Church Music* 27, no. 3 (March 1985): 13–16.

9. See Paul Tillich, *On Art and Architecture*, ed. John Dillenberger and Jane Dillenberger (New York: Crossroad, 1987).

10. See Stanley E. Fish, *Self-Consuming Artifacts: The Experience of Seventeenth-Century Literature* (Berkeley: Univ. of California Press, 1972).

11. See Kevin Hart, *The Trespass of the Sign: Deconstruction, Theology, and Philosophy* (Cambridge: Cambridge Univ. Press, 1989).

12. See Hal Foster, ed., *The Anti-Aesthetic: Essays on Postmodern Culture* (Port Townsend, Wash.: Bay Press, 1983).

13. Pierre Bourdieu, *Distinction: A Social Critique of the Judgement of Taste*, trans. Richard Nice (Cambridge, Mass.: Harvard Univ. Press, 1984).

14. See Immanuel Kant, *Critique of Judgment* (1790). For a critique of purist aesthetics that actually finds indirect warrant in some of Kant for nonpurist theories of

art, see Frank Burch Brown, *Religious Aesthetics: A Theological Study of Making and Meaning* (Princeton, N.J.: Princeton Univ. Press, 1989), pp. 47–76.

15. Tex Sample, *Hard Living People and Mainstream Christians* (Nashville, Tenn.: Abingdon, 1993), p. 115.

16. Ibid., p. 116.

17. Tex Sample, *White Soul: Country Music, the Church and Working Americans* (Nashville, Tenn.: Abingdon, 1996), pp. 41–54.

18. Ibid., pp. 157–62.

19. Thomas Day, *Why Catholics Can't Sing: The Culture of Catholicism and the Triumph of Bad Taste* (New York: Crossroad Books, 1990).

20. Sample, *White Soul*, pp. 27–68. The prior work of mine that enters into this discussion is found especially in the chapter "Sin and Bad Taste" in *Religious Aesthetics*, pp. 136–57.

21. This summary of Cone's views is based on personal conversation at a conference at the Wesley Foundation in Blacksburg, Va., in November of 1984.

22. John Wesley, Preface to *A Collection of Hymns for the Use of the People Called Methodists* (1780), in the *Works of John Wesley*, 26 volumes, vol. 7, ed. Franz Hildebrandt and Oliver A. Beckerlegge (Oxford: Oxford Univ. Press—Clarendon, 1983), p. 74. It must be admitted that Wesley goes on to assert that "the spirit of piety" is "of infinitely more moment than the spirit of poetry" (p. 75). He thereby demonstrates once again how hard it is for Christians to see artistic gifts as potentially gifts of the spirit, and to value a certain kind of aesthetic taste as conducive to what the Wesleys termed "Christian perfection."

23. See David Morgan, ed., *Icons of American Protestantism: The Art of Warner Sallman* (New Haven, Conn.: Yale Univ. Press, 1996); and Colleen McDannell, *Material Christianity: Religion and Popular Culture in American* (New Haven, Conn.: Yale Univ. Press, 1995).

24. With respect to music, this point is made in sharply contrasting ways in Day, *Why Catholics Can't Sing;* and in Sample, *White Soul.*

25. Franz Joseph Haydn, quoted in letter from Leopold Mozart to his daughter Nannerl, Feb. 16, 1785, in *The Mozart Compendium: A Guide to Mozart's Life and Music,* ed. H. C. Robbins Landon (New York: Schirmer, 1990), p. 386.

26. "One of Us," words and music by Eric Bazilian, on Joan Osborne, *Relish* (New York: Polygram Compact Disc, 1995).

27. Alyssa Katz, "Believe It or Not," *Spin,* May 1992.

28. This point is underlined by Marva J. Dawn, *Reaching Out without Dumbing Down: A Theology of Worship for the Turn-of-the-Century Culture* (Grand Rapids, Mich.: Eerdmans, 1995); and Neil Postman, *Amusing Ourselves to Death: Public Discourse in the Age of Show Business* (New York: Viking Penguin, 1985).

29. In the sphere of church music, as in other arts, the recurrent principles that have often been set forth as eternal "verities" can best serve as guideposts rather than as absolutes. For a valuable though relatively uncompromising treatment of these, see Quentin Faulkner, *Wiser than Despair: The Evolution of Ideas in the Relationship of Music and the Christian Church* (Westport, Conn.: Greenwood, 1996).

30. Nicholas Wolterstorff, *Art in Action: Toward a Christian Aesthetic* (Grand Rapids, Mich.: Eerdmans, 1980).

Chapter 2

1. See Samuel Laeuchli, *Religion and Art in Conflict* (Philadelphia: Fortress, 1980); and Gerardus van der Leeuw, *Sacred and Profane Beauty: The Holy in Art*, trans. David E. Green (New York: Holt, Rinehart and Winston, 1963).

2. Such vows, kept most strictly by monks of the Theravada tradition of Buddhism (as in Sri Lanka), are widely interpreted in such a way as to allow exceptions. For instance, Tibetan Buddhist monks (in the Vajrayana, or Tantric, tradition) now perform public sacred concerts using chant and dance, and they have long played wind, brass, and percussion instruments in religious ceremonies.

3. See John Renard, *Seven Doors to Islam: Spirituality and the Religious Life of Muslims* (Berkeley: Univ. of California Press, 1996); and Habib Hassan Touma, *The Music of the Arabs*, expanded ed., trans. Laurie Schwartz (Portland, Oreg.: Amadeus, 1996), pp. 152–67.

4. See John Baggley, *Doors of Perception: Icons and Their Spiritual Significance* (Crestwood, N.Y.: St. Vladimir's Seminary Press, 1988); and Gennadios Limouris, ed., *Icons: Windows on Eternity*, Faith and Order Paper 147 (Geneva: World Council of Churches, 1990).

5. For an edited survey of Christian artistic practices in the context of worship, see Robert E. Webber, ed., *Music and the Arts in Christian Worship*, vol. 4 of *The Complete Library of Christian Worship* (Nashville, Tenn.: Star Song, 1994).

6. Søren Kierkegaard, *The Book of Adler*, trans. Howard V. Hong and Edna H. Hong (Princeton, N.J.: Princeton Univ. Press, 1998), p. 174. One wonders whether Kierkegaard knew Augustine's long and admiring discussion of Paul's rhetorical art, in *On Christian Teaching*.

7. That Kierkegaard adopted several different stances toward art—by no means consistent with one another (in my view)—has often been pointed out. For one "state of the art" discussion of the matter, see Sylvia Walsh, "Kierkegaard: Poet of the Religious," in *Kierkegaard on Art and Communication*, ed. George Pattison (London: Macmillan, 1992), pp. 1–22.

8. Kierkegaard, *Practice in Christianity*, ed. and trans. Howard V. Hong and Edna H. Hong (Princeton, N.J.: Princeton Univ. Press, 1991), pp. 254–57.

9. Sculpted in marble, these figures were the work of a famous Danish sculptor, Bertel Thorvaldsen—an artist who once commented ironically that such religious feelings as he had, he owed to his teatime conversations with one Baroness Schubart. His lack of Christian piety should not be taken as an affront, he said; after all, he did not believe in Jupiter either. See Roger Poole, *Kierkegaard: The Indirect Communication* (Charlottesville: Univ. Press of Virginia, 1993), pp. 236–47. Oddly enough, Poole—who is largely uninterested in theology, and who sees irony even in the most sincere religious assertions of Kierkegaard—views the sculptures as more or less directly embodying Kierkegaardian principles and thinks that Kierkegaard would have gestured meaningfully toward them (and positively) on the occasions when he gave Friday communion discourses in the church. Poole makes no comment on the passage from Kierkegaard under discussion here.

10. Kierkegaard, *Practice in Christianity*, 255.

11. Ibid.

12. Ibid.

13. Ibid., pp. 255–56.

14. William Blake, "Aphorisms on the Laocoön Group," *Selected Poetry and Prose of Blake*, ed. Northrop Frye (New York: Modern Library, 1953), pp. 328–30. For an accurate reproduction of the Laocoön plate and Blake's comments, see *The Complete Poetry and Prose of William Blake*, rev. edn., ed. David V. Erdman (New York: Doubleday, 1988), pp. 272–75.

15. Blake, "To the Christians," from *Jerusalem*, ed. Frye, ibid., p. 303.

16. Blake, "A Descriptive Catalogue," ibid., pp. 376–77.

17. Blake has usually been regarded as someone who threw reason aside in order to embrace imagination and faith. That perspective on Blake now seems distorted. His mediating position—as no rationalist, but no irrationalist or "fideist" either—is something Jennifer Jesse shows convincingly in her as yet unpublished doctoral thesis, "The Binding of Urizen: The Role of Reason in William Blake's Religious Thought," The Divinity School, University of Chicago, 1997.

18. Blake, letter to the Reverend Dr. Trusler, Aug. 23, 1799, in *Complete Poetry and Prose*, p. 702.

19. For a valuable but rather technical and selective historical analysis of various Christian attitudes and uses of the arts, see Diana Wood, ed., *The Church and the Arts*, 1992; paperback ed. (Oxford: Basil Blackwell—Ecclesiastical History Society, 1995).

20. Quoted in John McManners, "Enlightenment: Secular and Christian," in McManners, ed., *The Oxford Illustrated History of Christianity* (Oxford: Oxford Univ. Press, 1990), p. 296.

21. See David Freedberg, *The Power of Images: Studies in the History and Theory of Response* (Chicago: Univ. of Chicago Press, 1989), pp. 162–66. Cf. Charles Garside Jr., *Zwingli and the Arts* (New Haven, Conn.: Yale Univ. Press), p. 91.

22. Augustine, *Confessions*, X.xxxiii.

23. Quoted and translated in Garside, *Zwingli*, p. 90.

24. Freedberg, *Power of Images*.

25. Ibid., pp. 162–88.

26. Freedberg himself, although intent on showing the power of images, and eager to find theological acknowledgment of the same, sometimes implicitly accepts the traditional hierarchical notion of images as spiritually "lower." He states, for example, that while the true mystic could rely only on holy texts and readily do without images, the assistance of images was nevertheless vital to those "who were incapable of reaching the purely spiritual heights" and who instead were engaged in "compassionate meditation" (Ibid., p. 173). One might well ask: Is the higher meditation and mysticism always image-less? Such a view would not be accepted by many Eastern Orthodox, of course, or even by some of the mystics discussed by Freedberg; but—to reiterate—the language of compromise and condescension creeps in repeatedly even in the defense of images, especially in the Western church. Freedberg takes up the topic in historical terms on pp. 378–428.

27. Ibid., p. 406.

28. Aidan Nichols, *The Art of God Incarnate: Theology and Image in Christian Tradition* (New York: Paulist, 1980), p. 5.

29. Tertullian, *De Idololatria*.

30. See Paul Corby Finney, *The Invisible God: The Earliest Christians on Art* (New York: Oxford Univ. Press, 1994).

31. See Hans Belting, *Likeness and Presence: A History of the Image before the Era of Art*, trans. Edmund Jephcott (Chicago: Univ. of Chicago Press, 1994), p. 26.

32. Ulrich Zwingli, quoted and translated in Garside, *Zwingli*, p. 90.

33. Timothy Gregory Verdon, ed., *Monasticism and the Arts* (Syracuse, N.Y.: Syracuse Univ. Press, 1984), p. 21.

34. See Sergiusz Michalski, *The Reformation and the Visual Arts: The Protestant Image Question in Western and Eastern Europe* (New York: Routledge, 1993); Carl C. Christensen, *Art and the Reformation in Germany* (Athens, Ohio, and Detroit, Mich.: Ohio State Univ. Press–Wayne State Univ. Press, 1979); and John Dillenberger, *Images and Relics: Theological Perceptions and Visual Images in Sixteenth-Century Europe*, Oxford Studies in Historical Theology (New York: Oxford Univ. Press, 1999).

35. John Calvin, *Institutes of the Christian Religion* (1559), I.XI.13; quoted and translated in Finney, *Invisible God*, p. 7.

36. Karl Barth, "The Architectural Problem of Protestant Places of Worship," originally published in the review *Werk*, no. 8, 1959; reprinted as an appendix to André Biéler, *Architecture in Worship* (Philadelphia: Westminster, 1965), p. 93. (Emphasis in the original.)

37. Quoted in Garside, *Zwingli*, p. 45. Cf. Jerome on a parallel passage in Ephesians 5:19, "We ought therefore to sing, to make melody and to praise the Lord more with spirit than the voice." There is reason to question Zwingli's interpretation of the passage in Colossians, which the NRSV, in keeping with most modern translations, renders in the following way: "Let the word of Christ dwell in you richly; teach and admonish one another in all wisdom; and with gratitude in your hearts sing psalms, hymns, and spiritual songs to God."

38. Quoted in Garside, *Zwingli*, p. 28.

39. See James McKinnon, ed., *Music in Early Christian Literature* (Cambridge: Cambridge Univ. Press, 1987), p. 3.

40. Ibid., p. 38.

41. See Johannes Quasten, *Music and Worship in Pagan and Christian Antiquity*, trans. Boniface Ramsey (Washington, D.C.: National Association of Pastoral Musicians, 1983).

42. For a historical discussion of such theological ideals for church music, see Quentin Faulkner, *Wiser than Despair: The Evolution of Ideas in the Relationship of Music and the Christian Church* (Westport, Conn.: Greenwood, 1996); see also an influential modern interpretation of these ideals in Erik Routley, *Church Music and the Christian Faith* (Carol Stream, Ill.: Agape, 1978).

43. Anon. ninth- or tenth-century Frankish clergyman, in *Scholia enchiriadis*, trans. Lawrence Rosenwald, in Piero Weiss and Richard Taruskin, eds., *Music in the Western World: A History in Documents* (Schirmer, 1984), p. 40.

44. See Robert F. Hayburn, ed., *Papal Legislation on Sacred Music: 95 A.D. to 1977 A.D.* (Collegeville, Minn.: Liturgical Press, 1979); and Friedrich Blume, Ludwig Finscher et al., *Protestant Church Music* (London: W. W. Norton, 1975).

45. Dietrich Bonhoeffer, *Life Together* (London: SCM Press, 1954), p. 50.

46. John Wesley, "Directions for Congregational Singing," from *Sacred Melody* (1761); reprinted in David W. Music, ed., *Hymnology: A Collection of Source Readings*, Studies in Liturgical Musicology, no. 4 (Landham, Md.: Scarecrow Press, 1996), pp. 139–40.

47. Pope Pius X, *motu proprio*, Section II.5, in Hayburn, ed., *Papal Legislation on Sacred Music*, p. 225.

48. Routley, *Church Music*, pp. 88–89.

49. See J. G. Davies, *Liturgical Dance: An Historical, Theological and Practical Handbook* (London: SCM Press, 1984).

50. Quoted in McKinnon, *Music*, p. 43.

51. See O. B. Hardison Jr., *Christian Rite and Christian Drama in the Middle Ages: Essays in the Origin and Early History of Modern Drama* (Baltimore: Johns Hopkins Univ. Press, 1965).

52. See Miri Rubin, *Corpus Christi: The Eucharist in Late Medieval Culture* (Cambridge: Cambridge Univ. Press, 1991).

53 Augustine, *On Christian Teaching*, trans. R. P. H. Green (Oxford: Oxford Univ. Press, 1997), Book 4, p. 105.

54. Among the vast number of literary studies of the Bible, see, for example, John Dominic Crossan's pioneering study, *In Parables: The Challenge of the Historical Jesus* (New York: Harper & Row, 1973); Robert Alter, *The Art of Biblical Narrative* (New York: Basic Books, 1981); Robert Alter and Frank Kermode, eds., *The Literary Guide to the Bible* (Cambridge, Mass.: Harvard Univ. Press, 1987); Stephen Prickett, ed., *Reading the Text: Biblical Criticism and Literary Theory* (Oxford: Basil Blackwell, 1991).

55. See Marjorie Reeves, "The Bible and Literary Authorship in the Middle Ages," in Stephen Prickett, ed., *Reading the Text: Biblical Criticism and Literary Theory* (Oxford: Basil Blackwell, 1991), pp. 12–63.

56. See McKinnon, *Music*, pp. 2–3.

57. The crucial role of music in Christian practice is made plain in Paul Westermeyer, *Te Deum: The Church and Music* (Minneapolis: Fortress, 1998).

58. Foreword to the *Geneva Psalter*, quoted in *Source Readings in Music History*, ed. Oliver Strunk (New York: W. W. Norton, 1950), p. 347.

59. Martin Luther, Preface to *Symphoniae jucundae* [1538], trans. Ulrich S. Leupold, in *Luther's Works* (Philadelphia: Fortress, 1965), 53:321–24.

60. For an early exposition of his idea, see Jon Michael Spencer, *Protest and Praise: Sacred Music of Black Religion* (Minneapolis: Fortress, 1990).

61. Ibid., p. ix.

62. "Sacred Music," *Constitution on the Sacred Liturgy*, Dec. 4, 1963, in *Vatican Council II: The Conciliar and Post Conciliar Documents*, ed. Austin Flannery (Northport, N.Y.: Costello, 1975), chapter 6, paragraph 112, p. 31.

63. Edward Foley, "Toward a Sound Theology," in his book *Ritual Music: Studies in Liturgical Musicology* (Beltsville, Md.: Pastoral Press, 1995, p. 123.

64. *Constitution on the Sacred Liturgy*, chapter 7, paragraph 122, p. 34.

65. For a useful and perceptive theological treatment of Christianity and the visual arts, see John Dillenberger, *A Theology of Artistic Sensibilities: The Visual Arts and the Church* (New York: Crossroad, 1986). See also Freedberg, *Power of Images*; and Yrjö Hirn, *The Sacred Shrine: A Study of the Poetry and Art of the Catholic Church*, 1909; reprint (Boston: Beacon, 1957).

66. See Joseph Gutmann, *Beauty in Holiness: Studies in Jewish Customs and Ceremonial Art* (New York: KTAV, 1970); and Gutmann, *No Graven Images: Studies in Art and the Hebrew Bible* (New York: KTAV, 1971); and L. Michael White, *The Social Origins of Christian Architecture*, 2 vols., Harvard Theological Studies 42 (Valley Forge, Pa.: Trinity Press International, 1997).

67. See White, *Social Origins*, 2:18–21.

68. See Finney, *Invisible God*, pp. 99–108.

69. Church historians are not the only ones to have paid less than adequate attention to the role of the arts in reshaping Christian identity vis-à-vis classical culture. Partly because classical education itself was so text oriented, even an illustrious historian like Charles Norris Cochrane could basically ignore the nonliterary arts in his impressive study, *Christianity and Classical Culture*, 1940; reprint (Oxford: Oxford Univ. Press, 1972).

70. See Otto G. von Simson, *Sacred Fortress: Byzantine Art and Statecraft in Ravenna* (Princeton, N.J.: Princeton Univ. Press, 1948).

71. Quoted in Rowland J. Mainstone, *Hagia Sophia: Architecture, Structure and Liturgy of Justinian's Great Church* (New York: Thames and Hudson, 1988), p. 10.

72. For art's role in shaping early Christianity and christology, see Margaret R. Miles, *Image as Insight: Visual Understanding in Western Christianity and Secular Culture* (Boston: Beacon, 1985); Thomas F. Mathews, *The Clash of Gods: A Reinterpretation of Early Christian Art*, rev. ed. (Princeton, N.J.: Princeton Univ. Press, 1999); and Robin Jensen, *Understanding Early Christian Art* (London: Routledge, 2000).

73. Quoted in Freedberg, *Power of Images*, p. 404.

74. Ibid., pp. 400–401.

75. See Belting, *Likeness and Presence*, pp. 4, 11.

76. See David Morgan, *Visual Piety: A History and Theory of Popular Religious Images* (Berkeley: Univ. of California Press, 1998); Morgan, *Protestants and Pictures: Religion, Visual Culture, and the Age of American Mass Production* (New York: Oxford Univ. Press, 1999); and Colleen McDannell, *Material Christianity: Religion and Popular Culture in America* (New Haven, Conn.: Yale Univ. Press, 1995).

77. See Melva Wilson Costen, *African American Christian Worship* (Nashville, Tenn.: Abingdon, 1993).

78. Quoted in Belting, *Likeness and Presence*, p. 1.

79. Bernard of Clairvaux, *Apologia ad Guillelmum*, quoted and translated in Umberto Eco, *The Aesthetics of Thomas Aquinas*, trans. Hugh Bredin (Cambridge, Mass.: Harvard Univ. Press, 1988), p. 8. See also Conrad Rudolph, *The "Things of Greater Importance": Bernard of Clairvaux's Apologia and the Medieval Attitude toward Art* (Philadelphia: Univ. of Pennsylvania Press), 1990.

80. Bernard quoted and translated in Eco, *Aesthetics of Thomas Aquinas*, p. 9.

81. Abbot Suger, "On What Was Done under His Administration," in *Abbot Suger on the Abbey Church of St-Denis and Its Art Treasures.*, ed. and trans. Erwin Panofsky, 2d ed. (Princeton, N.J.: Princeton Univ. Press, 1979), pp. 63–65.

82. Paul Tillich, "One Moment of Beauty," in *Paul Tillich, On Art and Architecture*, ed. John Dillenberger and Jane Dillenberger (New York: Crossroad Books, 1987), p. 235.

83. See, above all, Richard Viladesau, *Theological Aesthetics: God in Imagination, Beauty, and Art* (New York: Oxford Univ. Press, 1999); see also von Balthasar, *The Glory of the Lord*, vol. 4: *The Realm of Metaphysics in Antiquity* (San Francisco: Ignatius, 1989), pp. 317–412; Richard Harries, *Art and the Beauty of God: A Christian Understanding* (London: Mowbray, 1993), pp. 31–43; John Navone, *Toward a Theology of Beauty* (Collegeville, Minn.: Liturgical Press, 1996); Patrick Sherry, *Spirit and Beauty: An Introduction to Theological Aesthetics* (Oxford: Oxford–Clarendon, 1992), pp. 43–45; and Armand A. Maurer, *About Beauty: A Thomistic Interpretation* (Houston: Center for Thomistic Studies, University of St. Thomas, 1983), pp. 14–15.

84. See, for example, Harries, "The Invisible Made Visible," chapter 9 in *Art and the Beauty of God*, pp. 117–33; and Viladesau, *Theological Aesthetics*.

85. Such a move to see art as potentially sacramental is certainly warranted within Tillich's own concept of sacramentality. See Paul Tillich, *Systematic Theology*, 3 vols. (Chicago: Univ. of Chicago Press, 1963), 1:120–25.

86. Quoted in Jaroslav Pelikan, *The Christian Tradition*, vol. 2: *The Spirit of Eastern Christendom (600–1700)* (Chicago: Univ. of Chicago Press, 1974), p. 122.

87. Karl Barth, *Wolfgang Amadeus Mozart*, trans. Clarence K. Pott (Grand Rapids, Mich.: Eerdmans, 1986), pp. 55–57.

88. Ibid., p. 53.

89. This point, though never intended, can be deduced easily from the essays in Verdon, *Monasticism and the Arts*.

90. See James Luther Adams and Wilson Yates, eds., *The Grotesque in Art and Literature* (Grand Rapids, Mich.: Eerdmans, 1997).

Chapter 3

1. See Paul Kristeller, "The Modern System of the Arts," in *Renaissance Thought II* (New York: Harper & Row–Torchbook, 1965), pp. 163–227; and Wladyslaw Tatarkiewicz, "Art: History of the Concept" and "Art: History of Classification," in *A History of Six Ideas: An Essay in Aesthetics* (The Hague: Martinus Nijhoff, 1980), pp. 11–65.

2. The term "aesthetics" was invented in 1735 by Alexander Baumgarten, who was thinking of the Greek adjective *aisthetikos*, which means "perceptible, or concerned with perception."

3. See Immanuel Kant, *Critique of Judgment* (1790), Sections 1–22.

4. See David Carrier, ed., *England and Its Aesthetes: Biography and Taste* (Amsterdam: Overseas Publishers Association, 1997).

5. Friedrich Schlegel, "Ideas" (1800), in *German Aesthetic and Literary Criticism: The Romantic Ironists and Goethe*, ed. Kathleen Wheeler (Cambridge: Cambridge Univ. Press, 1984), nos. 46 and 52, p. 56.

6. Georg Wilhelm Friedrich Hegel, from *Lectures on Aesthetics*, in *Philosophies of Art and Beauty: Selected Readings in Aesthetics from Plato to Heidegger*, ed. Albert Hofstadter and Richard Kuhns (Chicago: Univ. of Chicago Press, 1964), p. 391.

7. See M. H. Abrams, *Natural Supernaturalism: Tradition and Revolution in Romantic Literature* (New York: W. W. Norton, 1971).

8. The extent to which various Romantics could be said to embrace some sort of Christian orthodoxy has always been difficult to determine, with their art and prose often vacillating in its leanings. See Abrams, *Natural Supernaturalism*.

9. See Robert Rosenblum, *Modern Painting and the Northern Romantic Tradition: Friedrich to Rothko* (New York: Harper & Row–Icon, 1975).

10. See Barbara Novak, *Nature and Culture: American Landscape and Painting 1825–1875* (New York: Oxford Univ. Press, 1980).

11. Friedrich Schleiermacher, *On Religion: Speeches to Its Cultured Despisers* (1799), 3d edition, 1821, trans. John Oman (New York: Harper & Row–Cloister, 1958), pp. 39, 143. In the first edition Schleiermacher had described religion as the "sensibility and taste" rather than "sense and taste" for the infinite.

12. Friedrich Schleiermacher, *On Religion: Speeches to Its Cultured Despisers* (1799),

trans., with intro. and notes, Richard Crouter (Cambridge: Cambridge Univ. Press, 1988), p. 158. As we will see, Schleiermacher could in fact at times make very bold claims about the religious importance of sacred art—particularly music.

13. See Andrew Wilson-Dickson, *The Story of Christian Music* (Oxford: Lion, 1992), p. 124.

14. Quoted in Hilary Fraser, *Beauty and Belief: Aesthetics and Religion in Victorian Literature* (Cambridge: Cambridge Univ. Press, 1986), p. 10.

15. John Henry Newman, "Poetry, and Reference to Aristotle's Poetics," in *Essays and Sketches*, ed. Charles Frederick Harrold, 3 vols. (London: Longmans, Green, 1948), 1:76.

16. John Henry Newman, *Discourses Addressed to Mixed Congregations* (London: Longman, Roberts, Green, & Longmans, 1849), pp. 185–86.

17. Ibid., p. 219.

18. See Hilary Fraser, *Beauty and Belief*, pp. 7–66.

19. John Keble, *Praelectiones Academicae*, trans. Owen Chadwick, in *The Mind of the Oxford Movement* (London: A. & C. Black, 1963), p. 70.

20. John Henry Newman, "Prospects of the Anglican Church," in *Essays and Sketches*, 1:358.

21. See George Pattison, "The Dream of a Christian Culture," in *Art, Modernity and Faith: Towards a Theology of Art* (New York: St. Martin's, 1991), pp. 30–53.

22. John Henry Newman, *The Idea of a University* (1852 section), ed. Martin Svaglic (Notre Dame, Ind.: Univ. of Notre Dame Press, 1982), p. 59.

23. John Ruskin, *Modern Painters*, vol. 2, part 3, sec. 1, chap. 2; discussed in Monroe Beardsley, *Aesthetics from Classical Greece to the Present* (New York: Macmillan, 1966), pp. 301–4, 306–7.

24. See Pattison, *Art, Modernity, and Faith*, pp. 54–77.

25. John Ruskin, *Works*, ed. E. T. Cook and Alexander Wedderbarn, 39 vols. (London: George Allen, 1903–12), 4:64.

26. John Ruskin, "The Relation of Art to Religion," in *Lectures on Art* (1870); reprint (New York: Allworth Press, 1996), p. 82.

27. Ruskin, *Lectures on Art*, pp. 82, 151.

28. Ibid., p. 108.

29. Ibid., p. 99.

30. Ibid., pp. 102–4.

31. Ruskin, *Works* 3:670. For an excellent account of Ruskin's impact on Victorian values and taste, see Linda Dowling, *The Vulgarization of Art: The Victorians and Aesthetic Democracy* (Charlottesville: Univ. Press of Virginia, 1996), pp. 25–49.

32. I am considerably indebted for my interpretation of Ruskin's religious views to John D. Barbour, *Versions of Deconversion: Autobiography and the Loss of Faith* (Charlottesville: Univ. Press of Virginia, 1994), pp. 53–72. See also Michael Wheeler, *Ruskin's God* (Cambridge: Cambridge Univ. Press, 1999).

33. Matthew Arnold, Preface to *God and the Bible* (1875), in *Complete Prose Works of Matthew Arnold*, ed. R. H. Super, 11 vols. (Ann Arbor, Mich.: Univ. of Michigan Press, 1970), 7:378.

34. Matthew Arnold, "The Study of Poetry" (1860), in *Essays in Criticism, Second Series* (London: Macmillan, 1888), p. 2.

35. See J. Hillis Miller, *The Disappearance of God* (Cambridge, Mass.: Harvard Univ. Press, 1963), pp. 212–69; for a sympathetic treatment of Arnold's pioneering attempts at what theologian Rudolf Bultmann (1884–1976) later called "demythologizing," see Nathan A. Scott Jr., *The Poetics of Belief: Studies in Coleridge, Arnold, Pater, Santayana, Stevens, and Heidegger* (Chapel Hill: Univ. of North Carolina Press, 1985), pp. 39–61.

36. Walter Pater, *The Renaissance: Studies in Art and Poetry*, 1st ed., 1873; 1893 text, with textual and explanatory notes, ed. Donald L. Hill (Berkeley: Univ. of California Press, 1980), p. 190.

37. In *Marius the Epicurean*, Pater has Marius propose an ideal existence, "a new form of the contemplative life," which would consist in "refining all the instruments of inward and outward intuition, of developing all their capacities, of testing and exercising one's self in them, till one's whole nature became one complex medium of reception, towards the vision—the 'beatific vision,' if we really cared to make it such—of our actual experience in the world." See Critical and Explanatory Notes in Pater, *The Renaissance*, p. 456.

38. Walter Pater, *Letters of Walter Pater*, ed. Lawrence Evans (Oxford: Oxford Univ. Press–Clarendon, 1970), p. 52.

39. Walter Pater, "A Child in the House" (1878), reprinted in *England and Its Aesthetes: Biography and Taste*, ed. David Carrier (Amsterdam: Overseas Publishers Association, 1997), pp. 67–68.

40. Ibid., p. 189.

41. Nathan Scott Jr. argues persuasively that Pater had a genuinely religious sensibility, even if without doctrinal convictions, and was by no means the wanton aesthete he has often been represented as being. See Scott, *Poetics of Belief*, pp. 62–89.

42. Clive Bell, *Art* (1913); reprint (New York: G. P. Putnam's Sons–Capricorn, 1958), p. 30.

43. One of the best accounts of the New Criticism remains Murray Krieger, *The New Apologists for Poetry* (Minneapolis: Univ. of Minnesota Press, 1956).

44. For a detailed discussion and critique of these features of modern aesthetic and literary theory, see Frank Burch Brown, *Religious Aesthetics: A Theological Study of Making and Meaning* (Princeton, N.J.: Princeton Univ. Press, 1989).

45. Clement Greenberg, "New Sculpture," in *Art and Culture* (1961); reprint (Boston: Beacon, 1965), p. 139.

46. This is the well-known dictum of Archibald MacLeish, found (ironically enough) in the poem "Ars Poetica," which obviously tried to mean something.

47. Numerous modernists have made assertions in keeping with a strict sort of purism—various New Critics, structuralists, and phenomenologists, or formalist art critics such as Clement Greenberg. But hardly anyone does so consistently. For an in-depth survey of art theories and their modern developments, see Francis Sparshott, *The Theory of the Arts* (Princeton, N.J.: Princeton Univ. Press, 1982). For an accessible treatment of modern literary theory, see Terry Eagleton, *Literary Theory: An Introduction* (Minneapolis: Univ. of Minnesota Press, 1983).

48. See Martin Heidegger, *Poetry, Language, Thought*, trans. Albert Hofstadter (New York: Harper & Row, 1971).

49. See Richard Foster, *The New Romantics: A Reappraisal of the New Criticism* (Bloomington: Indiana Univ. Press, 1962); Gerald Graff, *Literature Against Itself* (Chicago: Univ. of Chicago Press, 1979); and Krieger, *New Apologists*.

50. See R. S. Crane, ed., "Criticism as Inquiry," in *The Idea of the Humanities and Other Essays Critical and Historical,* 2 vols. (Chicago: Univ. of Chicago Press, 1967), and Crane, ed., *Critics and Criticism: Ancient and Modern* (Chicago: Univ. of Chicago Press, 1952).

51. Frye vacillates in the extent to which he sees it essential for literature to be hypothetical. In any case, his thinking is highly suggestive. See Northrop Frye, *The Stubborn Structure: Essays on Criticism and Society* (Ithaca, N.Y.: Cornell Univ. Press, 1970); Frye, *The Great Code: The Bible and Literature* (New York: Harcourt Brace Jovanovich, 1981); and Frye, *Words with Power: Being a Second Study of the Bible and Literature* (New York: Harcourt Brace Jovanovich, 1990).

52. *New Catholic Encyclopedia* (New York: McGraw-Hill, 1967), s.v. "Art."

53. T. S. Eliot, "Religion and Literature," in *Selected Essays,* 3d edition (London: Faber & Faber, 1951), p. 394.

54. Hans-Georg Gadamer, *Truth and Method,* 2d ed., revised, trans. Joel Weinsheimer and Donald G. Marshall (New York: Crossroad, 1989), pp. 84–85.

55. Ibid., pp. 86–88.

56. Ibid., p. 97.

57. Ibid.

58. See Brown, *Transfiguration*; and Brown, *Religious Aesthetics.*

59. John Dewey, *Art as Experience* (1934); reprint (New York: G. P. Putnam's Sons–Capricorn, 1958).

60. For a reading of the various sorts of theological significance of deconstruction in particular, see Kevin Hart, *The Trespass of the Sign* (Cambridge: Cambridge Univ. Press, 1989).

61. See Paul de Man, *The Rhetoric of Romanticism* (New York: Columbia Univ. Press, 1984); de Man, *The Resistance to Theory* (Minneapolis: Univ. of Minnesota Press, 1986); and Terry Eagleton, *The Ideology of the Aesthetic* (Oxford: Basil Blackwell, 1990); cf. Christopher Norris, *What's Wrong with Postmodernism* (Baltimore: Johns Hopkins Univ. Press, 1990).

62. See Fredric Jameson, *Postmodernism: Or, the Cultural Logic of Late Capitalism* (Durham, N.C.: Duke Univ. Press, 1991); and Jean-François Lyotard, *The Postmodern Condition: A Report on Knowledge,* trans. Geoff Bennington and Brian Massumi, Theory and History of Literature, vol. 10 (Minneapolis: Univ. of Minnesota Press, 1984).

63. See Eagleton, "From the *Polis* to Postmodernism," in *The Ideology of the Aesthetic,* pp. 366–415; Norris, *What's Wrong with Postmodernism*; and Wendy Farley, *Eros for the Other: Retaining Truth in a Pluralistic World* (University Park, Pa.: Pennsylvania State Univ. Press, 1996).

64. Jacques Derrida, *Memoirs of the Blind: The Self-Portrait and Other Ruins,* trans. Pascale-Anne Brault and Michael Naas (Chicago: Univ. of Chicago Press, 1993), p. 126. For a discussion of Derrida's most recent moves in and around theology, see John D. Caputo, *The Prayers and Tears of Jacques Derrida: Religion without Religion* (Bloomington: Indiana Univ. Press, 1997); Terence R. Wright, "'Behind the Curtain': Derrida and the Religious Imagination," in *Through a Glass Darkly: Essays in the Religious Imagination,* ed. John C. Hawley (New York: Fordham Univ. Press, 1996), pp. 276–95; and James K. A. Smith, "Determined Violence: Derrida's Structural Religion," *Journal of Religion* 78 (April 1998): 197–212.

65. The translator and publicists for Derrida's *Memoirs of the Blind* assiduously avoid any mention of religion or theology in the accompanying preface and promo-

tional blurbs. Nevertheless, here and in several other of his latest works, Derrida takes up religious themes with poignancy and intensity that is courting scandal once again, this time of the intellectual avant-garde. Many of the drawings and paintings that Derrida chooses to discuss in this volume, which originated in connection with an exhibition mounted by the Louvre Museum, are religious and even Christian, affording the Jewish and sometimes antitheological Derrida a chance to cross new boundaries and hazard new risks.

Chapter 4

1. I thank Richard Kieckhefer for pointing out to me that, in putting the matter this way, I must have had in the back of my mind Jean Leclercq's highly acclaimed study of monastic culture, *The Love of Learning and the Desire for God* (New York: Fordham Univ. Press, 1961), which I read twenty-five years ago.

2. If it is hard to know what to make of Derrida's content-less faith and almost purely structural religion, he would not be surprised, having referred to "my religion about which nobody understands anything." See Jacques Derrida, *Circumfessiones*, ed. Geoffrey Bennington and Jacques Derrida (Chicago: Univ. of Chicago Press, 1993), p. 154. See also James K. A. Smith, "Determined Violence: Derrida's Structural Religion," *Journal of Religion* 78 (April 1998): 197–212. For the most sympathetic and detailed treatment of Derrida's religious motives and motifs, see John D. Caputo, *The Prayers* and *Tears of Jacques Derrida: Religion without Religion* (Bloomington: Indiana Univ. Press, 1997).

3. Carroll Stuhlmueller, "Psalms," *Harper's Bible Commentary*, ed. James L. Mays (San Francisco: Harper & Row, 1988), p. 453.

4. Augustine, *Confessions*, trans. Henry Chadwick (Oxford: Oxford Univ. Press, 1991), X.xxvii.38, p. 201.

5. Augustine, *Confessions*, trans. Maria Boulding (Hyde Park: N.Y.: New City Press, 1997), X.vii.11, p. 244; and X.vi.8, p. 242.

6. Ibid., X.vi.8, p. 242.

7. Ibid., X.vi.9, p. 243.

8. Augustine, *City of God*, XI.iv.2, trans. John Healey (1610), in *An Augustine Synthesis*, ed. Erich Przywara (New York: Harper & Brothers–Torchbooks, 1958), p. 116.

9. For a probing discussion of Augustine's attitude toward creation and its beauty, see "Creation," in Carol Harrison, *Beauty and Revelation in the Thought of Saint Augustine* (Oxford: Oxford Univ. Press, 1992), pp. 97–139.

10. See Richard Harries, *Art and the Beauty of God* (London: Mowbray, 1993), p. 36. Although the Latin versions speak of *bonum* (goodness) rather than *kalos* (beauty) with respect to creation, the idea of the world's created beauty persisted in some form from antiquity to the present. In any case Augustine was convinced that the Septuagint (the Old Testament translated into Greek) was no less inspired than the Hebrew original. See Henry Chadwick, *Augustine* (New York: Oxford Univ. Press, 1986), p. 36.

11. See Umberto Eco, *Art and Beauty in the Middle Ages*, trans. Hugh Bredin (New Haven, Conn.: Yale Univ. Press, 1986), p. 56; see also Wladyslaw Tatarkiewicz, "The Aesthetics of St. Augustine," in his *History of Aesthetics*, vol. 2: *Medieval Aesthetics*, ed. C. Barrett (The Hague: Mouton, 1970), pp. 47–65.

12. See Søren Kierkegaard, *Either/Or* (1843), Part I.

13. Augustine, *Confessions*, trans. Boulding, VII.xi.17, p. 174.

14. Augustine, *Confessions*, trans. Chadwick, X.xxxiv.53, p. 210.

15. Ibid., X.xxxv.54, pp. 210–11.

16. Ibid., X.xxxiv.53, p. 210.

17. Ibid., X.xxxiii.50, p. 208.

18. Ibid.; cf. IX.vi.14, p. 164.

19. Ibid., n. 34.

20. Ibid., X.xxv.56–57, p. 212.

21. Ibid., III.ii.3–4, pp. 36–37.

22. Ibid., VI.viii.13, pp. 100–101; cf. Augustine *Soliloquia*, II. ii.18.

23. Alfred North Whitehead, *Adventures of Ideas* (New York: Macmillan–Free Press, 1933), p. 266.

24. Ibid., p. 267.

25. Ibid., p. 266.

26. Augustine, *On Christian Teaching*, I.xxxii.35.

27. Augustine, *Sermon 88.5.5*, translated in Margaret Miles, "Vision: The Eye of the Body and the Eye of the Mind in Saint Augustine's *De trinitate* and *Confessions*," *Journal of Religion* 63 (April 1983): 125–42.

28. Augustine, *Confessions*, trans. Boulding, VII.x.18, p. 174.

29. Augustine, *City of God*, XVI. viii.3.

30. For an illuminating discussion of this aspect, and others, of Augustine's theological aesthetics, see Hans Urs von Balthasar, *The Glory of the Lord: A Theological Aesthetics*, 7 vols.; vol. 2: *Studies in Theological Style: Clerical Styles*, ed. John Riches, trans. Andrew Louth et al. (San Francisco and New York: Ignatius Press and Crossroad, 1984), esp. pp. 127–29. See also, Robert J. O'Connell, *Art and the Christian Intelligence in St. Augustine* (Cambridge, Mass.: Harvard Univ. Press, 1978); and Carol Harrison, *Beauty and Revelation*.

31. Augustine, *Confessions*, trans. Boulding, VII.xiii.19, p. 175.

32. See Frank Burch Brown, "The Beauty of Hell: Anselm on God's Eternal Design," *Journal of Religion* 73 (July 1993): 329–56.

33. Augustine, *Confessions*, trans. Chadwick, X.xxvii.38.

34. Augustine, *Enarrationes in Psalmos*, 44.3; quoted in Harrison, *Beauty and Revelation*, p. 192.

35. See Harrison, *Beauty and Revelation*, pp. 215, 236.

36. See "Words: A Paradigm," in ibid., pp. 85–96.

37. Margaret Miles, "Vision": 125–42.

38. Augustine, *Enarrationes in Psalmos*, 99.5; quoted in ibid, p. 131.

39. Augustine, *City of God*, XXII.29, p. 1087.

40. Ibid., XXII.24, p. 1072.

41. Ibid., p. 1073.

42. Ibid., p. 1075.

43. For a sensitive and sympathetic treatment of this very point, see O'Connell, *Art and the Christian Intelligence in St. Augustine*.

44. Of the massive literature on metaphor, the book most immediately pertinent to the present matter is Mark Johnson, *The Body in the Mind: The Bodily Basis of Meaning, Imagination, and Reason* (Chicago: Univ. of Chicago Press, 1987).

45. Augustine, *In Jo. Ep.* 8.12, quoted in Harrison, *Beauty and Revelation*, p. 256.

46. T. S. Eliot, "Religion and Literature," in *Selected Essays*, 3d ed. (London: Faber & Faber, 1951), p. 394.

47. The dialectic of theology and art that I am describing here is one that has occupied my attention extensively—first in *Transfiguration: Poetic Metaphor and the Languages of Religious Belief* (Chapel Hill: Univ. of North Carolina Press, 1983), then in *Religious Aesthetics: A Theological Study of Making and Meaning* (Princeton, N.J.: Princeton Univ. Press, 1989). The issue is related, of course, to Kant's discussion of what the aesthetic symbol gives to thought, in the *Critique of Judgment* (1790), and to related discussions in the work of Paul Ricoeur, Karl Jaspers, and many others. My own emphasis is distinctive in that it stresses the interaction and mutual transformation of the artistic and the theological, or the symbolic and the conceptual.

48. Augustine, *On Christian Teaching*, trans. R. P. H. Green (New York: Oxford Univ. Press), I.xxxii.35, p. 25.

49. Ibid., I.xxx.34, p. 23.

50. Ibid., I.xxii. 21, p. 17; and I.xxxii.37, p. 25.

51. Ibid., I.xxxii.34, 35, pp. 24, 25.

52. Ibid., I.xxii.21, p. 17.

53. Ibid.

54. Ibid., I.xxxii.37, p. 25.

55. Ibid.

56. Augustine, *The Trinity*, trans. Edmund Hill, *Works of Saint Augustine*, part 1, vol. 5 (Brooklyn, N.Y.: New City Press, 1991), book 9, p. 278. (Hill utilizes his own subdivisions, which there is no need to indicate here.)

57. Ibid., Book 8, p. 252 (italics indicate scripture quotation).

58. Augustine, *The Trinity*, Book 9, p. 278.

59. Augustine, *Confessions*, trans. Chadwick, X.xxxiv.53, p. 210.

60. Ibid., X.xxxv.57.

61. E-mail correspondence with J. Gerald Janzen, May 21, 1999.

62. Nicholas Wolterstorff, *Art in Action: Toward a Christian Aesthetic* (Grand Rapids, Mich.: Eerdmans, 1980), p. 169; cf. pp. 78–83.

63. See Frank Burch Brown, "Varieties of Religious Aesthetic Experience," in *Religious Aesthetics*, pp. 112–35.

64. Simone Weil, *Gravity and Grace*, trans. Emma Craufurd (London: Fontana, 1963), p. 137. For carefully nuanced discussions and qualifications of such a position, see Patrick Sherry, *Spirit and Beauty: An Introduction to Theological Aesthetics* (Oxford: Oxford Univ. Press–Clarendon, 1992); and Richard Viladesau, *Theological Aesthetics: God in Imagination, Beauty, and Art* (New York: Oxford Univ. Press, 1999).

65. Clive Bell, *Art* (1913); reprint (New York: G. P. Putnam's Sons–Capricorn, 1958), pp. 68, 69.

66. Paul Tillich, "Art and Society," in *On Art and Architecture*, ed. John Dillenberger and Jane Dillenberger (New York: Crossroad, 1987), p. 33.

67. Richard Harries, *Art and the Beauty of God* (London: Mowbray, 1993), p. 101.

68. Alejandro García-Rivera, *The Community of the Beautiful: A Theological Aesthetics* (Collegeville, Minn.: Liturgical Press–Michael Glazier, 1999), p. 9.

69. Gerardus van der Leeuw, *Sacred and Profane Beauty: The Holy in Art* (New York: Holt, Rinehart and Winston, 1963), p. 337.

70. The list of transcendentals varies, as do theories of their significance. For a detailed and persuasive account of beauty as a transcendental, see Richard Viladesau, *Theological Aesthetics*, pp. 32–33, 125–34.

71. Letter to Henry Boys, June 29, 1937, quoted in Donald Mitchell, *Gustav Mahler: Songs and Symphonies of Life and Death* (Berkeley: Univ. of California Press, 1985), pp. 339–40; reproduced here with the kind permission of the Britten-Pears Foundation. The letters of Benjamin Britten are © The Trustees of the Britten-Pears Foundation and are not to be further reproduced without written permission. For an extensive and probing disussion of Mahler's "*Abschied*" itself, see Mitchell, pp. 327–432.

72. Although the "*Abschied*" is usually sung by a woman (mezzo-soprano), and to great effect, Mahler himself preferred that it be sung by a man (baritone). Clearly Mahler identified with the speaker in the poem, whose voice is represented in the singing.

Chapter 5

1. Augustine, *The Trinity, Works of Saint Augustine*, part 1, vol. 5, trans. Edmund Hill (Brooklyn: New City Press, 1991), pp. 247, 257.

2. See Matei Calinescu, *Faces of Modernity: Avant-Garde, Decadence, Kitsch* (Bloomington: Indiana Univ. Press, 1977), p. 234; see also Tomas Kulka, *Kitsch and Art* (University Park: Pennsylvania State Univ. Press, 1996), pp. 18–19. The exact etymology of the term "kitsch" is in dispute. One possibility is that it derives from the German verb *verkitschen*, meaning "to make cheap"; another that it comes from a German mispronunciation of the English "sketch," or else from an inversion of the French *chic*. See Kulka, pp. 17–19.

3. Milan Kundera, *The Unbearable Lightness of Being*, trans. Michael Henry Heim (New York: Harper & Row, 1984), p. 252.

4. A Czech woman whom I once observed standing in the church and praying in the direction of the Infant Jesus of Prague had on a plain coat with a deep pocket out of which her pet poodle kept poking its head, which somehow had a touching effect—like kitsch?

5. Janet Maslin, "*The Truman Show*: So, What's Wrong with This Picture?," *New York Times*, June 5, 1998; http://www.nytimes.com/library/film/060598truman-film-review.html.

6. Karsten Harries, *The Meaning of Modern Art: A Philosophical Interpretation* (Evanston, Ill.: Northwestern Univ. Press, 1968), p. 81.

7. Ibid., p. 82.

8. Robert C. Solomon, "On Kitsch and Sentimentality," *Journal of Aesthetics and Art Criticism* 49 (Winter 1991): 1–14; quotation on p. 1.

9. Max Horkheimer, "Art and Mass Culture," in *Critical Theory: Selected Essays* (New York: Herder and Herder), pp. 275, 281; cf. Clement Greenberg, "Avant-Garde and Kitsch," in *Art and Culture* (1961); reprint (Boston: Beacon, 1965). For a study of such attitudes, see Patrick Brantlinger, *Bread and Circuses: Theories of Mass Culture as Social Decay* (Ithaca, N.Y.: Cornell Univ. Press, 1983); and Paul R. Gorman, *Left Intellectuals and Popular Culture in Twentieth-Century America* (Chapel Hill: Univ. of North Carolina Press, 1996). For a positive assessment of popular culture, see John Fiske, *Understanding Popular Culture* (New York: Routledge, 1989); and Lawrence

W. Levine, *Highbrow/Lowbrow: The Emergence of Cultural Hierarchy in America* (Cambridge, Mass.: Harvard Univ. Press, 1988).

10. To be exact, the charge against the *"In Paradisum"* that concludes the Britten work is "artificial sweetness," which in the context connotes much the same thing as "kitsch." See James D. Herbert, "Bad Faith at Coventry: Spence's Cathedral and Britten's *War Requiem*," *Critical Inquiry* 22 (Spring 1999): 535–65. The Britten comes off favorably in comparison with Coventry Cathedral, where it was premiered in 1962.

11. The condemnation of Penderecki and Messiaen, for example, comes to me directly from the lips of a prominent contemporary British composer who will here remain nameless.

12. Colleen McDannell, *Material Christianity: Religion and Popular Culture in America* (New Haven, Conn.: Yale Univ. Press, 1995), p. 165.

13. James Lindsay, "Theology and Art," *Bibliotheca Sacra* 62 (1905): 479; quoted in McDannell, *Material Christianity*, p. 166.

14. See David Morgan, ed., *Icons of American Protestantism: The Art of Warner Sallman* (New Haven, Conn.: Yale Univ. Press, 1996); David Morgan, *Visual Piety: A History and Theory of Popular Religious Images* (Berkeley: Univ. of California Press, 1998).

15. McDannell, *Material Christianity*, p. 13.

16. The most exhaustive documentation and analysis of the social conditioning of taste remains Pierre Bourdieu's *Distinction: A Social Critique of the Judgement of Taste*, trans. Richard Nice (Cambridge, Mass.: Harvard Univ. Press, 1984).

17. Bob Roehr, "Cheap Shots: A Talk with Andrew Sullivan," *Christian Century*, Sept. 13–29, 1995.

18. *Russian Primary Chronicle*, quoted in Thomas F. Mathews, *Byzantium: From Antiquity to the Renaissance* (New York: Harry N. Abrams–Perspectives, 1998), p. 98; see also Linda Safran, *Heaven on Earth: Art and the Church in Byzantium* (University Park: Pennsylvania State Univ. Press, 1998), pp. 54, 88.

19. Precious Moments Web Site, http://www.preciousmoments.com/. Readers should seek out the web site, as I was unable to secure permission from PMI (Precious Moments, Inc.) to use any photographs of the chapel in the present book.

20. The doors, made of Philippine Nara wood, were carved by Butcher's assistant, his "understudy" Nelson Lete, guided by Butcher's drawings.

21. *The Making of the Precious Moments Chapel* (video), produced and directed by Jon D. Butcher, Precious Moments Chapel, Inc., 1994; 27 minutes.

22. See the Enesco web site at http://www.enesco.com/latest/gift/ggo10/ggo10abt.htm.

23. *The Precious Moments Chapel: A Keepsake Memory Book* (St. Charles, Ill.: Precious Moments, Inc., 1994), p. 2.

24. Ibid.

25. See "The Story behind It All," on the web site for Precious Moments Chapel (capitalized as in the original).

26. *The Precious Moments Chapel: A Keepsake Memory Book*; *The Making of the Precious Moments Chapel* (video).

27. Karsten Harries, *Meaning of Modern Art* (Evanston, Ill: Northwestern Univ. Press, 1968), p. 80.

28. Hans Belting, *Likeness and Presence: A History of the Image before the Era of Art*, trans. Edmund Jephcott (Chicago: Univ. of Chicago Press, 1994), p. 1.

29. See James W. Fowler, *Stages of Faith: The Psychology of Human Development and the Quest for Meaning* (San Francisco: Harper & Row, 1981), pp. 133–34.

30. Marva J. Dawn, *Reaching Out without Dumbing Down: A Theology of Worship for the Turn-of-the-Century Culture* (Grand Rapids, Mich.: Eerdmans, 1995).

31. Kundera usually takes that view; it is certainly that of Tomas Kulka in *Kitsch and Art*.

32. I owe this insight to my colleague E. Byron Anderson. See Dietrich Bonhoeffer, *The Cost of Discipleship*, 2d ed., rev., trans. R. H. Fuller (1959); reprint (New York: Macmillan, 1963), pp. 45–60.

33. Ellen T. M. Laan quoted by Natalie Angier, "Science Is Finding Out What Women Really Want," *New York Times*, Aug. 13, 1995.

34. Solomon, "On Kitsch and Sentimentality." See also Stephen Happel, "Common Sense, Kitsch, and Visual Culture: Meaning and Religious Identity in Contemporary Cultures," in *The European Legacy: Journal of the History of European Ideas* (Boston: MIT Press, 1999).

35. McDannell, *Material Christianity*, pp. 193–97.

36. Lee Smith, *Saving Grace* (New York: Ballantine, 1995).

37. Paul Ricoeur, *The Symbolism of Evil*, trans. Emerson Buchanan (Boston: Beacon, 1967), pp. 351–52.

38. The Christian putt-putt course and the art it displays appears to be a distant cousin to Michael Murphy's *Golf in the Kingdom*, a "mystical tale" from 1972, and to M. Scott Peck's *Golf and the Spirit: Lessons for the Journey*, which evidently takes a road more traveled. See Michael Murphy, *Golf in the Kingdom*, 1972; reprint (New York: Penguin–Arkana, 1992); M. Scott Peck, *Golf and the Spirit: Lessons for the Journey* (New York: Harmony, 1999).

39. Tim LaHaye and Jerry B. Jenkins, *Left Behind: A Novel of the Earth's Last Days* (Wheaton, Ill.: Tyndale House, 1995).

40. James Redfield, *The Celestine Prophecy* (Hoover, Ala.: Satori Publishing, 1993); and *The Tenth Insight: Holding the Vision* (New York: Time Warner, 1996).

41. Elisabeth Kübler-Ross, front cover blurb, second printing of Redfield's *Celestine Prophecy*.

42. Some readers will note a parallel with the Book of Mormon, which likewise purports to derive from documents preserved by ancient Native Americans and which relates the history of a tribe of ancient Israelites who sailed to America in about the year 600 B.C.

43. See George Steiner, *Real Presences* (Chicago: Univ. of Chicago Press, 1989), pp. 3–50.

Chapter 6

1. L & C Software promotion for Contemporary Christian Music and Donna Cori Gibson; internet site URL: csasso.hypermart.net/contempo.htm.

2. Augustine, *Confessions* X.xxxiii.49.

3. Augustine, *In psalmum cvi*, I, quoted in James McKinnon, *Music in Early Christian Literature* (New York: Cambridge Univ. Press, 1987), p. 159.

4. Karl Barth, "A Letter of Thanks to Mozart," from the Round Robin in the weekly supplement of the *Luzerner Neuesten Nachrichten*, Jan. 21, 1956, in Karl Barth, *Wolfgang Amadeus Mozart*, trans. Clarence K. Pott (Grand Rapids, Mich.: Eerdmans, 1986).

5. Karl Barth, "A Testimonial to Mozart," from the Round Robin in the *Neue Züricher Zeitung*, Sunday, Feb. 13, 1955; in Barth, *Wolfgang Amadeus Mozart*, pp. 15-17; quotation on p. 16.

6. From a review of Anonymous 4, *An English Ladymass: Medieval Chant and Polyphony* (Harmonia Mundi France, CD 907080, 1992). This and the following quotations come from uncopyrighted promotional materials distributed free of charge at live concert events.

7. To be precise, "Caravan" was composed in the 1930s by a member of Duke Ellington's orchestra, Juan Tizol, who played valve trombone.

8. I am referring to George Washington Blalock, 1869–1972.

9. For the most thorough documentation of the social conditioning of taste, see Pierre Bourdieu, *Distinction: A Social Critique of the Judgement of Taste*, trans. Richard Nice (Cambridge, Mass.: Harvard Univ. Press, 1984). Bourdieu unfortunately treats taste not only as socially conditioned but as, in effect, generated only by economic motivations and sustained only by the politics and powers of class. Bourdieu's sociological and economic reductionism is as dreary and monochromatic in its treatment of aesthetic value as it is fascinating and dazzling in its treatment of social factors affecting taste. For an equally brilliant yet likewise problematical analysis of the conditioning of taste and critical norms—this time more oriented toward literary theory and philosophy—see Barbara Herrnstein Smith, *Contingencies of Value: Alternative Perspectives for Critical Theory* (Cambridge, Mass.: Harvard Univ. Press, 1988).

10. For sociological perspectives, see Peter J. Martin, *Sounds and Society: Themes in the Sociology of Music* (Manchester: Manchester Univ. Press, 1995); and John Shepherd, *Music as Social Text* (Cambridge, Mass.: Basil Blackwell–Polity, 1991); for ethnomusicological perspectives, see John Blacking, *Music, Culture, and Experience*, ed. Reginald Byron, Chicago Studies in Ethnomusicology (Chicago: Univ. of Chicago Press, 1995).

11. Michael Eric Dyson, *Between God and Gangsta Rap: Bearing Witness to Black Culture* (New York: Oxford Univ. Press, 1996), p. 165.

12. Tricia Rose, *Black Noise: Rap Music and Black Culture in Contemporary America* (Hanover, N.H.: Wesleyan Univ. Press–Univ. Press of New England, 1994).

13. For the dual role of taste in uniting and dividing social groups, see Bourdieu, *Distinction*. For careful documentation and analysis of the role of musical styles and tastes in the shaping of religious identity and worship practices, see the work of Linda J. Clark, Joanne Swenson, and Mark Stamm on worship, music, and religious identity funded by the Lilly Endowment and concentrating on three representative congregations of the United Methodist Church. With the working subtitle of "God among Us," the research and analysis was presented in part at an extended conference on Worship, Music, and Religious Identity held at Boston University School of Theology, April 9-11, 1999, and will appear in due course in video, book, and possibly CD format.

14. See Charles Taylor et al., *Multiculturalism: Examining the Politics of Recognition*, ed. Amy Gutmann (Princeton, N.J.: Princeton Univ. Press, 1994); and David Theo Goldberg, *Multiculturalism: A Critical Reader* (Cambridge, Mass.: Basil Blackwell, 1994).

15. Martin E. Marty, "Music for the Ages," M.E.M.O. column, *Christian Century*, Nov. 2, 1994.

16. See John Renard, *Seven Doors to Islam: Spirituality and the Religious Life of Muslims* (Berkeley: Univ. of California Press, 1996), p. xiii and elsewhere. That Sufism is not entirely representative of Islam overall is something often glossed over by Muslims with Sufi leanings, as one sees in Seyyed Hossein Nasr, *Islamic Art and Spirituality* (Albany: State Univ. of New York Press, 1987).

17. For the fascinating genealogy of this saying, see the internet site of J. J. O'Donnell at ccat.sus.upenn.edu/jod/augustine.html.

18. For more on the eschatological dimension of worship, see Don E. Saliers, *Worship as Theology: Foretaste of Glory Divine* (Nashville, Tenn.: Abingdon, 1994).

19. Alejandro García-Rivera, *The Community of the Beautiful: A Theological Aesthetics* (Collegeville, Minn.: Liturgical Press–Michael Glazier, 1999), p. 2. For another Hispanic/Latino study that engages major issues in theological aesthetics, see Roberto S. Goizueta, *Caminemos con Jesús: Toward a Hispanic/Latino Theology of Accompaniment*, especially chapter 4, "Beauty or Justice?: The Aesthetic Character of Human Action" (Maryknoll, N.Y.: Orbis, 1995), pp. 77–131.

20. Ibid.

21. Ibid., p. 3.

22. See Charles Taylor, "The Politics of Recognition," in *Multiculturalism*, pp. 25–73.

23. See William Ian Miller, *The Anatomy of Disgust* (Cambridge, Mass.: Harvard Univ. Press, 1997).

24. Thomas Jefferson, *Notes on the State of Virginia* (1787); ed. William Peden (Chapel Hill: Univ. of North Carolina Press, 1954), p. 140.

25. Ibid.

26. Ibid., pp. 141–42. See Jan Ellen Lewis and Peter S. Onuf, eds., *Sally Hemings and Thomas Jefferson: History, Memory, and Civic Culture* (Charlottesville: Univ. Press of Virginia, 1999).

27. Immanuel Kant, *Observations on the Feeling of the Beautiful and Sublime* (1764), trans. John T. Goldthwait (Berkeley: Univ. of California Press, 1960), p. 97.

28. Ibid., p. 109.

29. Ibid., p. 110.

30. Ibid., p. 111.

31. See Partha Mitter, *Much Maligned Monsters: A History of European Reactions to Indian Art*, 1977; reprint (Chicago: Univ. of Chicago Press, 1992).

32. Edward W. Said, *Orientalism* (New York: Random House–Vintage, 1979).

33. See Immanuel Kant, *Critique of Judgment* (1790), many English translations.

34. Ibid., especially Section 29.

35. See ibid., Section 59.

36. See ibid., Sections 16, 42, 49, 52.

37. Letter to the author from David Brown, Dec. 3, 1999.

38. L & C Software promotional web site on Contemporary Christian Music.

39. F. W. King, tribute to John Coltrane at the web site of the African Orthodox Church of Saint John Coltrane, http://www.saintjohncoltrane.org/html/ bulletin.html.

40. Hans Kollwitz, Introduction, *Diary and Letters of Käthe Kollwitz* (1955), trans. Richard and Clara Winston, ed. Hans Kollwitz; reprint (Evanston, Ill.: Northwestern Univ. Press, 1988). p. 7.

41. *English Hymnal* (1906); 2d ed. (London: Oxford Univ. Press, 1933), p. v.

42. Tim Page, "*Satyagraha*: The Sense of Peace," in booklet accompanying the CD recording of Philip Glass, *Satyagraha* (1980), adapted from the Bhagavad-Gita, with text by Constance DeJong, New York City Opera, Orchestra, and Chorus, Christopher Keene, Director (Columbia/Sony M3K 39672, 1985).

43. Samuel Taylor Coleridge, *Biographia Literaria*, ed. J. Shawcross, 2 vols. (Oxford: Oxford Univ. Press, 1907), 2:242. Emphases in the original.

44. For an epistemology that places confidence in kinds of subjective awareness that disclose something about the reality that eludes narrowly empirical reflection, see Alfred North Whitehead, *Modes of Thought* (1938); reprint (New York: Macmillan–Free Press, 1968).

45. Kant, *Critique of Judgment*, Sections 57–58. I am the one who is remarking on the mysterious aspect of the connection, not Kant, as he is not much attracted to mystery.

46. See Rudolf Otto, *The Idea of the Holy*, trans. John W. Harvey (1923); 2d ed. (New York: Oxford Univ. Press–Galaxy, 1958), pp. 41–42, 62–63. For Kant's understanding of the sublime, both "mathematical" and "dynamic," see *Critique of Judgment*, Sections 25–29. Kant discusses a connection between sublimity and religious feeling, but in the process he appears to domesticate God—whom he acknowledges to be sublime—by reducing awe, and its necessary element of fear, to admiration and quietly reverent contemplation (Section 28). For a lucid discussion of musical sublimity, see Edward Rothstein, *Emblems of Mind: The Inner Life of Music and Mathematics* (New York: Random House–Times, 1995).

47. Georg Wilhelm Friedrich Hegel, *Aesthetics:Lectures on Fine Art*, trans. T. M. Knox (Oxford: Oxford University Press–Clarendon, 1975), 1:373 (original emphasis).

48. Ibid., p. 375. Hegel professes to be building on Jewish precedent, but he seems oblivious of the sublimity of nature invoked in the Psalms and in the book of Job.

49. Cf. Charles Wegener, *The Discipline of Taste and Feeling* (Chicago: Univ. of Chicago Press, 1992), p. 29; and Edmund Burke, "Introduction on Taste," in *A Philosophical Enquiry into the Origin of Our Ideas of the Sublime and Beautiful* (2d ed., 1759), ed. Adam Phillips (New York: Oxford Univ. Press, 1990), p. 22. At one point, Kant himself speaks of taste as uniting imagination, understanding, and spirit. See *Critique of Judgment*, Section 50, note 55.

50. David Hume, "Of the Standard of Taste" (1757), reprinted in George Dickie and R. J. Sclafani, *Aesthetics: A Critical Anthology* (New York: St. Martin's, 1977), p. 601.

51. Ibid.

52. Ibid., p. 602.

53. See Wesley Monroe Shrum Jr., *Fringe and Fortune: The Role of Critics in High and Popular Art* (Princeton, N.J.: Princeton Univ. Press, 1996).

54. See Robin A. Leaver and Joyce Ann Zimmerman, eds., *Liturgy and Music: Lifetime Learning* (Collegeville, Minn.: Liturgical Press, 1998); and Lawrence A. Hoffman and Janet R. Walton, eds., *Sacred Sound and Social Change: Liturgical Music in Jewish and Christian Experience* (Notre Dame, Ind.: Univ. of Notre Dame Press, 1992).

55. See Jan Michael Joncas, "What Instruments Are to Make Roman Catholic Worship Music?," in his book *From Sacred Song to Ritual Music: Twentieth-Century Understandings of Roman Catholic Worship Music* (Collegeville, Minn.: Liturgical Press, 1997), pp. 100-112.

56. I will pursue these ideas further in Chapter 8. This way of putting the matter is indebted in part to Joseph P. Swain, *Musical Languages* (New York: W. W. Norton, 1997), pp. 53–58. For more on music's theological meanings, see Clyde J. Steckel, "How Can Music Have Theological Significance?," in *Theomusicology*, ed. Jon Michael Spencer (Durham, N.C.: Duke Univ. Press, 1994), pp. 13–35; Albert L. Blackwell, *The Sacred in Music* (Louisville, Ky.: Westminster/John Knox, 1999); and Jeremy Begbie, *Theology, Music, and Time* (Cambridge:Cambridge Univ. Press, 2000).

57. George A. Lindbeck, *The Nature of Doctrine: Religion and Theology in a Post-liberal Age* (Philadelphia: Westminster, 1984).

58. Joyce Smith, "Commentary," *White Spirituals from the Sacred Harp*, recorded at an Alabama Sacred Harp Convention by Alan Lomax, 1959, New World Records, CD 80205–2.

59. For an accessible and eloquent argument for regarding singing as a fundamental Christian practice, see Don E. Saliers, "Singing Our Lives," in *Practicing Our Faith: A Way of Life for a Searching People*, ed. Dorothy C. Bass (San Francisco: Jossey-Bass, 1997), pp. 179–93. By way of support, Saliers fittingly invokes the Wesleyan claim that hymns form a body of "experimental [i.e. experiential] and practical divinity."

60. See Saliers, *Worship as Theology*, pp. 185–88; see also E. Byron Anderson, "'O for a Heart to Praise My God': Hymning the Self before God," in *Liturgy and the Moral Self: Humanity at Full Stretch before God*, ed. Anderson and Bruce T. Morrill (Collegeville, Minn.: Liturgical Press–Pueblo, 1998), pp. 111–25.

61. For a one-volume edited survey of Christian worship practices and issues, see Robert E. Webber, ed., *Twenty Centuries of Christian Worship*, vol. 2 of the *Complete Library of Christian Worship* (Nashville, Tenn.: Star Song, 1994).

62. See Joncas, *From Sacred Song to Ritual Music*.

63. "The Milwaukee Symposia for Church Composers: A Ten-Year Report," *Pastoral Music* 17, no. 1 (Oct.–Nov. 1992): 19–30.

64. *Music in Catholic Worship*, Statement of the NCCB Committee on the Liturgy (Washington, D.C., 1972; revised 1983), cited in Joncas, *From Sacred Song to Ritual Music*.

65. *Liturgical Music Today*, Statement of the NCCB Committee on the Liturgy (Washington, D.C., 1972; revised 1983), cited in Joncas, ibid.

66. "The Snowbird Statement on Catholic Liturgical Music," *Pastoral Music*, Feb.–March 1996, pp. 13–19.

67. Tex Sample, *White Soul: Country Music, the Church, and Working Americans* (Nashville, Tenn.: Abingdon, 1996), pp. 110–20.

68. For an extensive discussion of the ways in which sacred music can have and accrue cross-cultural meanings, see Blackwell, *The Sacred in Music*.

69. See Kathryn Tanner, *Theories of Culture: A New Agenda for Theology* (Minneapolis: Fortress, 1997).

70. Ralph Vaughan Williams, "The Music," from a Preface to the *English Hymnal*, pp. viii–ix.

71. John Keble, *Praelectiones Academicae*, trans. Owen Chadwick, in *The Mind of the Oxford Movement* (London: A. & C. Black, 1963), pp. 70–71. Quoted in Richard Harries, *Art and the Beauty of God: A Christian Understanding* (London: Mowbray, 1993), p. 15.

72. Preface, *English Hymnal*, p. iii.

73. John Murray Cuddihy, *No Offense: Civil Religion and Protestant Taste* (New York: Seabury, 1978). For certain parallel arguments based on considerations of legal theory, see Stephen L. Carter, *The Dissent of the Governed: A Meditation on Law, Religion and Loyalty* (Cambridge, Mass.: Harvard Univ. Press, 1996).

74. Paul Rozin, Jonathan Haidt, and Clark R. McCauley, "Disgust," in *Handbook of Emotions*, ed. Michael Lewis and Jeannette M. Haviland (New York: Guilford Press, 1993), pp. 575–94.

75. André Maurois (1885–1967), quoted in *1,911 Best Things Anybody Ever Said*, ed. Robert Byrne (New York: Fawcett–Columbine, 1988), p. 47.

76. See Philip H. Pfatteicher, *The School of the Church: Worship and Christian Formation* (Valley Forge, Pa.: Trinity Press International, 1995); and E. Byron Anderson, "Liturgical Catechesis: Congregational Practice as Formation," *Religious Education* 92 (Summer 1997): 349–62.

77. See Robert Webber, *Planning Blended Worship: The Creative Mixture of Old and New* (Nashville, Tenn.: Abingdon, 1998). Webber has recently preferred to speak of "convergent" rather than "blended" worship, since the latter term implies a goal of homogeneity that he never intended.

Chapter 7

1. Paul Tillich, "Contemporary Protestant Architecture," in *Paul Tillich on Art and Architecture*, ed. John Dillenberger and Jane Dillenberger (New York: Crossroad Books, 1987), p. 220.

2. In the interests of "full disclosure," I note that in 1984 I was commissioned to compose a work of music that was dedicated and presented to Mircea Eliade on the occasion of the 75th Anniversary Celebration of the American Academy of Religion— a quartet for piano, oboe, violin, and cello entitled *Ritual Compass*. (My brother was pianist on that occasion.) Whatever criticisms I express here regarding Eliade's theories will probably not disguise the fact that I am by no means neutral, let alone unsympathetic.

3. This chapter is a revised and expanded version of a plenary address ("Sacred for Whom?") given in multimedia form at the Sixth International and Interdisciplinary Conference on Built Form and Culture Research, University of Cincinnati, October 1997. The conference topic was "Making Sacred Places."

4. See Mircea Eliade, *Cosmos and History: The Myth of the Eternal Return* (New York: Harper–Torchbooks, 1959); *The Sacred and the Profane: The Nature of Religion*, trans. Willard R. Trask (New York: Harper & Row, 1961); *Myth and Reality*, trans. Willard R. Trask (New York: Harper & Row, 1963).

5. Eliade, *The Sacred and the Profane*, p. 28, Eliade's emphasis.

6. Ibid., p. 29, Eliade's emphasis.

7. Ibid., Eliade's emphasis.

8. Mircea Eliade, "The Sacred and the Modern Artist," in *Art, Creativity, and the Sacred*, ed. D. Apostolos-Cappadona (New York: Crossroad, 1984), pp. 179–83.

9. See, for instance, Thomas Barrie, *Spiritual Path, Sacred Place: Myth, Ritual, and Meaning in Architecture* (Boston: Shambhala, 1996).

10. See Mircea Eliade, *Yoga: Immortality and Freedom*, 2d ed., trans. Willard R. Trask (Princeton, N.J.: Princeton Univ. Press, 1969).

11. Mircea Eliade, *Shamanism: Archaic Techniques of Ecstasy*, trans. Willard R. Trask (Princeton, N.J.: Princeton Univ. Press, 1964).

12. For a discussion of sacred artistry, particularly the prophetic and the visionary, see Deborah J. Haynes, *The Vocation of the Artist* (New York: Cambridge University Press, 1997).

13. David Chidester and Edward T. Linenthal, Introduction to *American Sacred Space*, ed. Chidester and Linenthal (Bloomington: Indiana Univ. Press, 1995), p. 18.

14. Ibid., pp. 18–19.

15. See Laurence Sickman and Alexander Soper, *The Art and Architecture of China*, 3d ed. (New Haven, Conn.: Yale Univ. Press, 1968); Robert E. Fisher, *Buddhist Art and Architecture* (New York: Thames and Hudson, 1993); Henri Stierlin, ed., *Architecture of the World: China* (Lausanne: Taschen, n.d.); and Martin Palmer, *Travels through Sacred China* (San Francisco: HarperCollins–Thorsons, 1996).

16. The terminology of path, place, and node, which comes from Thomas Barrie, J. G. Davies, and others, is not specific to Chinese architecture.

17. I thank Judith Berling for pointing out this possibility to me.

18. For detailed evidence in support of this claim, see William H. Coaldrake, *Architecture and Authority in Japan* (New York: Routledge, 1996).

19. On Chinese religious pluralism, see Judith A. Berling, *A Pilgrim in Chinese Culture: Negotiating Religious Diversity* (Maryknoll, N.Y.: Orbis, 1997).

20. Robert Fisher, for example, writes: "As is often pointed out, despite its aesthetic qualities, East Asian Buddhist architecture was not integral to the religion, in the way in which Gothic or Baroque churches functioned in the West. In East Asia similar-looking buildings served secular and religious needs and what was placed inside constituted the primary difference among this assemblage" (*Buddhist Art and Architecture*, p. 110).

It is one thing to say that a style is not uniquely Buddhist, the way Gothic became uniquely Christian; it is another to conclude that it cannot function to create distinctly and distinctively spiritual perceptions. That Fisher makes the leap to the second assumption is clear from the fact that he does not explore any such perceptions. Yet he mentions that the "distinctive wooden temples" of Buddhism are featured repeatedly in Chinese landscape paintings. It seems evident that they are featured partly because of their acquired spiritual meanings and associations, to which they are in fact highly conducive. For a more sensitive interpretation of temple styles, see Palmer, *Travels Through Sacred China*.

21. See Barrie, *Spiritual Path, Sacred Place*; and Coaldrake, *Architecture and Authority in Japan*.

22. Richard Robinson and Willard Johnson, *The Buddhist Religion*, 4th ed. (Belmont, Calif.: Wadsworth, 1997), p. 185. Much of the resistance to Buddhism during the Tang dynasty was in fact specifically resistance to its residual Indian traits, its foreign or "barbaric" trappings—including monastic practices and what Emperor Wu-tsung called its "soaring towers" (presumably pagodas). The forms of Buddhism that persisted and later thrived in China—Chan and Pure Land, in particular—accommodated themselves more fully to Chinese culture. See Berling, *A Pilgrim in Chinese Culture*, pp. 50–55.

23. Fisher, *Buddhist Art and Architecture*, p. 111.

24. I am indebted to Thomas Barrie for reminding me of this much-documented fact.

25. Robert Thorp, *Son of Heaven: Imperial Arts of China* (Seattle: Son of Heaven Press, 1988), p. 101.

Chapter 8

1. Ted Hughes, "Crow," in *Crow: From the life and Songs of the Crow* (New York: Harper & Row, 1971), p. 24. The following poem by Sylvia Plath, "Black Rook in Rainy Weather," appears in her *Collected Poems*, ed. Ted Hughes (New York: HarperCollins-HarperPernnial, 1981), pp. 56–57.

2. If a reader happens to be aware of Plath's other poetry from the period, which includes much experimentation, it will not be a great surprise to discover the present rhyme scheme—although, to my knowledge, Plath never repeats it exactly, and comes close only in poems specially concerned with order. For a similarly hidden, and more complex, rhyme scheme in "East Coker, " from T. S. Eliot's *Four Quartets*, see Frank Burch Brown, *Transfiguration: Poetic Metaphor and the Languages of Religious Belief* (Chapel Hill: Univ. of North Carolina Press, 1983), p. 104.

3. In addition to the work of theologians of culture such as Paul Tillich, there is theological literary criticism of the sort represented at its best by Nathan A. Scott Jr. in such studies as *The Broken Center: Studies in the Theological Horizon of Modern Literature* (New Haven, Conn.: Yale Univ. Press, 1966); *The Wild Prayer of Longing: Poetry and the Sacred* (New Haven, Conn.: Yale Univ. Press, 1971); and *Visions of Presence in Modern American Poetry* (Baltimore: Johns Hopkins Univ. Press, 1993).

4. See Paul Tillich, *Dynamics of Faith* (New York: Harper & Row, 1957).

5. See James W. Fowler, *Stages of Faith: The Psychology of Human Development and the Quest for Meaning* (San Francisco: Harper & Row, 1981), pp. 184–213.

6. For more on literature, theology, and theodicy, see Larry D. Bouchard, *Tragic Method and Tragic Theology: Evil in Contempory Drama and Religious Thought* (University Park: Pennsylvania State Univ. Press, 1989).

7. Thomas Merton, *Contemplative Prayer* (1971); reprint (New York: Doubleday–Image, 1996), p. 84.

8. Ibid., p. 85.

9. Ibid.

10. Ibid., p. 84.

11. Samuel Johnson, "The Life of Waller," in *Johnson: Prose and Poetry*, ed. Mona Wilson (London: Rupert Hart-Davis, 1969), p. 848. For an illuminating discussion of the whole topic from the standpoint of Indian poetics, see Vijay Mishra, *Devotional Poetics and the Indian Sublime* (Albany: State Univ. of New York Press, 1998).

12. Dante Alighieri, *Paradiso*, from *The Divine Comedy*, trans. Allen Mandelbaum; (Berkeley: Univ. of California Press, 1984), XXXIII, lines 114–20.

13. In what follows, I am not attempting to work strictly with scholastic concepts of knowledge and aesthetic vision, which are highly technical and, in any case, much debated. See Umberto Eco, *The Aesthetics of Thomas Aquinas*, trans. Hugh Bredin (Cambridge, Mass.: Harvard Univ. Press, 1988), esp. pp. 49–63.

14. Jean Leclercq, *The Love of Learning and the Desire for God: A Study of Monastic Culture*, trans. Catharine Misrahi (1961); reprint (New York: New American Library–Mentor Omega, 1962), p. 213.

15. Benedetto Croce thought otherwise, having been put off by the intellectual abstractions of the final canto, but he is in the minority. See John Freccero, "The

Final Image," in his book *Dante: The Poetics of Conversion*, ed. Rachel Jacoff (Cambridge, Mass.: Harvard Univ. Press, 1986), pp. 245–57. William Anderson regards the final cantos as "unequalled in literature for their power, profundity, and beauty." See William Anderson, *Dante the Maker* (New York: Crossroad, 1982), p. 272.

16. See Karl Jaspers, *Truth and Symbol* (from *Von der Wahrheit* [1947]), trans. Jean T. Wilde, William Kluback, and William Kimmell (New Haven, Conn.: College and University Press, 1959); vol. 1 of *Philosophy*, trans. E. B. Ashton, in 3 vols. (Chicago: Univ. of Chicago Press, 1969–71), pp. 334–35; and Paul Ricoeur, *Symbolism of Evil*, trans. Emerson Buchanan (New York: Harper & Row, 1967), pp. 347–57.

17. Augustine, *The City of God*, trans. Henry Bettenson (Harmondsworth, Middlesex: Penguin, 1972), XXII.30, pp. 1087–88.

18. For various Hindu perspectives on what constitutes the peak of religious experience, and their aesthetic implications, see Vijay Mishra, *Devotional Poetics and the Indian Sublime*.

19. For an illuminating discussion of the Eternal Feminine in relation to Dante and Christian theology, see Jaroslav Pelikan, *Eternal Feminines* (New Brunswick, N.J.: Rutgers Univ. Press, 1990).

20. Henri J.M. Nouwen, *The Return of the Prodigal Son: A Story of Homecoming* (New York: Doubleday–Image, 1992), p. 43.

21. Pierre Teilhard de Chardin, *Hymn of the Universe* (New York: Harper & Row, 1965), p. 25.

22. Franz Liszt, untitled supplement to an article on religious music, posthumously given the title "On the Future of Church Music: A Fragment," quoted and translated (in part) in Conrad L. Donakowski, *A Muse for the Masses: Ritual and Music in an Age of Democratic Revolution, 1770-1870* (Chicago: Univ. of Chicago Press, 1972), p. 18.

23. Liszt, "Future of Church Music," as quoted in Paul Merrick, *Revolution and Religion in the Music of Liszt* (Cambridge: Cambridge Univ. Press, 1987), pp. 19–20; Liszt's emphasis.

24. Charles Trueheart, "Welcome to the Next Church," *Atlantic Monthly*, August 1996.

25. Ibid., p. 37.

26. Ibid., p. 50.

27. William Easum, *Dancing with Dinosaurs: Ministry in a Hostile and Hurting World* (Nashville, Tenn.: Abingdon, 1993), p. 81.

28. See Steve Miller, *The Contemporary Christian Music Debate: Worldly Compromise or Agent of Renewal?* (Wheaton, Ill.: Tyndale House, 1993).

29. "Life in the Fast Lane," an interview with Wayne Marshall, *BBC Music Magazine*, July 1998, pp. 24–28; quotation on p. 28.

30. I have not attempted to recreate the drift of Taylor's seriously playful "virtual discussion" of the "irreducible ambiguity" of fashion, surface, skin, postmodern signs, and the like in *Hiding* (Chicago: Univ. of Chicago Press, 1997), pp. 210, 211.

31. Tom Beaudoin, *Virtual Faith: The Irreverent Spiritual Quest of Generation X* (San Francisco: Jossey-Bass, 1998). For observations on the restless spirituality of the older, "Baby Boomer" generation, see Wade Clark Roof, *Spiritual Marketplace: Baby Boomers and the Remaking of American Religion* (Princeton, N.J.: Princeton Univ. Press, 1999).

32. Friedrich Blume, *Protestant Church Music* (New York: W. W. Norton, 1974), p. 30.

33. See Martin Luther, "Preface to the Burial Hymns" (1542); *Luther's Works*, vol. 53, ed. Ulrich S. Leupold, general ed. Helmut T. Lehmann (Philadelphia: Fortress, 1965), p. 327.

34. Ibid., pp. 327–28.

35. Ibid., p. 327.

36. See Blume, *Protestant Church Music*, esp. p. 29ff; Quentin Faulkner, *Wiser than Despair: The Evolution of Ideas in the Relationship of Music and the Christian Church* (Westport, Conn.: Greenwood, 1996); and Paul Westermeyer, *Te Deum: The Church and Music* (Minneapolis: Fortress, 1998), pp. 205–16.

37. See Hans Küng, *Mozart: Traces of Transcendence*, trans. John Bowden (Grand Rapids, Mich.: Eerdmans, 1993).

38. Charles Rosen, *The Classical Style: Haydn, Mozart, Beethoven*, 1971; reprint ed. (New York: Norton, 1972), pp. 366–75.

39. Martha Bayles, *Hole in Our Soul: The Loss of Beauty and Meaning in American Popular Music* (Chicago: Univ. of Chicago Press, 1994); see especially the chapter "Rock 'n' Rollers or Holy Rollers?," pp. 127–42.

40. Robertson Davies, *The Cunning Man* (Toronto: McClelland & Stewart, 1994), pp. 146–47. My thanks to William C. James for calling my attention to this passage.

41. Simon Frith, "Rhythm: Race, Sex, and the Body," in his book *Performing Rites: On the Value of Popular Music* (Cambridge, Mass.: Harvard Univ. Press, 1996), pp. 123–44.

42. George Steiner, *Real Presences* (Chicago: Univ. of Chicago Press, 1989), p. 217.

43. Ibid., p. 218.

44. For more on matters of music and meaning, see Joseph P. Swain, *Musical Languages* (New York: W. W. Norton, 1997); Stephen Davies, *Musical Meaning and Expression* (Ithaca, N.Y.: Cornell Univ. Press, 1994); Aaron Ridley, *Music, Value, and the Passions* (Ithaca, N.Y.: Cornell Univ. Press, 1995); Robert S. Hatten, *Musical Meaning in Beethoven: Markedness, Correlation, and Interpretation* (Bloomington: Indiana Univ. Press, 1994); Peter Kivy, *Sound and Semblance: Reflections on Musical Representation* (Princeton, N.J.: Princeton Univ. Press, 1984); Leonard Meyer, *Music, the Arts, and Ideas* (Chicago: Univ. of Chicago Press, 1967); Leonard Meyer, *Emotion and Meaning in Music* (Chicago: Univ. of Chicago Press, 1956); Peter J. Martin, *Sounds and Society: Themes in the Sociology of Music* (Manchester: Manchester Univ. Press, 1995). For the aesthetics of music and religious meaning in particular, see Albert L. Blackwell, *The Sacred in Music* (Louisville: Westminster/John Knox, 1999); Clyde J. Steckel, "How Can Music Have Theological Significance?" in *Theomusicology*, ed. Jon Michael Spencer (Durham, N.C.: Duke Univ. Press, 1994), pp. 13–35; Edward Rothstein, *Emblems of Mind: The Inner Life of Music and Mathematics*; and Jeremy Begbie, *Theology, Music and Time* (Cambridge: Cambridge Univ. Press, 2000).

45. Robert Walser, *Running with the Devil: Power, Gender, and Madness in Heavy Metal Music* (Hanover, N.H.: Wesleyan Univ. Press–Univ. Press of New England, 1993), p. 55.

46. Edward Farley, "A Missing Presence," *Christian Century*, March 18–25, 1998, p. 276.

47. I am paraphrasing observations passed on to me by my colleague Mick Smith, who has worked extensively among the peoples referred to.

48. Kathleen Norris, "Sinatra in the Bell Tower," *Christian Century*, March 18–25, 1998, p. 301.

Chapter 9

1. See James W. Fowler, *Stages of Faith: The Psychology of Human Development and the Quest for Meaning* (San Francisco: Harper & Row, 1981); and Fowler, *Becoming Adult, Becoming Christian: Adult Development and Christian Faith* (San Francisco: Harper & Row, 1984). The latter book describes the same stages, essentially, but identifies them as seven rather than as six.

2. Jonathan Edwards, *Images or Shadows of Divine Things*, ed. Perry Miller, 1948; reprint (Westport, Conn.: Greenwood, 1977), p. 136.

3. Cornel West, "Black Music and Youth," in *Prophetic Reflections: Notes on Race and Power in America*, vol. 2 of *Beyond Eurocentrism and Multiculturalism* (Monroe, Maine: Common Courage, 1993), p. 25.

4. Ibid., p. 52.

5. William Blake, letter to Mr. George Cumberland, July 2, 1800, in *Complete Poetry and Prose of William Blake*, revised edition, ed. David V. Erdman (New York: Doubleday–Anchor, 1988), p. 706.

6. Quoted in Matthew Fox, *Original Blessing: A Primer in Creation Spirituality* (Santa Fe: Bear & Company, 1983), p. 188.

7. Valuable as it may be in certain respects, this emphasis on "opening up" and "unblocking" as the central artistic "disciplines" disguises how much training of a more strenuous sort goes into even the most spontaneous of the spiritual arts, as seen in Zen calligraphy, for instance. Even so, considerable good can doubtless come from books such as Julia Cameron, *The Artist's Way: A Spiritual Path to Higher Creativity* (New York: G. P. Putnam's Sons, 1992). Quotation on cover; cf. p. 3.

8. Janet Maslin, film review, "Love Happens, and in Middle Age, Too," *New York Times*, Living Arts, June 2, 1995.

9. Jim Svejda, *The Record Shelf Guide to Classical CDs and Audiocassettes*, 5th rev. ed. (Rocklin, Calif.: Prima Publishing, 1996), p. 293.

10. I found this quotation on a billboard placed outside a used bookstore and have been unable to locate the exact source in Flannery O'Connor.

11. Howard Gardner, *Frames of Mind: The Theory of Multiple Intelligences*, 2d ed. (New York: HarperCollins–Basic Books, 1993), p. x.

12. For research and reflection on integrating the arts into theological education, see Wilson Yates, *The Arts in Theological Education* (Atlanta: Scholars Press, 1987).

13. See, for instance, Hans W. Frei, *The Eclipse of Biblical Narrative: A Study in Eighteenth and Nineteenth Century Hermeneutics* (New Haven, Conn.: Yale Univ. Press, 1974).

14. Deborah J. Haynes, *The Vocation of the Artist* (New York: Cambridge Univ. Press, 1997). It is significant, in this connection, that the Catholic theologian Karl Rahner pictured as one of the "highest possibilities" for the Christian life—a possibility as yet only rarely fulfilled—that "the same person should be both priest and poet in vocation." See Karl Rahner, "Priest and Poet," in *Theological Investigations*, vol. 3: *Theology of the Spiritual Life*, trans. Karl-H. Kruger and Boniface Kruger (New York: Crossroad, 1982), pp. 294–317; quotation on p. 294.

15. Nicholas Lash, *Easter in Ordinary: Reflections on Human Experience and the Knowledge of God*, 1988; reprint (Notre Dame, Ind.: Univ. of Notre Dame Press, 1990), p. 290.

16. Ibid., p. 291.

17. Professional musicians habitually talk to each other in precise musical terms that others might find opaque—as in this note my brother received from a former student who was studying the score of my brother's piano concerto: "Third movement, mm. 58–63, rhythmic intensity not matching harmonic intensity. I simply felt there was some kind of 'hole' here. The long-held note in the horns seems uncomfortably isolated (especially with all four on the same note), and with more than a measure rest between chords in the strings, and on such a dissonant chord. If the original idea was for the silence in the strings to be the source of tension, then maybe a more complicated rhythmic syncopation could be employed. Compare the second theme of the finale of Beethoven's 5th, where the potential 'hole' is filled with an ascending and descending dominant seventh arpeggio in the lower strings." (Mark Polesky to David Brown, e-mail correspondence, July 4, 1998; slightly edited.) No reader of this book will be surprised to learn that my brother actually regards that moment in which the horn tone is held and exposed to be quite transformative (at least potentially), revealing a new character to the main theme—and not at all a mere "gap" to be covered over, even in the manner Beethoven demonstrates so well.

18. Friedrich Schleiermacher, *Christmas Eve: Dialogue on the Incarnation* (1806), 2d edition, 1826, trans. Terrence N. Tice (Richmond, Va.: John Knox, 1967), p. 31.

19. James Baldwin, "Sonny's Blues," from *Going to Meet the Man*, 1957; reprinted in *Short Fiction: Classic and Contemporary*, 4th ed., ed. Charles Bohner (Upper Saddle River, N.J.: Prentice-Hall, 1999), pp. 69–89.

20. Wilfrid Mellers, *Bach and the Dance of God* (New York: Oxford Univ. Press, 1981), pp. 262–63.

21. Ibid., pp. 277–78.

22. Ibid., p. 280.

23. Ibid., p. 286; Mellers's quotation at the end is from Sir Thomas Browne.

24. Karl Barth, *Church Dogmatics*, 4 vols., vol. 3, part 3: *The Doctrine of Creation* (Edinburgh: T. & T. Clark, 1960), p. 297.

25. Ibid., p. 298.

26. Ibid., p. 299.

27. Ibid., p. 298. See also Karl Barth, *Wolfgang Amadeus Mozart*, trans. Clarence K. Pott (Grand Rapids, Mich.: Eerdmans, 1986), pp. 39–40, 56–57.

28. For ample though often indirect support of this point, see Wilfrid Mellers, *Beethoven and the Voice of God* (New York: Oxford Univ. Press, 1983). See also Albert L. Blackwell, *The Sacred in Music* (Louisville: Westminster John Knox, 1999) and Jeremy Begbie, *Theology, Music and Time* (Cambridge: Cambridge Univ. Press, 2000).

29. See Louis L. Martz, *The Poetry of Meditation: A Study in English Religious Literature of the Seventeenth Century* (New Haven, Conn.: Yale Univ. Press, 1954). See also Barbara Kiefer Lewalski, *Protestant Poetics and the Seventeenth-Century Religious Lyric* (Princeton, N.J.: Princeton Univ. Press, 1979).

30. S. Sankaran, *The Theories of Rasa and Dhvani*, 1929; reprint (Madras: Univ. of Madras Press, 1973), p. 3. See also Donna M. Wulff, "Religion in a New Mode:

The Convergence of the Aesthetic and the Religious in Medieval India," *Journal of the American Academy of Religion* 54 (Winter 1986): 673–88.

31. Wulff, "Religion in a New Mode," p. 3.

32. See V. Raghavan, *The Number of Rasa-s* (Madras: Adyar Library and Research Centre, 1967).

33. Wulff, "Religion in a New Mode," p. 674.

34. Raghavan, *Number of Rasa-s*, p. 30.

35. Ibid., p. 65.

36. Wulff, "Religion in a New Mode," p. 676.

37. Ibid., p. 680.

38. Timur Indyah Poerwowidagdo, "The Future of Christian Art in Asia," *Religion and Society* 34 (December 1987): 21–25; quotation on p. 24.

39. Ananda K. Coomaraswamy, *The Transformation of Nature in Art*, 1934; reprint (New York: Dover, 1956), p. 51.

40. Ibid., pp. 50–51.

41. Richard Temple, "The Painting of Icons," in John Baggley, *Doors of Perception: Icons and Their Spiritual Significance* (Crestwood, N.Y.: St. Vladimir's Seminary Press, 1998), p. 100.

42. John Baggley, "The Spirituality of the Icon Painters," in ibid., pp. 54–76; quotation on p. 55. See also Paul Evdokimov, *The Art of the Icon: A Theology of Beauty* (1972), trans. Steven Bigham (Redondo Beach, Calif.: Oakwood, 1990).

43. Josef Krips, notes to his 1963 recording with the London Symphony Orchestra of the Symphonies of Beethoven, quoted in Philippe Autexier, *Beethoven: The Composer as Hero*, trans. Carrie Lovelace, Discoveries Series (New York: Harry N. Abrams, 1992), p. 127.

44. While Leo Tolstoy somehow imagined that the Ninth Symphony is bad art that neither transmits the highest religious feeling nor engages the feelings of "people not specially trained to submit themselves to its complex hypnotism," his Christian taste by that point was notoriously eccentric. See Leo Tolstoy, *What Is Art?* (1896), trans. Almyer Maude (Indianapolis: Bobbs-Merrill–Library of Liberal Arts, 1960), p. 158.

45. Iris Murdoch, *Acastos: Two Platonic Dialogues* (New York: Penguin Books, 1986), pp. 62, 63.

46. Søren Kierkegaard, *Works of Love* (1847); ed. and trans. Howard V. Hong and Edna H. Hong (Princeton, N.J.: Princeton Univ. Press, 1995), p. 158.

47. Compare Karl Barth, *Church Dogmatics*, vol. 3, part 3, section 50, "God and Nothingness," which contains the extended meditation on Mozart's music.

48. Ibid., p. 297.

49. Isak Dinesen, "Babette's Feast," in *Anecdotes of Destiny and Ehrengard* (New York: Random House–Vintage, 1993).

50. See Clive Marsh, "Did You Say 'Grace'? Eating in Community in *Babette's Feast*," in Clive Marsh and Gaye Ortiz, *Exploration in Theology and Film: Movies and Meaning* (Oxford: Basil Blackwell, 1997), pp. 207–18. For an image of the ultimate santification of taste through sacramental grace, see the eschatology expressed briefly in verse in John Wesley's *A Plain Account of Christian Perfection*, 2d ed., 1776: "The creatures *all* shall lead to thee, / And all we taste be God."

Index